MODERN CAMBRIDGE ECONOMICS

THE POLITICAL ECONOMY OF UNDERDEVELOPMENT

MODERN CAMBRIDGE ECONOMICS

Editors
Phyllis Deane   Gautam Mathur   Joan Robinson

Also in the series

Phyllis Deane
The Evolution of Economic Ideas

Michael Ellman
Socialist Planning

Joan Robinson
Aspects of Development and Underdevelopment

THE POLITICAL ECONOMY OF UNDERDEVELOPMENT

Amiya Kumar Bagchi

CAMBRIDGE UNIVERSITY PRESS

CAMBRIDGE

LONDON NEW YORK NEW ROCHELLE

MELBOURNE SYDNEY

Published by the Press Syndicate of the University of Cambridge
The Pitt Building, Trumpington Street, Cambridge CB2 1RP
32 East 57th Street, New York, NY 10022, USA
296 Beaconsfield Parade, Middle Park, Melbourne 3206, Australia

First published 1982

Printed in the United States of America

Library of Congress catalogue card number: 81-10237

British Library Cataloguing in Publication Data

Bagchi, A. K.
The political economy of underdevelopment.
—(Modern Cambridge economics)
1. Underdeveloped areas—Economic conditions
I. Title II. Series
330.972'4 HC59.7

ISBN 0 521 24024 7 hard covers
ISBN 0 521 28404 X paperback

CONTENTS

	Series preface	*page* vi
	Preface	vii
1	Political economy and the study of social change in the third world	1
2	Methods of exploitation and the phenomenon of economic retardation	20
3	Underdevelopment in Latin America: historical roots	41
4	Colonialism in Asia: Indonesia, India, China	69
5	Growth and fluctuations in economically retarded societies	112
6	Rural classes, land reforms and agrarian change	147
7	Labour, capital and the state	179
8	Population growth and the quality of life in the third world	202
9	Planning for capitalism in the third world	220
	A guide to further reading	251
	References	254
	Index	277

SERIES PREFACE

The modern Cambridge Economics series, of which this book is one, is designed in the same spirit as and with similar objectives to the series of Cambridge Economic Handbooks launched by Maynard Keynes soon after the First World War. Keynes' series, as he explained in his introduction, was intended 'to convey to the ordinary reader and to the uninitiated student some conception of the general principles of thought which economists now apply to economic problems'. He went on to describe its authors as, generally speaking, 'orthodox members of the Cambridge School of Economics' drawing most of their ideas and prejudices from 'the two economists who have chiefly influenced Cambridge thought for the past fifty years, Dr Marshall and Professor Pigou' and as being 'more anxious to avoid obscure forms of expression than difficult ideas.'

This series of short monographs is also aimed at the intelligent undergraduate and interested general reader, but it differs from Keynes' series in three main ways: first in that it focuses on aspects of economics which have attracted the particular interest of economists in the post Second World War era; second in that its authors, though still sharing a Cambridge tradition of ideas, would regard themselves as deriving their main inspiration from Keynes himself and his immediate successors, rather than from the neoclassical generation of the Cambridge school; and third in that it envisages a wider audience than readers in mature capitalist economies, for it is equally aimed at students in developing countries whose problems and whose interactions with the rest of the world have helped to shape the economic issues which have dominated economic thinking in recent decades.

Finally, it should be said that the editors and authors of this Modern Cambridge Economics series represent a wider spectrum of economic doctrine than the Cambridge School of Economics to which Keynes referred in the 1920s. However, the object of the series is not to propagate particular doctrines. It is to stimulate students to escape from conventional theoretical ruts and to think for themselves on live and controversial issues.

JOAN ROBINSON
GAUTAM MATHUR
PHYLLIS DEANE

PREFACE

I undertook first to write a book on development economics at the suggestion of Jo Bradley, then with the Cambridge University Press. The editors of the Modern Cambridge Economics series approved of the idea. This book is the result. However, the immediate stimulus for writing on problems of underdevelopment was provided by the revolt of young students all over the world in the late 1960s. I was a witness of this revolt in Cambridge and in Calcutta, and I owe more to the challenge mounted by my students and their friends, than I know how to acknowledge properly.

The intellectual antecedents of the book will, I hope, be evident from the first chapter. But very directly I have benefited from the general climate of critical social science provided by my friends in Calcutta and other places, in particular by Gautam Bhadra, Amit Bhaduri, Krishna Bharadwaj, Nirmal Chandra, Pramit Chaudhuri, Barun De, Andre Gunder Frank, Ranajit Guha, Saugata Mukherji, Suzy Paine, Prabhat and Utsa Patnaik, S. K. Rao, Ranjit Sau, Amartya Sen and Asok Sen. I should like to record the debt I owe to editors of two outstanding weeklies, Krishna Raj and Rajani Desai of the *Economic and Political Weekly* and Samar Sen of the *Frontier*. During these years they have stoked the fires of radical, non-sectarian social science with unwavering courage and loyalty. In the actual writing of the book my greatest debt is to the editors of the series – particularly Joan Robinson and Phyllis Deane, who commented on more than one draft of the book. An early draft was read by Ashok Mitra, who, along with Joan Robinson, tried to keep me from straying too far from contemporary reality into the bylanes of history. Ranajoy Karlekar helped weed out obscurities in the final manuscript. Finally, I must thank an anonymous referee for helpful comments.

Bristol University and Jesus College, Cambridge, supplied me with the necessary facilities for browsing among books, and testing out my fledgeling ideas at an early stage. I would like to thank the authorities of the two institutions – and two friends in particular, Esra Bennathan and Moses Finley – who made this possible. The Centre for Studies in Social Sciences, Calcutta, provided me with the freedom and facilities to carry out my work in an unconstrained fashion. In particular, Arun Ghosh, the librarian of the Centre, was ever resourceful in finding books and materials. Subhendu Das Gupta helped with proof-reading and with arranging the references in an orderly fashion. The typists at the Centre, particularly Arun Sanyal, Asoke Sen Gupta and Gauri Bandyopadhyaya coped competently with the typing of more than one draft of the book. Arundhati Sen Gupta helped with the checking of the penultimate manuscript. I would like to thank them all.

During the time the book was in progress, I had to be away from home for considerable lengths of time. In spite of her own heavy teaching and research commitments, my wife, Ratna, forgave those long absences, and gave me unstinting support. I only hope that the outcome meets with her approval.

A. K. Bagchi

1

POLITICAL ECONOMY AND THE STUDY OF SOCIAL CHANGE IN THE THIRD WORLD

1.1 INTRODUCTION

The division of the world into a small group of rich nations and a large group of poor nations has been apparent to careful observers for a long time. The division of the poor nations between a very small group of affluent persons and the vast majority of very poor persons living continually on the brink of disaster is also apparent. However, there is no unanimity as regards the reasons for either the poverty of the poor nations or the wretchedness of the ordinary people belonging to the group of poor nations. This book aims to elucidate some at least of the historical origins of these cleavages among peoples and nations, and also to discuss the typical ways in which inequalities among classes and peoples are maintained and propagated.

Although in tracing the detailed effects of certain kinds of changes we shall employ economic analysis in the conventional sense, the analysis will by no means be confined to the domain of economic variables alone. Men engage in producing or procuring goods and services in order to support themselves; however, the framework within which they engage in such activities is provided by the society and polity they live in. One particular way of viewing social organization is to regard it as consisting of several classes which are interconnected with one another, but which are in fundamental conflict in respect of the rules governing distribution of goods and services. For example, in a slave society, the interests of masters and slaves are in obvious conflict in normal times. It can be argued that man's unceasing quest for mastery over nature, which provides him with the resources for earning a livelihood, can be hampered or encouraged by a particular kind of social organization. For example, those latter-day Hindus who believed that crossing the ocean was a sin were allowing a particular belief associated with a particular social organization to fetter their search for better sources of the goods they valued. In fact, one way of viewing social change is to regard it as resulting from interaction between 'the relations of production', that is, the relations between classes of men, grouped according to their relationships to the means of production, and the 'forces of production' which define the limits of man's power over the forces of nature in a particular society in a particular epoch.

This way of looking at social change was given a classic formulation by Karl Marx (see in particular, Marx's 'Preface' to *A Contribution to the Critique of Political Economy*, in Marx, 1859, pp. 20–1):

> In the social production of their existence, men inevitably enter into definite relations, which are independent of their will, namely relations of production appropriate to a definite stage of development of their material productive forces . . . At a certain stage of development, the material productive forces of society come into conflict with the existing relations of production, or – this merely expresses the same thing in legal terms – with the property relations within the framework of which they have operated hitherto. From forms of development of the productive forces these relations turn into their fetters. Then begins an epoch of social revolution.

Marx formulated the basic principles underlying the general process of social change propelled by conflicts between classes comprehended within a 'mode of production' – that is, a particular configuration of classes along with a certain postulated degree of development of productive forces. He also provided a detailed analysis of the contradictions implicit in the capitalistic mode of production at a particular stage of its development. But the notion that the process of economic or social change involves more than just economic variables, such as prices and quantities of output or 'factors of production', or the more particular notion that existing societies are characterized by conflicts between classes, were not Marx's inventions. Adam Smith was the author, both of *The Theory of Moral Sentiments* (1759) and of *An Inquiry into the Nature and Causes of the Wealth of Nations* (1776). Both Adam Smith and David Ricardo, following him, took it for granted that their society was divided into three classes, landlords, capitalists, and wage-earners, and that there were fundamental conflicts of interest between them. Smith recognized the manufacturers, owning machinery and buildings and setting propertyless wage-earners to work, as the class which was spearheading progress in England. And by advocating the abolition of legal monopolies and cumbersome restrictions on trade and manufactures, he objectively represented the interests of the industrial bourgeoisie. But he relentlessly exposed how merchants as a class and manufacturers of older types of staples 'conspired' against the interests of other people and how landlords used their bargaining advantage to depress real wages of labourers to the level of subsistence or even below (Smith, 1776, Book I, chapter VIII and Book IV, chapters II and III). Ricardo's theoretical system was a brilliant exposition of the conflict between the interests of the landlords on the one hand and the capitalists and workers on the other. Following Ricardo, first the 'Ricardian Socialists' such as Hodgskin and Bray, and then Marx, brought the conflict between capitalists and workers into primary focus (Marx, 1963, and Dobb, 1973, chapters 2–6).

The admission of class struggle as one of the main planks of analysis in political economy distinguishes both Marx and the classical economists from the general run of neoclassical economists who emerged after 1870 and who managed to conjure social classes away from the universe of discourse of economics. Indeed, the Austrian school of marginalism quite consciously took combating the influence of Marxism as one of their major tasks (Sweezy, 1975).

1.2 NEED FOR ANALYSIS OF DIFFERENT TYPES OF SOCIAL ORGANIZATION

When, after the Second World War, economists turned their attention to problems of economic development, many went back consciously to classical economics for concepts and even tools (see, for example, Lewis, 1954). But the majority of such economists tried to combine neoclassical and classical economics in an eclectic synthesis, and most refused to see existing societies as riven into classes and driven by their conflicts. In this book, I shall go back to the analysis of classical economists, including Marx, in a more whole-hearted fashion, because I would contend that actual historical change cannot be explained without bringing in conflicts between capitalists and workers, capitalists and landlords, capitalists of the ruling country and capitalists of the ruled nation, and so on. But, of course, neither in analysis nor in time can we wholly go back to the classics. For, in economics, with the work of Rosa Luxemburg, Kalecki and Keynes and their followers, we have a more extended analysis of problems of effective demand and capitalist crises than was attempted by Ricardo, Malthus or even Marx (see in particular chapter 5 below). In the analysis of social classes, Lenin and Mao Tse-tung have given us a finer typology of social classes than is available in the work of Marx and Engels (see chapters 6 and 7 below).

We have witnessed, since 1917, the emergence of a world-wide socialist bloc covering a quarter of the world surface and population, the latest additions to the bloc being South Vietnam and Cambodia (Kampuchea). We have seen the crumbling of all the formal empires controlled by Europeans or North Americans. The majority of the world population now belong to the so-called third world. This consists roughly of all those nations which are neither advanced capitalist nor affluent socialist. That is, it includes all the countries of Latin America except perhaps Cuba, all the countries of Africa and all the countries of Asia except Japan.

For understanding the development of third world countries, the delineation of non-capitalist modes of production and social formations is essential. For, at the time European merchant adventurers 'discovered' the third world countries, the latter generally had not become capitalist and were not on the path of transition to capitalism. Furthermore, most of these societies evolved along paths that are recognizably different from the paths of development of advanced capitalist countries such as Britain and France, or the USA and Canada. In their societies the property relations have not yet simplified themselves into those between capitalists and free wage-earners alone, or even between capitalists, landlords and free wage-earners. There are many segments of society with ties between people which are non-contractual in appearance and substance, and cannot be reduced to those simply between unattached buyers and sellers. It will thus be necessary to pay particular attention to precapitalist relations of production even when the dominant relations are capitalist in nature.

1.3 WESTERN EUROPEAN FEUDALISM AS A TYPE OF PRECAPITALIST SOCIAL FORMATION

The precapitalist formation which has been studied most intensively, in both its conceptual and historical aspects, has been western European feudalism. A mode of production and a social system which is claimed to have operated (albeit with variations from country to country both in respect of form and duration), from the eighth century A.D. to the nineteenth century A.D., cannot be defined by a short formula and even an approximate definition will not be universally accepted. But those who agree that such a society preceded the phase of industrial capitalism in Europe also generally accept that it had certain common characteristics. To use the formulation of Marc Bloch,

> the feudal system meant the rigorous economic subjection of a host of humble folk to a few powerful men. Having received from earlier ages the Roman *villa* (which in some respects anticipated the manor) and the German village chiefdom, it extended and consolidated these methods whereby men exploited

men, and combining inextricably the right to the revenues from the land with the right to exercise authority, it fashioned from all this the true manor of medieval times (Bloch, 1962, p. 443).

Having thus indicated that the feudal system in Europe could be traced back to at least two distinct ancestors, Bloch further elaborated the characteristics of feudalism in another passage:

A subject peasantry; widespread use of the service tenement (i.e. the fief) instead of a salary, which was out of the question; the supremacy of a class of specialized warriors; ties of obedience and protection which bind man to man and, within the warrior class, assume the distinctive form called vassalage; fragmentation of authority – leading inevitably to disorder; and, in the midst of all this, the survival of other forms of association, family and state, of which the latter, during the second feudal age, was to acquire renewed strength – such then seem to be the fundamental features of European feudalism (Bloch, 1962, p. 446).

At the core of the feudal economic system was the manor (Kosminsky, 1956, 'Preface'). The manor comprised mainly two types of land, one part cultivated by the lord of the manor directly (called the demesne), and another part cultivated by a class of dependent tenure-holders, serfs, villeins or bondsmen. The demesne was cultivated partly by the 'prebenders' or serfs attached to the lord's household, and partly by the other bondsmen, who would labour on it without payment for a specified number of days. The manor would also generally contain dependent artisans who would fashion farming tools, weave cloth for the lord's household and so on. The surplus received by the lord consisted of the surplus over the cost of cultivation (in real terms generally) of the demesne, taxes paid by the residents in the lord's domain, and the produce delivered by the tenure-holders. Not all tenure-holders were bondsmen; some held 'alloidal' tenures without the taint of villeinage. However, a freeman might be converted into a bondsman because that was the condition on which he would receive protection from the lord, or he might lose his freedom because he came to hold a dependent tenure. (For further details, see Titow, 1969, and Brenner, 1976).

The extraction of the surplus under feudalism was direct – not mediated by the market mechanism, although rudimentary local markets and long distance trade existed throughout the period of feudalism and, in particular, gathered strength in what Bloch calls the second age of feudalism. (The first feudal age comprised roughly the period from the ninth to the middle of the eleventh century; the second feudal age commenced in the middle of the eleventh century and went on till the thirteenth century in practically the whole of western

Europe.) The proportion of tenure-holders to the direct 'prebenders' of the lord tended to increase over time; however a group of free peasantry survived throughout the period. With depopulation of Europe in the Black Death epidemics of the fourteenth century, the objective position of the serfs and the peasantry improved, whereas the warring, extravagant lords felt the need for an ever-larger surplus to be extracted out of a reduced population. The rise of towns to which the serfs could flee, and the craving for luxuries supplied by the channels of eastern trade were two other factors causing tension and instability in the feudal system.

There are differences of opinion among economists and historians about the relative importance of the different factors in the final breakdown of feudalism (see Hilton, 1976). One group, following the historian Henri Pirenne, would ascribe a major importance to the rise of long-distance trade and the growth of a money economy. The feudal economy was basically a 'natural economy' and the operations of merchants and bankers introduced disturbing elements, and converted more and more of the obligations into monetary obligations. Demands were soon made for altering the feudal legal arrangements all down the line. However, many historians (including Marx) had claimed that trade relations which did not disturb the internal production relations within the manor would in fact strengthen the hands of the lord who could now have access to a new source of power – command over financial resources. Marc Bloch has provided corroborative evidence that the growth of trade and commerce in the second feudal age of western Europe, which went hand in hand with an upsurge of population, strengthened, rather than weakened, the feudal system. This does not mean that no importance is to be attached to the growth of transactions in money or the growth of trade as such in the final breakdown of feudalism. It just means that such factors can destabilize the society only if there are other factors that cause tensions in the production relations prevailing in the core system, viz. the manor in the case of western European feudalism.

In some recent articles on the transition from feudalism to capitalism in Europe, Robert Brenner (1976, 1978) has again emphasized the primacy of class relations and the strength of different classes (feudal lords, free peasants and serfs) in determining the outcome. In western Europe the feudal lords gave way (between the fourteenth and sixteenth centuries) in the face of resistance by peasants and erstwhile serfs. In eastern Europe, by and large, the feudal lords won the day and often managed to enserf a free peasantry. Economic factors, such as the pull of the demand for eastern grain in western

Europe, motivated the lords in renewed efforts at repression of the peasantry, but their success did not depend on such market factors alone.

Western European feudalism combined with the manorial system certain particular legal forms and certain types of political organization. Politically, the whole continent was divided up into principalities, dukedoms, etc. The rulers of these principalities were vassals of kings, but no single king or emperor exercised a unified authority over large territories. The whole society was hierarchically ordered, but the hierarchy resembled a pyramid with a rather flat top. Furthermore, the men at one level of hierarchy paid homage to superior levels usually only through the men at the next higher level of hierarchy. This feudal system also generally permitted the co-existence of royal and manorial courts, and secular and religious areas of jurisdiction. However, in this respect there were important differences even between neighbouring countries such as France and England.

The tendency on the part of some historians and social anthropologists to see the western European model of feudalism replicated in all precapitalist settings – such as the medieval kingdom of the Nupe in Nigeria (evocatively designated as a Black Byzantium by S. F. Nadel in a book of the same title), the chieftancies and principalities of Rajasthan in India (whose annals were culled by James Tod in 1829), the empire of the Mughals in India, and the long succession of Chinese empires – had led to the extreme reaction of rejecting 'feudalism' as a useful category for comparative study. Daniel Thorner, for example, examined the working of the state system in Rajasthan and in Mughal India, and found that 'using feudalism as a method of government. . . we have to conclude that neither the Rajput states nor the Muslim regimes of northern India were feudal' (Thorner, 1956, p. 150). He claimed that, in the Rajput states, the power of clans and kinship was much too strong, and the association of vassalage with holding of fiefs conferred by the liege lord much too weak, compared with the case under European feudalism. Contrariwise, in the case of the Mughal empire in its heyday, the power of the central government with its transferable civil and military service was much too strong. However, as against Thorner's view, it can be urged that power in many European feudal states, particularly in the early years, was associated with ties of kinship (Bloch, 1962, chapter IX) and that, in the later years of the feudal regime, the degree of political centralization in France was far greater than in the classic age of feudalism. Thus, some at least of the divergences between the archetype of western European feudalism and the political organization of Rajput states and of

Mughal India can be accommodated in the varying patterns of western European feudalism in its different phases of evolution and in the different areas under its sway.

In any case, the extraction of surplus in the form of rent in kind, performance of forced (*corvee*) labour, and money rent on the basis of *actual harvest* rather than as a ground rent on the *market value of land* as under capitalism, were characteristic of both Rajput states and Mughal India (for the distinction between feudal rent and capitalist ground rent, see Hindess and Hirst, 1975, chapters 4 and 5). However, in both the cases we find admixtures of a tribal organization (in the case of Mughals, various central Asian tribes or clans came to exercise power as functionaries in the central government and as subordinate rulers and landlords in particular regions) and the inter-penetration of the 'natural economy' of feudalism by a developing commercial and financial network. (In chapter 5 we refer to the salient characteristics of precapitalist production relations before colonial conquest of the third world.) In many African polities, such as the kingdom of Bunyoro in western Uganda, the chiefs enjoyed a considerable degree of autonomy in many respects and the ties of kinship, neighbourhood and communal organization were quite strong (see, for example, Beattie, 1967). In Chi'ng China and Mughal India, on the other hand, bureaucracy and centralization had developed much further than in the classic period of western European feudalism (for a balanced view of a social anthropologist regarding the nature of non-European societies, see Goody, 1971).

While we shall bear these qualifications in mind, we shall sometimes use the word 'feudalism' to connote a society in which landlords dominate over dependent tenureholders and peasants, and in which the predominant method of coercion is direct legal control rather than indirect control through market forces. Such usage is sanctioned by the writings of Lenin and Mao Tse-tung, the architects of the two greatest revolutions of this century. Many writers, including Mao, have also used the term 'semi-feudalism' to denote a situation in which the non-market power of landlords coexists with the market power of landlords (as employers of wage-labour), moneylenders and traders, and in which neither the peasantry nor the wage-earners are fully 'free' from various legal and customary disabilities.

1.5 PRECAPITALIST SOCIETIES OTHER THAN FEUDALISM: SOME ILLUSTRATIONS

Tribal or primitive communist organizations have been observed over several centuries in all parts of the world. They can be of several different types, pure food-gathering tribes living in forests, hunting, fishing and food-gathering tribes, nomadic tribes mainly subsisting off domesticated livestock, partly pastoral and partly agricultural tribes and tribes subsisting mainly on settled agriculture (cf. Marx and Engels, 1976, pp. 38–41; Sahlins, 1968, chapter 3, and Sahlins, 1974, chapters 2 and 3). The division of labour among tribal peoples tends to be rather rudimentary; even when the stage of settled agriculture is reached, the same person may perform several different functions. There may be a division of labour within the family rather than between families. But, of course, families in tribes are often extended kinship groups. In the relatively 'pure' forms of tribes, there is little class differentiation partly because of the small surplus above subsistence. There may be a tribal chief, who is an elected or hereditary head, and there may be certain families which are considered pre-eminent. But, in general, there are elaborate precautions among the members of the tribe to prevent differentiation on the basis of holding of wealth or property. These include communal ownership of the land to which the tribe stakes a claim, communal right to fruits of the hunt, periodic redistribution of wealth among the different families including periodic reallocation of land, periodic destruction of the items considered valuable among the tribesmen[1] and so on. Inequality among tribes generally took the form of enslaving defeated enemies, and subjecting women to the domination of males. But over whole continents, such inequalities apparently did not lead to any long-run process of class differentiation as between families or kin groups.

We shall later be concerned with certain aspects of the working of a tribal economy, such as the system of shifting cultivation (*jhoom* in India, *ladang* in Indonesia, *swidden* in Old English usage) and its replacement by a system of perennial cultivation of the same group of plots, either with rests at two to three year intervals, and/or with rotation of crops on those plots. However, it is important to note that most of the available descriptions of tribal economies come from necessarily incomplete historical evidence, or from observations of travellers and anthropologists in recent times. In the latter case, the tribal economies have already been penetrated by colonialism, or by a centralized state system, so that it is practically impossible to observe a tribal economy in a 'pure' form. Furthermore, the features picked out often serve as pieces in a preconceived model of 'primitive society', so

1 For description of ceremonies at which food or other goods were consumed and were redistributed among North American Indians, see P. Drucker, 'The potlatch', in Dalton, 1967; for a description of the elaborate ritual of gift exchanges serving a similar purpose, see B. Malinowski, '*Kula*: The circulating exchange of valuables in the archipelagoes of eastern New Guinea', in Dalton, 1967.

that it is necessary to avoid the idealistic trap of the model-builder.

The same observation is valid for descriptions of another type of social organization, viz. the village community, or communal ownership of property in general. Marx had, in his unpublished manuscript, *Grundrisse der Kritik der Politischen Okonomie*, clearly distinguished between three types of communal property in history:

> the real existence of the community is determined by the specific form of its ownership of the objective conditions of labour. The property mediated by its existence in a community, may appear as *communal property*, which gives the individual only possession and no private property in the soil; or else it may appear in the dual form of state and private property which coexist side by side, but in such a way as to make the former the precondition of the latter so that only the citizen is and must be a private proprietor, while on the other hand his property *qua* citizen also has a separate existence. Lastly, communal property may appear merely as a supplement to private property, which in this case forms the basis; in this case the community has no existence except in the *assembly* of its members and in their association for common purposes (Marx, 'Precapitalist economic formations', in Hobsbawm, 1964, p. 82; italics in the original).

Marx identified the second and the third forms with the ancient Roman and German forms of communal property, and the first form with the 'Asiatic' village community. Other commentators have also compared 'village communities of the East and West' and they have differed greatly about the typical character of village communities as observed in the eighteenth, nineteenth and twentieth centuries. The following characteristics seem to have been common to 'village communities' over most of pre-British and early British India: the villagers were governed by a local council, either a *panchayat* of all castes, or a *panchayat* of the major 'clean' castes, or a *panchayat* of the most powerful castes. While some land was individually owned, there was also some common land. Furthermore, transfer of land through sale was restricted in various ways. For example, in Maharashtra under Maratha rule, the purchaser of land in a village had to have the consent of the village headman as well as all the cultivators who were recognized as having a stake in the village (Kumar, 1968, pp. 26–7, and Fukazawa, 1972, 1974). Generally, the village or a group of villages had several artisan or service groups whose products or services were obtained by other villagers through a system of customary payments, including the right to enjoy the usufruct of certain specially allotted plots of land. In these transactions the landholding upper castes had the decisive voice. However, the 'village communities' were not by any means self-sufficient. They were involved in various cash transactions in buying salt, handicraft products, etc., from the outside world, and selling their grain and other crops which could be marketed outside the village or group of villages concerned. Furthermore, they had to pay taxes to the central or regional governments. Cash transactions were fairly common, though not very pervasive compared with the modern situation. Land transfers were also permissible, though certainly they were less frequent and more hedged about with customary restrictions than under British rule (for example, a landholder could rarely be sold up for realization of the debt of a moneylender, although his crops could be distrained).

When the British tried to create full private property in land, most of the communal rights were gradually eroded. But some features of the old community survived, although with gradually diminishing force, in the so-called *jajmani* system. 'Briefly, the *jajmani* system is a system of distribution in Indian villages whereby high-caste landowning families called *jajmans* are provided services and products by various lower castes such as carpenters, potters, blacksmiths, water-carriers, sweepers and laundrymen' (P. M. Kolenda, 'Toward a model of the Hindu *jajmani* system' in Dalton, 1967, p. 287). Here every serving caste (*kamins*) had its circle of *jajmans* or clients (who were really their patrons); this circle generally did not include the village as a whole. As the number of people in the serving castes grew, their bargaining position vis-à-vis the landowners tended to deteriorate, so that they had to eke out their income from the traditional occupation with some other work, or migrate. In a rudimentary form, the *jajmani* system could be found also among the Muslims. In Bihar, it was observed in 1901, that 'The exclusive right to employment by the people in the circle constituting a man's *brit* [i.e. traditional occupation] is so well established, that it is regarded as hereditable property, and with Muhammadans is often granted as dower' (Census of India, 1901, p. 473). The further advance of commercial relations into the countryside in the twentieth century rendered the system of customary payments practically unimportant. But, of course, the system of dependence of the landless lower castes on superior, landholding upper castes, which had a deeper foundation than the *jajmani* system has survived to a more significant extent (cf. Epstein, 1971 and Breman, 1974).

We have described these precapitalist forms in some detail, because western European capitalism transformed the third world countries partly by interacting with, and partly by destroying, such structures. When we come to discuss the processes of change in Asia and Latin

America, the modes of interaction and destruction will crop up extensively.

1.6 DIFFERENT PHASES OF CAPITALISM IN WESTERN EUROPE AND THE MEANING OF EXPLOITATION

Following Marx, we shall take the essence of the capitalist mode of production to be the predominant use of legally free but propertyless wage labour by owners of means of production for the purpose of making a money profit (cf. Marx, 1887, Parts II and III, and Dobb, 1963, chapter 1).

The surplus product is here realized by the owners of means of production typically in the form of 'surplus value', that is, the money value of output produced by wage labour (after allowing for the value of materials used up and the depreciation of capital stock) over and above the wages paid to labour.[2] Under the capitalistic mode of production, labour power itself becomes a commodity, to be sold and purchased in the market. Furthermore, production is here predominantly for sale rather than for direct use.

However, the mere development of trade or the use of money, or even the production of commodities for the market, is not evidence that capitalism has developed. For the capitalist mode of production to exist we must have the bifurcation of society into a group of propertied employers and a group of wage-earning proletariat, with the former employing the latter for the creation of surplus value in production. The competition between capitalists generally results in continuous accumulation of capital, and the development of techniques of production which produce more and more surplus value. But these latter characteristics must be regarded as the results of the development of capitalism rather than as its identifying marks.

An acquaintance with the ways in which merchants' activities, the breakdown of serfdom, the rise of wage labour and exploitation of colonies interacted to bring capitalism into being in western Europe could be suggestive in understanding the working of capitalism in the third world. However, it could be highly misleading to use actual western European patterns of development for predicting developments in the third world. For, since capitalism had triumphed in western Europe first and the western European capitalists had managed to subordinate the economies of the third world for their

2 Here we have ignored the distinction between 'value' and 'price' which figures so prominently in Marxian theory.

purposes, this central fact conditioned all the later developments in the dominated group of societies.

This recognition of the overriding nature of the initial conditions created by western Europe as the cradle of capitalism also shows why it is not very sensible to ask whether, independently of European contact, transition to capitalism could have taken place in other parts of the world. For, once the contact *had taken place* with a society which was further along on the capitalistic path, the lagging societies could not possibly develop in an autonomous fashion. In that respect, capitalism is probably far more of a contaminating system than all the systems that preceded it. We shall argue in the later sections that contact with western European capitalism retarded the development of anything resembling capitalism in third world countries.

In the western European context it is usual to distinguish between the mercantile (or commercial) and industrial phases of capitalism. In the era of mercantilism, in the Netherlands and England and even in France, most of the personal ties of dependence characteristic of feudalism gradually dissolved, and production came to be governed more by the pull of the market than by the needs of the manorial establishment. More and more people earned their living as wage-earners either in handicraft industry or in agriculture. Agricultural estates were increasingly managed for profit rather than for pomp or display of the military strength of the lord. In England and the Netherlands the feudal system had crumbled by the middle of the seventeenth century. Even in other countries, many of the feudal dues were commuted to payment in money and assumed the aspect of contractual payment. However, the population remained overwhelmingly agrarian, and, what is perhaps more important, most of the producers remained owners of their rather primitive, though slowly improving, means of production: In this era, 'trade was the great wheel driving the whole engine of society' (Glamann, 1974, p. 427). This was particularly true of international trade, which provided the surpluses for capital accumulation, the gold or silver or silver bullion for lubricating the process of exchange, the wherewithal and the incentive for increase in the tonnage of shipping and its quality, and the major vehicle for increase in the power of the new nation states of Europe. In this phase, what has been called 'profit on alienation' that is, profit made in procurement, transport and distribution of goods, was perhaps the biggest base of capitalist accumulation (cf. Marx, 1887, Part VIII, and Dobb, 1963, chapter 5).

The mercantile phase was succeeded by industrial capitalism, which was heralded by the Industrial Revolution in Britain. In England, and to a lesser extent, in such countries as France and the Netherlands, the stage for the rise of modern industry was prepared by deep-seated changes in rural society. Agriculture was converted into a mainly commercial activity and gave rise to a class of rural capitalists who employed landless rural workers working for a wage and invested capital in land (see Moore, 1967, Hobsbawm 1968 and Saville, 1969). Among the main characteristics of the Industrial Revolution in Britain were (a) the growth of steam power as the main source of energy for production, (b) the rapidly increasing use of machinery partly to assist labour and partly to supplant it, (c) the rise of large-scale factories where hundreds of workers were assembled under one roof, (d) the rapid decimation of handicraft industries, first in the cotton trades and then in woollen and other textiles, (e) the growth of a large-scale metallurgical and capital goods industry for supplying the needs of industry and locomotion, (f) the rise in the share of secondary industry both in national income and in the gainfully occupied population and the displacement of agriculture as the main source of livelihood and employment, and (g) the increasingly strict separation of employers owning the means of production in industry, agriculture and transport, and employees who earn their living by selling their labour power.

The succession of mercantile capitalism by industrial capitalism is primarily a phenomenon characterizing western Europe and, to a lesser extent, the USA. In the overseas offshoots of Europe, such as Canada or Australia, there was practically no phase of mercantile capitalism. Even in the USA, where the War of Independence was triggered off as a reaction to some of the mercantile policies of Britain, there was no great *internal* struggle against mercantile capitalism as there was in western Europe. (Of course, slavery might be regarded as the last remnant of the mercantile system; to that extent, the American Civil War marked the final struggle between mercantilism and industrial capitalism in the USA.)

The dependencies of the European countries in the third world and even formally independent countries such as the Latin American republics of the nineteenth century saw primarily one face of western European capitalism – and that was mercantile capitalism. Rulers took away a part of the product in the form of tribute, for which, of course, no payment was made; then merchants and chartered monopolies bought up products from peasants and artisans at prices which were absurdly low by internal and international standards, and various coercive devices and the closing of alternative markets kept these prices low; planters and mine-owners employed the local population and imported labour as slaves, serfs or other kinds of unfree labour, at wages which were often insufficient even to allow the workers to survive and reproduce themselves. The products of these mines and plantations then went directly or indirectly to service the growing capitalism of western Europe. These modes of extraction of a surplus in the colonies and other countries of the third world survived long after industrial capitalism had grown to maturity in western Europe and North America. Even when native capitalists succeeded Europeans in the third world countries, many of these methods of extraction of surplus from peasantry and semi-free labour were kept alive, at the same time as capacity was being built up in modern, mechanized industries. Thus there is no neat succession of stages of mercantile and industrial capitalism in third world countries. This, of course, would also follow from the fact that, as we shall see later, many features of precapitalist social organizations have remained intact side by side with the growth of commercial relations within the economies of the third world.

The process of extracting a surplus from the third world countries by the ruling classes – in particular the capitalist class – of the European and North American capitalist countries (and later on also of Japan) will be termed 'exploitation' in this book. We shall often qualify this as 'colonial' or 'imperialistic' exploitation in order to distinguish it from the exploitation of labour within the same country. 'Exploitation of labour' in Marxian economics has a precise meaning. In order to arrive at that meaning, we need Marx's definition of labour-power and its value. 'By labour-power or capacity for labour is to be understood the aggregate of those mental and physical capabilities existing in a human being, which he exercises whenever he produces a use-value of any description' (Marx, 1887, p. 167). 'The value of labour-power is determined, as in the case of every other commodity, by the labour-time necessary for the production, and consequently also the reproduction of this special article' (Marx, 1887, pp. 170–1). Assuming that the capitalist buys labour-power at its value, the surplus value is the excess of the value produced by this labour-power over the value of the labour power and the value of the raw materials used up in the process and the value of depreciation of the fixed capital. Exploitation of labour is the extraction of this surplus value by the capitalist by virtue of his ownership of the means of production without which labour power cannot produce value. More generally, exploitation of labour means the extraction of a surplus by the owners of the means of production over and above the wages of labour, the costs of raw materials or other current inputs and the amortization cost of fixed or durable capital. When we talk about exploitation in the international context, it means ultimately the appropriation of labour power of the exploited country by paying it less than the full value it produces.

1.7 THEORIZING ABOUT WESTERN ECONOMIC DEVELOPMENT AND THEORIZING ABOUT THE DEVELOPMENT OF THIRD WORLD COUNTRIES

In this book, particularly in the chapters delineating the evolution of underdevelopment (or, as we shall call it, 'retardation') in the third world, we shall be concerned with the analysis of social systems, and prices, outputs, incomes, balances of payments, and other entities familiar to the professional economist will not be the sole objects of interest. Only a minority among economists adopt a similar approach though there are books by Leo Huberman, Joan Robinson and John Eatwell which share this perspective, besides books by Marxists concerned with social evolution and revolution. (See in this connection Baran, 1962, Huberman, 1976, Robinson, 1971a, Robinson and Eatwell, 1974.) Furthermore, we share with classical economists, including Marx, a concern with analysis of explicit or implicit conflicts among social classes, because such conflicts are among the major propellers of history.

However, just as we cannot generalize the western European patterns of emergence of capitalism out of the shell of feudalism without analysis of the local-historical conditions in other continents or regions, so also we cannot use even the analytical framework of classical economists or their contemporary exponents without testing whether the special conditions they assumed to be valid held in the case of other countries.

One outstanding case illustrating the type of limitation we have in mind is the Ricardian theory of comparative costs. Ricardo explained the pattern of international trade by invoking the principle of comparative (labour) costs, which stated that if two countries A and B entered into trade relations, each capable of producing commodities X and Y, country A would sell the commodity in which its relative (rather than absolute) cost was lower, and correspondingly B would sell the commodity in which its own comparative cost was lower. Ricardo took trade between England and Portugal as his example. England sold textiles to Portugal, and the latter sold wine to England, according to the comparative cost principle. This was, for him, the natural order of things which could be realized by adopting universal free trade between nations. Adam Smith and Ricardo advocated the principle of free trade as against the mercantilist practice of protection of home production. England had already become the leading manufacturing nation of the world by 1815; and she had done so partly with the help of the despised mercantilist policies (including stiff tariffs on, and in some cases, outright prohibition of, imports of competing goods, and various types of protection and state patronage for English shipping under the Navigation Laws). She stood to gain by adopting the principle of free trade and forcing it on others whenever and wherever she could. The application of this principle to countries lacking an independent capitalist class, a substantial industrial base or independent state power doomed them to the position of suppliers of raw materials and grain.

Where the capitalists had any independent hold over state power or where the ruling classes were astute and strong enough to resist the pressures of British (or western European) capitalism, the free trade doctrines of the classical economists and their followers were rejected. Alexander Hamilton in the USA and Friedrich List in Germany advocated alternative policies for industrial progress in countries which were backward in relation to Britain (Hamilton, 1791, and List, 1857). They provided the rationale for protectionist policies which were already being pursued by all western European nations and by the USA (and were to be followed by other overseas offshoots of Europe such as Australia, Canada and South Africa). The policies of List were later generally adopted by nationalists in the third world countries as being conducive to economic development. However, two qualifications should be made regarding the unrestricted advocacy of Listian policies. First, List did not regard industrial growth as attainable by all countries. He envisaged the development of manufactures only for countries of the temperate zone, and relegated the colonial empires of Europe to the role of producers of raw materials and agricultural commodities. Since he believed that manufacturing production was subject to decreasing costs in the long run, he also postulated that the European countries and the northern part of the USA would grow faster than the tropical countries. (For an interesting interpretation of List, see De Cecco, 1974, pp. 9–12.) Secondly – and this is the more serious limitation from the point of view of today's third world countries – List's prescriptions needed for their effectiveness a capitalist class and a state apparatus capable of standing up to the challenge of the other developed capitalist countries, with some initial help given to the capitalists through the public exchequer. In particular, the capitalist class would be able to protect its home market and invade the colonial markets of other advanced capitalist countries and thus would be able to realize the economies of scale postulated – partly at the expense of other countries. With the vanishing of the frontiers of capitalism and the emergence of a dominant group of capitalist nations, Listian medicines would no longer sustain the growth of the weak capitalist classes of third world countries.

Neoclassical economics can offer little in the way of intellectual tools for even posing the problems of today's third world. The completely ahistorical nature of neoclassical economics, which takes a price-guided market system as the only 'rational' economy worth discussing is a first stumbling block. 'Money', for example, is endowed in neoclassical economics with all kinds of virtues which are to be found, if at all, only in the most developed capitalist societies. In actual history, 'money' has performed only a limited set of functions in most precapitalist societies, and even as a medium of exchange it has had clearly defined spheres of operation in such societies (see, for example, the articles by Bohannan, Thurnwald, Armstrong and Dalton, in Dalton, 1967). Again, 'monetization' or 'commercialization' has been regarded as a more or less automatic process, under which economic activities are brought into a uniform relation under the rationalizing influence of monetary exchange, and which, therefore, leads to the development of the economy. The more sophisticated analysts are aware of some of the costs exacted by the process, but they would argue that, nonetheless, when traditional attitudes have been overcome, and the undue influence of usurious moneylenders or exploitative middlemen have been eliminated, third world countries have definitely benefited from these changes (see, for example, Lewis, 1956, chapter III and Myint, 1965, chapter 3). Our argument will be that commercialization has been forced on many third world countries by using non-market coercion, and that the process of commercialization has often resulted in an economic structure which has acted as a brake on economic development; further, the process of commercialization generally led to the removal of surpluses from third world countries. Instead of developing these arguments in abstract, we shall demonstrate their general validity by analysing certain concrete historical processes.

1.8 THE PROSPECTUS FOR THIS BOOK

In this book we shall concentrate on the characterization of a state of economic underdevelopment or 'economic retardation' and on the diagnosis of its causes. In the next chapter we try to provide an analytic summary of the processes which keep the third world capitalist countries in a state of retardation. This will help clarify the principles which were used to select some particular historical developments for a somewhat detailed presentation. In the next two chapters we present certain aspects of historical development of societies in Latin America and Asia – societies which have been hybridized under the dual stress of the logic of evolution of its pre-existing social structure and of the buffetings of an evolving world capitalist system.

In chapter 5, the typical modes of growth and fluctuations of the third world countries under the influence of capitalist forces are analysed at a rather high level of abstraction. Behind these patterns of fluctuation and interaction lie the class configurations in towns and villages of the third world. In chapters 6 and 7 we provide an analysis of the class structures (particularly concentrating on the characteristics of the peasantry, the working class and the capitalist class of these countries), the class conflicts and the role of the state in the underdeveloped countries. One of the themes of this book will be the way in which the development of a particular class (most importantly the bourgeoisie) not only influences the character of income and power distribution within the country concerned but also determines the place of that society in the international hierarchy of capitalist countries. That in its turn influences the direction and magnitude of flows of resources (including people) between different countries.

We use the perspective presented in the earlier seven chapters, to deal with two topics of current interest: population growth and environmental damage caused by economic growth. The ways in which predatory capitalism damages the environment and the ills of capitalism and exploitation are foisted on to population growth as such form major themes in this chapter.

In chapter 9, we discuss what has been done in the name of economic planning in typical third world countries. The actual processes through which the stated aims of planning have been subverted, and governmental policies have mostly ended up by strengthening the forces for inequality, retardation and dependence are described.

In this book, we have concentrated on the non-socialist third world countries or on the non-socialist phase of the socialist countries of the third world. A discussion of the experience of socialist countries such as China or Vietnam would require a different focus. However, the literature on developments in socialist China has been signposted in 'A guide to further reading' appearing after chapter 9.

2

METHODS OF EXPLOITATION AND THE PHENOMENON OF ECONOMIC RETARDATION

2.1 CHARACTERIZATION OF ECONOMIC RETARDATION AND UNDERDEVELOPMENT

We regard third world countries as retarded, because, in respect of the ability to transform their production capacities so as to meet the growing needs of the population, they have fallen behind advanced capitalist countries on the two sides of the North Atlantic, and also Japan. We call them 'underdeveloped', because, not only does their actual development fall far short of their potential, but also because their capacity for exerting themselves to realize this potential is impaired by their internal social and political structure, and by the dominating effect of the advanced capitalist countries which limit their choices all the time. This usage was, of course, advocated a long time back by Paul Baran (1962).

Most social scientists today would readily agree that in order to assess the present and past performance of a particular society, income per head is not the only criterion. Yet in actual practice, some kind of index of income per head often serves as the sole criterion to characterize the 'underdeveloped', or rather the 'less developed', or 'developing' countries. This usage is not just an excusable over-simplification, but generally goes with a tendency to believe in certain simple causal mechanisms producing poverty and to ignore complications that might point to the existence of deep-seated social conflicts.

In this book, we shall take into account the social and political structures of the third world countries in order to place them relative to the advanced capitalist countries with whom they have had many decades, if not centuries, of a relationship of dominance and subordination. In such relationships, the position or the strength of the capitalist classes of the respective countries and their relative abilities to control resources yielding profit – particularly labour – and exploiting them efficiently, play a very important role. For in the era of domination of the world (barring the socialist countries of the twentieth century) by the advanced capitalist countries, it is the drive for more exploitation and more accumulation by the capitalists that provides the main dynamic of history until that drive is challenged by the peasants and workers affected by the whole process.

In the next two sections we shall describe the chief methods of exploitation that have been used by capitalists – both foreign and indigenous – in order to accumulate capital. The extracted surplus was often not invested in the country where it originated – and that is an integral part of the story of retardation and underdevelopment. (We discuss the typical class configurations of third world countries in chapters 6 and 7.)

2.2 CONTROL OF LABOUR AND THE PEASANTRY UNDER CAPITALISM AND COLONIALISM

Capitalists maintain themselves as capitalists and increase their power by extracting a surplus from labour and marketing it as surplus value. Given the level of productivity of labour, the higher the ratio of net value added to wages the higher, *ceteris paribus*, is the rate of profit (among other things, the capital per man and rate of utilization of capacity is taken as constant).[1] Given the rate of exploitation of labour (that is, roughly, the ratio of net value added to wages) and its productivity, the larger the labour force which the capitalists can use, the higher is their total income. Marx devoted about half of his *magnum opus, Capital*, Vol. 1, to the analysis of the ways in which capitalists extract surplus value from labour and try to increase the rate of extraction of surplus value. These included the practice of landlords (turned capitalist entrepreneurs) of using their tenants or serfs as labour power, and the attempts of capitalists to lengthen the working day, to lower wages even below the level at which labourers could subsist for any length of time, to use children as workers and shorten their poor lives, and, concurrently with all this, to deprive peasants and artisans of their land and tools, and convert them into members of the proletariat.

From the time of the Industrial Revolution onward, and, more particularly, after research and development techniques and product innovation had been made into a regular activity of capitalist firms and industries, there was also a struggle to raise the productivity of workers, and thus to raise the relative surplus value (the proportion of surplus value to the wage or cost of labour) realized by the capitalists (on the role of division of labour, modern machinery and modern

1 For definitions of 'labour power' and 'surplus value', see chapter 1.

industrial processes in making labour more productive and intensifying its exploitation, see Marx, 1887, chapters XIV and XV and Braverman, 1974). In the earlier phases of capitalist development (that is to say, up to the beginning of the eighteenth century in all capitalist countries and up to the beginning of the nineteenth century in nearly all countries except Britain), the extension of capitalists' power over labour and the intensification of exploitation of labour were the more important means of expansion of the base of capitalism.

In the third world, these two basic modes of exploitation and expansion remained the dominant ones until the onset of limited industrialization, starting from the third quarter of the nineteenth century. In fact, slavery and debt bondage, which died out in western Europe at the end of the Middle Ages, re-emerged in the non-white colonies and ex-colonies. In all these countries the European conquerors had to subjugate various types of precapitalist formations (Luxemburg, 1963, chapters XXVI – XXVIII). However, in many of the conquered societies, particularly in Asia, there were sectors involved in what Marx calls 'simple commodity production' and in multilateral exchange involving money, and very often Europeans came in first as traders who provided new opportunities for trade and employment of money to the proto-capitalist groups. But, of course, the conquering guns of the Europeans were never far from their measuring balances.

The Europeans generally established their suzerainty in territories which were already organized in states with a ruling group extracting a surplus from the ultimate producers. The conquerors could not simply displace the native rulers and take over; they also had to change the commodity composition of the surplus so as to make it internationally exchangeable. In effecting such redirection, force and political authority played a very important part.

Force was used by the rulers to deprive a large proportion of the population of access to means of production, although not all the labour so released could be fruitfully utilized. This led to an intensification of exploitation; labour was now subjected to the harsh routine of the quarries or plantations with the recompense of only a so-called subsistence wage. The theme that native workers need be paid only a 'subsistence' wage and no more, recurs frequently in the policy pronouncements of colonial administrators and businessmen (see, for example, Bettison, 1961, quoted in Harris, 1975). There was also a prevailing rationalization of low wages or of taxation designed to force people in colonial countries to work in the mines or plantations run by metropolitan capitalists, viz. that the natives would not work if they were offered, or allowed to retain, incomes that might leave them with a surplus above subsistence. This rationalization was, of course, primarily a myth to justify the extreme degree of exploitation practised by the alien rulers, but it gained a kind of authenticity because of the severe ill-treatment of the native workers who were then naturally reluctant to embrace the conditions imposed by their white masters. The myth will be further examined in chapter 6.

One basic device for keeping wages low was combination among the masters; this combination was sometimes explicit, but very often an agreement about the inborn 'inferiority' of the natives was enough. The monopsonistic and/or authoritarian control of labour and its ruthless exploitation has been the red thread running through the stories of all colonial and dominated countries.[2] We have already referred to the chattel slavery used in the American South, in the West Indies and Latin America up to almost the very end of the nineteenth century, and to the system of indenturing labour used prior to, and after, the peak period of slavery. Besides these systems of authoritarian control, in South Africa we witness from the end of the nineteenth century a system by which African peasants and tribesmen were forced out of their villages and confined in prison-like barracks in the interest of gold and capitalist profit. (For an early account of the 'discipline' imposed on African labour through what Rosa Luxemburg has called a 'peculiar combination between the modern wage system and primitive authority', see Bryce, 1897, as quoted in Luxemburg, 1963, pp. 363–4; for evidence of the forced depression of wages for black workers in South Africa, see Wilson, 1972).

In order to force labour out of the precapitalist relations under which they had access to a means of livelihood, however primitive it might be, capitalists had to restrict the scope of such access. In advanced capitalist countries, such precapitalist social formations gradually vanished; in colonial countries they never did, primarily because none of the countries made a full transition to industrial capitalism. While such precapitalist formations lasted, the metropo-

2 D. S. Landes has defined imperialist exploitation as 'the employment of labour at wages lower than would obtain in a free bargaining situation' or 'the appropriation of goods at prices lower than would obtain in a free market' (Landes, 1968). This is, however, too inclusive a definition of colonialism. As Adam Smith knew, there can really be no free bargaining between masters and men who are in an unequal bargaining position: 'Masters are always and everywhere in a sort of tacit, but constant and uniform combination not to raise the wages of labour above their actual rate' (Smith, 1776, vol. 1, pp. 59–60). The colonial situation is distinguished by the pervasiveness and persistence of non-market constraints (and not just constraints imposed by monopsony of labour) and the explicit nature of the legal and other sanctions used against workers and the peasantry.

litan capitalists not only exploited them through various devices such as taxation, purchase of products at prices that were lower than could be obtained in the best contemporary markets, and through usury and its supporting financial mechanism. These precapitalist formations also acted as reservoirs of labour which effectively subsidized the advanced capitalist sector by supporting the workers in their infancy and their decrepitude (when the capitalists had extracted the maximum out of the workers), and by keeping alive their families. After the worker had reached an age when he could earn some money and thus pay the taxes etc. imposed by the colonial authorities, he would leave home, earn his pittance, send some of it back home in order to enable the family to pay the hut tax or meet other cash obligations such as the interest due to the moneylender, visit his home to recuperate periodically and finally go back there to die. Meanwhile the capitalist entrepreneur could obtain the worker's services at a wage which was lower than was needed to support his family because the latter were gathering a miserable subsistence in the home village or tribal reservation. Such a process was most obvious in the British colonies of east and central Africa, such as Rhodesia or Kenya, but it could be observed also with respect to Amerindian labour in Latin America before and after its political liberation, and in the case of labour pressed into the jute mills, tea plantations and coal mines of India. The seasonal 'absenteeism' that British capitalists grumbled about in India was part of the system maintaining the low level of wages. (On Africa, see Arrighi, 1970a and Leys, 1976, chapter 2; see also chapter 7 below).

In many countries, particularly those of Asia, which had large populations, capitalist colonialism uprooted the native ruling class that consumed the better class of craft products, introduced machine-made products from the West and thus effectively decimated the traditional crafts; and the tribal people or peasantry were deprived of their customary access to land by making it a vendible asset and giving exclusive property rights to a very restricted set of individuals. An open or disguised surplus of labour emerged in the process. Low wages could then be rationalized on the ground that there was an excess supply of labour. The disguised or open unemployment in the agricultural or artisanal sector in the third world has been mistakenly attributed to the primordial scarcity of fixed and working capital. It is, in fact, the result of a colonial mode of exploitation in which traditional crafts were destroyed for the sake of extracting a surplus from the colonies but the surplus was not used to create alternative avenues of employment. A second type of misunderstanding has clouded the perception of the true nature of such unemployment. As we shall show in the next section, the operation of capitalist colonialism systematically curbs the growth of native capital and hence the drive to accumulate capital within the boundaries of the colony. This factor, allied with the continuous drain of surplus abroad, created a long-term problem of lack of employment.

It is now recognized that when unemployment of labour becomes chronic, the labour market is fragmented into a series of bargains between the masters and the men, with the masters naturally holding the whip hand.[3] Whatever the formal character of the bargain, in many third world countries, the condition of labour – particularly of unorganized labour – is depressed to a level at which it merely subsists. The more slowly growing the economy, other things remaining the same, the lower is generally both the level and the rate of growth of real earnings of labour. This is true not only for capitalist countries but also for countries containing major sectors characterized by precapitalist or mercantile methods of exploitation. (For a rigorous analysis of the connection between rate of investment, rate of growth of income and rate of growth of real wages under capitalist conditions, see Robinson, 1956). To take a bizarre but significant example, the living conditions and natural rates of growth of slaves were better in the southern United States than in the Caribbean islands and Brazil (see Curtin, 1969.) One major reason for the difference is probably that the American South was part of a fast-growing capitalist economy with a large volume of net inflow of capital, whereas the others were at best parts of dominated societies which acted as net transferrers of capital to western Europe and its overseas offshoots.

2.3 DOMINATION OF COLONIAL CAPITAL BY METROPOLITAN CAPITAL AND THE NETWORK OF UNEQUAL INTERDEPENDENCE

The metropolitan capitalists were competing among themselves all the time, and trying to fight off challenges from potential competitors. 'In that "struggle for existence" which provided the basic metaphor of the economic, political, social and biological thought of the bourgeois world, only the "fittest" would survive, their fitness certified not only by their survival but by their domination' (Hobsbawm, 1975, p. 116).

3 This was first formally recognized in the case of commodity markets, by Michael Kalecki who built up his theory of unemployment on the assumption that capitalists exercise monopoly power – particularly in the pricing of industrial products. See Kalecki, 1972a, which contains a selection of his relevant writings from 1933 onwards. For recognition of the formal point by a neoclassical economist, see Arrow, 1959.

When, at the end of the fifteenth century, the Spaniards and the Portuguese discovered the route to the Americas and the new route to Asia, the world outside Europe had already been divided by the two powers (by the Treaty of Tordesillas) in order to keep out other European powers from the territories they meant to conquer or dominate. The Portuguese and the Spaniards did effectively keep the other Europeans out of their spheres of influence until the end of the sixteenth century, although the Spaniards' control of the sea was increasingly challenged by the British, the Dutch and the French and their treasure-laden ships were the objects of attack of chartered and unchartered privateers.

With the entry of the English, the French and the Dutch into the fray using royally chartered monopoly companies, a new phase in the struggle of the western European powers for supremacy began. In effect, the power of the emerging nation states of western Europe was mobilized (although not always with the same degree of efficacy) behind the marauding seafarers of western Europe and their financiers. In Asia, particularly in the Indian Ocean and the littoral states, they directly faced the competition of Asian traders and shipowners. Naval and military defeat at the hands of the Portuguese and then the Dutch and the English eliminated most of the Asian traders' competition. Ironically enough, many Indian merchants financed the activities of the foreign intruders. The plunder of foreign peoples was rationalized in terms of racial superiority or the superiority of the Christian religion, and so from the beginning the right of the conqueror was converted into a permanent position of superiority over the non-white and non-Christian natives. (The conversion of the natives to Christianity did not improve their position much, except, in a few cases, as subordinate collaborators of the conquerors.) Hence there was no question of recruitment of the local proto-bourgeoisie into the ranks of the metropolitan bourgeoisie.

Capitalists of the dominant countries and the potential capitalists of the colonial countries are normally involved in a predator – prey relationship. Initially, in some countries such as India, there were alliances of convenience between conquering Europeans and some native merchants and financiers. But such alliances soon gave way to an unequal relationship within a structure of hierarchical control in which the levers of power were held by Europeans or other capitalists from dominant nations. Most of the surplus extracted by the foreign rulers and capitalists was transferred to the metropolitan countries or, from the nineteenth century onwards, to colonies of white settlement such as the USA, Canada, Australia, etc. This left little with which the local capitalists could expand their own capital base. In any case, in the process of expansion, the metropolitan capitalists closed many avenues of profit to the native businessmen who, perforce, ceased to be capitalists. Thus, in many cases, the local pressure for changes in institutions favouring industrialization could not surface effectively, because the capitalist strata who could give voice and substance to such demands had been stunted or eliminated altogether. It is only when advanced capitalism entered a phase of irreconcilable conflicts within its ranks, and local bourgeoisie or petty bourgeoisie of the third world could struggle for a bigger share of the surplus, that challenges to the older policies could materialize.

Through the conquest of the Americas by the Portuguese and the Spanish, and, following them, by the other European powers, and later on through the domination of the Asian trade with Europe and through the conquest of major parts of Indonesia and India, the European countries had already achieved dominance over world trade, finance and shipping by the end of the eighteenth century. Even in this mercantile phase of exploitation, the political or military authority of the European conquerors was backed by superiority in technology, applied science, organization and information systems. In the first place, important innovations in shipbuilding, navigation, weaponry and ammunition made possible European victories in the eastern seas (where they battled with the Arabs, the Indians, the Indonesians and, less successfully, with the Chinese and the Turks) and on the American *terra firma* (Parry, 1963, Part I, and Parry, 1974, Part III). In the second place, European capitalists enjoyed, through their very process of expansion at home and abroad, important economies of scale in finance, trade, transport, and managerial organization. These advantages were, of course, not available to any and every group of capitalists. Political control and deliberate discrimination were used to exclude outsiders abroad and at home. The monopoly companies created by European states by royal or parliamentary charter were the most public, but not necessarily the most successful, examples of monopoly power wielded by European capitalists to control resources and exclude potential competitors.

The role of the monopoly power, backed by political authority, that was exercised by European capitalists in suppressing the growth of native bourgeoisie has tended to be obscured by the attention paid to the character and role of the so-called 'comprador bourgeoisie' in such countries as China, India, Indonesia and Brazil. The extension of the bourgeoisie has a dual aspect – increase in the power of the class as a whole and the erection of barriers so as to keep it exclusive – without in the process losing its capacity to extend its control over resources. The metropolitan bourgeoisie might sometimes foster a subaltern native bourgeoisie in its own interest when it is struggling against precapitalist formations in the colonies. But it will try to suppress the collaborators if thereby it can increase its total surplus or stave off a threat to its dominance. Racial discrimination, which serves at one end to keep the non-white labour force in subjugation, also serves at the other end to exclude native capitalists from the most profitable avenues of investment. We have seen already that it might pay the metropolitan capitalists to preserve some precapitalist formations and utilize precapitalist methods of exploitation, in the sense that it thereby increases the expropriable surplus. But formation of native capitalist strata is largely thwarted.

In this book, we shall portray the relationships among the capitalists in terms of relations of dominance and subordination. The question still remains as to why the capitalist classes of North America and Western Europe are regarded as belonging to the block of dominant metropolitan bourgeoisie, whereas, let us say, the capitalist classes of South Asia are not so regarded. This subject is not yet as well researched as it should be. The provisional answer is that the early rise of nation states in Europe and their support for their native bourgeoisie served to mark out the latter as powerful on their own; and then open or covert racialism helped to cement the bonds between these initially dominant bourgeoisies and keep out the rest. Something quite similar seems to be happening in east Asia. After the Second World War, the Japanese capitalist class became one of the most aggressive (commercially, that is) in the world. The scattered fractions of the overseas Chinese bourgeoisie in Hong Kong, Singapore, Taiwan profited from Japanese dynamism, and the spin-off from the American–Vietnamese war, and had perforce to invest in industry since the Chinese mainland was closed to them for speculative purposes. Although the Second World War left bitter memories about the Japanese in the minds of the ordinary Chinese, there is no permanent racial barrier between the Chinese and Japanese bourgeoisie. This factor helped to consolidate a block of east Asian bourgeoisie and has acted as a stimulus to the growth of the east Asian economies of South Korea, Taiwan, Hong Kong and Singapore. The latter, of course, have benefited from other factors – such as acting as smuggling centres or supply bases for the American war machine in the east – but these alone would not explain the high rate of growth without bringing in the factor of effective integration with Japanese capitalism.

Racialism can have a paradoxical effect in helping preserve the identity of a subordinate bourgeoisie. One reason why Latin American capitalists, in spite of a longer history of political independence, have tended to merge again and again as subordinate strata of the North Atlantic bourgeoisie, whereas the South Asians have not, is that the former were socially conformable with the North Americans and Europeans but the latter were not.

To come back to our main story, by the inevitable logic of capitalist accumulation the countries under the sway of capitalism were brought closer and closer together. This became most obvious with the coming of the railways, steamships and telegraph systems linking the different continents. But the process had been gathering momentum from the second quarter of the fifteenth century when the Portuguese tried to find new routes to the East. The expansion of the network of interdependence under capitalist colonialism and imperialism is well summarized by the Russian revolutionary, Nikolai Bukharin (1972, p. 28):

International connections may grow in scope, spreading over territories not yet drawn into the vortex of capitalist life. In that case we speak of the extensive growth of world economy. On the other hand, they may assume greater depth, become more frequent, forming as it were a thicker network. In that case we have an intensive growth of world economy. In actual history, the growth of world economy proceeds simultaneously in both directions, the extensive growth being accomplished for the most part through the annexationist policy of the great powers.

This type of 'extensive growth' was easily accomplished by the European capitalist powers up to the end of the nineteenth century at the expense of the third world. It was when room for such expansion became extremely limited that the struggle for redivision of the formal and informal colonies among the advanced capitalist countries began in earnest, and what Lenin called 'imperialism, the highest stage of capitalism' was ushered in. We shall see in the next section that the process of capitalist expansion left permanent gaps and tears in the network of interdependence as far as third world countries are concerned.

For the present, we want to draw attention to the fact that the network of interdependence in physical space, and in the flows of commodities and surpluses, also established relations of unequal interdependence among capitalist groups and other groups (such as landlords) subserving the capitalist interests. The identities of the dominant and dominated partners in the third world countries were never in doubt: the political levers were in the hands of the foreign capitalists, the major enterprises were dominated by them and the direction of flow of net surpluses (for which no equivalent payment was made) was away from such countries. But within the group of European countries, the positions of different partners changed over time. Spain remained the formal sovereign of Spanish America from the beginning of the sixteenth to the beginning of the nineteenth century. But because of the incubus of feudal institutions in Castile (which were reinforced by the easy spoils of conquest), the surpluses extracted from the Americas ended up in Antwerp, Amsterdam or London. In the same way, Portugal surrendered most of her surplus to Britain and other advanced capitalist countries, although formally she retained political sovereignty over parts of her empire until the twentieth century. At a later stage, we see this process being repeated in Britain. Britain had the largest empire until the Second World War, extracted the biggest surplus from her formal and informal colonies, but then invested a major part of the proceeds in the USA, South Africa, Canada and Australia. The capitalist class staying at home or migrating to the white settlements gained enormously, but the home economy gradually fell behind.

The case of British investment overseas and its consequences for the home economy illustrates that we can have a situation where a capitalist class is strong, but its home base is weakened because of its global interests. In a much more attenuated form, the same phenomenon is observed with overseas Chinese and Indian traders and financiers in the interwar period, when they participated on a large scale in the trade and finance of south-east Asia and east Africa, but their home bases remained extremely backward. However, the converse phenomenon is rarely observed within the capitalist world economy. A society which fails to develop a strong native capitalist class tends to slip back in the race for domination. The gradual retardation of Argentina which we shall take up for specific discussion is a case in point. This is one reason why such crude indexes as the level of per capita domestic product or even income, or the degree of urbanization achieved are not reliable guides for projecting the future course of a society, for they leave out a crucial indicator: the strength of the native capitalist class (which may be composed of immigrants) in relation to the other classes in the home society, and in relation to the other capitalist classes with an interest in that economy.

The developments in Portugal, Argentina and Britain that we have referred to also indicate that even in peacetime the subordination of some capitalist groups to others across national boundaries goes on incessantly, as a result of competition between large and small capital, and between relatively advanced and backward segments of the capitalist class. But, of course, competition between capitalist classes can erupt into war, and the struggles of the dominated economies of the third world against their formal or informal rulers have led to wars of liberation. However, because of the head start of the European countries in the field of capitalism and the political hegemony obtained by them over the third world, it was hardly possible to talk about global 'competition' between metropolitan capitalists and capitalists of third world countries until the end of the Second World War. The continuous flow of surpluses out of the third world and the consequent failure to reinvest any major fraction of surplus value in the form of capital goods or working capital was a major factor perennially handicapping the third world countries and helping keep them retarded in relation to the advanced capitalist countries. We turn to the wider consequences of such failure of investment in the next section.

2.4 FAILURE OF INVESTMENT AND ASSOCIATED PHENOMENA OF RETARDATION IN THE THIRD WORLD

Accumulation of capital for the purpose of making a profit is characteristic of capitalism. There was little accumulation of capital in this sense in precapitalist societies, although there were massive investments in cities, palaces and temples, roads and irrigation works in such countries as India, China, Egypt and the Inca empire of South America. When the European powers conquered the Americas in the sixteenth century and parts of Africa and Asia in the sixteenth and seventeenth centuries, they systematically removed the fruits of labour to Europe or the new countries of white settlement; accumulation of capital in the conquered lands was hampered both by the removal of the 'surplus' (which often ate into the subsistence requirements of the people) and by the lack of a capitalist class to invest whatever surplus there might have been and increase the productive assets in the country. In this phase of mercantile capitalism in Europe, the aggregate rate of investment in the European economies perhaps remained low. Nevertheless, a large fraction of this investment owed its origin to the exploitation of the third world colonies.

In the phase of industrial capitalism in Europe and the USA, which developed in the nineteenth century, the densely populated countries of Asia were drawn much more closely into the network of exploitation of European capitalism. It was in this phase that the advanced capitalist countries began a systematic drive to capture the markets of the dominated countries. In Latin America, and much more massively in India, Egypt and China, handicraft industries were damaged by the onslaught of manufactures from western Europe (see Bagchi, 1976a). In contrast to the countries of western Europe, the destruction of handicrafts was not accompanied by a commensurate growth of modern manufacturing industries.

The reasons for this failure are several-fold. First, in European countries other than Britain and in the USA, Canada, Australia and South Africa, a considerable degree of state patronage, including tariff protection, guarantee of purchase by government agencies and financial help, was extended to help modern industries against the competition of manufactures from other countries, particularly British manufactures. As against that, third world countries were either forced or 'persuaded' to adopt free trade policies, so that investment in modern industries became unprofitable. Secondly, much of the investible surplus was transferred overseas, so there was a shortage of funds available to entrepreneurs who might venture into the field of manufacture catering to the home market. Many devices were used to transfer resources from the third world to Europe and thence to the white settlements of North America, Australia, etc. First of all, a major part was removed as a straight political tribute from such large colonies as India and Indonesia. The colonies were saddled with the 'cost' of conquering themselves – this may be called the payment for self-ransoming (a term used in a related context by Pearse, 1975). The colonies were also charged with the cost of defence against revolt or invasion by other powers; Indian revenues, for example, had to pay for the whole cost of defending the British Empire east of the Nile. The colonies also had to pay for the administrators imposed on them by the rulers.

The ruling country usually acted as the *entrepot* for the produce of the colonies, however distant they might be. Hence there was a restricted world market for the primary products of the colonies. The financial power of London enabled it to attract the produce of many other nominally independent countries in a similar way. The shipping services, banking (particularly exchange banking), insurance were monopolized by firms from metropolitan countries, often with direct help from the foreign rulers. Foreign firms also monopolized public utilities, extractive industries, foreign trade and processing industries in many cases (for India see Bagchi, 1972a; for French Madagascar, Dumont, 1966). The success of foreigners in these enterprises in the services or extractive industries largely depended on explicit or implicit barriers against the entry of natives into these fields (for

Indonesia, see Wertheim, 1959; and for India, Bagchi, 1972a).

When the British capitalists invested in railways in India or Argentina, they purchased their capital goods in their home countries, and there was little control on the values at which these purchases were entered in the books of the particular companies. A significant fraction of the loans to such countries as Turkey and the Latin American republics never found their way to those countries (Jenks, 1963, chapters 2 and 3; Cameron, 1961, chapter 15). The claims amassed by the foreigners against the colonial or semi-colonial countries – often on the basis of high monopoly profits reaped in those countries themselves and charging of exorbitant prices on the assets of the companies – all show up as 'foreign investment' in conventional accounts. As it happens, even conventional accounts show that most of the foreign investment by European countries went to the developed capitalist countries of today. There was in fact a massive net transfer of surplus from the third world countries to the metropolitan heartland, to be distributed thence to the white-settled colonies of the USA, Canada, Australia, South Africa, etc.

Careful computations of the true figure of transfer of capital (the nearest approximation is the computation made by Edward Long for Jamaica in 1774, which we have quoted in chapter 3) from the third world do not exist. Assuming that the major part of the surplus transferred took the form of unrequited exports, I have used the difference between merchandise exports and merchandise imports of such countries as India and Indonesia as a measure of the surplus transferred overseas without any return (see chapter 4 below). We should remember that such a measure may often be an underestimate of the surplus transferred, since it excludes the large expenditure incurred by the ruling foreigners in the colony itself for their security and consumption.

Apart from lack of state patronage and removal of surplus from the third world to the metropolitan countries, another factor which inhibited the growth of modern manufacturing was the slow growth of a native capitalist class. This was, of course, connected with the other two factors. The native traders or financiers who survived or even thrived in the colonies or semi-colonial lands acted as subordinate collaborators of the foreign capitalists (whose interests centred on the export–import sector) or as direct participants in activities connected with foreign trade. The condition for their survival was precisely that they should not venture into the hazardous field of modern manufacturing except where it enjoyed some overwhelming natural advantages.

The destruction of handicrafts thus led to the de-industrialization of many third world economies in the nineteenth century in the sense that the proportion of national income generated by, and the percentage of the population dependent on, industry of various kinds declined. Most of the population released in this process had to find an alternative means of livelihood in agriculture. In order to absorb all these people in agriculture, while giving them at least a standard of living which they had enjoyed before, massive investment in agriculture would have been necessary. However, such investment was not forthcoming either in the public or in the private domain. While some spectacular irrigation works were constructed in Egypt and India, such investment was quite small as a proportion of national incomes or domestic products of these countries. Furthermore, it was specifically designed to stimulate the growth of export crops, and to raise revenue for the government. The uncompensated costs imposed by such works on the local population in the form of the spread of such diseases as *bilharzia* and malaria, destruction of temporary wells or minor irrigation works, and eventual waterlogging and salinity, were ignored. Such investment further strengthened the hold of the metropolitan capitalists on the economy.

The phenomenon of de-industrialization was associated with the penetration of railway networks within the third world countries. The railways connected ports with points in the interior, and increased the relative distances between places in the hinterland, since very often the only connections they now had between themselves passed through the ports. The railway revolution thus turned the third world economies inside out and enormously increased the intensity of dominion of advanced capitalist countries over them. The accompanying stress on cultivation of exportable cash crops, on the vendibility of land as an asset, and on prompt payment of obligations to the state, landlords and moneylenders in cash, enormously increased the economic power of the landlord, the trader and the moneylender over the primary producer (the producer might be either the increasingly insecure, cultivating peasant or the vanishing artisan, or the most wretched of all, the landless labourer in the fields). The increase in the intensity of these internal methods of exploitation made investment in industry a decidedly less attractive proposition. In many third world countries, the displaced rulers of earlier times found a place in the colonial schemes as 'native princes', petty chieftains and landlords. They, along with the landlords and moneylenders (who primarily dealt in consumption loans), contributed to an increase in the share of consumption in that part of the surplus which was retained within these countries. Thus the stunting of native capitalist growth by the metropolitan countries found its own vicious logic in the proliferation of the spendthrift exploiters native to such societies.

The peasantry who lost their land or the artisans who lost their professions swelled the ranks of the unemployed. It then became easier for the landlords to treat them practically as serfs, and for the European planters in various lands to get them as indentured labourers. For, with a weak accumulation drive in the third world, the supply of labour often exceeded the demand for it.

While mercantile capital was exploiting the third world economies in the nineteenth century, primarily as a junior partner of industrial capital in Europe and North America, industrial capital in Europe and the USA was evolving towards 'monopoly capital' (Sweezy, 1964, chapter 14). Practically alone among the social scientists of his day, Marx had foreseen the rise of large monopolistic or oligopolistic production units on the basis of what he called the processes of concentration and centralization of capital. Under the process of concentration, the enterprise accumulates more capital either by ploughing back part of its profits or by raising more capital on the market. Under the second process an enterprise grows by absorbing other units of production through formal mergers and take-overs, or acquisition of the business of bankrupt firms. The incorporation of enterprises as joint-stock companies with limited liability facilitates both the processes enormously. In time, some business enterprises became the giant transnational corporations that straddle the capitalist world today. The difference between these monopolies and the monopolies incorporated by royal charter in the mercantilist phase is that the former are primarily producing and financing rather than trading and collecting organizations, and that they owe their position not so much to legal restrictions on the entry of rivals as to economies of scale in production, finance and management (see Baran and Sweezy, 1968, chapter 2; Galbraith, 1967, chapters 2–8, and Murray, 1972).

The phase in which industrial firms of capitalist countries acquire the character of monopolistic organizations is also the phase of imperialism as defined by Lenin.[4] In this phase, among other things,

4 We shall not deal with the Hobson–Lenin theory of imperialism directly, because while our focus is on the impact of western European and American capitalism on the third world countries and the development of the latter, the main purpose of Lenin's book on imperialism, as Lenin explained in his preface to the French and German editions, was 'to present, a *composite picture* of the world capitalist system in its international relationships at the beginning of the twentieth century – on the eve of the

'The export of capital, as distinguished from the export of commodities, becomes of particularly great importance, international monopoly combines of capitalists are formed which divide up the world, the territorial division of the world by the greatest capitalist powers is completed', and a struggle begins to redivide the world among the advanced capitalist nations, leading to world-wide conflagrations (Lenin, 1917; Dobb, 1940, chapter 7 and Sweezy, 1964, chapter 17). The export of capital from advanced capitalist to third world countries still takes a second place to the extraction of surplus from the latter, most of the re-investment going to other advanced capitalist countries or to countries with large white populations (see, for example, Thomas, 1967).

But the other aspects of monopoly capital affect the third world countries directly. The struggle among advanced capitalist countries, leading first to the Bolshevik Revolution of 1917 and, along with other factors, to the long crisis of the period between the two World Wars, gave the newly emerging capitalist and professional strata of the third world some room for manoeuvre on a political plane. Many third world countries consciously tried to adopt a programme of industrialization, partly under the stimulus of the slightly loosened hold of imperialism on the world and partly under the pressure of the severe depression of the 1930s which caused acute balance of payments crises. But most of them found themselves handicapped by the effects of the earlier history of exploitation and by their phase lag behind the monopoly capital of western Europe and North America. The lack of modern industry, de-industrialization and failure to invest in agriculture had left a large part of their population desperately poor and therefore unable to provide the enlarged markets that the minimum economic scale of many industries demanded. The same processes of exploitation had also deprived their populations of traditional skills, without endowing them with either new skills or literacy. There had been no opportunity either to build up those capital goods industries which are at the base of modern industrial development. During the period when the third world economies were integrated forcibly with the outside world, the earlier linkages between different parts of the economy were snapped, and the only links between different sectors were provided by the world market. As we shall see in chapter 6,

first world imperialist war' (Lenin, 1917, p. 181). Since Lenin's focus was on the explanation of the origins of the First World War, the conflicts among the imperialist powers received his primary attention, whereas in our case such conflicts figure only in so far as they bear on the development of the third world countries.

paradoxically enough, the spread of the market economy effectively forced many people off the market, when they faced a choice between starvation as an unsuccessful seller of unwanted labour power or unwanted commodities in the market, on the one hand, and scrounging a living out of various types of subsistence activities or a relationship of 'voluntary' bondage with a patron on the other. Thus when third world countries began their industrialization drive, they encountered various gaps in linkages and bottlenecks in supply.

In advanced capitalist countries, technological development had continued and the scales of output and spans of control of modern joint-stock companies had expanded enormously. These larger and technologically advanced corporations were hungrily looking for markets, and often they became the major beneficiaries of the tariff walls and import restrictions erected by third world countries in pursuit of industrial development.

The phase lag between monopoly capital in advanced capitalist countries and the embryonic industrial capitalism in third world countries had a doubly retarding effect on the latter because the industrial capital had at its base a structure of exploitation which remained basically mercantilist or even smacked of feudalism. Land continued to be monopolized by a small group of landlords who had little direct connection with production or, alternatively, who used various types of non-market pressures to get a surplus out of the tenants or labourers. Peasants also had traders and usurious moneylenders as other exploiters demanding a part of their output. Often the landlord himself was also the trader and moneylender. Some landowners began to behave like capitalist farmers consciously using new methods, wherever profitable. But they continued to use instruments of debt-bondage or non-market power when such use would advance their economic position or provide them with a more secure long-run return. Thus the existence of capitalist farmers in such countries has not always been associated with capitalist relations of production. Nor, of course, has the existence of capitalist relations in one sector of the economy led to its transformation into a full-fledged industrial capitalist economy.

In the following chapters the strength or weakness, the advance or retrogression of a class or country will be judged by looking at its position in relation to all the major constituents with which it is continually in contact: the capitalist classes of advanced economies, the economically advanced countries themselves, the other classes which make up the coalitions that rule the advanced capitalist countries, and the peasantry and workers whom the indigenous capitalist class exploits in collaboration with the capitalist classes of advanced countries. The relations of the third world and its capitalists with the socialist bloc are also relevant. The capitalist and other ruling classes of third world countries would enter into friendly relations with the socialist bloc so long as they see such relations strengthening their position vis-à-vis their own peoples or vis-à-vis other capitalist countries. Since they cannot remove the basic causes of retardation without destroying the effects of past history of exploitation, and, in effect, eliminating themselves (since they are an integral part of the present structure of exploitation) they will not progress in a genuinely socialist direction just because they have friendly relations with the socialist bloc. Thus no qualitatively new principles are introduced into the analysis of problems of individual third world countries through the recognition of the possibility of friendly intercourse between them and the socialist world.

2.5 CONTRADICTIONS OF CAPITALIST DEVELOPMENT IN THE COLONIAL AND POST-COLONIAL ERA

Summing up, we can say that capitalist colonialism and imperialism supported a mechanism of exploitation which had strong elements of usury, speculation and domination by landlords in its structure. Such a structure, which has been characterized sometimes as 'semi-feudalism' becomes particularly characteristic of the third world during the era of industrial capitalism in Europe. For, while industrial capitalism transformed the occupational structures of advanced capitalist countries, reducing agriculture to the status of the smallest sector in terms of both employment and income generated, in third world countries (including the ones which had already been subjected to colonial exploitation in the mercantile era of European capitalism) it led to a decline in the employment and income generated by industry (particularly in the nineteenth century), and a relative rise in the position of agriculture. Furthermore, in many third world countries, this was associated with a premature rise in the share of the tertiary sector in both income and employment generated (see Holub, 1970, for the experience of Asian countries in this regard).[5] This is because, on the one hand, many people who could not be employed in

5 The category, 'income from services' includes a variety of imputed incomes to people who are, for the most part, underemployed, and earnings of pimps, meddling bureaucrats or torturers in police cells, which are liabilities from a social point of view, and cannot therefore be treated on the same level as output of agriculture, industry, or transport.

agriculture or industry took up small-scale trade or other services as a last resort and swelled the ranks of the underemployed connected with these branches of activity, and, on the other hand, usury, high trading margins, profits from speculative trade, etc., went to swell the incomes of many who had little direct part in productive activities. (For connection between capital transfers and changes in occupational structure under capitalism, see Bagchi, 1972b; for the consequences of de-industrialization in the third world, see Bagchi, 1976a.)

Such antithetical results of the development of capitalism in advanced and retarded capitalist countries suggest that industrial capitalism is not a system that can be simply diffused through countries like, say, literacy. The typical paths of development in the past have *needed* some countries to *stay* retarded, transferring capital, providing cheap raw materials and markets for manufactures (particularly the lagging branches of manufactures, the more progressive lines finding markets in the more affluent countries), acting as reservoirs of cheap labour and sometimes – but more rarely – functioning as easy new frontiers to be conquered through very private (and often socially reprehensible) enterprise (as in Brazil today). Such a paradoxical perspective becomes plausible when we realize that capitalism is, of necessity, a deeply unequal system of domination of one class by another, of one nation by the ruling class of another. In chapters 3 and 4 we provide some histories of this unequal system in operation. In chapters 5–8 we delineate the logic of inequality as it works through economics, class relations, political alignments and the environment.

When third world countries attained political independence, some of the more naked forms of colonial exploitation and consequent capital transfer were ended. In the meantime, however, advanced capitalist countries had evolved new techniques of production, and huge conglomerate enterprises which straddled more than one nation. Although the scientific developments were often financed by the state in advanced capitalist countries, they were developed by the transnational enterprises. Through the system of patent rights and the development of knowhow closely guarded by the firms, much of the new technological developments came to be controlled by the transnationals and other firms based in advanced capitalist countries. The third world countries in most cases allowed the foreign firms to go on working within their frontiers and generally recognized the international patent laws, although in most cases the patents were held by foreign firms. On the other hand, they remained technically backward and failed to introduce an alternative spectrum of techniques, which would have required an alternative strategy of development altogether. Furthermore, many third world countries became dependent on 'aid' (mostly loans) from the advanced capitalist countries for solving their balance of payment problems. This 'aid' in turn created markets for the transnational corporations in the third world. Hence the third world countries were deeply penetrated by these Trojan horses of foreign firms, often acting in collusion with local collaborators.

These local collaborating enterprises were in many cases public sector corporations which found it easier to depend on transnationals than to alter the economic environment so as to prepare for technological independence. The transnationals in turn found third world public sector organizations more pliable and better endowed with financial resources than local private firms. Thus, in a strange inversion of the usual logic, a symbiotic relationship grew up between the monopolistic transnationals and local public sector enterprises, which were originally supposed to be spearheads in the third world countries' struggle for independence. Of course, dependence on transnationals, on foreign aid, and on advanced capitalist countries and the socialist bloc have led to a drain of resources from the third world, and produced new contradictions. The symbiosis of third world enterprises with transnationals or enterprises in the Soviet bloc has not cured the internal stresses in the third world social fabric. These external and internal contradictions portend further change in the disorderly progress of retarded societies through economic subjugation, political instability and revolution or counterrevolutionary authoritarianism.

Some of the other aspects of the relations of third world economies to transnationals and foreign capital in general are dealt with in chapters 5, 7 and 9 below.

3

UNDERDEVELOPMENT IN LATIN AMERICA: HISTORICAL ROOTS

3.1 INTRODUCTION

In this chapter we shall first describe the typical social and exploitative institutions inherited by Latin America at the beginning of the nineteenth century when Spanish and Portuguese rule ended in all mainland countries of Latin America. We follow this up with a brief review of the development of three large countries of the region, viz. Argentina, Brazil and Chile. Their history has a special interest in highlighting the constraints on autonomous national development and social progress under the aegis of international capitalism even when the countries are formally independent.

3.2 DEPOPULATION IN AMERICA UNDER EUROPEAN RULE AND THE RISE OF THE ATLANTIC SLAVE TRADE

In the early sixteenth century the Spaniards overthrew the Aztec empire in Mexico and the Inca empire in Peru. Their superiority lay in the military arts rather than in the arts of production, and, in their conviction that they were ethnically superior to the Amerindians, they conquered by guile and force (see Parry, 1973, chapters 3–5; and Parry, 1963, chapters 3–7). The *conquistadores* wanted to exploit the labour of the indigenous population and make fortunes as quickly as possible.

However, excessive and inefficient exploitation of Amerindian labour, combined with the outbreak of epidemics, led to the decimation of the Amerindian population. This exploitation took the following main forms. (i) The Amerindians were confined to special villages and their labour was commandeered for use by the Spanish officials and settlers. (ii) The local people were uprooted from their villages and sent to work in the mines of Mexico and Peru, where they died in their thousands. (iii) The Indians were deprived of their best pieces of land, and of essential sources of water supply, which the

Spaniards occupied, so that the income of the former declined. (iv) The local people were often compelled to grow crops which were unfamiliar to them, and which were not fully adapted to their careful system of irrigation (for a description of the pre-Columbian system of irrigation, see Price, 1971). (v) The Spaniards introduced livestock farming in well-populated areas. The Indians often practised shifting cultivation with long rotational cycles, or irrigated agriculture with careful allocation of water and the fields. Naturally, the horses, cattle and sheep owned by the Spaniards 'ate up' the Indians.

According to Borah and Cook, the Amerindian population of New Spain (Mexico and parts of central America) numbered between 20 and 28 million in 1519 – a very high figure indeed.[1] From this level, the Indian population of New Spain fell to a mere 1.075 million in 1605. The Carib Indians, who numbered about 300,000 in 1492, and who tenaciously resisted the Spanish invaders, were practically wiped out (see Rich, 1967).

The demographic disaster in Spanish America coincided with a serious demographic reversal in Spain (Parry, 1973, pp. 230–3), so that even were the Spaniards willing to replenish the active work force in Latin America, Spain could not re-populate the land with her own inhabitants. This disaster reinforced the social retardation that had set in in Spain in the wake of the inflow of precious metals. While the rich Spaniards lived as grandees on the fruits of the American plunder, the other western European nations took advantage of their parasitism by destroying the local manufactures of Spain and taking over many branches of Spanish trade. The nascent capitalism of Catalonia was smothered by the decadent feudalism of Castile, and Spain suffered a long-term retardation in comparison with the Netherlands, England and France (see Borah, 1951, Elliott, 1963, and Israel, 1974).

Spain needed exploitable labour to carry on her empire and this labour was increasingly supplied by Africans transported as slaves across the Atlantic. The Arabs had traded in African slaves for a long time before the west African coast was invaded by Portugal and other European nations (Oliver and Fage, 1969). But these slaves were used mostly as servants in the court, as mercenary soldiers or as domestic servants, rather than as the mainstay of the exploited labour force and their numbers were far smaller than those involved in the Atlantic slave trade, particularly in the late eighteenth and nineteenth

1 For comparison, it should be noted that, as late as 1800, the two countries of western Europe with the highest populations, viz. France and Germany, had populations of 26.9 and 24.5 million respectively. See Glass and Grebenik, 1965, table 7.

centuries. The Portuguese were the first European nation to make slave-raids on the west coast of Africa or to purchase slaves from African chiefs on the coast, from the early fifteenth century onwards. They were soon joined by other European nations when a demand for slaves arose in the Caribbean plantations, in Spanish America, and in Brazil, which was under Portuguese rule.

This trade in human beings was rationalized by racialism. A class society needs an ideology of inequality in order to maintain the status quo (Mason, 1970, chapter 1, and Robinson, 1972, chapter 4). Racialism is a special kind of divisive and inegalitarian ideology; it is an ideology of domination over the majority of human beings on the basis of skin colour (white versus black or brown), the shape of the nose, and the texture of hair. When the European navigators and pirates began first to explore the Caribbean islands, they regarded the autochthonous population as material for either enslavement or extermination. In the early years of settlement of such islands as Barbados and St Christopher by the British, white servants were press-ganged to emigrate to these islands as indentured labourers. But such workers soon left the plantations to set up as freeholders, and proved too expensive for their masters. Negro slaves were then imported in vast numbers to convert the Caribbean islands into vast sugar plantations run on the basis of slave labour justified by racialism (see Dunn, 1973).[2] The apparent freedom of the Latin conquering peoples from racialism, as evidenced primarily by the ease with which they tolerated miscegenation between white males and black or brown females, has been shown to be largely a myth (Boxer, 1973a, chapter 11, and R. Bastide, 'Dusky Venus, black Apollo' in Baxter and Sansom, 1972). Bartolomeo Las Casas, who earned the sobriquet of the 'Apostle of the Indians', by passionately pleading the case for banning the enslavement of the Indians, had to combine his plea with toleration of the fate of chattel slavery for black Africans (for contemporary justification or denunciation of Spanish rule in America and for evaluation of the various policies pursued by Spain to 'protect' and segregate the Indians, see Hanke, 1969a, section III).

The racialist ideology served the purpose of justifying not only

2 Some writers have tried to represent racialism as basically an after-birth of the need to use slaves in the Caribbean and on the mainland of America (see, for example, Williams, 1944 and Oliver C. Cox, 'Race and exploitation: A Marxist view', in Baxter and Sansom, 1972). But the attitude that non-European and non-Christian peoples were *ipso facto* inferior to Europeans was already there among the early European navigators to Africa and America. Of course, the racialist doctrine was given a new 'scientific' basis in the nineteenth century by thinkers as diverse in range and ability as Count de Gobineau and Charles Darwin (see Curtin, 1971).

Negro slavery, but also other modes of exploitation of labour. At a later stage, carefully propagated doctrines of superiority of whites served to keep the oppressed peoples divided among themselves. Racialism and similar ideologies based on caste and religion are among the most potent instruments still preventing exploited groups from uniting together. Several Latin American governments have had an official policy of encouraging European immigration with the objective of 'whitening' the race (see Dumont, 1965, chapter 3, and Mason, 1970). At another level, racialism was used by the conquering European capitalists to exclude native merchants and financiers from the most profitable opportunities of trade and investment in India, China and Indonesia.

According to Philip Curtin (1969, table 77), during the whole period of the Atlantic slave trade, lasting from, say, 1451 to 1870, about 10 million slaves were transported across the Atlantic.[3] Of these, almost 2 million were imported into the Americas over the period 1801–70 – that is, after slave trade had been declared illegal in the British Empire! Of the total number of slaves imported, Spanish America accounted for 1.6 million, Brazil for 3.6 millions, British colonies and ex-colonies (including the USA) for 2 million, and the French Caribbean for 1.6 million.

The trade in slaves increased from the late seventeenth to the nineteenth century as a result of the rapidly expanding market for sugar and other tropical products in Europe, and the competition among plantation owners and their need to cut down costs as much as possible. Furthermore, under the brutal conditions of exploitation, particularly in the Caribbean and Brazil, slaves failed to reproduce themselves, so that fresh supplies were continually needed to replenish the stock of worn-out and dying slaves. The net imports of slaves into Jamaica, for example, between 1731 and 1775 amounted to 266,320, but the net increase in slave population between 1730 and 1778 amounted only to 136,369 (Sheridan, 1965, tables 1 and 2; see also Sheridan, 1976). Since there was no large-scale manumission or migration of slaves, this state of affairs indicates that capitalist enterprise in the eighteenth century was now eating up whole African communities, after killing off millions of Amerindians in the sixteenth century. In this enterprise – which was so profitable for plantation-owners and for the European metropolis and so disastrous for everyone else – an average human being was valued in Jamaica at slightly more

3 Curtin's estimates are on the conservative side. Anstey has indicated that for important sectors of the slave trade Curtin's estimates may have to be revised upwards by 10 per cent or more. See Anstey, 1975 and 1977.

than twice the value placed on a typical unit of livestock on the plantations (see Sheridan, 1965, tables 6 and 7). The conditions in the plantations on the islands under Spanish rule were probably much worse.[4]

The slave trade and slavery were highly profitable to individual slavers and planters, and also to the advanced capitalist countries – particularly Great Britain. Although the early demands for African slaves originated in the Spanish colonies, Spain was herself unable to supply these slaves. The trade was carried on mainly by nationals of other countries. For Spanish colonies this was organized under *asiento* (licence) by Portuguese, Dutch, French and British shippers. These nations, of course, supplied their own colonies as well. Thus production by means of slave labour and the slave trade became joint enterprises of western European capitalists. As the British gained naval supremacy of the western, and later of the entire, world, they also became the leading 'slavers', carrying off the major share of the profits from the slave trade.

The slave trade and the slave-based plantations formed vital links in the overseas flows of commodities and capital supporting the Industrial Revolution in eighteenth-century Britain. Slavers obtained slaves through raids in which they enlisted the support of African chiefs, and sold them to the planters in the Caribbean and South America. These slaves were 'paid for' by providing the chiefs and other collaborators with consumer goods produced in Britain. The planters produced rum, sugar and other tropical products which were sold to Britain and the northern British colonies (which became the USA later on). The northern colonies in turn provided the planters with foodstuffs, timber, animals, etc., and obtained many of their manufactures from Britain. Normally the West Indian colonies had an export surplus with Britain, and the northern colonies had an import surplus which was partly covered by capital exports from Britain. This sort of pattern, in which the 'colonies of exploitation' (West Indies in this case) have an (unrequited) export surplus and the colonies of European settlement

4 Jamaican plantations, as the outposts of British capitalism, were more heavily capitalised than the average plantation on other islands. This proved a handicap when slavery was first abolished in the British Empire and West Indian sugar lost its special tariff advantages in Britain. Spanish colonies in the Caribbean evaded the British embargo on slave trade far into the nineteenth century. They thereby passed the cost of breeding the slaves on to the African societies, and enjoyed lower costs per slave than the British colonies (in the period between abolition of slave trade and of slavery). When free trade in sugar was introduced at last, the slave-produced sugar found a ready market in Britain. Thus it is one of the ironies of capitalism in advanced countries that it thrived on slave-produced cotton (imported from the southern USA) and slave-produced sugar.

have an import surplus which is covered by capital exports from the metropolis becomes much more pronounced in the nineteenth century, as we shall see in chapter 4. For most of the eighteenth century, colonial trade provided the most dynamic element in British export trade, which in turn helped expand the market for British manufactures. Furthermore, British capitalists controlled practically all the links in the production and trade of the West Indian colonies (as opposed, for instance, to the case of North America); this rendered them among the most valuable possessions Britain had (Saul, 1960, pp. 7–8; and Deane and Cole, 1967, p. 34).

The gains made by the ruling country from a colony are not always easy to compute. The usual balance of payments data are often quite useless for computing such gains. For, in such computations a metropolitan country is often credited with the performance of non-existent services (where the payment by the colony is really a political tribute) or the nationals of the metropolitan country exercise an effective monopoly on the supply of certain commodities and services and the monopolistic element in the payments made by the colony cannot be separated out. We shall discuss such problems in greater detail in chapter 4. For Jamaica, we are fortunate in the possession of a contemporary computation by Edward Long, a leading planter, which is comprehensive in the sense that it takes account of all the ways in which Britain earned an income from that colony (see table 3.1).

Table 3.1 *Annual income of Great Britain from the Jamaica trade, 1773 (figures in pounds sterling)*

Freight inwards and outwards	414,600
Insurance	20,000
Commissions, brokerage and other charges	260,000
Profit on merchandise trade	130,357
Profit on the slave trade	125,142
Absentees, expenditures	200,000
Interest on borrowed funds	35,000
Transport of merchants, planters and servants	4,500
Balance paid to North America and remitted to Great Britain	45,321
Balance paid to Ireland and remitted to Great Britain	14,244
TOTAL	1,249,164

Source: Edward Long, *The History of Jamaica* (3 vols., London, 1774), vol. 1, p. 507, quoted by Sheridan, 1965, as table 9.

To these profits must be added that portion of the annual income 'which was not repatriated but held in idle balances, reinvested or lent out locally', and the total would then come to £ 1.5 million per annum (Sheridan, 1965, p. 305). Sheridan concluded that 'from 8 to 10 per cent of the income of the mother country [i.e. Britain] came from the West Indies in the closing years of the eighteenth century, and probably a larger percentage in the period preceding the American War of Independence' (Sheridan, 1965, p. 306).[5] In the following, we shall mostly be concerned with Latin America which also imported slaves from Africa. How were the African societies affected by the slave trade?

The West African societies suffered terribly from the operations of the fishers of men. The absolute depopulation of the favourite hunting-grounds of the slave traders was severe enough. But even more important was perhaps the intensification of wars fought with firearms and the retarding effect of the channelling of economic activities towards the forcible enslavement and export of human beings. In this phase of West African history, when the Europeans chose to operate through chiefs rather than rule the African states directly, the effect of western man on the internal structure of these societies could not have been profound. The example of Europe slave-raiders was not likely to be considered worth looking up to either. 'Read book and learn to be rogue as well as white man' went a common west African saying (quoted by J. D. Hargreaves, 'Relations with Africa', in Goodwin, 1965, p. 246). For similar reasons, the western impact on the culture of Angola or Congo was also entirely superficial, or simply bestial (cf. Boxer, 1973a, chapter 4).

In the Caribbean islands, after the formal abolition of slavery, a peasant society gradually grew up. But its growth was hampered by the existence of European-owned plantations, in whose interest the development of peasant agriculture was often deliberately throttled, as in Guyana (Adamson, 1972, chapters 1–3): a landowning peasantry would demand higher wages for working on the plantations and would resist the oppression of the planters in a more determined fashion. In

5 There is considerable controversy surrounding the question of why Britain took the lead in abolishing so profitable an enterprise as the slave trade and slavery itself. Eric Williams has successfully demolished the view that it was simply the pressure exerted by a group of humanitarians in England that effected the miracle. But for full understanding of the issues involved, it would be necessary to look beyond the narrow economic interests of slavers and plantation owners towards the larger interests of industrial capitalism; the latter needed to free capital from more backward-looking enterprises and to demolish the mercantile system of which slave trade and slavery were such important components. For a balanced summary of the debate and a bibliography, see Hopkins, 1973, pp. 112–16.

several colonies, the plantations were kept practically intact by importing indentured labourers. When these labourers in turn became free, they merged with the general mass of ex-slaves and other indigenous peoples. But, of course, the 'plurality' in the society created by colonialism was carefully nurtured in the interests of the ruling classes.

In West Africa, a new chapter in colonialism began with the 'scramble for Africa' at the end of the nineteenth century, that was the prelude to the first imperialist world war. There also the majority of Africans were converted into peasants, and the usual mercantile methods of exploitation were deployed (see chapter 2). However, the major arena of exploitation of peasantry in the nineteenth century shifted to Asia – to India, Indonesia and China. We discuss the underdevelopment of societies peopled predominantly by formally free peasants in chapter 4. But we shall take up certain specific illustrations from West Africa again in our chapters on class structure and the nature of the state in retarded societies. We now turn to the mainland of South America, to see how Spanish and Portuguese colonialism up to the beginning of the nineteenth century and the 'voluntary colonialism' of the era of liberalism led to many of the problems of underdevelopment today (for an authoritative account of developments in West Africa see Hopkins, 1973; see also Rodney, 1973).

3.3 LATIN AMERICAN SOCIETY UNDER SPANISH RULE AND AT THE TIME OF LIBERATION

After the conquest of Mexico and Peru, the Spanish *conquistadores* were rewarded by the Crown with *encomiendas*, which were essentially the right to exact tribute in the form of goods, money, or, most important of all, labour from the Indians who were 'entrusted' to the *encomenderos*. Hernan Cortes, the conqueror of Mexico, had, officially, the right to exact tribute from 23,000 tributaries, and in actual fact from many more. A grant of land to the *encomendero* was made separately and was not tied up legally with the *encomienda*. Nor was an *encomienda* meant to be heritable except by special permission. Thus by separating the control over labour from the control over land, the Spanish Crown tried to prevent the emergence of great landed chieftains who might challenge the central authority. The ban on Indian slavery was also probably motivated by the same consideration, although theological arguments might have played their part. The Spanish Crown, over the course of the sixteenth century, succeeded in asserting its authority over the *conquistadores*, and in largely preserving the personal liberty of the Indians (except those who had already been enslaved during the course of conquest, or those who had been later enslaved as rebels). But it needed Indian labour for working the inhospitable mines and for public works. It then resorted to *repartimiento* (division) of Indian labour, under which officials had the right to allocate labour for 'public' purposes, which also included work on private estates and ranches and, of course, on private mines, mainly of silver and mercury, in Mexico and Peru. Mercury mining was horrible in its effect on living workers and even more in killing off miners. The apologia was then used that forced labour, called *mita*, had been exacted also by the Inca rulers in Peru whom the Spaniards overthrew (see Whitaker, 1941).

The Spanish Crown appointed officials called *corregidores*, to guard the interests of Indians. They used their position to exploit the latter, who had to pay tribute to the *encomenderos* or other private lords, and to satisfy the greed of the *corregidores* (who bought up the goods produced by Indians at low prices and sold to them the goods they had to buy, at high prices, and who took bribes for exempting particular Indians from the obligations of *repartimiento*). However, the Spanish Crown did try to prevent the emergence of centres of local power under the *criollos* (that is, Americans born of Spanish ancestors). The society remained extremely hierarchical, with authority exercised by various kinds of royal officials – centred on towns – with estate-owners lording it over the Indians in the interior – but in theory, subject to supervision and correction by royal officials. *Criollo* and immigrant European merchants made fortunes and then married into the established landed families, and the sway of a narrowly based ruling class over the whole society was consolidated (Halperin-Donghi, 1975, chapter 1). Indians retained a large part of their land, although many of them effectively became *peones* – bound under debt bondage to particular estate-owners. Indians were also divided up into segregated communities, which made it difficult for them to unite and revolt effectively against Spanish rule, although the whole of Spanish colonial history was interspersed with heroic revolts and resistance by the Indians.[6]

Spain, in spite of her steep decline as a military power in Europe, retained her possessions on the American mainland until the beginning of the nineteenth century. During this period, enormous

6 For descriptions of society under Spanish rule, and of attempts to exercise royal authority over the local rule by *criollo* estate-owners, see Parry, 1948, 1973, 1974 and Israel, 1974; for the effect of Spanish rule on the solidarity of the Indians, see Gibson, 1969; on general issues of the nature of the society in Latin America, see Frank, 1971 and Luis Vitale, 'Latin America: Feudal or capitalist?', in Petras and Zeitlin, 1968.

quantities of silver, gold, sugar, hides, etc., were exported to Europe, silver taking pride of place. The value of exports from Spanish America greatly exceeded that of imports, since most of the Spaniards in control went there primarily to make enough money to be able to cut a figure back at home (Furtado, 1972, p. 13). The extravagance of the royal treasury in Madrid also had its share in these developments. But because of various restrictions put on trade and because of difficulty in communications, some local manufactures, such as textiles and leather products, grew up in Spanish America.

Spain and Spanish America were involved in a recession in the seventeenth century, partly stemming from decline in silver production but mainly from depopulation of Indians; this left a permanent imprint on the structure of society. Royal or official demands on Indian labour through the instrument of *repartimiento* were gradually restricted. On the other side, Indians abandoned much of their land, and sought the 'protection' of powerful *criollo* estate-owners. Indian reserves became reserves of bonded labour for the estate-owners. Thus the typical Latin American institution of hacienda with its necessary complement of peonage or hereditary debt-bondage of the Indians grew up, although, in theory, such institutions did not have royal sanction behind them. In parts of Spanish America, such as central Peru, where the control of the colonial authorities was necessarily loose, almost from the beginning, the *conquistadores* tried to combine the ownership of land with control over the Amerindian peoples. Thus a structure of society tended to be built up which was much nearer the traditional pattern of a feudal economy in Europe, except that the landlords were the subjects of the Crown rather than vassals, and their aims were mercantile rather than to extend political power for its own sake. But the condition of the subject Amerindian peoples was often much more servile than that of the serfs of Europe (Bauer, 1975, chapter 1).

In the eighteenth century, under the Bourbon monarchs of Spain, attempts were made to assert Crown authority, and at the same time to stimulate production and trade. Some of the more irksome restrictions on trade such as a prohibition on direct trade between Peru and Mexico were removed in 1774. With partial recovery of the Amerindian population, with increased flows of silver from the mines, and increase in demand emanating from an industrializing Europe, Spanish American production and trade also recovered. This naturally benefited the *criollos* and Spaniards controlling trade and production. They began to smart under the tighter administration brought in by the Bourbon monarchs. The benefits of freer trade and the example of the thirteen colonies of the United States, whose struggle for independence had been actively assisted by France and Spain, opened the eyes of the *criollos* to what they could gain out of full independence and freedom to trade with whomever they liked. Thus was set the stage for the wars of liberation of the Spanish colonies from 1810 onwards.

Except in Mexico, the call for the revolt was generally given by upper-class *criollos* immediately after Napoleon's usurpation of power in Spain. Only in Mexico did the struggle for independence start also as a struggle for a more just social order. There a parish priest, Miguel Hidalgo, led the Indians in revolt in 1810 with the cry of freedom and land. He was quickly captured and defeated. But his banner was taken up by another priest, Jose Maria Morelos. Morelos' revolt, too, was defeated by a union of the army, the church, the *criollo* land-owners and the Spanish Crown (Galeano, 1973, pp. 57–8, Paz, 1961, and Wolf, 1973, pp. 8–9). But Hidalgo and Morelos remained beacons for all later revolutionary movements in Latin America.

The wars of independence against Spain were wars for attainment of power by the *criollo* elite led by the great landowners and merchants. Ultimately, everywhere in liberated Spanish America power fell into their hands. The landowners wanted free trade with the outside world, particularly Britain, and the enjoyment of power in their own locality. The continent disintegrated into numerous states connected only through the international market. They all produced primary products on the basis of traditional Indian or Spanish techniques, and were competitive rather than complementary with one another.[7] This situation was aggravated by the adoption of 'liberal' policies at home and abroad. In return for their support of the local revolts against Spain, and because of their ability to supply the wants of the landowners and merchants, the British easily acquired a dominant position. The merchants who had earlier acted as agents of Spanish principals often switched over to being agents of British firms (Halperin-Donghi, 1975). The flood of British manufactures destroyed the handicrafts that had grown up on the basis of the internal market in Peru, Mexico and the interior provinces of Argentina. The adoption of a 'liberal' ideology by the ruling classes led to the removal of the protective barriers erected by the Spanish Crown around the surviving Indian communities and to their wholesale expro-

7 Alexander von Humboldt, the German traveller, estimated the values of agricultural produce, minerals and manufactures in New Spain at the end of the eighteenth century at 30 million, 25 million and between 7 and 8 million pesos respectively (Parry, 1973, p. 318).

priation. At the same time, most of the land became concentrated in the hands of an oligarchy (Bauer, 1975). We shall study the consequences of these developments in some detail in the case of two Spanish American republics, Argentina and Chile, and the single Portuguese American state, Brazil, which became a monarchy on liberation from Portuguese rule, and a republic on the abdication of Dom Pedro Segundo in 1889.

While exploitation in Spanish America was centred on mining, Portuguese Brazil started out as primarily a colony based on tropical agricultural products. The leading item among these products was sugar, but ancillary activities, particularly cattle-breeding, grew up in the areas not monopolized by the sugar plantations (Furtado, 1971, Parts I and II; Boxer, 1973a, chapters 4 and 5). Then for about fifty years starting in the last decade of the seventeenth century, Brazil had a 'golden age', when gold was discovered and quickly exhausted in Minas Gerais (Boxer, 1969). This gold benefited the gold-diggers from the state of Sao Paulo, and other mining entrepreneurs following on their trail, and, later on, the royal treasury at Lisbon. But Portugal was already involved in a semi-colonial relationship with Britain, and much of the gold found its way eventually to the London market (see R. Davis, 'English foreign trade, 1700–1774' in Minchinton, 1969, and Fisher, 1969). There is here an exact parallel to what happened to Spanish silver in the sixteenth and seventeenth centuries and for substantially the same reasons: in the era of emerging capitalism, a country which does not transform its own society fast enough in the direction of capitalism is likely to become dependent on the advanced capitalist countries with which it is linked through trade relationships. During the period immediately preceding the birth of industrial capitalism in Britain, Brazilian gold was extremely useful to her in lubricating her internal payments mechanism and in settling her trade deficits with the East and the Baltic countries. Thus the importance of exploitation of colonies under capitalism has to be assessed in a global perspective, rather than as a phenomenon that relates to the colony and the directly governing country alone.

The Brazilian colony of Portugal from the beginning depended greatly on the import and use of slaves. Portugal had been a slave-owning country before her colonial conquests began, and theological sanction was given to her thriving slave-raiding expeditions on the West coast of Africa by the Papal Bull of 1454, which gave the Portuguese a permit to 'attack, subject and reduce to perpetual slavery the Saracens, Pagans, and other enemies of Christ southward from Capes Bojador and Non, including all the coast of Guinea' (quoted in Rich, 1967, p. 309). With command over slave-raiding stations in West Africa exercised by Portugal, Brazil became a predominantly slave-owning society, with the plantation-owners in the countryside, and slave-traders, and foreign merchants at the ports, on top. There were adventurous elements among this upper crust, particularly among the inhabitants of the State of Sao Paulo, but their adventures often consisted in illegal raids in Spanish and Portuguese American territories in search of Amerindian slaves.

When Portuguese Brazil formally became independent of the 'mother country', it was a society divided between an upper crust of people of Portuguese extraction and masses of slaves, ex-slaves and poor peasants of Amerindian, African and mixed origins at the bottom. The vast majority of the population were not only poor but also bonded in some way to their owners and 'patrons' (cf. D. Aulden, 'The population of Brazil' in Hanke, 1969a). There were some important regional differences as between the North East, where the sugar planters and *fazenderos* (estate-owners) settled down into a typical semi-feudal pattern of existence, and the southern parts, particularly Sao Paulo, which was the home of the *bandeirantes*, slave-raiders, smugglers and discoverers of gold in Minas Gerais. But the undoubted enterprise of the latter remained mercantile in nature, and very much tied to a slave-using, and race- and class-divided agrarian society.

3.4 FROM 'VOLUNTARY COLONIALISM' TO THE DRIVE FOR IMPORT-SUBSTITUTING INDUSTRIALIZATION: ARGENTINA, BRAZIL AND CHILE

Of the three countries we have taken up for study, the ruling class in Argentina, up to 1914, followed, in an extreme form, the twin policies of strengthening the position of a landowning oligarchy and virtually unresisting adaptation to the forces transmitted by advanced capitalism in Britain and other metropolitan countries. The Chilean ruling class and then the Chilean masses (in the twentieth century) engaged in periodic struggles to attain national autonomy in economic life – struggles that usually ended in tragic failures. The Brazilian case falls in between these two extremes – in some respects the ruling class followed more adventurous economic policies than in Argentina but, because of their unwillingness to change the social structure radically, could not ultimately escape the logic of international capitalism.

3.4.1 *Export-dependence and arrested industrialization in Argentina*

Argentina proclaimed her independence by declaring the port of Buenos Aires open to the trade of all nations. Buenos Aires had prospered in the eighteenth century as the inlet for trade in goods and slaves (for a long time illegal) to Paraguay and Upper Peru or Bolivia, and as the outlet for the leather and tallow produced by the feral cattle of the pampas; the opening of *saladeros* or factories for producing salt beef, used for feeding soldiers and slaves in Brazil and the Caribbean, increased its profit. The *porteños* (those who lived in the port of Buenos Aires) went in wholeheartedly for free trade and became suppliers of dairy livestock and agricultural products to the outside world, in exchange for the flood of manufactured goods from Britain.

Argentina had a vast, practically unpopulated, prairieland. The new rulers decided to 'engross' most of this land, and, beginning with Rosas, the dictator of Argentina in the 1830s and 1840s, the rulers gave away huge parcels of land to a few influential families, practically free of cost (see Rennie, 1945, pp. 70–1 and 137–40).[8] Thus was laid the basis of a highly unequal distribution of land.

As in other parts of Latin America, political struggles among different groups of the ruling classes, and lack of adequate transport facilities linking the hinterland with the ports at first protected some of the handicrafts and local industries that had grown up under Spanish rule. But the 1860s witnessed a marked change in this respect. The 'liberal' economic policy which had earlier on been professed by many politicians could now be enforced by an effectively centralized government at Buenos Aires. An active policy of collaboration with foreign business interests and of encouragement of immigration from Europe was pursued. Leading liberals and educators such as Alberdi and Sarmiento propagated European-style education and styles of living, including dress, in the hope of 'civilizing' the Argentine people. The 1860s also saw the rapid spread of railways outside Europe and North America, and Argentina shared in this. The decade marked a quickening of the rate of migration of Europeans, a stream which assumed the proportions of a flood by the first decade of the twentieth century (see Woodruff, 1966, tables III/4 and III/5). 'Liberal' Argentine governments and publicists prepared the ground for this integration of the Argentine economy to the world capitalist order as a supplier of primary products. The Sociedad Rural, an organization of the more

8 Adam Smith (1776) gave a lucid analysis of the beneficial effects of the lack of 'engrossing' or monopolization of the land in the thirteen colonies of the USA. The analysis can be applied in reverse to derive the wage-depressing, inegalitarian consequences of the 'engrossing' of land in republican Argentina.

'progressive' *estancieros* (estate-owners), was founded in 1866, and played an important role in preparing the *estancieros* for profitable innovations in livestock or arable farming, and in shaping government policy to favour the *estancieros*.

Before the acceleration of the flow of migrants and foreign capital into Argentina from the 1860s onwards, the agricultural economy was dominated by the crude processing of the meat, fat and hides of the traditional *criollo* cattle of the open Argentine pampas. Short-horn cattle and fencing of the fields were introduced by English ranchers such as Newton and Miller, but these innovations did not make much headway. The Argentine landlords could see their sheep and cattle multiplying without much investment of effort or capital, and Argentina imported cereals from abroad. With immigration of Spaniards, Italians, Germans and Swiss into the economy, land could be better cultivated, and better varieties of cattle could be raised. These immigrants showed the way towards a more intensive use of land, and the *estancieros* followed in their wake, generally by using tenancy arrangements, rather than cultivating the land themselves. As a result, the amount of tilled land per head increased from 0.13 acres in 1865 to 7.7 acres in 1914 (Jefferson, 1926, p. 43).

The developments in Argentine agriculture and industry after the 1860s can be regarded as the adaptation of an open, export economy to the expanding world trade of the late nineteenth century under the impulse of immigration of southern Europeans and the direction of advanced foreign capital based in London. With the help of the immigrants, Argentina began to utilize her land better – raising maize, wheat and linseed. From being a net importer of wheat, she changed over to become an exporter of wheat and other cereals on a large scale (see J. Colin Crossley, 'The River Plate countries', in Blakemore and Smith, 1974). In the meantime, imported breeds of cattle were bred for their meat, which was now processed in *frigoroficos*, or chilling plants, particularly after the export of live cattle to European countries fell off because of official restrictions. Sheep farming prospered, particularly in the south, which was 'conquered' by driving out or exterminating the Patagonian Indians in the late 1870s. The principal industries of Argentina before the First World War were based directly or indirectly on agriculture. These were sugar milling in the interior, flour milling, refrigeration of meat, breweries and dairy industries, with some tanning and some weaving of cloth (see Martinez and Lewandowski, 1911, part III, chapter II). These latter industries were mostly concentrated in Buenos Aires (see, for example, Mulhall, 1896, pp. 365–6).

Large-scale immigration from Europe did modify the Argentine social structure but its extremely inegalitarian character survived, particularly in rural areas. Except for a small fraction of immigrants who came with some capital and were settled on model colonies such as Esperanza, most started as tenants. Tenancy contracts in the cattle-raising belt normally specified that over a three-year period only three crops, wheat, maize or linseed, could be grown and at the end the land had to be sown with alfalfa, which was the best fodder for fattening cattle. As land values increased, standard rentals rose from 10 to 12 per cent to 25 to 30 per cent by 1912 or so. The rental could even go up to 50 per cent and approximate the conditions prevalent in poor underdeveloped countries (see, for example, Scobie, 1960, pp. 8–9). Tenants had less and less chance to become owners and the typical landholdings of immigrants were small. The census of 1937 revealed a high degree of tenancy, particularly in the cattle and wheat belts. In 1948, Carl Taylor concluded from his observations that, while existing tenants had acquired more farm equipment and some pure wage-earners had become tenants, it had remained as difficult as ever to become a property-owning farmer, and that very large family estates remained the norm, the top families owning several large estates each (Taylor, 1948, chapters I, II, and pp. 190–204; and Germani, 1966). In the meantime, the mestizos and Indians who had been *peones* in the colonial and early republican era became the lowest stratum of this society under the dual impact of their own initial landlessness and the racialist ideology favouring whites in employment.[9] Thus the initial 'engrossing' of uncultivated land by the oligarchy permanently affected the rural class structure and naturally also influenced the urban class structure.

Partly owing to lack of access to land, most of the immigrants came to settle in urban areas. A small minority among them formed the top crust among Argentine businessmen, below the British businessmen and managers, who normally did not settle down in the country. The rest of the immigrants in the urban areas became artisans, tradesmen and workers in the services and the agriculture-based industries.

In the adaptation of the Argentine economy to the needs of the expanding world trade of the late nineteenth century, while the immigrants supplied the bulk of the additional labour force needed, the direction and entrepreneurship were largely supplied by capitalists

9 Even in the 1880s when Mark Jefferson visited the sugar *ingenios* of the interior province of Tucuman, the typical worker was virtually a serf. In order to ensure the control of the owners, laws were passed requiring every worker to show proof of gainful employment, and employers were authorized to realize any advances made to the workers directly out of their wages (Jefferson, 1926, pp. 32–3).

and managers from advanced capitalist countries, particularly Britain. Naturally they exacted a stiff price for these services. The first Argentine railway, 39 kilometres in length, was built with local capital. The next railway, the Ferrocarril Central Argentine, was built by a British company, for which the government guaranteed a rate of return of 7 per cent, besides allowing the cost of construction to be 60 per cent above the initial estimate. The company was also granted three miles of land free on both sides of the track, 'liberal tax exemptions and a guarantee against rate fixing until 15 per cent was being earned on the stock' (Rennie, 1945, p. 153; see also Ferns, 1960, pp. 325–6). Other railway companies, mostly foreign, were given even greater concessions. Apparently, in spite of considerable effort, the Ferrocarril Central Argentina (and other foreign railway companies) could not interest the rich Argentina families as investors (Ferns, 1960, pp. 334–5). Their abdication of responsibility led to payments abroad to make up artificially created deficits below guaranteed interest, to watering of capital, to the inflation of the cost of acquisition of new assets by railway companies, and to unduly high railway rates. All these phenomena occurred also in the case of railways in Brazil, but probably on a lesser scale, and we shall not dwell on them separately. Such inflation of so-called 'foreign investment' (at the cost of the host country) is also met with in nineteenth-century India, except that there the ruling class was foreign and the colonialism was not 'voluntary' (see Rennie, 1945, pp. 155–7; for Brazil, see Graham, 1968, pp. 57–60).

The consequences of acceptance of direction by foreign capital are illustrated by the Argentine foreign exchange and monetary policy in the period 1880–1914. Argentine imports, particularly of capital goods, were greatly dependent on foreign borrowings. In an advanced capitalist economy, investment expenditures normally expand with national income, even if foreign loans are not forthcoming. By contrast, in Argentina, in the 1890s, while incomes went on expanding, imports of capital goods (which were practically synonymous with investment in fixed capital) declined drastically, because foreign borrowings (which had been substantial in the 1880s) also declined (see Ford, 1962, chapters VI–IX). Investment thus depended more on the enterprise and willingness to lend of foreign investors rather than on the initiative of the Argentine rich. Their habits of extravagance in private and public life did not help either (see Scobie, 1968).

From the 1870s onwards, Argentina, in common with most other countries, used gold for international payments and for settling foreign debts. From 1881 to June 1884, the Argentine peso was convertible into gold; but from 1884 to 1899 Argentina kept her paper peso inconvertible and then, until the First World War, adopted gold as the medium of both internal and external payments (see Ford, 1962; and Williams, 1920).

The Argentine ruling class, which derived its main income from agricultural exports, allowed the peso to depreciate freely as the volume of paper currency rose, for such depreciation increased their peso incomes. When inflows of foreign funds or increases in exports aggravated domestic booms, or when outflows of foreign capital or decreases in exports caused a recession, no counteracting measure was adopted. During the regime of inconvertible paper money, prices rose faster than wages in Argentina, thus redistributing incomes in favour of employers. When, around the end of the century, the Argentine peso began to appreciate and threatened to redistribute incomes in favour of wage-earners, the government decided to make the peso fully convertible into gold again.

On the eve of the First World War, Argentina had apparently achieved a high per capita income comparable, say, to that of Italy in Europe. But the structure of that income was peculiar for a country at her level of income or industrialisation: agriculture (and livestock farming) contributed 37 per cent, manufacturing 14 per cent and services fully 49 per cent of Argentine GNP (Scobie, 1964, p. 177). Furthermore, while accumulated 'foreign investment' in Argentina was estimated as £384 million around 1908, she was paying at least £18 million net in order to service that debt (probably more, since the average rate of return was taken as 6 per cent), and she generated an export surplus of around £24 million annually out of exports of £73 million in order to support that drain (Martinez and Lewandowski, 1911, pp. 227, 233, and 363). Argentina's exports became concentrated on a few products; and she depended for about 20 per cent of her exports on one single market, Great Britain. British citizens also accounted for the bulk of the investments in the country, including those in the crucial meat-packing industry and in the railways. This dependence on a few agricultural exports, and the intimate tying up of the interests of the great landowners and British traders and investors, caused severe problems from the late 1920s onwards as the world capitalist economy became involved first in an agricultural, and then in a general, depression.

With the coming of the depression, the Argentine ruling class had to adopt measures which proved protective for manufacturing industries. However, lack of foreign exchange and the virtual non-existence of domestic industries making industrial capital goods limited investment in industry. Furthermore, the dependence of the Argentine landed oligarchy on the British market forced it to give concessions to foreign exporters of industrial goods at the very moment when Argentine industry needed state patronage most. Under the Roca–Runciman pact, Argentina was forced to 'buy British' in exchange for promises of maintaining her market for wheat, wool and beef. Further concessions were extracted by Britain as the depression lingered (Scobie, 1964, pp. 183–4). However, the depression did force some industrialization in Argentina, and, by 1939, according to one estimate, the share of agriculture in GNP had declined to 23 per cent, and that of construction and manufacturing had increased to 27 per cent, while that of services remained more or less constant at 49 per cent (Scobie, 1964, p. 279; see also Furtado, 1972, chapter 11). The crisis of the 1930s revealed Argentina as a dominated capitalist country, vulnerable to pressures emanating from advanced capitalist countries and unable to steer her destiny autonomously. The Second World War ended the domination of Argentine economic life by British interests, only to usher in the USA as the new overlord in the economic sphere. The post-Second-World-War period has been characterized by stop–go cycles – primarily governed by external influences – that are familiar in many third world countries. We will take up the discussion of such phenomena in chapter 5 below.

3.4.2 *Nationalism and the curse of mineral exports in Chile*

At the time of liberation from Spanish rule, Chile's social structure was set in a pattern very similar to that of the rest of Latin America (see McBride, 1936; Frank, 1971; and Bauer, 1975). Chilean landed estates were known as *fundos*; and Chile developed her peculiar form of bonded labour in the shape of *inquilinaje*. *Inquilinos* were tenants who were obliged to put in labour services, in return for a small allotment of land. The Chilean landowners had earlier on been producing livestock products for the Peruvian market; over the course of the eighteenth century, demand shifted towards wheat, and the landowners acquired a greater degree of control over the settled land. With these developments, there occurred a regression from payment of cash rents by tenants to payment in the form of services. By the beginning of the nineteenth century *inquilinos* had become hereditary farm servants.

As in other parts of Spanish America, Chilean Indians had suffered a severe demographic decline as a result of Spanish conquest. But the Araucanian Indians resisted the conquerors all the way, and, before the nineteenth century, had restricted Spanish occupation to the north of the river Bio-Bio. As in Argentina, so in Chile, the last resistance of the Indians was overcome in savage wars of extermination during the nineteenth century.

Perhaps because Chile was relatively inaccessible to Europe in the first half of the nineteenth century, the government was, for a time, able to follow a protectionist policy for fostering modern industry (Rippy and Pfeiffer, 1948). It also tried to encourage Chilean shipping by a system of differential import duties on goods carried in Chilean ships. Under the governments of Bulnes and Montt (1841–61), efforts were made to open up coal mines, and to build telegraph lines, roads and railways. Railways were built through state help and without much participation of foreign capital (Frank, 1971, p. 83). Even in this phase, foreign enterprise played an important part. With the help of British capital, William Wheelwright, an American, provided Valparaiso with various port and town facilities, founded the Pacific Steam Navigation Company, to link the ports of Chile with Peru, Panama and Europe, and built the first telegraph line in the country (Pendle, 1971, pp. 145–6).

Chile was forced gradually to accept the regime of free trade from the 1860s onwards. In 1864, for example, the laws protecting native Chilean shipping against foreign competition were abolished. In spite of this, particularly under the stimulus of the War of the Pacific (1879–82), in which Chile came out victorious against Peru and Bolivia, metal-making industries producing ploughs, threshing machines, railway wagons, and steam locomotives expanded. However, paradoxically enough, victory in the War of the Pacific, and the further addition to the already rich mineral wealth of Chile as a result of that victory undid the residual autonomy of Chile in economic matters.

Chile had exported copper first in 1749, and her copper output increased over time. For the three decades starting in 1851 Chile became the top copper-producing nation of the world. In this phase native (Urmeneta) and immigrant (Charles Lambert and his son) Chilean entrepreneurs were responsible for some innovations in the copper-mining industry. But when the richest copper ores ran out, the Chilean entrepreneurs were apparently unable to solve the technical problems of reducing the huge reserves of porphyry ores economically, and the disadvantage of being a rather small and isolated capitalist country showed up (although this smallness and isolation had to some extent protected her) (see Gedicks, 1973).

As a result of the victory in the War of the Pacific, Chile acquired sovereignty over nitrate producing territories in the north but promptly lost control over the mines to foreign, particularly British, nationals. When the areas producing nitrate were within Peru and Bolivia, it was Chilean workers and businessmen who operated the mines and carried on as the main traders in the ports. Then Peru decided to nationalize the nitrate mines and Chile went to war with Peru and Bolivia in the name of free enterprise and private property. In the meantime, British businessmen, among whom the most sinister figure was John Thomas North, bought up the Peruvian bonds which were in effect titles to the mines, at knockdown prices, with the help of credit extended by the Bank of Valparaiso and other Chilean banks. When Chile won the war, she had to honour the titles – particularly because international recognition of her claims to the new acquisitions depended on placating the big foreign powers (see Galeano, 1973, pp. 156–7, Blakemore, 1974, pp. 522–3, and Mamalakis, 1971).

After the rise of nitrate as the major export-earner in the Chilean economy, the traditional Chilean oligarchy became more firmly linked and subordinated to the dominant capitalist classes from advanced capitalist countries. A dramatic conflict between the interests linked to foreign business and the spokesmen of autonomous development took place during the presidency of Balmaceda. Balmaceda tried, though in a halting and confused manner at first, to prevent the complete takeover of Chilean nitrate and the nitrate-producing territory by foreign businessmen, develop railways under some degree of state control, encourage domestic manufactures (including the processing of Chilean minerals at home) and undertake extensive public works. These policies led to a rise in real wages, and threatened the interests of established foreign capitalists, the church and the landowning oligarchy. Almost symbolically for nineteenth-century imperialism, the vested interests fomented a rebellion in the navy in 1891. The rebels were able ultimately to occupy Santiago and overthrow the government. President Balmaceda committed suicide. (For the history of the civil war see *Encyclopaedia Britannica*, tenth edition, vol. 27. For interpretations of the reasons for the conflict, see Frank, 1971, p. 93; and articles by Pike, Necochea and Blakemore, in Hanke, 1969b, section v.) The rebels succeeded not only because of foreign backing but also because the dominant section of the ruling classes was behind them.

A new phase of expansion of copper production and export in Chile began in the early twentieth century, when the US corporations, Anaconda and Kennecott, acquired ownership rights over the huge low-grade ore deposits in the Norte Chico and established the Gran Mineria. In the earlier phases, enterprises had been small, and technology fairly simple. In the second phase, exploitation was based on large-scale, capital-intensive technology. The Anaconda-owned Chiquicamata mine, for example, had by the 1960s a production capacity of over 100,000 tons of copper ore per day, and had produced between 1913 (the year it started) and 1958 a total of 6 million tons of copper (over 300 million tons of oxide ore had been removed; Blakemore, 1974, p. 532). While the scale and the technology of Gran Mineria were impressive, capital came out of the profits made in Chile. Between roughly the First World War and the victory of the Unidad Popular led by Salvador Allende (in November 1970), Anaconda and Kennecott together had taken out of Chile $ 4 billion, whereas their total nominal investment in Chile was at most $ 800 million (the real investment was a lot less) (Galeano, 1973, p. 159).

Pointing out that both Anaconda and Kennecott were built up by immigrants into the USA with little initial capital of their own, Norman Girvan asks why immigrants into Chile could not achieve similar feats (Girvan, 1972). The explanation would lie in factors internal to Chile and in the general pattern of advance of capitalism which progressed furthest in the dominant capitalist countries such as the USA. In the first place, Kennecott and Anaconda could draw directly on the much vaster base of technological innovations, and of economies of scale, production and management, which they transferred to Chile. In the second place, the Chilean upper class, which was an amalgam of landowners, bankers, large-scale traders and industrialists, had come fully to depend on foreign capital for major innovations. For breaking out of their dependence, they would need to change the highly unequal social structure, with precapitalist relations surviving in agriculture. This they were naturally unwilling to do.

Chile's dependence on copper and nitrate increased until the depression of 1929 led to a disastrous contraction of export earnings. Her rulers had to find substitutes for imports of both manufactures and foodstuffs. This was the beginning of an industrialization process under state patronage. Over the period 1929–47, the increase in the proportion of industrial income to total GDP was greater in Chile than in Argentina, Brazil, Mexico or Colombia. But the initial percentage of industrial output in Chile was lower than in the other countries except Colombia. However, the formation (in 1939) of CORFO, an agency for promoting domestic production, which was responsible for an electrification plan, for establishing a steelworks and for other measures of industrial development, also played a part in the industrialization drive (Furtado, 1972, chapter 11).

In many ways import-substituting industrialization accentuated class conflicts in Chile as in other Latin American countries. We shall briefly review the major postwar economic developments in Argentina, Brazil and Chile in section 3.5.

3.4.3 *Sugar, coffee, and enforced industrialization in Brazil*

Brazil became independent as a separate empire under the rule of the Crown Prince of Portugal, in the aftermath of the migration of the seat of the Portuguese empire to Rio de Janeiro, when Napoleon occupied Portugal. Britain played a decisive role in getting Portugal to recognize, in 1825, the independence of Brazil. The new Empire promptly (in 1827) signed a commercial treaty with England, in effect duplicating in Brazil 'those special privileges which Britain had long enjoyed in her trade with Portugal' (Humphreys, 1965, p. 632). Brazilian society continued to be based on slavery: Brazil imported 1.15 million African slaves between 1801 and 1870, in addition to the 2.5 million she had imported by 1801, and emerged as the top slave-importing territory in the world (Curtin, 1969, p. 268). The Brazilian upper class, while they went 'liberal' in other ways, were reluctant to abolish the slave trade and slavery. The former was abolished, under British pressure, in the 1850s and the latter, effectively, only in 1889 (Graham, 1968, pp. 163–4; for descriptions of slave trade and slavery in nineteenth-centrury Brazil, see articles collected in section 4 of Hanke, 1969b; and for analysis of forces leading to the ultimate abolition of slavery, see Emilio Viotti da Costa, 'Why slavery was abolished', in Hanke, 1969b).

The economy of Brazil remained basically agrarian, the small manufacturing sector suffering further under the impact of the free import of machine-produced manufactures from Britain. The sugar plantations in the north and north-east of the country survived, but became backward in comparison with the rising sugar industries of Indonesia or many of the Caribbean islands. Coffee plantations then came up in the area near Rio de Janeiro and the Paraiba valley and spread towards the southern states of Sao Paulo, and even down to Parana. Up to the 1880s or so, many of the large coffee plantations were based on slave labour, and so some of the most persistent opposition to the abolition of slavery came from these 'dynamic' regions; later the problem of labour supply was solved by the flood of immigrants arriving from southern Europe. Between 1887 and 1900, the state of Sao Paulo received more than a million immigrants (see Galloway, 1974, pp. 356–67; and Furtado, 1971, chapters 20, 22, 24). The eventual domination of the Brazilian economy by coffee (Brazil became the leading producer and exporter of coffee in the world) had serious consequences in the twentieth century.

Apart from coffee and sugar, the most important manufacture to develop in the nineteenth century was the cotton textile industry, which grew mainly on the basis of the home market. The entrepreneurs in the textile industry pursued highly restrictionist policies, based upon a self-justifying assumption of a narrow and inelastic domestic market. The industry also remained unprogressive in technology and dependent entirely on imports of machinery and knowhow (see Stein, 1955).

Much of the infrastructure and other accessories for the nineteenth-century growth in Brazil, including railways, port facilities, other public utilities and banking were provided by British enterprise. Even the legendary Baron Maua, who was a daring innovator in many fields, was an Anglophile and had close British connections (Graham, 1968, chapter 7). British domination in business and other fields was enthusiastically supported by many liberal 'sepoys' among the native upper class (Graham, 1969). The inflow of capital supporting the foreign enterprise is inflated to an unknown extent, as in the case of other third world countries, by the arbitrary writing up of capital, by the overvaluation caused by effective tying of loans and purchases to the major imperialist country and by similar other factors. Nonetheless, even the nominal inflows of capital rarely came up to the cost of servicing the foreign debt (Furtado, 1971, p. 175n).

Coffee prices in the world market fell drastically from 1893 to 1899. Credit inflation, however, supported further expansion of coffee production, causing a glut. The coffee planters of Brazil persuaded the governments of the coffee-growing states to adopt a price-boosting or 'valorization' scheme (under the Taubaté Agreement of February 1906). The government under this scheme purchased any surpluses in the market, with the help of foreign loans. The loans were serviced by a new tax levied in gold on every bag of coffee exported. The expansion of plantations was also to be discouraged (see Furtado, 1971, chapters 30–33, for a stimulating analysis of the crisis in the coffee economy and the consequences for Brazilian industrialization).

However, this defence plan of the coffee planters kept prices steady and provided an incentive for extension of plantations. For example, between 1925 and 1929 coffee production grew by almost one hundred per cent. However, exports did not expand correspondingly, primarily because consumption per head in the chief export market, the USA, levelled off. As a result, stockpiles of coffee were already very high when the world crisis of 1929 broke out. Within two years (1929–31) prices of coffee exported fell from 22.5 to 8 cents a pound. After trying to indulge in the luxury of a convertible currency, and exhausting the foreign exchange reserves accumulated earlier, the Brazilian government had to devalue the currency. In the meantime, the federal government took upon itself a new valorization scheme under which coffee stockpiles were financed with internal credit and the stocks withheld were destroyed. This scheme, together with the depreciation of the currency, led to a transfer of losses from coffee growers to consumers (who paid in the form of higher prices both for imported and domestic goods). The effective increase in deficit financing by the government also helped maintain money incomes. If the depression in the coffee sector had been allowed to run its course, with the eventual abandonment of plantations and large-scale unemployment of coffee workers, money incomes would have declined more drastically. This factor made import-substitution in Brazil a more powerful engine of industrialization than in countries such as India, where the government did not try to protect the money incomes of the people, but responded to the situation by enforcing the principles of orthodox public finance (see chapter 4).

3.5 THE POSTWAR CRISIS OF IMPORT-SUBSTITUTING INDUSTRIALIZATION AND AUTONOMOUS DEVELOPMENT IN LATIN AMERICA

In almost all big Latin American countries, the growth in demand and the interruption of supplies of manufactured goods experienced during the Second World War intensified the drive towards industrialization through the process of import substitution. But the transition to the postwar world was marked by *apparently* different types of development in different countries.

In Brazil, the regime of Getulio Vargas gave a name, Getulismo, to a populist style of government, stressing amelioration of social conditions and a high rate of growth – particularly in industry. His regime straddled the 1930s and the Second World War. In Argentina, an extremely conservative regime, which won power through a coup in 1930, ruled until 1943, when a pro-labour, anti-American colonel, Juan Peron, helped topple that regime. Peron claimed to represent the interests of the *descamisados* (the shirtless people) primarily in the towns, and during the first few years of his rule the organized workers made notable gains. But a balance of payments crisis and inflation forced him to compromise with his earlier principles. He was overthrown in 1955 by the military. This was only the beginning of a series of coups, mildly democratic regimes and rule by military juntas, which paralleled the stop–go cycles in economic life that we take up for further analysis in chapter 5. Meanwhile in Brazil, the basic tenets of Getulismo were adhered to by a succession of Presidents, until, in 1964, frightened by prospects of agrarian reform and concessions to labour, the established interests in land and industry encouraged the military to take over power.

In the case of both Argentina and Brazil, the motives for right-wing military coups included both the prevention of social changes which might threaten the power of the oligarchy with its interests in land and industry, and the threat to US interests posed by expansionist and *etatist* policies (that is, policies offering state patronage to development programmes in all fields) pursued by populist regimes. Most of the populist regimes were at best mildly reformist. But after the Cuban revolution of 1958, the fear of communism shadowed all existing regimes in Latin America, and further darkened the vision of the White House in Washington as regards that backyard of American power. In Chile, the threat both to the established social order and to American interests came near to being realized under the regime of Salvador Allende, and so the suppression of that threat by the military coup of Pinochet naturally assumed the bloodiest form in the gory history of Latin America since the Second World War (see Niedergang, 1971, Pendle, 1971, Petras and Zeitlin, 1968, and Scobie, 1964.)

The Chilean case illustrates how difficult it is for a small retarded capitalist country to win national control of her own resources in this era of domination by a few advanced capitalist countries, and how the battle for national autonomy, if carried far enough, becomes merged in the battle for social revolution. Two American companies, Anaconda and Kennecott, came to control the most valuable resource of Chile, viz. copper, from the mining to the marketing stage. Throughout their history, these companies ploughed back only a fraction of the final value of copper or the profits made by them into the Chilean economy. On the other side, the USA, one of the biggest buyers of Chilean copper, imposed tariffs on it during periods of slump in the copper market, but denied to Chile the extraordinary profits that should normally have resulted in a rise in prices in periods of boom, by buying copper at controlled prices. The Chileans tried to market their own copper in the 1950s. But the experiment was abandoned as soon as it ran into trouble, partly deliberately engineered by the monopolistic interests in copper. The government of Chile tried to bribe the copper companies to invest more in the industry, but the latter simply reaped the higher profits without carrying out investment on the promised scale because such investment did not fit in with their world-wide plans. The regime of President Frei gave another bribe in the form of inflated prices for 'Chileanization' of part of the copper mines, but this had no better effect on company performance than earlier measures. The nationalization of copper mines by Allende in 1971 at a price which was fixed after allowing for various kinds of illegal appropriation by the companies was an act of national self-defence, transcending class interests (Gedicks, 1973, Girvan, 1972, Griffin, 1969b, pp. 149–73, and Johnson, 1973, chapter 4). The American copper companies fought the Chilean government in various world courts and in the world copper market. The traditional oligarchy of Chile teamed up with American interests and ultimately succeeded in overthrowing the popularly elected Allende regime in 1973. The new regime 'compensated' the copper companies on a generous scale, thus paying back part of its debt to its US patrons (for an account of the various American attempts to prevent Allende from gaining power and then to topple him, see BRPF, 1972).

We shall take up the analysis of the class structure supporting the economically retarded societies of the third world in detail in chapters 6 and 7. Here we note two characteristics of the Latin American upper classes that seem to explain the chronic political instability and its solution by extremely authoritarian methods. The first is that these classes are generally an amalgam of ruling groups in land, banking and industry, and have not been formed by new groups which have an interest in breaking the power of the traditional oligarchs. Growth in industry did not occur through the bursting asunder of the traditional social fabric. Instead, the traditional ruling classes themselves engaged in new economic activities, to the extent that this could be done while retaining their monopoly of land and government, and incorporated the few new industrialists into their ranks (see, for example, Frank Safford's study of entrepreneurship in Colombia in Hanke, 1969b, and Pike, 1968). The situation did not change radically during the intensive process of import substitution in the 1930s and after (see Johnson, 1967–68).

Another notable characteristic is that, from the last half of the nineteenth century onwards, economic life in the Latin American countries has been largely guided by the enterprise and requirements of the dominant capitalist country of the day – Britain up to 1914, and the USA since the 1930s, with a short interregnum in between. In such a situation, even the members of the upper classes have not had much leeway for action. However, sometimes they gave away even the freedom of manoeuvre they had for the furtherance of short-run sectional interests (cf. section 3.4.1 and Rock, 1975). The control of government has then been seen as an instrument for gaining an advantage over rival native groups, and perhaps as a bargaining weapon in the unequal contest with foreign capital. Hence sudden changes in government have been brought about even for adjustment of claims as between different members of the ruling coalition, and authoritarian measures have been used (for a lucid explanation see Kling, 1968). When a threat has been posed to the established order by the exploited classes, then, of course, both the traditionalists and 'modernizers' among the rulers have combined, with moral and material help from the USA and her allies to impose an 'orderly' solution by bloody methods. Latin American rulers and their powerful Big Brother to the North, have thus shown the way to authoritarian rulers of other third world countries.

The issues of class composition and class domination are vital for understanding the course of development in the third world. Hence we take these up separately in chapters 6 and 7.

4

COLONIALISM IN ASIA: INDONESIA, INDIA, CHINA

4.1 INTRODUCTION

In this chapter, we shall analyse the impact of capitalism on the economies of China, Indonesia and the subcontinent of India, which in 1970 accounted for about 1,543 million out of the total population of 2,564 million of the less developed countries; the last figure represented a little less than three quarters of the total world population of 3,632 million (the estimates are taken from Bairoch, 1975, pp. 6 and 246). Indonesia was the major colony of the Dutch until 1949; and India the most important colony of the British up to 1947 (we shall call the joint territory of India, Pakistan and Bangladesh, by the pre-independence designation of India or British India), while China became one of the most important bones of contention for imperialist powers, until her liberation by the Communists in 1949. These three countries together provided the major fraction of the surplus extracted by the colonial powers from the third world until 1914. Hence for understanding both the mechanics of capitalist colonialism on a global scale, and for assessing the nature of the present predicament of the peoples of India and Indonesia, and the background of the Communist revolution in China, a quick review of the way capitalist colonialism exploited and moulded their societies is essential.

4.2 THE RULE OF INDONESIA BY THE DUTCH IN THE PHASES OF MERCANTILE CAPITALISM AND INDUSTRIAL CAPITALISM

The Indonesian archipelago was the most important source of spices for Europe in the mercantile period. For cloves, nutmegs and mace, the most valuable spices, the Moluccas were practically the only source. The Portuguese managed to control the major part of the spice trade from Indonesia in the sixteenth century, but in the seventeenth century the Dutch wrested control from them and set about enforcing a far more effective monopoly in the sale of Indonesian spices than the

Portuguese had managed to achieve. As in other areas of the globe, trade, piracy and war were closely linked with European expansion. The builder of Batavia and the founder of the Dutch empire, Jan Pieterszoon Coen, wrote in 1614 to the Directors of the Dutch East India Company (known by its Dutch initials as VOC): 'Your Honours should know by experience that trade in Asia must be driven and maintained under the protection and favour of Your Honours' own weapons, and that the weapons must be paid for by the profits from the trade; so that we cannot carry on trade without war nor war without trade' (quoted by Boxer, 1973b, p. 107).

By employing their superior firepower and naval strength, and by playing one local ruler against another and one claimant for a throne against another in the widely dispersed kingdoms or sultanates of Indonesia, the Dutch managed to subjugate most of that archipelago between 1609 and the beginning of the eighteenth century (for detailed accounts of Dutch conquest and rule up to 1800, see Boxer, 1973b; Furnivall, 1967, chapter II; Parry, 1974, chapter 5; and the chapters by G. B. Masefield and E. E. Rich in Rich and Wilson, 1967). The Dutch did not accept the responsibility of direct rule except in the part of Java where Batavia was located. But they exercised suzerainty over all the islands, and tightly controlled the trade and production of spices. They forbade the production of high-value spices to all except a specified few and compelled the latter to grow them in required quantities. Thus the production of nutmegs was limited to the small Banda Islands and that of cloves to Amboyna. The system was policed by annual inspection tours, or 'Hongi' raids, in which all production in excess of Dutch requirements was destroyed. These measures at first led to a drastic decline in the output of spices. Then the Dutch took to prescribing the amounts of particular crops to be grown by the different islanders. They appointed 'regents' to enforce their decisions, except in the part of Java where they ruled directly. 'Regents' were former chiefs who had acknowledged Dutch sovereignty, or traitors who had been recognized as rulers. The VOC levied a political tribute (*contingenten*) from the islanders, generally in the form of spices, indigo and cotton yarn. But it also exacted forced deliveries (called *leveringen*) of whole crops of certain products, generally spices or other crops, naturally at abnormally low prices (Parry, 1974, pp. 110–11).

Because of the increasing popularity of coffee in Europe the Dutch tried to get the Indonesians to cultivate the crop, at first by compulsion. And then when the crop became popular in Indonesia, and coffee prices in export markets were considered too low, the Dutch tried to restrict its cultivation, as they had done with the valuable spices. As in the case of the latter, the Dutch paid absurdly low prices for the coffee they 'bought' as forced deliveries. In 1777, for example, because of exactions by the 'regents', the VOC officials in their private capacity, and arbitrary deductions by the VOC itself, the cultivator of coffee had to supply 240 to 270 pounds, for every pikol of 126 pounds shipped, and he received payment for only 14 pounds of coffee, presumably at the depressed domestic price of Indonesia! (Furnivall, 1967, p. 40).

The Dutch, by monopolizing all the important items and routes of external trade in Indonesia and eliminating all rivals, also naturally raised the prices of imports, which included such necessities as textiles and rice. They managed in addition, to choke off indigenous industries either by selling imported stuff forcibly or denying them their usual sales outlets. Many of the islands suffered considerable depopulation under Dutch rule. It is difficult to find one redeeming feature of this period of Dutch rule, which seems to have merited all the strictures of Adam Smith against rule by a monopoly company (Smith, 1776, vol. 2, pp. 126–36). However, the control of major branches of the spice trade enabled the Dutch to reap fabulous profits (in some cases, the profit margins on spice trade exceeded a thousand per cent), and doubtless fed that stream of Dutch finance which eased the birth of the new industrial system in Britain.

Dutch rule in Indonesia suffered an eclipse during the Napoleonic Wars, when Indonesia was occupied by the British. But the latter handed the islands back to the Dutch in 1816. By then industrial capitalism was beginning to spread out from Britain and Belgium to other western European countries. In this phase, the Dutch began to take a more direct part in administration and in the production decisions of the Indonesian peasant.

The first part of this period was dominated, as far as economic policy was concerned, by the 'culture system'.[1] This was introduced by Governor Van den Bosch in 1830. Its essence was the expropriation of a certain percentage (generally a fifth) of total labour and land in a village for the production of valuable export crops (coffee, sugar, etc.). The villagers could either deliver the stipulated share of the crop to the government or could set aside a stipulated fraction of the land for producing the crops (generally under strict supervision) to be delivered to the government. These exports were channelled through a monopolistic trading organization, Nederlandsche Handelma-

1 Our account of developments in Indonesia from 1816 to 1939 is based mainly on Boeke, 1946; Furnivall, 1967; Geertz, 1963; R. J. Van Leuwen, 'Indonesia' in Lewis, 1970; and Wertheim, 1959.

atschappij or NHM for short. The 'culture system' lasted formally for more than thirty years, after which Dutch private planters achieved through contracts what the government had sought to accomplish through direct expropriation of land and labour of the Indonesian (primarily Javanese) peasants. The private sugar plantations (generally controlled by large joint-stock companies) usually entered into $21\frac{1}{2}$ years leases with the villagers. The sugar estate planted one third of the cultivated land of the village in sugarcane.

> The cane occupied these fields for about fifteen months; after eighteen months the land was returned to the holders and another third of the village's land was taken for sugar, and so on around the cycle. But, as the new cane planting usually took place before the old one was harvested, any particular field was in sugar about a half rather than a third of the time; or to put it aggregatively, about one-half of the village's land, now one-third, now two-thirds, was in sugar, and half in peasant crops – either rice, or dry-season second crops such as soya or peanuts (Geertz, 1963, pp. 86–7).

Over the course of the nineteenth century, coffee was replaced by sugar as the major export crop of Indonesia, and a larger and larger fraction of Java's land was planted in sugarcane. In spite of a great deal of labour intensification for cultivation of rice and resort to dry crops requiring only small amounts of water, Java had to import increasing quantities of rice to meet the subsistence requirements of a growing population. By imposing a tremendous burden on the Indonesian people, the Dutch succeeded in (a) extracting, on a long-term basis, a very large fraction of the produce of the Inner Islands of Indonesia and (b) keeping the surplus from passing straight into the hands of the British (as happened in the case of the surplus extracted from Brazil by Portugal in the seventeenth and eighteenth centuries). This latter objective was achieved by monopolizing the external trade as much as possible. The Indonesian surplus helped the Dutch in overcoming the state of relative backwardness in modern industry with which they had started after the Napoleonic Wars.[2]

I have not found any estimate of the value of the surplus extracted by the Dutch (and, to a much more limited extent, by other advanced capitalist powers), from Indonesia. Such an estimate should ideally include the kinds of items Edward Long listed in his estimate of British profits from the possession of Jamaica (see chapter 3 above). As I have pointed out earlier (in chapter 2) such figures have not been computed

2 It is a curious commentary on the objectivity of bourgeois academic scholarship that in the account of industrialization of the Netherlands by Jan Dhondt and Marinette Brouwier in Cipolla, 1973, the role of the surplus extracted from Indonesia does not find even a fleeting mention.

for most countries, and I have used instead the excess of merchandise exports over merchandise imports as a minimal measure of the surplus extracted. In ordinary international accounts, if a country shows a persistent surplus of exports over imports, then the balance accumulates as (a) claims against foreign countries or (b) reserves of gold or foreign currencies. If we scrutinize Indonesian or Indian balance of trade accounts up to 1939, we find that while both countries had persistent balance of trade surpluses, Europeans were all the time accumulating claims against them in the form of ownership of private capital and holdings of public securities of various kinds. The basic reason was that the Europeans were appropriating the export surplus in various ways (mainly as a political tribute, or as a return from monopolized occupations and monopolistic enterprise) without much of a return. This is why the export–import gap provides in these cases a measure of the unrequited export surplus from these countries.

Table 4.1 provides the estimates of the export surplus generated by the Netherlands Indies. In spite of the entry of some British and American capital into Indonesia, particularly in the twentieth century, most large-scale enterprises continued to be owned by the Dutch. For most of the nineteenth century, the Netherlands accounted for almost half or more of the exports from Indonesia. But she accounted for a much smaller fraction of imports into Indonesia, for she was not a major exporter of either the manufactured goods or the foodstuffs that Indonesia imported in large quantities. Much of the exports by Indonesia to the Netherlands were re-exported. Taking everything together, the Dutch doubtless reaped the lion's share of the surplus extracted from Indonesia by foreigners. In the fourteen years from 1865 to 1878, the national exchequer of Holland made a clear gain of £18 million from the colonial administration of Indonesia (Britannica, 1881, p. 819). But this is only a fraction of the total export surplus generated by Indonesia – or appropriated by the Dutch from that country. Apart from increasing the fund for accumulation (and consumption) of capitalists in the Netherlands, the Indonesian surplus also served to balance the external payments accounts of the metropolitan country. This function is analogous to that performed by the Indian trade surpluses in the payments accounts of the British Empire, except that its importance was probably greater in the case of the Netherlands. For, unlike the British, the Dutch were not a leading manufacturing nation until the First World War, and a large part of their total external earnings came from direct exploitation of Indonesia and control of her external trade.

The annual export surplus of Indonesia in the years 1876–80 was 51

Table 4.1 *Exports from and imports into Netherlands Indies of merchandise in selected years, and five-year averages from 1876 to 1930 (million guilders)*

Year or five-year period (annual average)	Exports	Imports	Export surplus on merchandise account
	(1)	(2)	(3)
1830–34	20	15	5
1835	32	16	16
1840	74	26	48
1845	64	27	37
1850	58	24	34
1855	79	32	47
1860	99	44	55
1865	101	40	61
1870	108	44	64
1875	172	108	64
1876–80	180	129	51
1881–85	189	142	47
1886–90	185	130	55
1891–95	206	162	44
1896–1900	227	170	57
1901–05	275	197	78
1906–10	414	258	156
1911–15	643	407	235
1916–20	1339	685	654
1921–25	1417	817	600
1926–30	1501	994	507
1929	1443	1052	391
1933	468	318	150
1938	658	478	180
1940	882	432	450

Note:
(a) For international comparison, £1 sterling can be taken as equivalent to 12 guilders or florins over most of the period: see Furnivall, 1967, p. xxiii.
(b) Although nowhere is the basis of computation of the figures specifically mentioned, the values of exports are assumed to be f.o.b. and of imports, c.i.f.

Sources: For the period up to 1875, Furnivall, 1967, pp. 171, 207; for the period 1876 to 1930, Wertheim, 1959, p. 101, and for 1929, 1933, 1938 and 1940, Boeke, 1946, pp. 22 and 26.

million guilders, roughly £4.25 million. The estimated population of Java, Bali and Lombok, which generated most of the exports, was about 19 million in 1877 (Boeke, 1946, chapter II). Thus every inhabitant of these islands contributed about 4 shillings to the export surplus. If the income per head in these islands can be taken as about £3, which was the income per head in British India around 1900, then more than 6 per cent of the Indonesians' income was taken away abroad every year. Over time, the ratio of export surplus to total exports increased, and came to form more than a third of total exports by the beginning of the twentieth century. Since the importance of export crops themselves seemed to have increased over time, the degree of exploitation also seems to have risen. Indonesia continued to be a vital adjunct of the Dutch economy until the Japanese invasion altered the situation completely. According to one estimate, the total foreign capital invested in plantations, railways, shipping companies, banks, etc., operating in Indonesia in 1929 came to about 4,000 million guilders of which the Netherlands owned about two thirds. In that year, the 'Indonesian connection' is estimated to have generated an employment of 150,000 persons or about one tenth of the Dutch working force (see La Valette, 1938a and 1938b). Besides this, 241,000 Europeans (mostly Dutchman) lived in Indonesia in 1930 (Furnivall, 1967, p. 347).

The systematic extraction of a large proportion of the fruits of labour in Indonesia was achieved at the cost of retarded development of the colonial society. This retardation became much more pronounced in the era of industrial capitalism in Europe. Taking up the most important manufacture of the earlier era, viz. cotton textiles, we find that already by the end of the eighteenth century Javanese exports of cotton goods had been eliminated by exports of Indian textiles, which also made some inroads on the Javanese domestic market. Furthermore, in the eighteenth century the VOC obtained forced deliveries of cotton yarn from the Indonesians, often paying little more than half the market price in Java, and thus thwarted this branch of the industry (Matsuo, 1970, chapter 1). But on the whole, before the coming of machine-made cotton goods from Europe, the Indonesian textile industry had managed to carry on and supply most of the domestic needs. The situation changed radically in the nineteenth century: the value of imports of cotton goods increased from 3.9 million guilders in 1830 to 35.7 million guilders in 1900 (Furnivall, 1967, pp. 130 and 207). Nothing was done to halt the process of destruction of native handicrafts until the beginning of the twentieth century. Then half-hearted measures were proposed but could not make any headway against the resistance of Dutch plantation-owners who feared that encouragement of industry would raise wages. Finally, the depression of the 1930s compelled the government to adopt some measures for fostering small-scale industries, as a policy of unemployment insurance (Matsuo, 1970, pp. 19–21).

We have already seen how estate agriculture was promoted by the Dutch government by compelling Javanese villagers to grow cash crops either under the name of taxation (the 'culture system') or under the system of long-term leases of village land. This led to the growth of cash crops, partly at the expense of the growing of paddy and partly through the application of more labour. The leases were supposed to be voluntary, but were in fact forced on the villagers by village headmen and officials – with the incentive of the advance of several years' rent to the impoverished peasantry. Under the Agrarian Law of 1870, European planters were given long leases of 'waste lands', that is, all lands that were not already cultivated. This measure helped confine the peasantry to their original villages, and secured a captive, low-wage labour force for the sugar factories. With little capital at their disposal and with a rising population, the peasantry changed over, where there was scope for such a change, from *ladang* (shifting cultivation), to *sawah* (annual, intensive cultivation) and then applied more and more labour to the same quantity of land. This is the process that Geertz has called 'agricultural involution' (Geertz, 1963).

In the Outer Islands, because Dutch rule was indirect for a long time, the control of European planters on the land and labour was a little less absolute. Even there, through contracts with the local sultans who leased their land to them and through the use of such laws as a Police Regulation (which gave masters the right to penalize servants for breach of contract), and a Coolie Ordinance, which gave employers 'effective legal control over their imported labourers' (Furnivall, 1967, p. 182), the planters acquired firm control over large tracts of land and the labourers employed there. Still, the native landholders in the Outer Islands did better than in Java, because (a) they had more land available, and (b) since the exactions on them by Dutch planters were not as severe, they could save and invest more, and diversify their output.

In spite of the fact that the Dutch imposed various restrictions on alienation of land from the Indonesians and that most contracts were made with the village as a unit rather than with individual peasants, there was considerable differentiation among the Javanese peasantry, with the majority of the residents in a village being either landless or poor peasants and a small minority owning the major fraction of the land (Wertheim, 1959, pp. 111–14). However, until the end of the First World War, few of the rural rich could invest as capitalists since there were few channels of investment other than the purchase of land.

The emergence of a unified capitalist class was also inhibited by deliberate Dutch policy. The Dutch had in the very beginning destroyed the commerce of Mataram and hence the most important base of operations of Javanese businessmen. By monopolizing all external trade and driving its claws deep into the sphere of production, the VOC completely eroded the base of an Indonesian capitalist class. Dutch policy, both at a governmental and private level, favoured the 'Foreign Orientals', mostly Chinese, as intermediaries in the bazaar and as petty traders serving the local markets. But in order to prevent Indonesian dissatisfaction at the possible loss of land to the 'Foreign Orientals', various laws were passed to limit the power of moneylenders over debtors, and banning the alienation of land owned by Indonesians to others. By using other laws regulating the movement and residence of 'Foreign Orientals', the Dutch authorities managed to segregate the former from the general Indonesian population (see Fairbank, Reischauer and Craig, 1969, pp. 733–4, and Furnivall, 1967, pp. 45–8, 213–14, 239–42).

Thus was born the 'dual society' described by Boeke. According to his apologia, the eastern peoples were incapable of reacting rationally to economic incentives, or adopting profit maximizing behaviour.[3] As we have seen above, the basic reasons for the apparent difference in the behaviour of the Indonesians, the Chinese and the Europeans – where such differences did exist – lay in the fact that the last group systematically monopolized all profit-earning opportunities and all highly-paid posts and kept the Indonesians without education and without hope for control of their own assets. (Even in 1938, 92.2 per cent of higher personnel in government and 83.97 per cent of all controlling staff among administrative personnel were Europeans: Wertheim, 1959, p. 149.)

In such circumstances an Indonesian business community was slow to emerge, and slower to develop. The use of imported yarn allowed a small textile sector to develop in the twentieth century. A putting-out system soon developed under the stimulus of some government encouragement to small-scale industry from the 1920s onwards, and under the compulsion of the effects of depression of the 1930s, which led to a disastrous fall in the value of agricultural exports and hence made

3 For a representative selection of the opinions of Dutch economists and policy-makers, including Boeke, see Indonesian Economics, 1961. For a critique of such theories, see Wertheim, 1959, and Higgins, 1971.

industrial investment more attractive than before, the process of formation of an Indonesian business community, not entirely confined to landownership, accelerated (Matsuo, 1970, pp. 20–48, and Geertz, 1963). But this community still remained extremely small and singularly unprepared for the role of leadership in the economic sphere to which it was catapulted in 1949 by the successful outcome of the Indonesian struggle for independence.

4.3 INDIA IN THE EARLY YEARS OF BRITISH RULE–EXPLOITATION THROUGH THE MERCANTILE SYSTEM

In the nineteenth century, the Dutch constructed probably the biggest system of plantations in any colonial territory, but they did it not with slave or indentured labour, but with peasants and formally free labourers. Even when direct government compulsion on peasant production was abolished and when formally free trade was in operation, the essentials of the system remained unchanged.

In some ways, the British in India behaved very similarly to the Dutch. The British East India Company which conquered India was a legally chartered monopoly like the VOC. Like the Dutch, the British also organized plantations for producing indigo, sugar, coffee, tea and rubber. But they managed to get a much greater fraction of peasant output through indirect taxation and through purchase of commodities from the peasants and sale of manufactures. The British may indeed be regarded as the real founders of modern neocolonialism, for both in Latin America and in India in the late nineteenth century they depended more on economic power and political influence than on direct use of political power at every stage for obtaining the lion's share of the surplus of the dominated economies.

But in the initial sixty years or so of British rule in India, monopoly and levy of political tribute were the major instruments of exploitation. The effective British conquest of India began in 1757 with the defeat of the Nawab of Bengal by Robert Clive, primarily because of the treachery of the Nawab's Commander-in-chief. From then until 1813 is the purely mercantilist phase of the exploitation of India. For, during this period, the East India Company enjoyed a monopoly of trade between Europe and the East, including India and China. In 1813, the Company's monopoly of trade between Europe and India was abolished, but it retained the monopoly of trade with China, which was in turn abolished in 1834. The East India Company ruled India until 1858, when, because of the great mutiny by its Indian troops marking the first national war of independence in India, the task of ruling India was taken over directly by the British Parliament. The period 1813–34 may be characterized as that of transition to exploitation through free trade. The period 1858–1914 saw the zenith of that system of exploitation. The policy of free trade was augmented in this period by the public works policy of the British Indian government, which helped open up India fully to the influence of the world capitalist market, and provided new levers for extracting the surplus from India. Finally, the period 1914–47 marked the end of the colonial exploitation of India by the British and the beginning of neocolonial exploitation by advanced capitalism in general. I shall divide this brief analysis of the economic impact of British rule in India into two sections: in the first section, I shall primarily be concerned with the period 1757–1858, and in the next with the period 1858–1947, but there will inevitably be some overlapping of themes between the two sections.

The East India Company conquered Bengal in 1757, but for a few years they tried to rule through their local puppets. This proved impossible because of the greed of the European servants of the East India Company and other private British traders, who flouted all laws in order to increase their profits. The British gradually assumed all the formal powers of a ruler. In 1765, they acquired from the titular Mughal Emperor the *dewany*, i.e. the charter to collect the land revenue of Bengal. They kept most of the basic features of the Mughal land revenue system but raised the proportion of the produce collected as revenue enormously. Anthony Lambert, a British trader writing in 1795, recognized this quite clearly. In the first year of the Company's *dewany*, the revenue came to Current Rs. 27,857,485:

> This exhibits the revenue nearly doubled since Akbar's reign, or, rather (from a much later period) since the Subaship of Suja Khan, the expiration of which was nearly coeval with the fall of the Mogul empire. The annual revenues of Bengal, and its tribute, had continued nearly uniform from the establishment of the empire by Akbar, to its dismemberment in the reign of Mohammed Shah. But, in less than forty years after this event, we find the revenue nearly doubled (Colebrooke and Lambert, 1795, p. 232).

Partly as a result of the misrule under the system introduced by the East India Company, a succession of terrible famines led to a decline of the population by about a third over the years 1769–71. But the actual revenue collections in the immediately succeeding years, instead of falling, rose above pre-famine levels (Dutt, 1963, p. 47).

Thus in terms of tax exaction, the British proved much harsher than the earlier Mughal rulers. Furthermore, a major fraction of the tribute formally exacted by the Mughals had come back through various channels to stimulate the demand for the local products of Bengal, whereas very little of the tribute levied by the British came back that way. On the contrary, the operation of the monopoly of the East India Company and the associated European merchants meant that the post-tax output of the Indians was paid for at very low prices indeed.

> While Europe has demanded more productions from India, it has returned less in money and commodities. The English Company has drawn from Bengal a greater tribute than was remitted to Delhi; and, for the purchase of production required by Europe, Bengal has ceased to receive what formerly replaced the tribute it paid. It is immaterial whether the tribute has been drawn from the money of circulation, or its manufactures; either, ultimately becomes a tribute of labour (Colebrooke and Lambert, 1795, pp. 221–2).

The Company not only taxed the land. For decades together, it monopolised the manufacture and sale of salt, and production and sale of Bengal opium, a crucial item of the Company's commerce with China, remained a Company monopoly throughout its rule. Wherever it had any direct interest in production, it depressed the wages of the producers to levels that often went below subsistence and deprived them of freedom of choice of occupation or employer. For silk goods it substituted the production of raw silk and compelled the weavers under its control to give up silk weaving when the sale of raw silk in Europe proved more profitable than the sale of silk goods.

Throughout this first phase, the trade under the control of the Company was riddled with restrictions – most of them harmful to the Indian interest. Thus, for example, the import of Indian cotton goods into England was restricted by duties and by sumptuary regulations. Most of the imports of such goods into Britain were re-exported. Much more damagingly, Indian cotton goods produced in India had to pay considerably higher duties than cotton goods imported from England (see Dutt, 1963, chapter XVII; Sinha 1970, chapter 3; and Trevelyan, 1835). This proved crucial in the period when the Indian handloom industry was overwhelmed by the competition of British goods, that is, during the period 1815–30: internal custom and transit duties were not abolished until 1836.

The exploitation of India during the period 1757–1813 was carried out with the East India Company as the legal monopolist, but with the active assistance of a number of private European traders whose co-operation proved very important in the trade with China. During this period, the Company's trade and tribute included Indian cotton goods and other handicraft products as well as agricultural materials such as raw cotton, indigo and opium. Part of the surplus realised through the trade and revenue system in Bengal was utilized to extend the British dominion over the rest of India and to balance the trade account with China (with whom Britain normally had a deficit until about the first quarter of the nineteenth century). The rest of it was transferred to Britain as unrequited export surplus in goods or bullion. Since after acquiring dominion over India, the East India Company and private traders could appropriate Indian goods as tribute of profits without really paying for them, Britain did not any longer have to send bullion to India to balance her accounts. Instead, bullion was now sent out from India either to China or to Britain.

The existing estimates of the external 'drain' or unrequited exports from Bengal or British dominions in general put it at an aggregate of £38 million for the period 1757–80 (Sinha, 1927, pp. 51–2), £1.78 million annually over the decade from 1783–84 to 1792–93 (Furber, 1951, pp. 312–16), and between £3 million and £4 million per annum around the years 1813 to 1822 (Prinsep, 1823, pp. 63–4 and 64n.). Taking a detailed estimate of Colebrooke for the output of agriculture as the base (see Bagchi, 1973c), the external drain from Bengal could be put at about 3 to 4 per cent of the gross domestic material product. If we add another 2 or 3 per cent as the expenditure on the wars of conquest incurred by the East India Company in this period, we can see that at least 5 to 6 per cent of resources of the ruled land were siphoned off from any possibility of investment. If we compare this waste with the 7 or 8 per cent of national income invested by Britain during the period of her Industrial Revolution, we can begin to gauge the magnitude of the damage inflicted by this period of British rule on the Indian economy – particularly when we remember that the period was punctuated by wars, famines, and arbitrary exactions by British tax collectors.

Some orderliness was introduced into the revenue system and administration by the reforms of Cornwallis in the 1790s, but at the expense of raising the rate of exploitation attained through torture and force, and excluding Indians from all responsible or highly-paid posts. The revenue system introduced by Cornwallis in Bengal was different from the so-called *ryotwari* system that found favour with other officials such as Elphinstone in Bombay or Munro in Madras. However, all these systems had the common characteristic of making land an alienable commodity without creating full private property in it, and providing a large surplus in the hands of the British rulers with very little expenditure in recompense. These systems endured, with little modification, throughout the British period.

In respect of the formal organization of external trade and its commodity composition, the period 1813–58 witnessed two major changes. First, as already mentioned, the East India Company lost its monopoly of trade between India and Europe, and between China and Europe, in 1813 and 1834 respectively. Then, as we have also noted, the internal transit and town duties in most parts of India were abolished in 1836. These measures ushered in the era of formal free trade in India: this has been called a system of 'one-way free trade' (Dutt, 1949), for this did not involve any reciprocal concessions either by Britain or by other countries trading with India. The position of the East India Company was in many respects taken over by a small group of European business firms ('agency houses' – later transformed into 'managing agencies') which controlled practically all the external trade (barring a portion of this trade in western India) and much of the wholesale internal trade, especially in exportable commodities. Secondly, India ceased to be a leading manufacturing country of the precapitalist era and was reduced to the position of a supplier of agricultural goods and raw materials to the industrializing economies of the West, particularly Britain.

The long process of de-industrialization of India started with the catastrophic disappearance of cotton manufactures from the list of exports of India and the meteoric rise and the steep ascent of cotton manufactures in the list of her imports – almost exclusively from Britain. For more than seventy-five years up to 1913, India remained the major importer of cotton goods from Britain, often taking more than forty per cent of the British exports. For example, in 1886, the exports of cotton goods from the UK amounted to £68.9 million (Mitchell and Deane, 1976, p. 304); in the fiscal year 1886–87, Indian imports of cotton yarn and cotton goods produced in the UK amounted to about £28 million (O'Conor, 1887). In terms of quantity of cotton piece-goods, the proportion of Indian imports to British exports was generally even higher. Other rural or urban manufactures were ruined partly by the rise of alternative sources of supply and by government restrictions. Thus the manufacture of saltpetre was ruined by the rise of the Chilean nitrate industry and by rigorous and oppressive methods of licensing and inspection by the government. The gun-making industry of Monghyr was ruined by the discriminatory licensing policy of the government and withdrawal of all government custom. The de-industrialization of India, along with government policies relating to land and land revenue led to a structure of society which has often been characterized as 'semi-feudal'.

4.4 THE SYSTEM OF FREE TRADE, PUBLIC WORKS AND THE SPOLIATION OF INDIA

While the British took over much of the Mughal system of land revenue administration, they altered the whole basis of revenue assessment and the mode of collection of that revenue, and thereby effected some fundamental changes in the production relations on land. The Mughals had assessed land revenue on the area *actually* cultivated, whereas the British assessed land revenue on the basis of the amount of land a person was *entitled* to cultivate. The Mughals had calculated the revenue in cash, but often collected it in kind. The British calculated the revenue in cash and collected it in cash. Under the Mughals, although land changed hands as between peasants, and as between various title-holders to the rent from land, normally failure to pay rent in time or to repay other kinds of debt did not lead to the loss of land. Since the assessments were based on actual output, there was a built-in flexibility in the system. The notional rent was in fact rarely collected in full. Since the Mughal system evolved over two centuries, since customs varied as between different parts of the country, and since different parts of the country were affected in different degrees by the growth of commerce and monetary transactions, there were many exceptions to the generalizations mentioned above, but these were recognised as exceptions rather than the rule.

The system introduced by the British made revenue demands inflexible in terms of cash. It also permitted the sale of land or rights to collect rents for realization of arrears of revenue or the dues of the superior tenure-holders. As a corollary, British law allowed moneylenders to sell up peasants and 'zamindars' (the superior tenure-holders) for the failure to repay a debt and the interest accumulated on it. But the British by no means introduced full private property in land. For a start, arrears of rent or government revenue demand were allowed as a prior claim on the land, and thus restricted the rights of other creditors. Secondly, titles to land were complicated by the recognition of rights of a whole series of intermediate tenure-holders, the claims of many of whom were overlapping. Thus when the British government wanted to favour the European planters in Assam and encourage them to open up tea gardens, they gave them land on 'fee simple' terms on the British pattern, with the government as the only claimant to land revenue.

There were two basic variations on the British Indian system of land revenue. The first was the Permanent Settlement of Bengal under which the government farmed out the right to collect revenue to a handful of *zamindars*, and gave the latter special powers over the actual cultivators, most of whom were initially degraded to the position of tenants. In return, the *zamindars* had to pay a fixed sum to the government which was fixed in perpetuity in certain areas (although the government managed to raise its collections marginally over time by levying certain special imposts). In the temporarily settled *zamindari* areas, the same system prevailed, except that the revenue demands were revised at, say, thirty-year periods. Under the other basic variation, the *ryotwari* system, various layers of intermediary rights grew up over time, although such areas probably escaped the extremes of proliferation of intermediary tenures that plagued the *zamindari* areas.

Various theories, including the theories of the French Physiocrats and English utilitarians, were invoked by the British law-makers and administrators to justify particular levels and systems of revenue collection in India (see, for example, Stokes, 1969 and Guha, 1963). But, in actual fact, the revenue settlements were dictated mainly by considerations of expediency, ease of collection and maximization of government revenue in the long run, subject to the constraint of avoiding any costly revolt. Under most forms of revenue settlements, revenue collections went up from year to year, whatever the state of the weather, or the level of prices. In fact, a rise in revenue collection was *ipso facto* taken to be proof of prosperity of a region!

Under the system introduced by the British, the cultivators were forced to raise crops that would enable them to pay rent in money, and they had to intensify labour on the fields and extend the margin of cultivation. They could no longer treat pasture as an untaxed capital asset, for if they claimed any right they had to pay rent on it as on the cultivated land. Since the cultivators were left with very little surplus, they could not maintain the fertility of soil or replace their main capital stock and consumer durable, viz. cattle (see Bagchi, 1976c).

Under this system, in the agricultural sector, most of the cultivators, whether formally landless or not, were reduced to near-subsistence level. Landlords and moneylenders emerged as the lords of the countryside licensed by the British *Raj*. Moneylenders had been lending money to cultivators and revenue-farmers, and in some cases even acquiring titles to land, before the British came into the picture. But, as we have mentioned above, usually there were safeguards against the proletarianization of the actual producer. The landlord or the moneylender was interested in directly appropriating a part of the labour of the cultivator (or artisan) in the form of goods and labour services rather than in depriving him of his basic productive equipment. Under British rule, with the compulsion to pay land revenue fixed in money and with the removal of restrictions on transfer of land and on usuary, the situation changed drastically. The process of deindustrialization of India, particularly of those regions where handloom production for export markets had been formerly extensive, further depressed the position of the cultivator. Although formally a free market in labour was legalized in 1843 with the abolition of slavery, in actual fact the labourer, faced with the prospect of unemployment and starvation, often chose to opt out of his profitless freedom, and bind himself to a landlord, with the hope that the latter would give him a subsistence wage.

The policies the British pursued in other areas did little to alter these production relations centring on land. Marx wrote in 1853:

> There have been in Asia, generally, from immemorial times, but three departments of Government: that of Finance, or the plunder of the interior; that of War, or the plunder of the exterior; and finally, the department of Public Works . . . Now, the British in East India accepted from their predecessors the department of finance and of war, but they have neglected entirely that of public works
>
> (Marx, 1853, p. 33).

However, the last deficiency in the running of the state on the pattern of Oriental despotism was already being remedied when Marx wrote. The East India Company started in the 1820s by restoring and extending the East and West Jumna canals of pre-British times. The work was later extended to the excavation of the Ganges canal, and a start was made with the irrigation system in the Punjab. In the south, the ancient irrigation works based on the Cauvery were renovated and extended. In 1854, the first few miles of the two trunk railway systems in Western and eastern India, viz. the Great Indian Peninsula Railway and the East Indian Railway, were opened for traffic.

The work of extending the railway system received a new impetus after the assumption of direct power to rule over India by the British Parliament. The British manufacturing interests, for commercial reasons, and the British civilian and military authorities in India, for reasons of internal security and military expediency, pushed the construction of railways forward, very often with loans raised in England. By the beginning of 1914, India had 34,000 miles of railways. In the same year, the total amount of area irrigated by government works in India including Burma came to 25 million acres (Anstey, 1952, pp. 614 and 616).

Before I discuss the wider economic impact of railways and irrigation works in India, let me note that but for certain military railways built in the north-western part of India, and certain protective works constructed by the government in the late nineteenth and early twentieth centuries, the public works were eminently profitable to the government in a commercial sense. There was a period when the government guaranteed a certain minimum rate of interest on the capital invested by the railway companies, but there was virtually no check on expenditures incurred, so that the companies could easily convert profits into losses and mulct the state of millions of rupees. Even when construction of railways under guarantee ceased, the purchase of materials and equipment, the financing and administration of railways remained concentrated in British hands. In contrast to what happened in Britain, the USA or other advanced capitalist countries, no railway equipment industry grew up on the basis of railway building in India, since the state pursued a policy of free trade, with a strong bias towards the purchase of British goods for the railways. The irrigation works constructed by the Government were generally strictly commercial propositions; the most profitable of them yielded a rate of profit far higher than the market rate of interest.

A notable effect of these public works was to convert India into a major supplier of raw materials and foodgrains for Europe and many of its colonies overseas. The route alignments and rate structures of railways were such as to make it cheaper to transport goods from the ports to the interior and back rather than between points in the interior. India was opened up to the inflow of manufactures, primarily from Britain; in return, she supplied raw cotton, jute, indigo, hides and skins, oilseeds and wheat to western countries, to South America, and, later on, to Japan. The large-scale irrigation works in western Uttar Pradesh, Punjab and Sind were particularly important in supporting the exports of raw cotton and wheat.

The gross command area of these large-scale works did not always equal the net increase in irrigated area; for, they often displaced the earlier irrigation works in the form of wells and ponds, which were under the direct control of farmers and which supported agricultural practices that paid due attention to crop mixtures and the preservation of soil fertility. Moreover, while the canals helped expand the exportable surplus of foodgrains and commercial crops, they displaced dry crops such as millets or pulses. The millets were often the staple food of the poor, and pulses were a very important source of protein. Furthermore, the payment of water rates, the raising of the assessed value of the land, the pressure to grow commercial crops – all these factors increased the indebtedness of the cultivators to moneylenders and traders and, consequently, the control of the latter over the former (Whitcombe, 1972, chapters II and IV). Because large-scale alienation of land to moneylenders led often to disaffection among the cultivators, the Government of India was compelled to impose restrictions on the transfer of land from cultivators to non-cultivators (Nanavati and Anjaria, 1951, chapter XII). However, this often meant simply that landowners themselves became moneylenders (if they were not already functioning in such a dual capacity) and the position of the actual cultivator did not improve. Apart from the effect of large-scale irrigation aggravating such social cleavages, it also caused widespread problems of waterlogging, salinity and alkalinity, which rendered millions of acres infertile (see Whitcombe, 1972).

Besides constructing railways, irrigation works and port facilities, the British in India opened up coal and mica mines, tea plantations and coffee plantations and, from the 1850s onwards, they also began to build up a large jute mill industry. They ran indigo and sugar plantations in the areas of settled agriculture. For the recruitment of labourers in the tea gardens, they used a system of indentured labour, under which the condition of the labourers approximated to that of slaves. The same system was used to export Indian labour and replace the erstwhile slaves in the West Indian and Mauritian sugar plantations. Indian indentured labour was also exported to Natal, Malaysia, Ceylon and Fiji (Tinker, 1974). The planters interested in indigo and sugar generally gave advances to peasants and induced and coerced them to grow indigo or sugarcane. Their oppressive methods led to the so-called 'Indigo Mutiny' in Bengal proper in the 1860s; but they continued the same practices in other parts of India until the First World War at least. In these activities they were often assisted by the *zamindars*, from whom they leased in part of the land or the *zamindari* rights. Thus the British, with one hand introduced private property rights and abolished slavery, and with the other hand helped strengthen many of the precapitalist relations of bondage on the fields, plantations and in the mines. Such relations of bondage in turn shored up the system of excessively long hours of work and primitive working conditions for factory labour.

From the 1850s onwards, mostly in western India, an Indian capitalist class began to build up a cotton textile industry, partly supplying the lower counts of yarn to Indian handloom weavers, partly exporting such yarn to China, and partly supplying the coarser varieties of cloth to the Indian market. Their example was taken up in other parts of India, and Indian capitalists also acquired some interest in coal and mica mines, and in tea and coffee plantations. But modern enterprises in manufacturing, mining and plantations, and in banking, shipping and insurance in 1914 were mostly under European control, with cotton mills in western India providing the only major exception. The growth of this comparatively small modern industrial sector hardly made an impact on the basic framework of Indian society, which remained dominated by colonialism, landlordism and usurious moneylending interests.

In the period from the 1850s up to 1918 or so, India played an extremely important role in squaring the British imperial balances.[4] She not only generated vast surpluses in her aggregate balance of trade accounts; she had a deficit with Britain in her balance of payments, and a large surplus with the rest of the world. Thus Britain was able to use Indian surpluses to balance her accounts with third countries and to smoothly effect capital transfers to the latter. In the later part of the nineteenth century, in particular, Indian exports to Latin America, and to continental Europe became vital for financing British deficits with the USA and Europe (Saul, 1960, chapters III–IV).

These trade relations were consonant with the international investment pattern that developed in the nineteenth century, centred primarily on Britain – and, to a smaller extent, France. Britain built up foreign assets worth about £4,000 million by 1914. Most of this investment was concentrated in the USA, Canada, Australia, New Zealand, and South Africa (see Simon, 1967 and Thomas, 1967). The mechanism of international trade and investment in the nineteenth century in effect served to mop up the surpluses of today's underdeveloped countries – particularly the Asian countries – in order to transport, feed and equip the white settlers of the temperate-region colonies. The formal policy of free trade pursued by Britain was an integral part of this mechanism. India was the biggest market for Britain's cotton goods, which in turn were the single largest item of British exports until almost the end of the nineteenth century. This was especially important because tariff barriers restricted the export of British goods to other developed capitalist countries – particularly western Europe, the USA, Canada, Australia and South Africa. In order to prevent retaliation against exports of Indian primary products to countries outside the British Empire, Britain had to enforce a policy of free trade in India. (For a fuller discussion of the nineteenth century interconnections of growth and underdevelopment, see Bagchi, 1972b).

Such a policy went hand in hand with systematic discrimination against Indians in both official and unofficial British policy. Indian

4 The triangle of trade relations between Britain, China and India in the era preceding the Opium War is described in section 4.6.

industrialization was thwarted through the policy of 'one-way free trade' (see the preceding section), the stunting of the Indian capitalist class by means of political and racial barriers against their entry into business, and through the draining away of resources as political tribute and as monopolistic rents of foreign enterprises. This thwarting in turn led to further drain of surplus product through many vents. We have discussed above how the flow of unrequited export surplus in colonial or semi-colonial countries can be approximately measured as the difference between merchandise exports and merchandise imports. In table 4.2 are given the export surpluses of India from 1871/72 to 1938/39. As the population subject to exploitation grew and as the economy became ever more subject to the influence of international capitalism, the export surpluses also grew until the interwar period. This export surplus rarely fell below a sixth, and sometimes exceeded a fifth, of Indian exports. This period was marked by several devastating famines and epidemics, costing millions of lives. Setting aside the cost in human lives, the other costs of exploitation of India can perhaps be approximated by the cumulative difference, over time, between the actual income controlled by Indian citizens and the income they could have enjoyed if India had been allowed to pursue the same in-

Table 4.2 *Export surplus of British India on merchandise account,* 1871/72 to 1938/39

Period	Annual average value (Rs. '000)
1871/72 to 1875/76	212,258
1876/77 to 1880/81	223,513
1881/82 to 1885/86	278,199
1886/87 to 1890/91	254,143
1891/92 to 1895/96	313,010
1896/97 to 1900/1901	200,854
1901/02 to 1905/06	413,759
1906/07 to 1910/11	477,700
1911/12 to 1915/16	527,993
1916/17 to 1920/21	457,401
1921/22 to 1925/26	617,417
1926/27 to 1930/31	509,101
1931/32 to 1935/36	173,854
1936/37 to 1938/39	304,200

Source: Based on Bagchi, 1976c, Table 2 (original data from *Annual Statements of the Seaborne Trade of British India*).

dustrializing policies as Canada and Australia were pursuing and if the systematic discrimination against Indians in government, business and the sphere of foreign trade and finance had been ended.

Most of whatever growth occurred in India up to 1914 was concentrated on either raw or crudely processed agricultural commodities. (Besides cotton and jute mills, tea and coffee plantations, and coal and mica mines, the only modern industries of any significance to begin their life in this era were sugar mills, a steel mill and paper mills.) In the absence of domestic industrialization, Indian producers of primary commodities became extremely vulnerable to international business cycles. Among other things, India and China were used as dumping grounds for depreciating silver (during the period 1872–94 in the case of India, and up to a much later period in the case of China) when the advanced capitalist countries adopted gold as their monetary standard. In any financial crisis, generally the banks, exporters, importers and the wholesale merchants covered themselves adequately, and the brunt of adjustment was borne by the ultimate producers whose credit was cut off while the prices obtained by them fell precipitously (Triffin, 1969).[5]

4.5 THE CRISIS OF THE BRITISH EMPIRE AND THE FIRST PHASE OF IMPORT-SUBSTITUTING INDUSTRIALIZATION IN INDIA

Throughout the nineteenth century in India, handicraft industries declined, while large-scale industry made but a feeble beginning. The result was almost certainly a net decline in the proportion of the population engaged in industry (see Bagchi, 1976a). The effective rate of gross investment as a proportion of national income could hardly have exceeded the 5 per cent which is conventionally taken to be

5 The situation was not exactly symmetrical for primary producers from advanced capitalist countries (including white colonies). For, in the latter, the trade in primary products was in general controlled by indigenous capitalist groups, so that the redistribution as a result of credit contraction occurred as between two indigenous groups, rather than as between a foreign group and an indigenous one. Moreover, the primary producers in white colonies typically operated with much larger volumes of capital at their command and had effective political lobbies to fight the bankers and the foreigners. In non-white colonies, the primary producers were mostly small peasants who were at the mercy of everybody else. Thus decline in the price of raw cotton had very different implications for the producers of the Indian Deccan, or the Egyptian *fellaheen* and the owners of large cotton plantations in the southern USA. This is one of the reasons why the usual terms of trade calculations (in which prices at the border are used) are so misleading for unravelling the process of redistribution as between classes and countries.

needed just to maintain capital intact. This was not because of any absolute shortage of finance for investment in the hands of the tiny native capitalist class or in the hands of the foreign capitalist class. It is simply that under the policy of free trade and with an economic environment where mass poverty was endemic, it was not profitable to invest in domestic industry for supplying the home market.

The First World War revealed starkly how shaky Britain's supremacy in the capitalist world had become. The crisis of the British empire and the growth of the nationalist movement in India opened up new opportunities in that the British Government was compelled to modify its free-trade policy in significant ways. But the situation did not change radically. War time shortage of capital goods apart, investment in modern industry continued to be limited by the relative lack of profitability springing from the constriction of the home market, rather than by a shortage of raw materials, labour, finance, or even local entrepreneurship (though almost certainly the base of the local business class had been broadened by the forced disengagement of most British businessmen in India from their normal business pursuits). (For development of the argument, see Bagchi, 1972a).

Beginning with the First World War, India's links with the UK were loosened, and she entered into a situation of multilateral dependence on the advanced capitalist countries. However, the passage from unilateral to multilateral dependence was slow for several reasons. First, much of the interwar period was one of recession and instability for the capitalist world, so that the USA, the new overlord, retreated into an isolationist position – except, of course, that her 'special relationship' with Latin America grew in strength. (This was the period when many Latin American countries including Argentina gradually passed from the British to the American sphere of influence.' Capitalist instability was increased by the lack of a clear directing centre and by the renewed struggle of Germany to succeed to the position that Britain was forced to vacate. (The rise of the Soviet Union further weakened the capitalist world and increased its internal contradictions.) Secondly, in east, south, and south-east Asian markets (including India and China), Britain was competing with Japan. And the USA, to a large extent, acted as Britain's ally. Britain had to grant some concessions to Indian capitalists, partly in response to the nationalist struggle, and partly in order to counter the Japanese threat. In the third place, the depression of the thirties seemed to presage for Indian capitalists a final state of independence. Their assets grew faster than those of the British capitalists in India, and much of the public debt of India held in Britain was liquidated. As it turned out, this promise proved to be an illusion, and it led to a new kind of multilateral dependence on the advanced capitalist camp. But the onset of this latter process was delayed by the interval of loosening of older types of colonial ties.

The Government of India was granted a measure of fiscal autonomy after the First World War, and it adopted a policy of 'discriminating protection' with effect from 1924 onwards. Protective tariffs began to be used to shelter some existing Indian industries against foreign competition. (But imports from countries of the British Empire – including, of course, Britain – were accorded a preferential treatment.) Tariff protection was not intended as a promotional measure and was not accompanied by other measures of state assistance on any scale. Furthermore, the latter half of the 1920s was already marked by depression in world agriculture, and in 1929 the great depression of the 1930s set in. Agricultural prices declined to levels below those obtained even before 1914, and they declined far more precipitously than industrial prices. Thus the money and real incomes of the average Indian declined at the time tariff protection really made its mark. The government's taxation and expenditure policies, instead of cushioning the decline in money incomes, aggravated it. In attempting to balance its budget, and protect India's 'credit' abroad (in reality, the prices of existing securities of the Indian government held by bondholders in Britain), the Government of India slashed its expenditure as its revenues fell. (In this, its policy was in strong contrast with that of the Brazilian government; see chapter 3 above.) There occurred a redistribution of incomes within India in favour of fixed-income groups and people deriving their incomes from sources other than agriculture. Such redistribution helped stimulate the demand for industrial consumer goods. But the growth of industries remained tied to a basically stagnant economy, and government policy did little to ensure sustained growth. By the end of the 1930s, India achieved a fair degree of self-sufficiency in the basic consumer goods produced by industry, and also in such crude producer and intermediate goods as pig iron, steel and cement (see Bagchi, 1972a, chapters 7–13). This phase of import-substituting industrialization did not strain the supplies of labour, capital or entrepreneurship. Beyond strengthening the Indian capitalist class, and filling some obvious gaps in the industrial structure, it did not usher in a period of sustained growth either.

In the interwar period, India's value to Britain and the advanced capitalist world as a source of surplus declined considerably (cf.

table 4.2 above). During the First World War and for a few years after it, the British Government had forced India to contribute massively to the British war effort (including an *ex gratia* payment of £100 million) and had foisted on India a very great increase in the external public debt. Since most of this debt was held by British stockholders, the British Government had an important stake in Indian fiscal and monetary policies (for evidence of the concern of the Government of India to protect British imperial interests and British stockholder interests, see Keynes, 1973, p. 13). By the end of the 1920s, the excuses for and the feasibility of, raising new loans for India in London had been well nigh exhausted. However, India's importance as the centrepiece of the British Empire in the East still remained. The position of the foremost supplier of export surpluses to the imperial system was now taken by Malaysia, whose tin and rubber helped Britain to square her accounts with countries outside the sterling area (Kahn, 1946, chapters XI–XV). The Indian empire was a declining asset in other respects too, for, the finances of the Government of India were often embarrassed, and British businessmen's pickings from governmental expenditure and borrowings were nowhere near as large as they had been before the First World War.

There was probably little actual transfer of British-owned assets to Indians before the Second World War. But Indians were more active than Europeans in the field of new enterprise, and their share in industrial capital grew. Conflicts of interest in industry, banking and shipping between Indian and European capitalist groups were starkly revealed. The upsurge of a nationalist movement forced the British government to make some concessions to Indian capitalists, whose alliance they sought to purchase thereby. Nevertheless, as we have mentioned above, the freedom of manoeuvre that the Indian capitalists enjoyed during this period proved to be short-lived. Large international companies and cartels had already began to dominate world capitalism, and India could not escape their grip, particularly in fields characterized by advanced and rapidly changing technology. The Imperial Chemical Industries set up a manufacturing plant in India at the end of the 1930s, and companies like General Motors set up assembly plants for cars. On the other side, Indian firms entering new fields of industry (such as the manufacture of textile machinery, or railway locomotives) sought the collaboration of foreign firms for plant design and process knowhow, as well as the use of licences and patents.

These tendencies became accentuated during the Second World War, in spite of restrictions on investment imposed by the policies of the Government of India. From the War, Indian industry emerged with the first phase of import substitution, in which basic consumer goods industries predominated, essentially complete and with huge unsatisfied demand for new equipment, and new facilities for building up consumer goods industries. Between 1946 and 1951, much of the wartime backlog of demand for capital goods was worked off, and India embarked on her series of Five Year Plans which were expected to bring her to the door of self-reliance.

Few economists at the time noticed that between 1937 and 1946 India had exchanged a state of unilateral dependence on Britain for that of multilateral dependence on the advanced capitalist countries. This latter type of dependence was caused by her earlier history and by her socio-economic structure. As a backward, predominantly illiterate country, India lacked the base for autonomous technological development or for successful imitation of techniques developed abroad. With a poor population and a social structure dominated by a weak and far from homogeneous capitalist class, the market for the better types of consumer goods, particularly durables, remained extremely restricted. The state apparatus precariously balanced the interests of the landlords, monopoly capitalists, professional classes, and collaborationist elements in the upper classes. Hence government policy was never radical enough to release agriculture from conditions of semi-feudal bondage, and lay a firm base for assured growth. India had in effect made a transition from the demand-constrained stasis of colonial times to the multiply-constrained three-legged race of a neocolonial, retarded society. We attempt a theoretical analysis of this latter type of growth in chapter 5, and analyse the typical class structures of neocolonial, semi-feudal, retarded societies in chapters 6 and 7.

4.6 THE DECADENCE OF THE CH'ING EMPIRE AND THE COLONIAL AND SEMI-COLONIAL EXPLOITATION OF CHINA IN THE PERIOD UP TO 1895

Even as late as the eighteenth century, the unified, aloof empire of China, ruled by the Ch'ing (Manchus) since 1644 excited the admiration of Europeans. Francois Quesnay thought that 'such an empire as that of China is equal to what all Europe would be if, the latter were united under a single sovereign' (F. Quesnay, 'Despotism in China', in Schurmann and Schell, 1967). China was a country with a huge bureaucracy manned by scholar officials. The latter were generally recruited from the ranks of landlords who in turn exercised most of the local power which was not appropriated directly by the imperial officials. We shall use Joseph Needham's phrase 'bureaucratic feudalism' to characterize Chinese society as it was before European penetration changed it drastically (J. Needham, 'The past in China's present' in Needham, 1969; see Balazs, 1972, for a different characterization).

This society was basically agrarian, supporting an elaborate bureaucracy and highly exploitative landlords. Artisanal production, specialized crafts and their guilds had developed on a large scale; the use of money had been widespread at least since the eighth and ninth centuries, and merchants accumulated large volumes of capital and carried on long-distance trade. Many of the signs of existence of private capitalist strata are discernible by the end of the eighteenth century. These included marketing of crops on a large scale, the widespread borrowing and lending of money, the growth of private enterprise in textiles, the payment of rent in cash, and so on. Development in techniques of production in agriculture and industry supported the growth of private enterprise.

However, this primitive capitalism remained on a tight leash. While licensed salt merchants might amass great wealth, the state and the landlords would tax or regulate the merchants down to size whenever they threatened to become too powerful. And the prosperity of particular merchants depended on official favour.[6] When Europeans came to trade in China, for example, the Chinese government licensed some selected Chinese merchants (the so-called 'Hong merchants') to handle the trade with the foreigners under the supervision of government officials. As the imperial government became weaker in relation to the foreigners in course of the nineteenth century, many of the Chinese merchants in the so-called 'treaty ports' became agents of the foreigners, thus exchanging one set of patrons for another.

Under the system recognized by the Chinese imperial authorities until 1842, the foreigners could trade only through the intermediation of the Co-hong or the guild of Hong merchants (see Morse, 1909 and Greenberg, 1969). They refused to enter into any 'equal' trading relations with the foreigners, and Canton was the only port where they were allowed to trade. In 1793, Lord Macartney was sent as an envoy by the King of England to China, with magnificent presents, hoping for the opening up of trade. Emperor Ch'ien-lung accepted the presents as

6 For developments in textile manufacture and in the rice trade, see Myers, 1965, and Chuan and Kraus, 1975, respectively. For the relation of state to private enterprise, see Lattimore, 1960, and Balazs, 1972. For a summary of technical developments, see Mark Elvin's paper in Perkins, 1975.

'tribute' from the English King but was constrained to observe that 'our celestial empire possesses all things in prolific abundance' (Fairbank, Reischauer and Craig, 1969, p. 77). Nothing came of that embassy. The next British embassy of Lord Amherst in 1816 did not even receive an audience from the Emperor, partly because the British were then involved in an aggressive war against Nepal, a tributary of China.

In the meantime, the lure of profits to be made from trade with China was increasing for the British. With the progress of the Industrial Revolution in Britain and the continued stagnation of the Chinese economy and society, the ability of the latter to defend itself against British designs was declining all the time. In the period up to 1830, the profitability or necessity of trade with China had little to do with the direct results of the Industrial Revolution (except in so far as the growth in incomes in Britain increased the demand for Chinese tea). In the eighteenth century, there was a profitable market for Chinese handicrafts, and, much more importantly, for Chinese tea in Britain and other European countries. There was, however, no corresponding demand for European goods in China. Hence Britain had an adverse balance of trade with China, which was met by the export of bullion. After the conquest of Bengal, Indian textiles and silver obtained from Indian exploitation served to square Britain's balance of trade with China. Their place was increasingly occupied by exports of raw cotton and opium from India. Opium, as a habit-forming drug, could be sold without meeting a saturation level. But trade in opium was under an imperial ban in China (proclaimed in 1796) and the British East India Company used private European traders to smuggle the drug into China.

As early as 1786, Lord Cornwallis, the then Governor General of India, was pleading for the East India Company to extend special facilities to private traders trading between India and China (although theoretically the Company enjoyed a monopoly of trade both with China and India). For this was the only way of transferring the vast tribute of Bengal to England without losing heavily through exchange depreciation, and of at least partly meeting China's bill for tea and other goods bought by Britain and other European countries (Greenberg, 1969, chapter II and Singh, 1966, p. 38). The East India Company kept up the polite fiction that its ships could not be used for exporting opium to China. But it did everything in its power to push the sale of the drug, by monopolizing its production in Bengal (it could not yet control its production in central and western India), regulating prices, and assisting the private European smugglers.

As a result, the shipment of Indian opium to China grew from

49,619 chests (of $133\frac{1}{3}$ lbs) in the decade 1801–10 to 276,143 chests in the decade 1831–40 (the estimates are based on Tan Chung, 1973, table xv.)

The growth of exports of opium and, to a much smaller extent, of raw cotton from India soon led to a situation in which China was having to pay for her imports with silver, thus reversing the direction of flow of bullion.

By 1828, exports of European goods paid only for about a quarter of the purchases of tea by the East India Company, the rest being paid for by exports of Indian raw cotton and Indian opium (Greenberg, 1969, p. 13). The British traders thus succeeded in obtaining their profits from both China and India by inducing a change in their structures of production. Both China and India were gradually reduced to the status of exporters of raw materials or primary products, such as tea, cotton, opium and raw silk. By 1828, private traders accounted for more than two thirds of the total trade and acted as the carriers of silver from China to Britain. The China trade became the channel of remittance by the East India Company from India to London.

> This was partly because a considerable proportion of the Company's territorial revenue was obtained in kind, in such goods as could be sold profitably only in Canton; partly because by remitting through China via the Country Trade [i.e. the intra-Asian trade as distinguished from trade with Europe] the Company was able to gain a large advantage from its control over the rate of exchange of its bills (Greenberg, 1969, p. 15).

The Company and the private European traders thus participated in a collective monopoly of foreign trade between China, India and Europe. The dominant British private traders in the China trade, as in the case of Indo-British trade, were only a few in number. Two British firms, Jardine, Matheson & Co., and Dent & Co., came to control two thirds of the British trade in China. On the eve of the Opium War, the British in their turn controlled two thirds of the foreign trade of China.

With the growth of imports of opium and the drain of silver, China was involved in a fiscal crisis. Furthermore, since copper was the normal medium of exchange for the poorer people whereas silver was the unit of account for most payments, the drain of silver meant a rise in its value in relation to copper and increased hardship for the Chinese peasantry and other toiling people. The state naturally tried hard to enforce the ban on the import of opium.[7] On the other side, the abolition of the formal monopoly of the East India Company in the

7 The contact with the foreigners had already produced collaborationists who wanted to enter into a compromise with foreigners. The gains of corrupt officials from the system of opium smuggling made many of them drag their feet over the execution of official policy. See in this connection, Opium War, 1976, chapter 3.

trade between China and Europe removed the last restraint on the British side on trade with China, and private European traders began to chafe at the restrictions on 'freedom of trade' imposed by the Chinese system of licensed foreign trade.

At the end of the 1830s, the Chinese authorities appointed an incorruptible and vigorous official in the person of Lin Tse-hsu in order to enforce the ban on opium trade. Lin tried first to persuade the British to abjure smuggling in the name of international law and common morality. When these appeals did not produce the desired effect, he adopted sterner measures, including confiscation of smuggled opium. The British replied with guns and a naval blockade. The military and naval technology of the dominant capitalist power easily proved superior to the war junks and shore batteries of the Chinese. The latter were compelled to sign the first of the series of unequal treaties, the Treaty of Nanking. Under its provisions, the monopoly of foreign trade by the Co-hong merchants was abolished, Hong Kong was ceded to Britain, and five more ports, including Canton and Shanghai, were opened to British trade; further, a 'fair and regular tariff' on trade was promised. The British also exacted an indemnity of 21 million dollars (Fairbank, Reischauer and Craig, 1969, pp. 128–46; Greenberg, 1969, chapters VII and VIII; and Opium War, 1976).

The Treaty of Nanking was followed in rapid succession by the British Supplementary Treaty of the Bogue, the American Treaty of Wang hsia, and the French Treaty of Whampoa. These treaties reinforced one another, for the privileges obtained by one foreign power were also claimed by other like-minded foreign powers under the so-called 'most favoured nation clause'. The rest of the nineteenth century was a story of escalation of first Western, and then Japanese, demands on China for various kinds of privileges including rights of extraterritoriality. The second Opium War of 1856–60 was fought under the most frivolous excuse of redressing 'an insult to a British flag lowered by Chinese police from a Chinese-owned vessel registered at Hong Kong' (Fairbank, Reischauer and Craig, 1969, p. 169). In this war, the French joined the British, their arch rivals in European diplomacy at the time, to share in the kill. Chinese defeat in the war resulted, among other things, in the formal handing over of Chinese customs to the supervision of the foreign powers, represented by a British official, the opening up of the whole of China to penetration by foreign traders, and the payment of an indemnity of 8 million taels.

In the 1850s and 1860s, China was convulsed by a series of peasant revolts, which included the Muslim rebellion in the north-west, the revolt of the Nien and, most important, the Taiping Rebellion (see Chesnaux, 1973; and Taiping Revolution, 1976, for accounts of these revolts). The Taiping Rebellion has been called the greatest peasant revolt in history. It was a direct response to the humiliation suffered by the Chinese at the hands of the foreigners beginning with the Opium War. But it was also in the great tradition of Chinese peasant revolts of earlier times, which, however, generally led only to a dynastic change and not to any fundamental changes in society (see Mao Tse-tung, 'The Chinese Revolution and the Chinese Communist Party' in Mao, 1967, vol. II, for an analysis of the significance of these revolts). This rebellion was inspired by a millenarian Christian ideology, and had staunchly egalitarian ideals. It failed because it could not create a state apparatus which was essentially different from the Ch'ing regime it was fighting. The French and the British, after humiliating the Ch'ing in the second Opium War, jointly helped it to crush the Taiping revolt.

Until Japan's bid to carve out a separate sphere of influence in China and detach actual territories from the Empire changed the rules of the game, the Western imperialist powers pursued a dualistic policy:

> From time to time one country or another thought it necessary to chasten a too obdurate China. Once chastened, however, China's incompetent Manchu government had to be put back in business again, for it could not be expected that future demands would be carried out if the government was too weak to carry them out. Thus there emerged an interesting principle: for international purposes, the ideal government of China was a government strong enough to carry out orders, but not strong enough to defy orders (Lattimore, 1960, pp. 104–5).

This policy of the imperialist powers and the system of treaty ports which limited the direct impact of the foreigners to the coastal regions, effectively restricted the impact that industrial capitalism could have on China throughout the nineteenth century. The absence of any railways linking the coast with the interior further circumscribed such impact.[8] A clear distinction thus emerged between the 'comprador

8 One important reason for the differences in the degree of foreign domination of India and of China lay in the relative degrees of strength of the Mughal and Ch'ing emperors at the time the Western capitalist powers made a bid for conquest. 'While China, even in the days of her weakness maintained a political unity, and the Emperor was able to enforce his authority in the most distant provinces and the viceroys "trembled and obeyed", in India by 1740 the Imperial authority had completely broken down . . . In China the issue had to be fought out in every case with the central government, while in India the British and French companies dealt with local governors, viceroys, and princelings and were therefore able to exert pressure on them' (Panikkar, 1970, pp. 93–4). The Chinese Empire also disintegrated when the western powers and the Japanese could play one viceroy or general against another in the pursuit of their self-interest.

bourgeoisie' in the treaty ports in subservient alliance to the foreign capitalists, and 'the national bourgeoisie' in the interior. The distinction between the two, however, became a little blurred in the Republican period.

Until the 1880s, the predominant methods of exploitation of China by the Western powers were mercantilist in nature. Opium, which was a product of India, rather than of the industrialized economies of Europe, remained extremely important as an item of import into China and source of profit to the British businessmen and the British Indian government until the very end of the century. According to one estimate, Indian exports of opium to China and the Straits Settlements (most of the opium from the Straits Settlements found its way to China) grew from about £8 million per year in the second half of the 1850s to more than £10 million in the second half of the 1870s, the peak period of opium exports to China.[9] According to Chinese official statistics (see Hsiao Liang-lin, 1974, tables 2 and 9a) imports of opium varied between £8 million and £12 million per annum during the period 1867–94; though quantities imported declined from a peak of 83,000 chests in 1883 to 18,000 chests in 1913, the value never went down below £4 million before 1914.

Although opium was the produce of Indian cultivators, they were not willing partners in the exploitation of China. Rather, they as producers and the Chinese as consumers were yoked to the same system of oppression. The system of government supervision over the cultivation of opium has been summarized as follows:

> The opium industry in Bengal is a Government monopoly, and the districts are divided into two agencies, Bihar and Benares, which are under the control of officials residing respectively at Patna and Ghazipur . . . Anyone who chooses may enter the industry, but cultivators are obliged to sell the opium exclusively to the Government agent at a price fixed beforehand by the latter, which is approximately 3s.6d. per lb., the government selling it at about 11s. per lb (Britannica, 1884, p. 789).

Adding 45 per cent to 11s. we get 16s. as the landed cost of opium in China; import duties and *likin* (local tariffs) would make the price still higher for the Chinese consumer. The Indian producer thus obtained at most one fourth of the landed cost and less than one fifth of the price paid by the Chinese consumer. The Indian peasant often had to be coerced to cultivate opium, through a combination of advances and the threat of loss of land in case of failure to fulfil government

9 The estimate is based on Royal Commission on Opium, 1894, Appendix XII, pp. 390–1.

obligations in time. The greatest beneficiaries of the system were the British Indian Government and the British business firms dealing in the drug. But quite a few Indian capitalists in western India also made their fortunes in the opium trade.

The legal and illegal import of opium soon led to 'import substitution' in the product. Even before the first Opium War, extensive cultivation of opium had begun in China. After the war and the increasing crisis of the Ch'ing empire, the output of the poppy crop spread enormously, particularly in the south-western provinces of Szechwan and Yunnan. (See the evidence of W. B. Spence, British Consul at Ichang, in Royal Commission on Opium, 1894, Appendix XII.) Landlords and merchants, and officials taxing the crop (and retaining a part of the 'squeeze' from the traders and peasants), came to acquire a vested interest in it, and peasants were compelled, often under share-cropping arrangements, to cultivate the crop. Long before the trade in the drug was banned officially (which happened in the early twentieth century), China had become practically self-sufficient in it. Chu Teh remembered with bitterness the deterioration in the condition of the people which forced them to take up the cultivation of poppy (in the late nineteenth or early twentieth century) (Smedley, 1972, p. 43). The taking of opium continued to spread among the people throughout the period of warlordism, Kuomintang militarism and Japanese aggression succeeding the fall of the Ch'ing in 1911 (Chen, 1969) and was stopped only by the communist victory in 1949.

As in the case of India, the most important traditional handicraft, namely, spinning of cotton yarn and weaving of cotton cloth, was adversely affected by imports of machine-made goods from abroad. As a result of imports of yarn, the traditional spinning industry definitely declined. But this cheap imported yarn arrested the decline of the handloom industry. Further, the competition from foreign cloth led to unemployment among handloom weavers, whose wages declined, thus restoring a degree of competitiveness to the handloom industry (see Feuerwerker, 1970, and Kang Chao, 1975). But even if the handloom industry might have been helped by cheaper yarn and lower earnings of weavers, there must have been a net contraction in employment in the cotton handicraft sector, because handspinning required more labour than hand-weaving. A similar contraction must have occurred also in other branches of handicrafts. These developments were probably much less severe than in India because of factors mentioned elsewhere. But since the growth of modern mechanized industry was on a smaller scale than in India, the effect this had in countering the de-industrialization caused by decline of traditional handicrafts was also weaker (see Bagchi, 1976a).

The trade in opium illustrates how advanced capitalist countries have in the past moulded the production and consumption structures of whole subcontinents and have impeded their progress. In the Chinese case, the depredations of advanced capitalism aggravated the contradictions of a feudal–bureaucratic society. The disintegration of the empire in turn provided opportunities for banking firms and other enterprises from the imperialist nations to make extraordinary profits. On the British side, for example, Jardine Matheson and Company, which was one of the main beneficiaries of the first Opium War, acted in concert with the Hong Kong and Shanghai Banking Corporation to mulct the Chinese treasury. The former gave accommodation to corrupt officials, who would float loans on behalf of the empire, and the latter would arrange for the underwriting and floatation of the loans (see, for example, Collis, 1965, chapter 3). The guarantee for the loans was generally provided by Chinese customs or specially designated internal taxes. In this way, most of the fiscal resources of the empire came to be mortgaged to foreigners, and its downfall was hastened. The operations of foreign firms in China in this respect were very similar to those of French and British financiers in Egypt, except that, because of the sheer size of the country and the intensity of interimperialist rivalry, China escaped the fate of actual conquest by any particular power.

4.7 THE FINAL PHASE OF IMPERIALIST AND SEMI-FEUDAL EXPLOITATION OF CHINA

The specific mode of exploitation associated with industrial capitalism, viz. through the setting up of manufacturing enterprises using machine-based methods, had its beginning in the final phase of disintegration of the Ch'ing regime. In 1894, Japan attacked Korea, which had recognized China as her suzerain. China tried to defend her territorial claims, but the Japanese destroyed the Chinese navy in a naval engagement. By the Treaty of Shimonoseki, signed in 1895, China ceded Formosa, the Pescadores and the Liaotung Peninsula; and Korea, under the guise of independence from China, became a Japanese colony. Thus began Japan's protracted aggression against China and her persistent effort to convert north China, including Manchuria, into a Japanese colony. Japan also exacted an indemnity of 200 million taels, which was increased to 230 million taels, when she had to give up her claims to the Liaoning Peninsula (in north China) under Russian–German–French pressure. The commercial part of the treaty gave Japan, and therefore other imperialist powers, the additional privilege of carrying on 'industries and manufactures' in the treaty ports. The payment of indemnity by China did not cease there. The Boxer Rebellion, which was a nationalist and conservative movement directed against the foreigners, broke out in 1898, and all the imperialist powers joined together in suppressing it. They then stipulated the payment of an indemnity of 450 million taels (Outline History, 1958, pp. 272–3).[10]

The Treaty of Shimonoseki opened up the field of manufacturing enterprises to foreigners, and the British and the Japanese took the greatest advantage of this opportunity. Before this, a section of the bureaucrats and landlords, of whom Tseng Kuo-fan and Li Hung-chang were the most important, tried to promote industries with a modern technological base, without, however, endangering the inherited structure of society. The enterprises thus promoted came to be known as *Kuan-tu shang-pan* enterprises, that is, they were government-supervised and merchant-managed. They comprised munition factories, steamships, telegraph lines, and, later, cotton mills. They were, however, too few in number, too dependent on foreign help and too conservative in conception to be effective agents for the industrialization of China. They derived much of their profit from officially protected monopolistic privileges or special tax concessions, and much of their capital and management from the comprador capitalists in the treaty ports. They were the direct ancestors of the system of 'bureaucratic capitalism' spawned by the Kuomintang, which we shall discuss below (see Feuerwerker, 1958, and Outline History, 1958, chapter 42).

The Treaty of Shimonoseki was followed by a scramble for railway concessions. They were both the formal imprint that a particular region belonged to the sphere of influence of a particular foreign power, and an excuse for extending the spheres of influence of respective powers. To some extent, the foreign claims tended to offset one another, for a concession often informally or verbally extended by

10 The period of payment was stipulated as 39 years. With accrued interest it would have amounted to 980 million taels (Outline History, 1958, pp. 272–3). Some of the indemnity was later waived by foreign powers because of defeat in the First World War (as in the case of Germany), because of socialist revolution in the home country (as in the case of Russia), or as a concession to the Kuomintang government. But some part was also used to spread the light of Western education and ideologies, in the hope of making the Chinese – particularly the upper class Chinese – see things through western eyes, through such institutions as the American-built Tsinghua University (Smedley, 1972, p. 56).

a high central official or a provincial governor with only ill-defined areas of jurisdiction could be set against other concessions whose claims to legality were equally uncertain. The imperialist powers generally insisted on treating all such vague, dubiously legal, concessions as treaty obligations (Willoughby, 1920, chapters I and X; see also Allen and Donnithorne, 1962, chapter VIII). The British and the Russians were early in the field with their respective railway concessions. Those two old partners in the game of milking China, Jardine Matheson & Co., and the Hong Kong and Shanghai Banking Corporation, set up the British and Chinese Corporation to build railways in China, with Jardine, Matheson looking after the contracting side, and the Hong Kong and Shanghai looking after the finances (Allen and Donnithorne, 1962, p. 139 and Collis, 1965, chapters 3 and 5). Other foreign powers used similar instruments but also direct state power to extract and execute railway concessions. By the end of the First World War, the foreigners owned and operated some of the most important railways in China such as the South Manchuria Railway (Japan), Chinese Eastern Railway (Russia), Yunnan Railway (France), and Shantung railway (Japan – then Germany) (the particular power involved is mentioned within brackets). In other cases also, foreigners generally exercised a large measure of administrative control: it was often stipulated formally that certain top supervisory posts should be held by foreign engineers and accountants (Willoughby, 1920, chapter XX).

When the Ch'ing empire was overthrown by revolutionary nationalists under the leadership of Sun Yat-sen in 1911, the imperialist powers tried to ensure that China stayed within their sphere of control. The older imperialist powers at first wanted a unified China, under the control of the traditional scholar officials, generals and landlords. Yuan Shih-kai, who undid the work of the nationalists and usurped supreme authority for himself enjoyed the support of the western powers (Collis, 1965, chapter 6). But once the empire was formally broken up into territories of different warlords, the imperialist powers did everything to accelerate the process by throwing their support behind particular warlords. In this way, Japan gradually consolidated her hold on north China, and by the end of the 1920s converted Manchuria into a puppet state.

Under Sun Yat-sen, the Kuomintang made an effort to unite all of China under the nationalist flag. But after his death, and after the victory of the Kuomintang over the northern warlords, Chiang Kai-shek turned against the Communists. In effect Chiang emerged as the supreme warlord, basing his power on the landlords, control over regional warlords, and support of the western imperialist powers. In 1931, Japanese militarists began their final thrust to occupy all of northern China. The Communists, under the leadership of Mao Tse-tung, survived several extermination campaigns launched by the Kuomintang, and retained a base in north-west China. When Japanese aggression escalated, the Communists fought the aggressors much more tenaciously than Chiang Kai-shek and in the process extended their political control in Japanese occupied areas.

The Kuomintang regime emerged from the Second World War apparently stronger than ever with enormous stocks of military equipment and assured flows of American aid. But their refusal to carry out any basic reforms, particularly in the field of land relations, their preference for killing Communists and other democratic elements to fighting the Japanese, their unwillingness to tax the rich and hence their inability to control inflation, and the rampant corruption at all levels of the army and the administration had robbed them of all popular support and sapped their real power irremediably.[11] The village-based Communists then encircled the Kuomintang strongholds, and ultimately compelled the Chiang Kai-shek clique to seek refuge in Taiwan, under American protection. A unified China came into being again in 1949 after the lapse of half a century, under the leadership of Mao Tse-tung and the Communist Party of China.

This very brief sketch of the political history of modern China indicates how quickly China's economy and society must have changed since 1895, so that a Communist regime could replace the Ch'ing empire within a period of 38 years. The operations of foreign capitalists backed by their governments contributed greatly to this outcome. At the same time, the earlier resistance of Chinese society against foreign penetration, represented by the confinement of the foreigners to the treaty ports and the later popular resistance to many of the activities of foreign capitalists and missionaries kept alive a strong sentiment for patriotic unity against foreigners. One example of this resistance is provided by the slowness of railway construction in China after the initial scramble for concessions.

The total rail mileage in China, including Manchuria, came to only 12,000 miles in 1942. Their organization was highly regionalized, and might be considered inefficient from the point of view of a truly national transportation system (see Sun, 1955). Both the slow growth of railways and decentralization of their control had their positive

11 On the inefficiency and corruption prevalent in the Kuomintang regime, see Stilwell, 1948, and Belden, 1973.

aspects. The Chinese people, often led by patriotic landlords and national capitalists, resisted the building of railways by foreigners in the interest of foreigners. The decentralization itself was sometimes the result of assertion of local, basically patriotic, interest, against the pressure of the imperialists, exerted through Peking. The slow development of the railways (and the alignment of major railways along existing waterways) continued to limit the direct influence of the foreigner to the littoral provinces, and prevented the conversion of all surviving native capitalists into collaborators, or the wholesale destruction of local handicrafts. In these respects, China differed greatly from India (cf. Smedley, 1972, pp. 65 and 90).

But in spite of the limits placed on the operations of foreigners by imperial and popular resistance, the amount of 'foreign investment' in China mounted rapidly in the twentieth century. Foreign investment, as conventionally computed, grew from 787.9 million US dollars in 1902 to US $ 1,610.3 million in 1914 and US $ 3,242.5 million in 1931. Great Britain remained the leading investor until the early 1930s, but Japan rapidly rose to be the leading 'creditor' nation, particularly after 1931 when she became master of Manchuria and North China (Remer, 1933, p. 76). Sectorwise, transportation accounted for 33.0 per cent and 26.1 per cent of the total foreign investments in 1914 and 1931 respectively, thus indicating the importance of railway investments. The next important category was 'general purposes of the Chinese government', which accounted for 20.5 per cent and 13.2 per cent of the foreign investments in 1914 and 1931 respectively. In 1914, 'imports and exports' made up 14.9 per cent of the total foreign investments. Manufacturing formed only 6.9 per cent of foreign investments in 1914, but 11.6 per cent of the total in 1931. These foreign-owned manufacturing firms dominated modern coal mining, cotton weaving, electric power generation and cigarette making, among others (Feuerwerker, 1968, p. 16).

If we look at the growth of modern manufacturing in the Japanese-occupied or Kuomintang-ruled China, in percentage terms it might look impressive, because the base was very small. But in absolute terms the growth was not very striking. In table 4.3 we give figures of looms and spindles in place in India and China in 1912 and 1936. These figures show that in about the best year of Kuomintang rule the Chinese cotton mill industry was much smaller than that of India, which was a colonial country, with a smaller population. Furthermore, while the contribution of modern industry to national income in the 1930s has been estimated to be about 7 per cent in India,

Table 4.3 *Spindles and looms (in '000s) in the cotton mills of India and China*

		Spindles	Looms
India	1912–13	5,737	83
	1936–37	8,441	178
China	1912	738	2
	1936	5,635	58

Sources: For India, *Reports of the Bombay Millowners' Association*. The figures are underestimates by between 5 and 10 per cent. For China, Chang, 1966, and Kang Chao, 1975.

it has been estimated by an apologist of Kuomintang achievement in industry to be only 3 per cent.[12]

The conditions of the factory workers in these modern industries with little labour legislation or supervision of existing factory laws, and of artisans in the languishing handicraft industries were as inhuman as possible. Shanghai, the biggest centre of foreign-owned industry became a byeword for the state of its slums and its working class poverty. In agriculture, the conditions of ordinary cultivators were as desperate as in most of India. Tenancy was widespread in China, but more extensive in south China than in the north (see Tawney, 1964). Under the impact of the terrible famines in north China from 1928 to 1933, there were huge land transfers from the peasantry to the landlords, and in Shensi, for example, insecurity of tenancy became a serious problem. Civil officials, army officers, landlords had close links in most parts of China, and this facilitated their exploitation of the peasantry. The breakdown of civil authority and the increased scope for arbitrary decisions, and the growing commercial involvement of the landlords led to more intensive exploitation of the peasants (see Selden, 1972).

In Kwantung in southern China, Chen Han-seng (1936) found in the 1930s extreme degrees of incidence of tenancy and exploitation of the peasantry through share rents, taxes, payments for 'feasts' and other forms of exactions. There were many payments to the landlords which were outside the contract or lease agreement, and the terms of the contractual agreement could be altered by asserting non-market

12 The estimate for India is from Sivasubramonian, 1965; the estimate for China is from Chang, 1966.

power and exercising violence[13] (see also Smedley, 1972, p. 16, and Selden, 1972, pp. 6–7). In various parts of Kwangtung, rich merchants would lease land from the clans and then sublease it to others. Sometimes this subleasing extended as far as five stages. In the negotiations for lease by rich merchants, various kinds of threat were used against the weaker landlords, such as the threat of higher taxes (where merchants were in league with office-holders) or employment of hired toughs to forcibly harvest the crop (Chen Han-seng, 1936, pp. 49–56).

Generally speaking, the commercial exploitation of peasants was more intense in those parts (such as Kwangtung or Fukien) where commercialization had proceeded furthest. These were also generally areas which had been penetrated most deeply by foreign capital, particularly foreign banking capital. The collaboration of the various Chinese governments with such capital was generally rationalized in the name of 'modernizing' agriculture or industry.[14] Foreign banking capital operated through the Chinese merchants or landlords but often also directly to affect the conditions of production and distribution in the countryside (IPR, 1939, section III). Foreign industrial capital also intervened directly in some cases. For example, the British-American Tobacco Company subsidized the introduction of tobacco-growing in Shantung. Tobacco was generally more labour-intensive than other crops; it was found (by Chen Han-seng) that if labour costs were included, tobacco was less profitable than the competing crops. But if labour costs were neglected, tobacco was more profitable. However, as was found in the case of many other cash crops in the third world, the peasantry grew the crop because they had to earn *cash* to meet their obligations and because there was not enough work for them at the going wages (see Allen and Donnithorne, 1962, pp. 169–73, Wiens, 1975, and 'Tobacco marketing in eastern Shantung' and 'Foreign industrial capital and the peasantry in Hunan' in IPR, 1939).

13 The difference between the Indian and Chinese situations was that in India, generally all contracts for share tenancy were verbal, and written agreements were an exception. There was also perhaps less explicit resort to violence (for British rule was far more 'orderly' and exploitation was far better organized in India). Otherwise the shares obtained by landlords (ranging usually from 50 to 75 per cent), the exploitation exercised through usury and through the purchase of poor peasants' products at low post-harvest prices often as repayment of loans, and the control exercised by the gentry in the triple capacities of landlord, moneylender and merchant were very similar in the two cases.

14 What Chu Teh said of the conservative reformers of 1898 would apply with minor modifications to all the bourgeois reformers coming later: 'they planned to modernize the country on a capitalist basis while leaving the peasants in their old servitude under the landlord. They spoke of agrarian reforms, but these meant nothing but the introduction of such things as Egyptian or American long-staple cotton seeds which the landlords could buy and sell to their tenants' (Smedley, 1972, p. 52).

The other characteristics associated with widespread and insecure tenancy, domination of peasantry by landlords and merchants and stagnating agricultural production (as evidenced most starkly by the frequency and virulence of famines) were also found in China. Peasants' access to markets on their own was limited, the prices obtained by them on their products were at the mercy of the merchants who thrived on speculation, and the rates of interest charged on loans to the peasantry were extortionately high (rates ranging from 36 to 60 per cent being quite common).[15] Under the Kuomintang, co-operatives were sometimes organized to tackle some of these problems. But these came again to be dominated by landlords and merchants and acted as vehicles for channelling the banking capital to the countryside and obtaining a share of the rural surplus in that fashion. For example, in Wusih, cooperatives organized for instructing the farmers in the use of improved silkworm eggs for producing better raw silk remained under the control of merchants and had to compete with landlords owning silk filatures, who set up their own egg-producing stations (see 'Silk filatures and silkworm cooperatives in Wusih', and 'Trade capital and silk farming in Wusih', IPR, 1939).

The Kuomintang tried to bring all the forms of exploitation under their control by organizing bureaucratic structures over which the four ruling families (the three families of Chiang, Soong and Kung, and the family of Chen brothers) presided. The apex of this structure of 'bureaucratic capitalism' was provided by their monopolistic control of organized banking in China (except for the field left open for the foreign banks). Usually, T. V. Soong or H. H. Kung was the finance minister of the regime, and Chiang, Kung and Soong together controlled the four government banks, the Bank of China and the Central Bank of China. These banks were used to monopolize trade and distribution of many goods, or to extract 'commissions' from those who were allowed to conduct business on their own.[16] Kung and his wife also speculated on the foreign exchanges with full inside knowledge. Corruption even extended to trade by top officials and generals in Japanese goods across the border between free and occupied China. The Chen brothers, who controlled the bureaucracy

15 Attempts have been made from time to time to depict the Communist revolution as a 'mistake' and the Kuomintang or even Japanese controlled China as only mildly exploitative, where things would have gone right if only marginal reforms had been carried out in time. One such notable attempt is Myers, 1970. But both Myers' data-base and his analysis have been subjected to searching criticism by Payer, 1975, and Wiens, 1975.

16 They even exacted 'squeeze' from the industrial co-operatives organized by Rewi Alley, Edgar Snow and Nym Wales to help restore the production of some basic industrial products in free China after the Japanese had occupied most of the important industrial centres, including Shanghai (see Snow, 1958, Part 2, chapters 23 and 24).

of the Kuomintang, were also later given charge of the Farmers' Bank of China, which enriched the gentry through the so-called 'farmers' cooperatives' and contributed greatly to the sharpening of contradictions in the countryside. Education in foreign countries, which became popular in China after 1900, helped to create the new class of bureaucrats controlling the governmental apparatus of the warlords and the Kuomintang (Chen, 1969).

The capitalist framework of international payments and trade in this disintegrating society contributed greatly to its final break-up. China continued to be on the silver standard both internally and externally throughout the period up to 1934. Since silver depreciated continually in value during this period, this was translated into a persistent tendency towards inflation and the living standards of workers and peasants fell. After the First World War, silver prices rose for a time because of international shortage. This led to a crisis of circulation because of the shortage of coin within the country, with resulting depression in trade and production. Essentially the monetary developments were completely at the mercy of movements in the international market.

In the 1930s, China experienced a serious drain of silver, and the country was again faced with a payments crisis. The solution was found in 1935 by introducing currency notes inconvertible into silver, and linking the international price of the inconvertible currency, *fapi*, first to sterling and then to the US dollar, and keeping sterling and dollars as reserves. The reform was carried out with the advice of foreign experts and had the support of British banks (Chang, 1958). The Kuomintang government, however, soon resorted to the printing of notes as the major method of defraying its expenditures. The inflation released by these policies has become one of the textbook illustrations of hyperinflation in modern times: '100 fapi could buy two oxen in 1937, one in 1938, a pig in 1939, a sack of flour in 1941, a chicken in 1943, two eggs in 1945 . . . and not even one grain of rice in 1949' (CR, 1975, p. 10).

The development of contradictions in China was analysed by Mao Tse-tung from 1926 onwards; this analysis was the cornerstone of his revolutionary strategy.[17] The key features of this analysis are a clear

17 The articles and monographs we have in mind are the following in particular: 'Analysis of the classes in Chinese society' (March 1926), 'Report on an investigation of the peasant movement in Hunan' (March 1927), 'Why is it that Red political power can exist in China?' (5 October 1928), 'A single spark can start a prairie fire' (5 January 1930), 'How to differentiate the classes in the rural areas' (October 1933), 'On tactics against Japanese imperialism' (27 December 1935) in Mao Tse-tung, 1967, vol. I, and 'The Chinese Revolution and the Chinese Communist Party' (December 1939) and 'On New Democracy' (January 1940) in Mao Tse-tung, 1967, vol. II.

delineation of the class structure in China at different points of time, with a subtle perception of the shifting alignments between different classes at different junctures of history. In his mature analysis of rural classes in 'How to differentiate classes in the rural areas' written in October 1933, for example, Mao distinguished between five rural classes: the landlords, the rich peasants, the middle peasants, the poor peasants and the workers. In defining a particular class he took into account not only its direct ownership of land or lack of it, but also its ability to use other means of exploitation than owned land, or its chief source of livelihood. Thus Mao recognized that landlords could use clan or school property for their own profit, and nominal owners of land could be exploited through the market mechanism, particularly when they had to sell part of their labour in order to make ends meet.

Mao distinguished between national bourgeoisie and comprador bourgeoisie (that is, those who were agents of foreign capitalists) and regarded comprador bourgeoisie and the big landlords as enemies of the revolution. But he noted that because of conflicts of interest between the imperialist powers, some sections of the comprador bourgeoisie might be willing to further the anti-Japanese war to a certain extent (Mao Tse-tung, 'The Chinese Revolution and the Chinese Communist Party' in Mao, 1967, vol. II). He knew that the national bourgeoisie were a vacillating class, but he wanted to enlist their support in a common struggle for national liberation. However, he was quite firm that leadership in this struggle must be vested in the working class in the towns and villages.

The disintegration of the Chinese bureaucratic feudalism started in the nineteenth century. It was accelerated with the fall of the Ch'ing empire. The weak bourgeoisie of China tried to control the revolutionary forces for a time. But soon the rise of the warlords, the continued strength of the landlords in the countryside and towns, and the continued meddling by imperialist powers (whose recognition or lack of it could make or unseat a particular ruler) sealed the prospects of a bourgeois democratic society. Naked Japanese aggression on the one hand strengthened Chinese nationalism and, on the other, helped to break the social structure down at a rapid rate. The Chinese Communists by joining the patriotic struggle of the people in a wholehearted fashion and by showing themselves as the leaders of the vast majority of the exploited people were able ultimately to topple the corrupt, landlord- and warlord-dominated, regime of the Kuomintang (for a graphic foreshadowing of the break-up of the semi-feudal, semi-colonial society of China, see Mao Tse-tung, 'A single spark can start a prairie fire', in Mao, 1967, vol. I).

5

GROWTH AND FLUCTUATIONS IN ECONOMICALLY RETARDED SOCIETIES

5.1 INTRODUCTION

In chapters 3 and 4, we recounted the experience of development of some major underdeveloped regions of the world in the period up to the Second World War. In the present chapter, we discuss certain general features of the development of these economies in their colonial and post-colonial phases. We start with an analysis of the real (as against monetary) aspects of changes in production structures in these societies in the phase of *export-led exploitation.* Then we turn to the monetary and fiscal institutions that supported this mode of exploitation. Next we turn to the policy of import-substituting industrialization in its different phases and describe the typical features of fluctuations of retarded societies in the later phases of the import substitution process. Then we follow the implications of typical stabilization policies recommended and enforced by such agencies as the International Monetary Fund and the World Bank in such societies. Finally, we end up with a critique of the export-led growth strategy often recommended by economists of orthodox persuasion for the underdeveloped countries. Many of the earlier policies imposed on the retarded societies are now again being recommended by apparent well-wishers of such societies, and it is necessary to expose the consequences of such recommendations. Furthermore, few underdeveloped societies have entirely sloughed off the modes of exploitation that prevailed in the nineteenth century and thereafter; the modes of exploitation of the most advanced among the retarded societies are amalgams, in different proportions, of the different modes that we discuss in this chapter and that we referred to in chapter 2.

5.2 THE IMPACT OF CAPITALISM ON THE STRUCTURE OF PRODUCTION OF UNDERDEVELOPED COUNTRIES WITH SETTLED AGRICULTURE IN THEIR PRE-COLONIAL PHASE

A typical third world economy with settled, rather than shifting, cultivation, before contact with European capitalism would be almost entirely agrarian. The development of productive forces in such an economy would take the form primarily of acquisition of new skills and use of new techniques for cultivation of crops or production of goods without any great increase in the use of fixed capital. However, such an economy would also be characterized by a centralized state, and by long-distance trade within its borders. Most of these economies would be endowed with a handicraft sector which would produce the simple tools and consumer goods needed by the peasantry. This sector would also produce luxuries for the landlords, the nobility, the bureaucracy and the court. In some cases, such as China, India or the Ottoman Empire, there was considerable development of foreign trade and of monetary transactions within the country and with foreigners. However, the basic structure of production would be dictated by the internal needs (including the needs of the domestic exploiters) of the country or the Empire, rather than by the dictates of foreign trade or the requirements of rulers based in a foreign land.

Viewed from outside, such an economy may appear to have considerable slack in it, with underutilized land and unemployed labour. The fact that landlords or noblemen have a large number of retainers, or that considerable resources are devoted to social ceremonies, or that vast amounts of land are used as pasture may be taken as evidence of such a slack. But, in fact, in many cases, the 'surplus' of labour or land turns out to be illusory: the employment of retainers is essential to the maintenance and smooth functioning of a landlord-dominated society, the expenditure of resources in social ceremonies is often an essential part of redistribution within the society, and the reservation of vast amounts of land as pasture or cultivable waste is necessary to maintain the fertility of the soil and the productivity and number of the domestic animals (cf. Allan, 1971; and Pearson, 1957).

When European capitalists burst on the scene as conquerors, or as traders turned conquerors, the balance of this economy was upset. The Europeans appeared with a demand – either paid for in money, at least in the beginning, or exacted as tribute – for particular types of goods; it had to be met by changing the structure of production. The change in the structure of production could not be effected without upsetting the existing social relationships, for (a) the economy was not geared to the production of commodities for the market, except as a subsidiary activity, and (b), where the demand was for tribute, it could not be met without depriving some sections of the population of their earlier earnings. Thus the impact was rarely, if ever, a costless adjustment to an increased monetary demand.[1]

1 The 'vent for surplus' models of growth of international trade of the third world, of which Myint, 1958, is an example, are thus fundamentally mistaken. For, they assume

When the structure of demand was forcibly changed, very often open unemployment of labour or open underutilization of land or particular types of capital appeared. Thus, in the case of India in the nineteenth century, the fall in the demand for traditional handicraft products led to the massive displacement of labour previously engaged in such industries. There was no automatic redeployment of such labour in agriculture. For such redeployment to take place, there had to be adequate and compensating demand for the agriculture products and there was no mechanism to guarantee this. Furthermore, such redeployment would require massive investment in the agricultural sector. With continuous drain of resources from underdeveloped countries, with a stunted native capitalist class and with a government which was run in the interest of the colonial power, neither of the above-mentioned conditions were generally fulfilled.[2] On the other side, if the peasantry of a region are kept busy trying to grow the crops that would enable them to meet the demands of the state and allow them to subsist on their existing allotments of land, they would be prevented from taking up new land for cultivation. Such 'waste land' could then be given away to foreign planters.

In the semi-colonial economies of nineteenth century Latin America, and in non-white colonies, we notice two dominant types of production organization, viz. centralized plantations directly run by foreign capitalists, and peasant-cultivated holdings indirectly controlled by foreign capitalists and their subordinate collaborators. There was a mixed type, such as the indigo estates of India, the sugar estates of Indonesia, or the sugar *engenhos* of north-eastern Brazil, where peasant agriculture was subordinated to the needs of the central sugar mill.

The plantation economies were often created on the basis of slave labour. In other cases, land was given away practically *gratis* to plantation-owners (as in the case of Dutch-owned coffee-plantations in Indonesia or tea plantations in India), who were helped in various ways to keep the wages of labour low and labour itself as unfree as possible.[3] Restricting the peasants' access to land was generally an

---

that the third world economies were already adapted to production for the market at the time of European incursion and they ignore the costs that the European traders and conquerors exacted in compelling such economies to throw up a surplus.

2 Hymer and Resnick, 1969, discuss the process of transfer of labour and other resources from handicrafts to agriculture under the impact of capitalist colonialism. But they make the mistake of assuming that full employment prevails throughout the process.

3 Baldwin, 1956, offers a travesty of a theory to explain the low wages of labour in plantations and blames its meagreness on the high degree of capital-intensity of processes

essential part of this policy package. Mining enterprises were organized in very similar ways. However the plantations or mines originated, most of the value-added in such enterprises was generally concentrated in the hands of the foreign capitalists. The capital invested in such enterprises was generally accumulated out of the dominated economies, after remitting most of the profits abroad. The techniques used there evolved in a capital-using direction, partly because that was the way things were moving in metropolitan countries, and partly because it was easier to control the various branches of these enterprises (such as the growing of the crop, its processing, the transport of the product, and its induction into the trading channels) by using some sophisticated equipment and control methods.[4] Foreign capitalists, *qua* capitalists, had little regard for the intrinsic needs of the countries in which they were operating.

5.3 THE MONETARY AND FISCAL MECHANISM SUPPORTING EXPORTED-LED EXPLOITATION OF PEASANT AGRICULTURE

When the plantations were mainly based on wage-labour or slave-labour, surplus value from labour was directly extracted in the production process. In the colonial economies of India or Indonesia, most of the plantations were controlled by foreign capital and were often vertically integrated from the stage of growing of the crop to the marketing of the product, at least up to the point of shipping it abroad. There were then buying organizations in the major consuming countries which distributed the product. Such organizations themselves often controlled plantations in the colonies. Fluctuations in the market for the product were directly passed on to the workers in the plantations in the shape of fluctuations in their employment and wages. This sequence would apply also to such mineral products as Chilean copper, after it came to be controlled by giant transnationals such as Anaconda and Kennecott. When the fortunes of such enterprises fluctuated, government revenues and other incomes indirectly generated by them would also fluctuate, and this would greatly affect the states of such essentially mono-export economies as Chile or Peru (where guano played the role that mineral nitrate and

---

of production. The truth is the other way round: it is the forcible cheapening of labour and land that enables the plantation-owner to accumulate capital and adopt capital-intensive techniques.

4 The control functions of advanced production techniques have generally been ignored in the literature. A notable exception is Braverman, 1974.

copper played in Chile) or Ceylon (where tea became the dominant export).

Where the export crops were produced by peasants or by plantations which had a dependent peasant economy surrounding and supporting them, the method of exploitation was more indirect. Here the fiscal arm of the colonial state, and various devices for controlling the process of circulation and exchange, played a more vital role than in the case of pure plantation economies or mineral-based economies. One major source of revenue was the land tax, and another was the poll tax, or hut tax, particularly in African economies. These taxes helped to break up or subordinate pre-capitalist formations where they survived, and to compel the subject peoples to work in plantations, quarries or public works (generally road- or railway-building).

The colonial powers generally introduced their own legal tender, including bank notes, and drove out or subordinated any earlier monetary mechanism that had developed. In the process many indigenous bankers lost much of their business, including the highly profitable business of lending to the state, to the foreign capitalists. Usually at the level of small transactions many of the earlier types of currency survived, for ordinary people were too poor to buy goods in units of Spanish dollars, gold sovereigns, or even full silver rupees. Examples of such survivals were *cowries* (a special type of sea-shells) in India, and strings of copper cash in China (see Cooke, 1863). However, tax payments or payments to foreigners had to be made in the legal tender or an internationally accepted medium. Ordinary people lost heavily in exchanging the medium of smaller denominations for the medium of higher denominations; when there was a drain of bullion, the exchange rate turned increasingly against those using smaller denomination coin. When deposit banking was introduced by capitalists from advanced capitalist countries – often with the patronage of the colonial government – the banks usually discriminated in favour of capitalists from imperialist countries, and in favour of operations involving export and import of goods.[5]

After the entry of European capital and colonialism, most com-

5 The following passage from the report of the directors of the European-controlled Agra Bank for the year 1874 is most revealing about the role of 'modern' banks in supporting the basic processes of exploitation in a colonial country. 'The first portion of the year, owing to the high value of money in India, consequent upon the famine which then prevailed in that country, was favourable to profitable working; but the same cannot be said of the latter half, when, from the reaction which generally follows upon extreme prices, money was comparatively abundant, and more difficulty was experienced in employing it to advantage' (See Agra Bank, 1875).

modities and instruments of production became saleable. Cultivators and artisans were suddenly faced with the threat (often realized) of losing control over their basic means of production because of failure to fulfil obligations specified in terms of money. This was a radical departure from the precapitalist regimes under which failure to fulfil financial obligations did not normally lead to the loss of land or other means of production.

With the coming of capitalist colonialism, then, peasants were compelled to devote all their energy to the earning of money. This usually meant the production of exportable crops. The peasants were often tenants of a landlord who retained half or more of the crop. They were indebted to moneylenders who held them in debt bondage in return for the consumption loans extended to them year after year. The moneylender (who was also the landlord in many cases) bought up the produce of the peasants at abnormally low post-harvest prices. The petty middlemen (themselves often moneylenders) who bought the products from the peasants were generally indebted to wholesale merchants in the towns. The wholesale merchants in their turn were indebted to banks controlled by capitalists from advanced capitalist countries. The exporters who bought the goods from wholesale merchants were often indebted to banks and business houses in London, Amsterdam, Lisbon or Paris. This kind of chain could be observed both in direct colonies and in semi-colonial countries.

Any adverse movement in the demand for exportable products in world markets (generally controlled from metropolitan countries) could be passed back down the chain from business houses or banks in the metropolitan countries to exporters and banks in the colonial or semi-colonial countries, and then to the wholesale merchants in the same group of countries. The wholesale merchants in their turn passed the loss down to the middlemen, who in turn passed it to the peasants directly or indirectly through the landlords. In the process some export houses, wholesale merchants and many middlemen and landlords would go to the wall. But most of the loss would be borne by the ultimate producers, the peasants. Conversely, the gains resulting from an improvement in the markets for exportable products of the third world would be retained mostly by the operators near the final product outlets, that is, by the banks and business houses in advanced capitalist countries, by the export houses and exchange banks in the third world, and, to a lesser extent, by the wholesale merchants, petty middlemen and landlords, while the peasants would benefit only marginally if at all.

The long-term factor underlying these transactions was the compulsion exercised on the peasant to produce as much as possible of the exportable product, so that the total surplus value extracted by the ruling capitalist country and the capitalists from the dominating metropolitan country could be maximized. The stick that was used here was the tax obligation coupled with complete destruction of all rights in means of production which were not protected as unencumbered private property. Thus the expansion of exports by most low income countries in the period before 1914 must be seen as a response not only to expanding demand from the industrializing nations of Europe (part of this increased demand was itself pulled by the exploitation of the colonies) but also to the pressure of the ruling power for more revenue and of the businessmen from the advanced capitalist countries for more profit. Capitalists from advanced countries instigated a huge investment in trasport, linking the ports to the interior, and, in a few cases, some investment in perennial irrigation, in order to facilitate the export. They also controlled the major trading and financing organizations so that the flow of exports could be altered according to their own convenience. The depression of home demand caused by the continual drain of surplus value from the third world and its failure to industrialize kept the domestic absorption of exportable products low. Conversely, the sluggish growth of home demand combined with the policy of free trade, enforced in most third world countries, made it almost impossible for private investors to build up manufacturing industries.

In the period up to 1914, the third world acted essentially as an adjunct to the advanced capitalist countries, supplying them with raw materials, food crops for industrial labour and a surplus for investment in the frontier economies of the white-settled colonies. The latter also produced and exported primary products to the west European metropolis. But they differed from third world economies in several respects: they were net receivers rather than net transferrers of capital, they adopted deliberate policies facilitating industrialization and other ancillary policies meant to insulate their economies against fluctuations in the international economy as much as possible, and they were guided by a developing capitalist class whose primary interest lay in their host economies (even though many of the capitalists originally were immigrants). Even the fates of the migrants from third world countries and from Europe were different. The former went first as slaves and then as indentured labourers and became the most exploited part of the plantation economies of the Caribbean, southern United States, Mauritius, Ceylon, Malaysia, etc. The European migrants became either free wage labourers, farmers, artisans or industrial white collar workers in the USA, Canada, Australia, or Argentina. In South Africa they became the top crust in a rigidly racist society.

The growth in exports of primary products from third world countries was thus at the expense of industrialization of these countries and also at the expense of other crops or products primarily meant for domestic consumption. The majority of the inhabitants of the third world gained but marginally from this growth, and many of them actually lost out through unemployment, and through deteriorating supply conditions of some of their staples (such as millets, maize or paddy). Hence this phase should be characterized as that of *export-led exploitation* of the third world, rather than as that of export-led growth.

The monetary and financial institutions in their international as well as domestic aspects supported this pattern of exploitation. Most of the western European countries and the USA adopted the gold standard after the 1870s; but India, China and, to a lesser extent, Indonesia continued to use silver as the primary medium of exchange. During this crucial period, India and China effectively absorbed the increasing outputs of silver mines controlled by capitalists based in metropolitan countries, and helped to keep up their sagging profitability. Since the price of silver dropped precipitously from the 1870s to the 1890s, this meant that India surrendered any price advantages she might have derived from increasing demands for her exports from the European and American nations. Continual depreciation also created an enormous uncertainty in the sphere of international trade, and greatly increased the cost of servicing of foreign debts, generally contracted for in terms of gold, and, in the case of India, also the cost of payment of the tribute to Britain.

Ultimately, when the supply of gold from British-controlled gold mines increased, India was forced to adopt the so-called gold exchange standard, or rather, the sterling exchange standard, under which the Government of India held sterling balances in London as 'backing' for rupee issues in India (see Keynes, 1913, chapter 2, for an apologetic, and De Cecco, 1974, for a critical account of the gold exchange standard). These balances were used (a) to counter any pressure against the external value of sterling, and (b) to stabilize the operations of the London money market. Not only India, but many other underdeveloped countries, some of them nominally independent (such as Argentina) accepted an arrangement under which the external value of their currency and even the internal monetary policy were geared to the interests of the financial centre of London. The major European countries on the gold standard, such as France,

Germany or even Austria–Hungary, took measures to protect their economies and their exchange rates against fluctuations in exports and imports. But the exchange rates, the prices and the levels of economic activities of non-white colonies and the semi-colonial economies of Latin America remained fully vulnerable to changes in demands for their exportables, or changes in the supplies of silver and gold, and changes in the financial policies of the metropolitan countries. The operations of the major financial institutions, which withdrew credit from the third world countries whenever a panic or a stringency occurred, aggravated the instability of the latter. In effect, the cost of adjustment required by the gold standard (of which the sterling exchange standard was an essential adjunct) was borne mainly by the dominated countries (Ford, 1962, chapters 1–4; and Triffin, 1969).

5.4 INDUSTRIAL INVESTMENT IN THIRD WORLD COUNTRIES IN THE EARLIER PHASES OF IMPORT SUBSTITUTION

Some modern manufacturing industry, particularly cotton textiles, sugar, and other industries based on processing of primary products, began to grow up in the larger-sized third world countries such as Argentina, Brazil and India before the First World War. Increases in money and real wages of workers in advanced capitalist countries rendered some lines of industry there unremunerative and helped the third world countries to start up their own production. In countries with a large handicraft sector, the new industries grew partly at the expense of handicrafts, so that the net addition to industrial employment was generally meagre or even negative. Import substitution in manufactures really started in the bigger third world countries only in the interwar period and gathered strength during the depression of the thirties. (For description of typical patterns, see Helleiner, 1972, chapter 6.)

According to the conventional wisdom of economics, industrial growth in these countries has in the past been limited by the shortage of capital and entrepreneurship (see, for example, Lewis, 1956, or Kindleberger, 1965). But close examination of the evidence relating to India or China does not bear out the theory that shortage of finance was a major constraint on growth of manufacturing industry in the period up to the Second World War (Bagchi, 1972a; and Riskin, 1975). Even after the drain of a huge surplus abroad and the leakage of potential savings into the conspicuous consumption associated with a landlord-dominated society, there was enough finance in the hands of indigenous capitalists and of foreign capitalists operating locally to sustain a much higher rate of investment in industry than actually occurred in these retarded societies.

The question of lack of entrepreneurship as a constraint on industrial growth is more complex. One result of economic retardation under capitalist colonialism was to thwart the growth of a native capitalist class. But, for import substitution in the early phases, it was often enough to imitate the successful and avoid the mistakes of the failures, without possessing any outstanding pioneering qualities. In many industries it turned out that knowledge of finance and marketing possessed by the native traders was the crucial ingredient for success. What deterred industrial investment was the possibility of making a high rate of profit in money-lending, landownership and trading and the relative lack of profitability of manufacturing in the absence of effective state patronage.

The degree of profitability of the simple types of manufacturing was in the long run largely a matter of the size of the market and its rate of growth. Here the rate of exploitation of the workers and the peasantry and the rate of reinvestment of the surplus in the domestic economy were key variables. A high rate of exploitation would constrict the market; a low rate of reinvestment of the surplus would slow down the rate of growth of that constricted market. A high rate of growth of population would have partly counteracted this growth. But given the monopsonistic control over labour exercised by employers in the third world and widespread underemployment and unemployment, quickening population growth often merely tightened the employers' control over labour – without noticeably widening the market for industrial consumer goods. Where agriculture is dominated by landlords, depending mainly on feudal methods of exploitation, the demand for capital goods naturally varies directly with the *rate of growth* of industrial consumer goods and the demand generated by the need for replacement of worn-out capital goods. A rise in the rate of growth of consumer goods output through import substitution could be expected to stimulate the output of capital goods. But here economies of scale, 'learning by doing' and start-up costs generally afforded an enormous advantage to established producers. Without some direct state patronage and protection, capital goods production on any significant scale could start or survive in very few countries indeed.

The immediate stimulus for substituting domestic manufacture for imports was generally provided by the cutting off of the earlier source of supply caused by the First World War, and by the imposition of tariffs on imported manufactures by the government. The established foreign businessmen or the foreign manufacturers supplying the country before the imposition of import tariffs were often the first to take advantage of the situation. Such manufacture often led to a larger expenditure of foreign exchange in the form of components, royalties, technical fees and remittance of profits than if the so-called import substitution had not taken place. Apart from foreigners, the other groups taking advantage of the increased opportunities for profitable investment in manufacturing industry are generally indigenous traders who have some connection with trade in the particular products involved.

The typical response of aggregate investment to import substituting opportunities can be approximated by some variant of the 'capital stock adjustment hypothesis' (see Matthews, 1959 for a discussion of this hypothesis). At the moment of introduction of tariff protection, there is a certain aggregate demand at the post-tariff prices that can be supplied either by internal production or by external trade. So long as the investors in the aggregate are unable to build up capacity which is equal to this internal demand, there is scope for entry by another investor (assuming that the industry is not characterized by strong economies of scale). Initially there is a large shortfall of domestic capacity from domestic demand, so in industries where a viable unit requires only a moderate amount of finance, investment is likely to be quite brisk. Since investment decisions are decentralized, and initially the demand prospects for a single firm appear rosy, there may in fact be such a high rate of investment in the industry that actual capacity far exceeds the capacity needed to supply the domestic market at the initial post-tariff price (cf. the discussion of investment in the Indian sugar industry in Bagchi, 1972a, chs. 1 and 12). Then, of course, there will be a reaction, and potential investors will look for other avenues of investment.

In a closed economy, if investment in several interrelated industries occurs at the same time, at a sufficiently high rate, then their joint impact may raise the rate of industrial growth sufficiently to create the expectation of continued growth. However, in typical third world economies between the two World Wars, investments in different manufacturing industries were rarely sufficiently bunched, and in the few cases in which they were, their stimulating effect was damped by other factors. For one thing, if the per capita income is very low and expenditure on basic consumer goods produced by industry (such as cotton textiles, sugar or paper) forms only a small fraction (such as 10–15 per cent) of total national income, even a large percentage increase in industrial production alone will mean a small percentage increase in national income, and this may be swallowed up by the next downturn in the harvest. Secondly, the multiplier effects of the investment will be greatly damped because most of the equipment has to be bought from abroad. In the case of large-scale participation by foreign enterprises and the tying of equipment purchases to the dominant metropolitan country, there also occur enormous leakages of profits and other payments abroad.

To these general problems of stimulating industrial growth in third world economies were added, during the interwar period, certain difficulties that arose out of a continuation of the prewar framework of international payments and finance and associated government policies and other difficulties that were caused by the general crisis of the capitalist economies. Although during the First World War the gold standard mechanism broke down, in general, third world economies continued to have their exchange rate and monetary policies dictated by the metropolitan countries. Both India and China, for example, had to go through a period when the external values of their currencies appreciated, to their detriment, because they continued to use silver as the medium of international circulation and because US policies caused a scarcity of silver in the world market. After the War also India's fiscal policy continued to be governed by considerations of her rating as a creditworthy country in the London money market rather than by the requirements of domestic development. For the sake of maintaining this creditworthiness (which in effect meant protecting existing British holders of Indian government securities against any capital loss), the Government of India pursued a policy of balanced budgets even when deficit financing would have helped stimulate the economy. In an underdeveloped economy with various precapitalist structures impeding smooth increases in production, and with large gaps in the supply lines of complementary inputs, naturally, government expenditure cannot have as much of a stimulating effect as in an advanced capitalist economy. But in most large third world countries the slack was so great in the depth of the depression that expansion of government expenditure or even its maintenance at a steady level *could have had* a significant expansionary effect on industrial output. This was illustrated by the experience of Brazil which we have touched upon in chapter 3.

By contrast, in India during the depression the Government, in pursuit of balanced budgets and preservation of its reputation abroad for financial soundness, slashed its own expenditure and thus deepened the contraction of money incomes in India. (Ironically enough, the creditworthiness of the government was never tested again in the London money market, for the government of British India never again raised a loan abroad.) Furthermore, in order to support the external value of sterling and generally the British balance of payments, the Indian government repaid a large part of the public debt of India held abroad, precisely during the worst years of the depression, and thus aggravated the deflationary effect on India. Other examples of similar monetary policies which had perverse effects on the third world countries but which gave at least temporary succour to the metropolitan countries could be cited from the experience of other dependent countries during the same period. During the Second World War, for example, the British government incurred enormous expenditures in India simply on the promise of paying part of it back at some future date. At the same time, in a short-sighted attempt to conserve all the resources for the war effort, the British government prevented the shipping of essential capital goods and construction materials to India from Allied countries, in spite of American pleading to the contrary (see Mitchell, 1942, and Sayers, 1956). India, and many other countries situated similarly, paid the price in terms of virtually unchecked inflation and unnecessarily thwarted industrial growth during the War.

During the interwar period, the capitalist world went through a series of crises which provided opportunities to the third world countries to devise some policies in their own interest, but which also rendered the economic environment generally unfavourable for sustained growth. Most of the capitalist countries, except the USA, really did not experience a strong boom even during the 1920s. This led to cut-throat competition for markets for industrial products among these countries, and made it doubly difficult for potential investors in the third world to enter these fields. Then from 1926–27 onwards a world agricultural depression set in, and depressed money incomes throughout the third world. The depression of the 1930s followed, in which the outputs and prices of manufactures, minerals and plantation products fell, and in which the prices of agricultural products fell far more steeply than those of industrial products. This meant that the money incomes of the majority of producers in the third world fell – often by as much as 50 per cent. Since the terms of exchange turned against agricultural products, their real incomes also crashed, even when their agricultural outputs did not fall. But, paradoxically enough, by concentrating incomes in the hands of fixed-income (often urban) groups, this situation expanded the markets for some of the more expensive types of industrial goods, such as fine cloth, cement for urban housing, and sugar.

The confusion created by the crisis of the advanced capitalist economies could have been overcome and in fact turned to the advantage of third world economies if there had been proper planning to correct the earlier pattern of growth, and to co-ordinate the development of industry and agriculture, so as to really build a self-reliant economy. But, outside the Soviet Union, planning in this epoch primarily meant patronage of private enterprise. Left to itself, with the stimulus of tariff protection and state patronage in other forms, private investment took place in a haphazard fashion, and followed the pattern of demand that had been imprinted by the earlier history of export-led exploitation. Such a course doomed the third world economies to be backward and inefficient imitators of advanced capitalist countries, and, as we have seen in chapter 2, this type of imitation would never allow the laggards to overtake the leaders and will instead doom them to a condition of continual retardation.

Of course, there were differences between different third world economies in the degree of success of the import substitution process. The earlier the process could start in an economy, the higher the incomes per head, the higher the levels of wages and earnings of the general run of the peasantry, the more developed the indigenous capitalist class and the larger the absolute size of market of a particular economy, the greater would be the growth-stimulating effect of import-substituting industrialization. Other things being equal, a larger population would lead to a bigger market, which is why it was generally the bigger economies which embarked earlier on the course of import substitution. Given the same population size, and the same degree of inequality of distribution of incomes, a higher income per head would imply the existence of sizeable markets for a larger range of goods and hence the existence of opportunities for investment in a wider spectrum of industries. A partial exception would seem to be the development of luxury goods, for which, given the same income per head, a more skewed distribution of incomes would create larger markets. To the extent that the better types of cloth, sugar, cement, newer types of domestic utensils (including bread-making equipment in Latin America) can be considered luxuries, a decisive shift of income distribution towards urban and fixed-income groups probably stimulated investment in such industries. But for precisely the same reason, the growth-stimulating effect of such investment could not last long: this range of goods could not be widely diffused among the majority of the population and the market for the goods contracted again when the terms of exchange shifted towards agriculture and rural income groups.

The first stage of import substitution in the industrial consumer goods sector was generally accompanied by domestic production of some basic and capital goods such as iron and steel, non-ferrous metals, ships, locomotives and the simpler types of machinery. The state often actively helped this process (particularly from the Second World War onwards) by subsidizing the setting up of plants in this sector, often with an eye to military needs. But since the basic framework of economic activities remained geared to private needs and private profitability, the state could only partially control the pattern and growth of expenditure in the economy, and thus could not fully guarantee the necessary markets for capital goods industries. Profitable investment in capital goods industries catering to the consumer goods sector requires as a consistency condition the prospect of a minimum steady demand for capital goods, and that in turn requires (apart from the minimum replacement needs) a steady *increase* in the demand for consumer goods supporting a steady rate of net investment in consumer goods industries. There are capital goods industries which cater to other capital goods industries, but if the capital goods sector grows through the development of such industries alone, then (barring the *import* of capital goods for the consumer goods sector), the proportion of investment to national income will have to rise continually, creating untenable imbalances in a private enterprise economy. As it turned out, the growth of investment in capital goods industries in third world economies was soon inhibited by (a) the inability of the state to guarantee adequate growth in demand, (b) the lack of experience of the capitalist and managerial class in producing modern capital goods and the consequent rise in gestation lags and costs, and (c) the ingrained prejudice against domestically produced substitutes for imported machinery – a prejudice that was apparently justified by their high costs, and by the inability of the domestic producers to catch up with technical advances in related fields abroad.

5.5 THE LATE PHASE OF IMPORT SUBSTITUTION IN THIRD WORLD ECONOMIES AND ITS DIFFICULTIES

The early period of import-substitution has often been identified as the 'easy' phase and the late import-substitution period as the 'difficult' phase of import-substituting industrialization (Felix, 1968, and Hirschman, 1968). (The early phase lasted in the case of India until the middle of the 1950s, in the case of major Latin American countries such as Argentina, Brazil or Mexico until the end of the 1940s). The development of capital goods industries, however, is a difficult proposition in either phase. In fact, because the experience of making capital goods is totally lacking in some cases in the early import substitution phase, it may well be more difficult to undertake their production successfully in the early than in the late phase – though in other cases, the greater degree of sophistication of the capital goods needed in the late phase may take it more difficult to substitute imports by domestic manufacture. However, there is little doubt that import substitution in the consumer goods sector in the late phase presents a greater number of difficulties than in the early phase.

In the early phase, import substitution takes place in the production of such goods as cotton and woollen textiles, construction materials, sugar, leather goods, and so on. The markets for such goods are large enough in many underdeveloped countries to support several firms exploiting the available economies of scale to the full. Generally the machines and knowhow can be procured from abroad without large and continuing payments for patents, licences, etc., being involved. (The machinery-suppliers often act as consultants for setting up the plants. This may involve 'packaging' of the technology, which costs more and bequeaths less knowledge to the host country than if the latter were entirely free to choose and to learn by making mistakes.)[6] In the 'difficult' import substitution phase, the domestic markets for the basic consumer goods having been more or less saturated, the capitalists search for new products to produce. These happen to be sophisticated consumer goods (mostly durables) developed for the affluent societies. The economies of scale in the production of many such durables, such as cars, are considerable, and a plant has to produce on a scale which is often larger than the national markets of most third world countries (cf. Pratten, 1971). They also involve the use of more skilled manpower than is available in even large-sized third world countries (cf. Vernon, 1970). Moreover, they are increasingly tied to the original developers of the products and techniques in the advanced capitalist countries through patents, and through unpatented knowhow and 'software' available only through the network of the master firm. These problems are aggravated by the fast development of transnational corporations which bring more and more independent firms and product lines under their all-embracing control. Since in the late stage of import substitution the product

6 For discussion of the problems of choice of techniques by third world economies see Bagchi, 1978, and chapter 9 below.

frontier of the third world comes nearer that of the advanced capitalist countries, the ability of firms based in the latter to keep control over as many markets as possible is much greater.

One of the consequences of the iron grip of the firms in the advanced capitalist countries on the products characteristically taken up in the late stage of import substitution is that the overt payments to the parent firms in the form of royalties, technical and consultancy fees, dividend remittances and under-cover payments in the form of inflated transfer prices for various components and materials are rather large (cf. Vaitsos, 1974). Very often a rapid rate of import substitution in such products leads to a rise in the ratio of imported intermediate imports to net value added in industry and aggravates the balance of payments crisis instead of alleviating it.

In the current situation, most third world countries find that the more they try to industrialize through import substitution, the more they become dependent on advanced capitalist countries for technology, product development and managerial expertise. Had these countries been able, from the beginning of the import substitution process, to adopt a policy akin to that of Japan, which rigidly excluded the entry of foreign firms and foreign private capital while permitting the purchase and imitation of foreign techniques in every field, they might conceivably have avoided their present fate. But they were unable for political reasons to introduce such a proviso, or to adopt the other policies which led to a fast development of the technological and educational base in Japan.

Most of the third world countries more or less stumbled into the late import substitution phase. The capitalists in these countries were unwilling to explore the possibility of developing the markets for the older types of consumer goods by lowering their prices (this would have required a cut in production costs through research and development, and the lowering of profit margins). Instead, they looked for new avenues where profit margins would be high and could be easily protected against raiders. The production of consumer durables proved ideal from this point of view, particularly since governments in the third world could be easily persuaded to impose stiff tariff and quota restrictions on the import of luxury consumer goods. The multinationals wanted to protect their markets in the third world, and the easiest method of doing that was to set up production facilities in such countries behind tariff walls. The willing collaboration of native capitalists in the host countries afforded them the necessary political protection.

What we have characterized as a state of dependence in the name of industrialization has been deliberately adopted as a model by Brazil and has even been advocated as an exemplar to other countries. After a fairly fast rate of industrialization along the path of import substitution, Brazil entered a period of stagnation in the early 1960s. After a military coup, the ruling Brazilian junta adopted a policy of turning the income distribution against the workers and in favour of the rich. Apart from encouraging the growth of capitalism, this authoritarian policy also had the aim of increasing the demand for consumer durables such as cars, refrigerators, air conditioners, and so on. Brazil's rulers enjoyed several advantages in pursuing their policy. Under Vargas, Kubitschek and Goulart a large capital goods industry had already been built up, partly under direct state ownership and partly under the control of foreign capital. Brazil also contained a large hinterland which was ripe for capitalist development (although such 'development' often meant absolute disaster from the point of view of the Amerindian populations of the interior). After the 'disciplining' of the economy under the deflationary policies pursued over the years from 1964 to 1967, foreign private capital was responsive to the red carpet spread out for it under the military regime. The consumer durables which had already proved the fastest-growing subsector in earlier cycles again became a pace-setter in the Brazilian 'miracle' of 1968–75. The price for this miracle has been an extreme degree of inequality of income distribution, a very large foreign indebtedness, effective denationalization of major sectors of the Brazilian economy, and a rigorous suppression of civil and political liberties for the people (see Bacha and Taylor, 1978, Bergsman, 1970, Furtado, 1973, and Wells, 1974, and 1977; and chapter 7 below). The enthusiasm of foreign capital for Brazil and the resulting economic growth helped to counter some of the demand-depressing effects of the policies pursued by the military regime and diffuse the gains of growth a little more widely than was thought probable at the beginning of the 1970s.

Other third world countries, however, even if they are prepared to pursue unequalizing policies, cannot ensure large enough markets or tempting enough frontiers for foreign capital. They are also likely to fall foul of the difficulties inherent in relying on consumer durables as the major generator of growth much earlier in the story than Brazil. The most important consumer durable, the private motor car, is subject to strong economies of scale, particularly for the standard models. Because of the general effect of learning through production, and because of such changes as standardization of equipment for longer runs of production, replacement of batch production by production in continuous runs, automation of processes, and so on, the economies of scale also tend to increase through time. Furthermore, the cost of model changes in the car industry are considerable, running to several million pounds for each model change. The steeply rising price of petroleum is another inhibiting factor. The economies of scale are not as large in the case of other consumer durables nor are their initial capital requirements as high as in the case of cars, but changes in models and production processes are important and expensive (see Pratten, 1971). Furthermore, the third world countries are greatly dependent on the advanced capitalist countries for techniques and knowhow; and they are increasingly faced by huge conglomerates transcending national frontiers as sellers of the technology and controllers of marketing outlets, so that their area of choice and bargaining power are more restricted. To what extent they can use the power of the national state and the alternative source of the Soviet bloc for countering the monopoly power of the transnational firms is a question that merits more general discussion, and we shall take it up in chapter 7.

As a result of the factors mentioned above, although the outputs of particular consumer durables in individual third world countries grow very fast when they are first introduced as import substitutes, they also tend to taper off quickly (cf. Felix, 1968, and Bagchi, 1975). Furthermore, the model changes of consumer durables mostly originate abroad, and most firms producing such durables in the third world find it unprofitable to produce all the components of any model at home. Most of them also have to pay either their parent firms or their foreign collaborators, for the knowhow, patented processes and so on. As a result, import substitution along these lines causes a drain on foreign exchange earnings, and in fact aggravates balance of payments crises.

As a remedy for recurrent balance of payments crises and for the thwarting of growth resulting from import substitution, the policy of 'export-led growth' has often been advocated in recent years. We shall take up an analysis of the implications of such a policy in the concluding part of this chapter. Before that, we shall analyse the typical cyclical patterns observed in a third world economy. Two of the major sources of such fluctuations are fluctuations in agricultural output and balance of payments crises. These in turn are related to the basic weaknesses of the industrial or 'modern' sector of a third world economy in relation to the precapitalist relations and models of exploitation prevailing in the agricultural and trading sectors of the economy and the dominated character of the capitalist and managerial class controlling the modern or industrial sector.

5.6 HARVEST FLUCTUATION AND CYCLES IN A RETARDED ECONOMY

In pre-industrial economies, harvest fluctuations were major determinants of the ebb and flow of economic activity, and of prices (see Braudel and Spooner, 1967). Third world countries in the phase of import-substituting industrialization are not pre-industrial economies in the sense in which, say, Austria was a pre-industrial economy in the seventeenth century. They possess an industrial sector in which employment is concentrated in factories, and for some of them (such as Argentina, Brazil or Mexico), industrial income accounts for more than 25 per cent of total national income. But most of these economies are characterized by relative inelasticity of agricultural output in the short run. What is as important is that the weather and other natural factors remain the predominant influence conditioning potential output, and man-made inputs as yet play a subsidiary role in the agricultural sector. The relative inelasticity of agricultural output is also due partly to the failure of internal accumulation which has characterized the evolution of third world economies (see chapter 2 above) and partly to the survival of precapitalist modes of exploitation in such economies – a survival ensured by the logic of working of the weak capitalism of such economies (see section 5.2 above, and chapters 6 and 7 below). Furthermore, the per capita incomes of third world economies being generally very low, a given percentage fluctuation in the supplies of foodgrains in such economies has a much more pronounced effect on relative expenditures on foodgrains and industrial consumer goods than in the more affluent capitalist countries. Hence harvest fluctuations deserve a separate treatment in the context of the third world.

Changes in agricultural output can be expected to affect industrial growth in several ways. First, agriculture is the source of major raw materials such as cotton, sugarcane, jute, sisal, groundnuts, etc., and any shortfall in their output adversely affects the output of agriculture-based industries. Secondly, for most third world economies agricultural products are major earners of foreign exchange. A decline in export earnings, unless it is offset by increased foreign credits or grants, affects the availability of imported capital or intermediate goods, and can lead to a major contraction of economic activity all round. We look at the general problem of balance of payments crises in the next section. Thirdly, contraction in agricultural output will affect the demand for industrial goods both because incomes of peasants, landlords, etc. are affected directly, and because, through a rise in prices of agricultural products, real incomes of other sections of the people are affected. Fourthly, because expenditure on foodgrains forms such an important part of the budgets of third world peoples, and because landlords and merchants together generally exercise a monopolistic hold over the supply of agricultural crops in the markets, a decline in the output of such crops can act as a signal for speculative price rises and start off a process of inflation, or can further feed an inflationary spiral. In this section we shall largely be concerned with analysing the impact of changes in incomes of different classes because of harvest failures and of changes in prices brought about by the actions of landlords in the context of harvest fluctuations.

In accord with Engel's law, in typical underdeveloped economies, the elasticity of demand for foodgrains with respect to expenditure has been found to be less than unity. But, in the short run, the estimated expenditure elasticity has often turned out to be unity or even larger than unity (Rudra and Paul, 1964, Ramsunder, 1965 and Weisskoff, 1971). The elasticities of demand for foodgrains with respect to changes in their own prices have been usually found to be negative, but less than unity in absolute value. A fall in agricultural output, particularly of foodgrains, *ceteris paribus*, leads to a rise in prices of agricultural goods, and a rise in money incomes accruing to agriculture. In the urban areas (especially among poorer people), an increase in expenditure on foodgrains leaves less income to be spent on other consumer goods and generally leads to a lower fraction of income being spent on industrial consumer goods. In the rural areas, the poorer peasants and agricultural labourers who are net buyers of foodgrains in the market are affected in the same way as the urban poor, and their expenditure on non-agricultural consumer goods falls. The money incomes of landlords and richer farmers who are net sellers of foodgrains on a large scale go up. This may lead to an increase in demand for industrial consumer goods on their part, especially for luxuries or durables such as radio sets, refrigerators, or even cars (the exact designation of 'luxuries' will depend on the degree of affluence of the particular economy). The net effect on marketed surplus of foodgrains of a fall in the output of foodgrains will have an important bearing on the demand of the urban sector for industrial consumer goods. If the farmers' expenditure elasticity of demand for foodgrains is high, a fall in agricultural output that boosts their money income will result in a steep fall in the marketed surplus, and this will in turn adversely affect the demand for industrial consumer goods.

In theory, a fall in the output of foodgrains can lead either to a net decline or a net increase in the demand for industrial consumer goods, depending on the relative weights of the increases in demand by the rich landlords and farmers (and possibly traders) benefiting from the shortage and the decreases in demand by everybody else. The necessities produced by industry can be predicted to suffer a contraction in demand, but the demand for luxuries may go either way. T. N. Krishnan found that in the case of India, sales of mill-made cloth were inversely related both to own prices and to prices of foodgrains, thus suggesting that the factors depressing industrial demand (in the rank of necessities) as a result of increases in foodgrains prices were stronger than those tending to boost demand for industrial consumer goods (Krishnan, 1964, chapter 4).

How does this kind of inverse relationship affect industrial investment and growth in the short run? Prabhat Patnaik, following Kalecki, has built a model of investment behaviour in an attempt to answer this question (Kalecki, 1972a and Patnaik, 1972b). Essentially, in this model, the level of agricultural output determines the marketed surplus available for supporting workers in industry, on the one hand, and the demand for luxury consumer goods on the part of the landlords and the rich farmers, on the other. As a first approximation, it is assumed that workers spend a fixed proportion of their wage on agricultural goods. However, every industrial or urban worker must consume a minimum level of foodgrains in order to survive. If government expenditure and the private investment induced by it reach a level at which total urban employment is too high in relation to the marketed surplus of foodgrains, the foodgrains component of workers' wages will fall below the acceptable minimum; this will then cause urban and industrial unrest. In this situation, if we rule out import of foodgrains to augment supplies, the government will try to cut down its expenditure. This will result, with a lag, in a fall in private investment, and the degree of capacity utilization in industry will also fall, further depressing investment in the private sector.

In an economy in which private investment is at best sluggish (in the sense that its response to increases in profitability or sales is limited), the government can try to ensure a certain aggregate rate of growth by allowing its own expenditure to grow at a given rate. But if the target rate of growth is significantly different from the trend rate of growth of agricultural output, then, as can be seen by a simple extension of the argument in the preceding paragraph, fluctuations in aggregate output can arise, even if agricultural output does not actually fluctuate. Harvest fluctuations, of course, will aggravate such problems. The mechanics of such fluctuations will be similar to those of Hicks' theory of the trade cycle, where the rate of investment is a function of past changes in sales, but is subject to a ceiling imposed by the rate of growth of the budgets of the ordinary people of the third world (after any backlog of unemployment has been worked off) (Hicks, 1950). Only by a fluke would changes in the rate of growth of agricultural output, changes in private investment and changes in capacity utilization in various subsectors of the economy be in balance and be so synchronised as to avoid cyclical fluctuations. The market does not provide a mechanism for such fine tuning – certainly not in a retarded economy.

Two other possibilities that may conceivably ensure smoother operation of the system are (a) that the government may try to determine the rate of growth of agriculture itself and (b) that the private sector should reallocate its investment to the same end. Governments in most import-substituting economies have in fact tried to do that, after realizing that sluggishness of agricultural output was a major hurdle in the way of ensuring a steady and high rate of economic growth. In the 1930s, third world governments reacted to the drastic fall in exports of agricultural products and their prices by shifting resources towards industry. This left a legacy of relative neglect of agriculture in many economies. In those cases in which governments tried to encourage agricultural growth, they came up against obstacles posed by the landlord-dominated class structure, the nature of the state and the history of retarded economies.

Many third world governments are greatly dependent on the output of agricultural crops for their revenue, for a major part of their tax revenues is derived from indirect taxes, such as excise duties, export taxes, sales taxes, and so on. A decline in agricultural output, therefore, often squeezes government resources precisely when such resources are required for developing agriculture and stimulating the economy. So long as this situation continues and the government is unable to tax the rich, especially the rural rich, a fiscal crisis will stand in the way of developing agriculture.

For most colonial governments, development of agriculture as a whole had a low priority. Whatever research or building up of irrigation facilities had taken place had been concentrated on export crops – including plantation crops. The new governments were ill-equipped by their general inheritance to build up infrastructure facilities that would benefit the general run of the peasantry.

Attempting to introduce new methods or crop varieties from the top, rather than motivating the peasantry to find their own solutions still remained the dominant approach. The programme of introduction of high-yielding varieties of seeds supported by intensive utilization of fertilizers, was introduced under the initiative of the US government, and the Ford and Rockefeller Foundations (see chapter 6 below). This programme has remained confined to a few crops, such as wheat, paddy and hybrid maize. Even for such crops the diffusion of the programme among small peasants has been incomplete, because of lack of access to credit, irrigation facilities, and the domination of peasants by landlords, traders and moneylenders who deprive them of the fruits of the new technology. Hence in many economies the agricultural innovations have taken predominantly a form that benefits the rich landowners, by making a saving of capital or labour, without necessarily raising the rate of growth of agricultural output – and, particularly, of staples predominantly consumed by the poorer sections of the people (see Grunig, 1969 and Janvry, 1973).

We now turn to the question of the extent to which productive investment by capitalists in agriculture is likely to be induced by a shortage of agricultural output, raising its price in relation to that of industrial output. Since the demand for foodgrains is inelastic with respect to changes in price, traders can expect to *increase* their money returns by restricting supplies and by raising prices. This course is facilitated by the usual rules of extension of credit by the banking system. Bank loans are granted on the basis of security of existing assets (including stocks of commodities) valued at market prices. If prices rise, the values of assets offered as security also rise, and hence the amounts that can be borrowed by the holders of commodity stocks also go up. Imposing restrictions on the types of commodities that can be financed by bank loans (known as 'selective credit control'), as has been attempted in many underdeveloped countries, is not very effective. The reason is that the trader is often also an industrialist and landlord, or has strong connections with landlords, and simply switches the activities which he finances out of his own funds and the activities against which he takes bank loans (cf. Dehejia Committee, 1969).

Whether the traders and landlords find it profitable also to invest in assets increasing the productivity of agriculture depends on their appreciation of future trends of relative prices of agriculture and industry, on their access to land, on existing tenurial arrangements and on their appreciation of effectiveness of government policy. In a poor society, a sudden increase in the output of foodgrains is likely to result in a glut, and prices of farm products will fall drastically. If the government operates a price stabilization programme or guarantees a ratchet below farm prices by buying up any surplus at the minimum guaranteed price, some landlords and traders may undertake investment in productive assets. But this will increase the money incomes of groups which are recalcitrant to taxation, and will pose an inflationary threat. Moreover, landlords and traders may try to blackmail the government to raise farm prices, by threatening to curtail supplies. In this case, the programme of price support will prove costly from a fiscal point of view. It will also prove costly to the other classes, such as industrialists with no interest in trade in agricultural products, industrial workers, and small peasants and agricultural labourers from whom incomes will be transferred to the landlords, rich farmers and traders.[7] Also, investment in land in underdeveloped countries is a highly localized operation, and is hampered by local power exercised by landlords, by tenurial arrangements peculiar to each locality, by the need to adapt to the particular soil and water supply conditions, and so on. Hence not everyone who is willing to invest in land can in fact gain access to it. The restrictions surrounding land as a commodity in typical retarded economies impede capitalist accumulation in agriculture.

5.7 BALANCE OF PAYMENTS CRISES IN THIRD WORLD ECONOMIES IN THE PHASE OF IMPORT SUBSTITUTING INDUSTRIALIZATION

In the preceding section, we have largely ignored the relation of agricultural growth and industrial investment in third world economies to their balances of payments. When agricultural growth falters, the supply of exportables falls, and the import demand for agricultural commodities, especially foodgrains, goes up. On the other hand, a rise in domestic investment and industrial output generally induces a rise in demand for imports of consumer goods, intermediate goods and capital goods. In the phase of late import-substituting industrialization, direct imports of consumer goods and the simpler types of capital goods are eliminated. Then a rise in domestic investment induces a steep rise in imports of intermediate goods and more

7 Analogy with US price support programmes is inappropriate here: there is a major difference between stabilizing at most 10 per cent of GNP with transfers from the other 90 per cent (as in the US case), and stabilizing anywhere between 30 and 60 per cent of GNP with transfers from the other income groups as in the case of underdeveloped countries.

sophisticated capital goods. These two sets of factors, acting together or separately lead to frequent balance of payments crises. In the present section, we shall deal with certain typical patterns of adjustment in the face of balance of payments crises and scrutinize some of the policies that have been suggested for meeting them in third world economies.

Most third world economies cope with balance of payments problems by resorting to a variety of controls – such as exchange control, multiple exchange rates, quota restrictions, import tariffs, subsidies on exports, and so on. One persistent lobby consisting of the IMF, the World Bank, GATT, advanced capitalist governments and economists of the neoclassical school has pressed the underdeveloped countries to move towards greater free trade and, as a step towards that, to devalue their currencies. The pressure for devaluation has been particularly great when a third world country has had to seek assistance from international agencies and from foreign governments in order to meet its balance of payments deficits.

On orthodox reasoning, for the third world as a whole, devaluation of their currencies is not normally a very sound procedure. For, in the case of the typical products (barring perhaps petroleum among the important commodities) exported by the third world, the price elasticity of demand is taken to be generally low. But for a particular third world country, the partial price elasticity of demand of an exportable can still be high, if it is assumed that its competitors will not fully match any slashing of the international price of its exportables caused by the devaluation (for the orthodox theory, see Robinson, 1937, and Haberler, 1949). So for particular countries at particular times devaluation could make sense, if, of course, exports responded positively to the increase in domestic price caused by the devaluation.

But it is not enough to look at the exports alone in order to find out the effects of devaluation. When we look at the characteristics of import demand in a third world economy and the circumstances that typically trigger off devaluation, it is found to result in a depression in the economy (see Cooper, 1973). We assume that the demand for importable is not very responsive to increases in costs in domestic currency resulting from devaluation, at least in the short run. We also assume that, at the moment of devaluation, at the going prices there is a potential balance of payments deficit, part of which is met by an inflow of foreign assistance, and part of which is repressed by exchange control. If, after devaluation, all quantitative controls are removed, the balance of payments deficit may well grow larger than the actual deficit before devaluation. Hence often the bait of increased official 'aid' (including loans) and increased inflow of private foreign capital is dangled by the international agencies and the US bloc to entice an underdeveloped country to devalue and to adopt more liberal trade policies. But the actual granting of such aid is generally conditional not simply on devaluation by the country in difficulties but also on its continued good behaviour, particularly as regards the rights of private property, foreign and national (see Hayter, 1971, Konig, 1973, and Payer, 1974).

The elasticity of demand for imports in third world economies is likely to be low when imports consist mainly of raw materials (including oil), semi-processed products, and capital goods. This is the general pattern in the stage of late import-substituting industrialization. In those cases where a major part of foodstuffs is imported (as was the case for Sri Lanka, for example) their substitution by domestic products is also likely to take a long time. On the other hand, the supply of exports – mostly consisting of primary products, processed agricultural materials or semi-manufactures – is often rigid in the short run. Hence devaluation may result in a worsening of the trade balance, measured in the domestic currency. This will then have a recessionary effect on domestic output, since the net leakage (i.e. imports – exports), in the national income identity (when all quantities are measured in domestic prices),

$$\text{National income} = \text{consumption} + \text{investment} + \text{exports} - \text{imports},$$

will increase. If government expenditures are curtailed at the same time (since excessive government expenditure leading to inflationary pressures, which may be contained by direct control, is often blamed for 'overvaluation' of the exchange rate), this will have a further recessionary impact.

Paradoxically enough, this recessionary impact is often accompanied by a price rise which starts an inflationary process, or which aggravates an existing state of inflation. First, the prices of imports rise more or less proportionately with the rise in the price of foreign exchange, if originally imports were not repressed by quantitative controls. If they were originally repressed by quantitative restrictions and if these restrictions still operate, domestic prices may rise faster than the price of foreign exchange. Only if imports rise substantially after liberalization will import prices rise less than proportionately to the price of foreign exchange. Monopolistic control over foreign trade is generally an additional barrier against increased imports and lower prices for foreign goods (cf. Amjad, 1977). As for exports, so long as the major exports of the country concerned form only a small part of the world supply of the corresponding commodities, the foreign currency prices of exported items will not be affected by devaluation. In that case, domestic prices will rise in the same proportion as the price of foreign exchange is raised by devaluation. In case the country does export a significant fraction of the world supply of a particular exportable, the exporters will normally try to reap a competitive advantage by lowering the foreign currency prices concerned. But it is unlikely that they will lower the foreign currency prices by the full extent to which the currency is devalued. In that case, domestic prices of exportables will also rise as a result of devaluation (Reddaway, 1963).

The rise in prices of importables and exportables will affect all the prices directly or indirectly linked with them. The costs of production of all the commodities into which imported raw materials or equipment enter will rise. The prices of goods which are substitutes for exportables are likely to rise in sympathy. In fact, in those cases in which exportables enter directly into the consumption baskets of ordinary people, a rise in their prices will act as a major factor redistributing income away from wage-earners and towards property-owners (cf. Reddaway, 1963, Diaz Alejandro, 1965, 1970, chapter 7 and Zuvekas, Jr, 1966, 1968).

In the farming sector, while the prices of farm products rise as a result of devaluation, the wages of farm workers rise only with a lag, if at all. This is especially true in countries where there is a surplus of labour in rural areas, and farm labour is not unionized. Thus there is a redistribution of incomes in favour of property owners as against farm workers and poor peasants (who have to earn at least part of their living by selling their labour and who have to buy at least a part of their foodgrains in the market). If the prices of farm products rise more than those of domestic non-farm products as a result of devaluation, there may be a redistribution of income away from industry towards agriculture. But within the non-farm sector itself, prices of products will rise first, and even if the cost of living of non-agricultural workers rises, the wages of such workers will rise only with a lag. Thus in this sector also, there will be a redistribution of income in favour of property owners.

To the extent that, with an inelastic supply of exportable products as a whole, the curtailment of the demand on the part of wage-earners and other poor consumers leads to an increase in the net supply of exports to the world market, it could be argued that in fact the purpose of devaluation, viz. the elimination of the balance of payments deficit, will be achieved by such regressive income redistribution (assuming that an increase in exports does not lead to a precipitate fall in foreign currency price). However, since there is a fall in the real incomes of the poorer people all round, this may also lead to a decline in the degree of utilization of capacity of those industries which cater primarily to domestic mass consumption. These industries may, of course, then be compelled to search for markets abroad, but it is precisely for such products (such as cotton textiles) that price elasticity of world demand is likely to be rather low and competition among third world countries very stiff.

Even if devaluation succeeds temporarily in ameliorating the balance of payments problem by creating a recessionary situation and redistributing income in favour of property-owners, its beneficial effects are unlikely to be long-lasting. For one thing, as a result of the speculative activities of traders and of the price–wage spiral in organized industry (which is characterized by various degrees of monopoly), the inflationary process will soon erode the competitive advantage gained through devaluation. But there are other factors working to widen the balance of payments deficit. The property owners in underdeveloped countries tend to spend a large part of their incomes on products (such as consumer durables) which are normally more import-intensive than the products consumed by the poorer sections of the people (we are here neglecting those years in which foodgrains have to be imported on a large scale). So when a redistribution takes place in their favour, the import bill tends to go up again on consumption account (cf. Diaz Alejandro, 1965, Hazari, 1967, and Zuvekas, Jr, 1968). Furthermore, the expected new investment also tends to be more import-intensive than the current production of wage-goods.

So a measure of devaluation or some equivalent measure redistributing income in favour of property-owners is very likely simultaneously to create a general recession in the economy and to stimulate import demand so as to wipe out the gains of devaluation in respect of the balance of payments. Then a further dose of deflation may be necessary to close the widening deficit. The IMF policies (such as devaluation accompanied by curtailment of bank lending and curtailment of government expenditure) enforced in many countries of Latin America and in Turkey have been rightly criticized on the ground that in trying to cure inflation and chronic balance of payments problems, they strangled the growth of the economy itself. But it is also clear that, given the typically low elasticities of supply of exportables, and of demand for imports and the high propensity to import on the part of property owners, an unstable growth process is hard to avoid in retarded economies (cf. Zuvekas, Jr, 1968, and Bagchi, 1977).

During import-substituting industrialization, much of the trouble starts from the fact that the capitalist classes of retarded economies adjust to the gaps left by the shifting of the demand of the advanced capitalist countries away from the agricultural exportables of these countries, instead of restructuring their activities to the requirements of the peoples working in them. The restructuring, of course, would have run against the logic of domination implicit in international capitalism. Only Japan was able to create a relatively autonomous capitalist base in the era of industrial capitalism in Europe, and for that she had rigidly to exclude foreign capitalists from domination of any part of her economy and to try and carve out an overseas empire for herself. The weak capitalist classes in third world countries suffered from a profound ignorance of their own economies, and from the failure to develop a base for technological or managerial innovation, or for adaptation of techniques borrowed from other economies. Their almost hereditary state of dependence on the capitalist classes of advanced capitalist economies makes for a 'tunnel vision' on their part. They look at the potential for development in their own economies partly with the eyes of their masters, and their view of the outside world and its opportunities is also limited by the continued presence of the erstwhile imperialist power. Thus, for example, Indian firms continue to have a larger number of foreign collaboration agreements with firms based in the UK than with firms of any other country, long after the UK has ceased to be a leader in any major field of *technological* development (as distinct from scientific advance). Similarly, the capitalist classes of retarded economies accentuate the rural–urban differentials of colonial times by continuing to foster development of enclaves of modern enterprise, while failing to develop the productive forces in the countryside except in a very limited fashion. Their almost blind imitation of the new products and technologies developed abroad, combined with other growth-inhibiting factors, pauperize vast numbers and leave a broad swath of population out in the cold. Thus 'import-substituting industrialization' of this type means segmental development accompanied by devastation of new areas.

The third world capitalists fail (a) to develop production techniques for their internal needs either in industry or in agriculture, (b) to transform production relations in agriculture so as to get rid of precapitalist types of bondage and usury, and (c) to use the state apparatus to effectively counter the power of foreign capitalist classes and their home governments. Hence they cannot determine their own course except within very narrow limits. Capitalist accumulation in such economies cannot raise itself by its own bootstraps.[8] The capitalist class and its mode of exploitation have to acquire a certain degree of dominance both in relation to the economy and polity it operates in, and in relation to advanced capitalist economies, for its rate of accumulation to be at least approximately determined by its own actions. The logic of dominance and the drive on the part of all capitalist classes to acquire control over more capital funds and more labour power are all the time establishing connections between the rates and the patterns of accumulation of different capitalist economies (see chapter 2 above). Hence the rate of accumulation of any single capitalist economy can never be determined by internal factors alone. But in the case of advanced capitalist countries, the capitalist class in a particular economy is not simply reacting to impulses received from abroad, but is also sending out impulses on its own. Indeed, the capitalist class of a leading capitalist–imperialist nation (such as Britain in the nineteenth century and the USA after the Second World War) in effect directs the activities of a number of other economies.

The dependence of the capitalist classes of retarded economies on advanced capitalist nations for techniques, products and modes of organization and marketing, and their failure to develop the productive forces of any but selected segments of the population act as severe constraints on their long-run growth. In some respects, the growth of all capitalist economies is logically viewed as a series of short-run investment booms which stay connected so long as capitalist relations of production continue to be reproduced. However, in the case of advanced capitalist economies these short-run movements do help to shift the binding constraints by changing product types, techniques, and modes of organization in the fields of management, finance and marketing. In the case of the retarded economies there are few internal factors acting to shift the constraints outward, impulses of growth remain primarily exogenous in nature, and hence any upward surge remains peculiarly vulnerable to any exogenous change such as harvest failures, changes in the conditions of the export markets, or changes in techniques of production abroad. Thus the cyclical phenomena analysed above can be viewed as both corroborative

8 Cf. Robinson, 1971b, p. 13: 'The point of view embodied in the acceleration principle suggests that investment keeps up with the expected rate of growth of sales. But the rate of accumulation is itself the main determinant of the rate of growth of income, and therefore of sales. Carrying itself by its own bootstraps is just what a capitalist economy *can* do.'

evidence and consequences of the general phenomenon of retardation with which we were concerned in earlier chapters.[9]

5.8 ADVOCACY OF EXPORT-LED GROWTH AND EFFICIENT NEOCOLONIALISM

The difficulties faced by the third world in industrializing by the path of import substitution have prompted many economists and policy makers to advocate that the third world should abandon the vain hope of changing its economic structure by trying to replace imports by domestic production and should attempt to export as much as possible. Since the major part of world trade originates as exports to and imports from advanced capitalist countries, this would in effect mean re-integrating the third world more fully into the international economic order centred on advanced capitalism.

The ideological basis for this attack against policies fostering import-substituting industrialization and against intervention in economic life by the state through the use of direct controls has been provided by neoclassical economics (see Bagchi, 1971b). The argument runs roughly as follows: physical controls over allocation of resources and quota restrictions on imports distort the effective relative prices in an arbitrary way, and misdirect resources. In particular, quota restrictions and tariffs on imports, without any corresponding subsidies to exports, create an arbitrary advantage for products primarily directed towards the internal market. While it is true that some domestic industries might need encouragement in their early phases, a regime of restricted trade turns these industries into

9 The recurring balance of payments deficits of third world economies were financed, until the end of the 1960s, largely by official grants, or, more frequently, loans from the advanced capitalist countries, the World Bank and its associate, the International Development Authority, and, to a lesser extent, by grants and loans from the socialist countries. Latterly, particularly for such countries as Indonesia and Brazil, loans from private banks and other private financial institutions have played a major role in bridging balance of payments deficits. Much of the official grants and loans, such as aid under PL480 of the USA, has been given as consumption grants. Where the grants and loans have been given ostensibly to aid investment, governments of third world economies have simply used them to support private and public consumption. Of course, much of the aid was in the nature of military assistance, particularly to repressive regimes, and was meant to be spent unproductively. The apparently low cost of official 'aid' has been very deceptive: the costs have been pushed up by various forms of tying of aid, and repayment obligations have often eaten up the major part of export earnings, so that new 'aid' has had to be given to repay the old, thus creating an international phenomenon of debt bondage. On various aspects of aid policies, see Vanek, 1967, Hayter, 1971, and Griffin, 1973, Newlyn, 1973, and Papanek, 1973.

permanent 'infants'. In this way, the country loses the advantages of specialization in the international market, and fails to reap the benefits of developing those sectors in which it happens to have a comparative advantage. One of the first requirements for getting the country out of the regime of distorted price structures and thwarted growth is to remove the disadvantages under which industries producing exportables suffer and to let the bracing air of international competition blow through the economy. The list of recommendations, of course, does not stop here but often extends to the whole field of economic policy (see, as an example, Little, Scitovsky and Scott, 1970). I will here deal only with that part of the recommendations that concentrates on exports as the leading sector in the growth of third world economies.

We have already examined (in section 5.2 above) the problems that a strategy based on promotion of export of primary products has created for third world economies in the past. In spite of a short primary commodity boom in the early 1970s, most of the problems facing agricultural exports are as they were in the nineteenth century. Some of them have in fact been aggravated. Advanced capitalist countries have become net exporters of foodgrains to the third world and synthetic materials have partially or completely replaced such products as indigo, cotton, jute and sisal. The demands for such beverages as tea and coffee have reached saturation points in many countries (see Helleiner, 1972, chapter 2). Thus the bargaining positions of the third world countries exporting primary agricultural products may have worsened over time. In fact, because of lack of political organization among themselves, because of the power of monopsonistic buying organizations in advanced capitalist countries, and because of threats of retaliation by advanced capitalist countries, the third world has been unable to develop any bargaining strength by organizing international cartels in primary products[10] (cf. Clairmonte, 1976). One result of this failure was a severe decline in the terms of trade of third world countries after the Second World War – a decline which persisted until the end of the 1960s (see Bairoch, 1975).

Even were these countries to try and export more primary and manufactured products to their main markets, viz. the advanced capitalist countries, they would come up against severe barriers in the latter. Beet sugar is protected against cane sugar, many agricultural and livestock products produced by advanc-

10 Petroleum remains the only case in which the price could be raised through cartellization by third world countries. In its case, the collusion of giant oil companies based mainly in the USA and one or two western European countries has been suspected.

ed countries are heavily protected against imports of similar products from third world countries. Not all the barriers against trade take the explicit form of tariffs or quota restrictions, and it is much more difficult to overcome informal but effective barriers against trade (see Massel, 1973). The exports of such simple manufactures as textile products, leather goods, labour-intensive engineering goods from the third world come up against even more severe barriers to entry into the affluent capitalist countries. In spite of many pious resolutions adopted at international conferences, particularly under the auspices of UNCTAD, the progress achieved in opening the markets of advanced capitalist countries to exports from the third world has been very limited. With a major recession engulfing the capitalist world, further progress in this direction seems unlikely. Under prodding from UNCTAD, the developed capitalist countries adopted the so-called Generalized System of Preferences, under which there was a general cut in tariffs or liberalization of quotas on imports from the third world. However, the system is so hedged around with qualifications that in 1975 it was predicted that 'the actual expansion of preferential trade in the future might be negative' (Iqbal, 1975, p. 37).

For some years past, transnational corporations and buying agencies based in countries such as Japan and the USA, have utilized the low labour costs and favourable treatment accorded to capitalist enterprises in such enclaves as Hong Kong or Singapore, or such semi-colonies as South Korea and Taiwan, to get part of their supplies fabricated for export to the advanced capitalist countries. The practice has also spread to such countries as Yugoslavia, Mexico, Brazil, the Philippines and India. Such subcontracting on an international scale, or such relocation of plants in low-wage economies for export to advanced capitalist countries as well as other countries has been seen by many economists as the vehicle for a new variety of export-led growth. However, even the advocates of such growth point out the severely limited scope for such subcontracting. 'If one judges by present-day Mexico, Taiwan and Korea, the countries where international subcontracting has the greatest importance, then the gross value of international subcontracting exports will probably reach at the most 5–15 per cent of the total value of exports' (Sharpston, 1975, p. 130). Moreover, in the cases of both subcontracting to nominally independent concerns and production by subsidiaries or branches of transnationals for export purposes, the proportion of value-added in third world countries to total price of the product tends to be rather low. For comparable products, the proportion is lower for third world countries than for similar subcontracting or export production by subsidiaries in the developed capitalist countries themselves (Sharpton, 1975 and Watanabe, 1976).

International subcontracting for export is unlikely to be a major vehicle for development of skills and transfer of technology. For a start, only the simplest operations are subcontracted out. Very often, the subcontractors use only traditional skills and the lowest-paid labour – the labour of young women in such activities as garment-making, for example (Kreye, 1977). Attempts to transfer more sophisticated skills come up against diseconomies of small scale, and the rapid obsolescence of production processes in advanced capitalist countries. There is also increasing trade union resistance against the attempt of transnational corporations to evade claims for higher wages by actually shifting or threatening to shift production locations.

Advanced capitalist classes, in order to overcome the crisis of worldwide inflation and stagnation, will definitely try to utilize low-wage locations for some of their investment. Such investment will tend to link the third world closely to the international capitalist system. The problems of a low level of development of productivity of the majority of the population, of growing unemployment and underemployment in most countries, of the depression of demand because of poor levels of living will not be solved by subjecting the third world to an even more rigorous thraldom to advanced capitalism. It is ironical that while advanced capitalist countries continue to use massive state patronage for fostering both technology-intensive industries such as nuclear power, electrical equipment, aircraft, petrochemicals, motor vehicles and keeping alive such poor relations as textiles, shoe-making, etc. (see for example, Burn and Epstein, 1972), economists based in those countries should advocate the unhindered development of comparative advantage in the third world. The third world countries took a wrong turn, when, in trying to correct the imbalances imposed on them by nineteenth-century colonialism, they imitated the techniques, products and organizational methods of advanced capitalist countries; such imitation, which came to be known as the policy of import-substituting industrialization, for want of a better name, produced its own contradictions. However, the resolution does not lie in yet another dose of forced orientation towards world capitalism; it lies in the development of economic structures, techniques and organizations that will foster the growth of these economies inward and will produce strong *internal* connections between different sectors of the economy and different occupational groups. The logic of capitalist exploitation and domination has hindered such a development so far.

6

RURAL CLASSES, LAND REFORMS AND AGRARIAN CHANGE

6.1 INTRODUCTION

In the third world, most people live in villages. In 1960, only 16.7 per cent of the third world population lived in towns with 20,000 persons or more (Bairoch, 1975, table 44). By 1980 this percentage may be 23.

Most rural people derive their livelihood from land. But they do not all derive this livelihood in the same way, and there are definite conflicts of interest between different groups. We aim in this chapter to analyse how rural people can be grouped into classes depending on their relation to the means of production, such as land, farm animals, and other agricultural implements and inputs.

6.2 THE LENIN–MAO SCHEME FOR ANALYSING RURAL CLASSES AND LATENT CLASS CONFLICTS

In most third world countries, there is a class of people who do not labour on the land and often do not even manage it, but nonetheless derive an income from the land. These are the 'landlords'. They may or may not live in the villages. In most countries, there are also a class of rural people who have nothing except their own labour to offer for sale and who make a living thereby if the offer is accepted. These are the landless labourers. In between the landlords and the landless labourers, there are many other families who have some right to the fruits of the land as owners, managers, tenants, etc. A scheme propounded by Lenin (1920) and further developed by Mao Tse-tung (1926, 1933) will help us in arranging these intermediate groups, analysing their interrelations with one another and changes in their relative positions with changes in state policy, market phenomena and technology (for a comparative analysis of Lenin's and Mao's schemes of classification, see Patnaik 1976).

In this scheme, the landlord derives his income from the rent of the land which is cultivated by tenants. He is distinguished from the rich peasant by the fact that the latter derives his income mainly from the surplus produced by hired labour, although some part of the income of the rich peasant may also accrue from the rent on the land leased out. The rich peasant may work on his own land, but the major part of his income is derived from the surplus of the output of hired labour over the wages of such labour. After the rich peasant comes the middle peasant who cultivates his own land mainly with family labour, but may also hire supplementary labour, particularly for peak-season operations. Then come the poor peasants who cultivate some land, either owned or rented, but who *have* to sell part of their labour power in order to earn a subsistence. Finally, there come the rural proletariat who derive their livelihood entirely from the sale of their labour power. Most of their working time is generally spent as agricultural labourers on other people's farms. We shall sometimes lump together the last two categories simply as 'poor peasants', and the context will make it clear when we have the more restricted definition of poor peasants in mind.

This scheme of classification is flexible enough to accommodate various complexities. For example, landlords and rich peasants may also earn income from moneylending or from commercial pursuits. Whether they will be classified as moneylenders, traders or landlords depends on whether land rent is their main source of income or not. Furthermore, some absentee landlords may derive their income from urban occupations such as trading, factory employment, etc. Whether they will be regarded as landlords or workers will depend partly on their relative incomes from their two roles (cf. Chandra, 1975) and partly on their objective interest in retaining landlordism or abolishing it. This last has to be judged in the context of the evolution of the whole society and on the state of political struggle. If the society is undergoing rapid development, so that opportunities outside rural areas are opening up fast, then at least the smaller landlords may find it convenient to sell their land and use the proceeds in other ways. On the other hand, if a strong political movement poses a challenge to the established interest in the towns as well as the villages, then the petty absentee landlord too may be forced to agree to the curbing of powers of property even though it may harm his immediate interest in the countryside. If neither of these developments takes place, the absentee landlord may continue to be an exploiter in the countryside even while he agitates for workers' rights in the town.

There are many other cases in which the interests of the same group of people in their different roles may be in conflict. For example, a landlord may lease his land out to sharecroppers and at the same time earn an income from consumption loans extended to them. Suppose in this case, a productivity-increasing innovation is introduced. If the proportionate share obtained by the landlord remains the same, then the rental income of the landlord will go up but so will the income of the tenants who will now borrow less from the landlord. It has been argued (Bhaduri, 1973) that, under certain conditions, the consequent fall in the usury income of the landlord will be greater than the rise in his income from rent and in that case the landlord will not allow the innovation in question to be introduced on the land rented out. Whether this will happen will depend on a number of factors such as whether the landlord can alter the rental share in his favour, whether the productivity-increasing innovation is financed by public expenditure or by the landlord himself, at what rate the market for the product is expected to develop and so on. The Lenin–Mao classification scheme can be easily adapted to analyse such problems of conflict within the same group or as between classes.

The Lenin–Mao scheme can be most easily applied where private property in land is clearly defined, and where labour power is extensively bought and sold in the market. Where these conditions do not obtain, but the rural society is nonetheless undergoing a greater degree of commercialization, the scheme can be easily modified. For example, in early twentieth-century Russia, communal property in land had not yet been abolished in all cases and some of the residual claims of the feudal lords on peasants' labour and land still remained. In this situation, it was difficult to get an exact notion of how much land a peasant operated or how much labour he actually hired in. To meet this situation Lenin used a dual criterion, involving the land operated by a peasant's family and the number of horses – the main implement of production apart from land and labour – owned by the family (Lenin, 1899, 1900a and b, 1903, 1908a and b). In the same way, the transition from precapitalist relations to capitalist relations of production in other parts of the contemporary world can be handled by identifying the emerging categories of rich peasants, middle peasants and the agricultural proletariat.

6.3 TRANSITIONAL OR MIXED FORMS AND STRATIFICATION SYSTEMS

The polarity between the landlords or rich peasants and the agricultural labourers is overlaid in most parts of the world by various kinds of *stratification* systems. That is, groups of people are distinguished not by their class positions as defined above, but by criteria derived from ethnic, religious or other kinds of distinction (cf. Stavenhagen, 1975, chapter 2). For example, in India, among the Hindus, people are stratified by caste. The system of caste distinctions differs from one part of the country to another. But, in most parts, the priestly or warrior castes are supposed to be at the top and the castes associated with menial tasks such as scavenging, or even working in leather, are supposed to be at the bottom. These latter castes were often regarded as untouchable by the superior castes. From that degrading characterization followed various other personal and social disabilities of these 'low-caste' people. The Government of India has legally abolished untouchability and many of the social disabilities associated with it, but the practice of denying many ordinary civil rights to these groups (who are now called *harijans*) persists in many regions.

There have been many incidents of violent conflict between the *harijans* and other castes in recent years and also between the intermediate castes themselves. While not all these conflicts originate in economic causes, underlying all of them there are conflicts about access to land, to public resources and to political patronage over jobs, credit and so on. The *harijans* in most cases are landless (this is true of many tribal groups which have been incorporated into the larger society), and their oppressors have generally been landlords belonging to superior castes. In some cases, the up and coming rich peasants and capitalist farmers have been in conflict with the earlier dominant section of landlords over possession of land or possession of political power and greater control over public resources. Since again the rich peasants and erstwhile landlords often belong to different castes, these class conflicts have taken the form of caste conflicts.

In a similar fashion, in many parts of Latin America, the landless or poor peasants belong mostly to the ethnic group of Amerindians, whereas the richer landowning employers either actually have or claim to have predominantly European blood in their veins. The latter are called *ladinos* in Mexico and Guatemala (Stavenhagen, 1975, part III). These real or supposed ethnic distinctions correspond in most cases to the distinction between the landless or poor peasants and the employing landowners, between farmers mainly growing maize and those growing more widely marketed crops, between groups with little access to state patronage and those obtaining the lion's share of it, and so on.

We can see then that the stratification systems very often reinforce the class relations brought about by the working of the market. As between agricultural labourers and their employers or landlords, they help to sustain relations of personal bondage and thus impede the development of free wage labour. In a situation of chronic unemployment in rural areas, since labour power cannot be sold at a given wage in unlimited quantities, employers can keep the labourers' wages low and circumscribe their personal freedom in many ways (Bagchi, 1973b). Even when such chronic unemployment has not surfaced, workers are often kept in a situation of bondage through chronic indebtedness to the employers and through the use of extra-market, and often extra-legal, coercion. Stratification systems can help the employers to perpetuate the relations of personal bondage of the workers or tenants who belong to particular castes, communities, or ethnic groups.

Occasionally, the classes which feel that the existing structure does not allow them to exploit their opportunities in full try to use the stratification system to mobilize political support and fight other classes which stand in the way. In India, many of the conflicts of the castes which count rich peasants among their members with other castes – either below them or above them in the hierarchy – can be traced to such origins. These stratification systems partly blur the distinctions between the different classes. But they can also be used to sharpen the antagonism between the classes and clarify the class relations further.

Such transitional phenomena can occur not only in countries which have long been characterized by settled agriculture and predominantly peasant populations, but also in countries where tribal systems are even now in the process of being replaced by systems of individual peasant proprietorship. Such is, for example, the case with the Ivory Coast or Ghana (Stavenhagen, 1975, part II), or such was the case in Kenya at the time of independence (Leys, 1976, and Njonjo, 1975). In the Ivory Coast and many other parts of West Africa, before the coming of European rule, while there were well-defined areas of tribal occupation of land, the right of private property did not exist. Gradually with the introduction of cash crops such as cocoa and coffee, and immigration of foreigners into areas occupied by such tribal groups as the Agni, rights of private property have developed – sometimes alongside community rights (where there was abundant land) and sometimes in violation of such rights. Along with this has gone the development of various categories of agricultural labour and tenants who may have long-term or seasonal contracts with the owners of land and who may share in the output produced in different proportions. Where the ratio of labour to cultivable land is small or where the labourers have organizations of their own, tenant shares or wages tend to be high and where the situation is reversed, the tenant shares or wages tend to be relatively low. A recognizable class structure with rich, middle and poor peasants and agricultural labourers is developing in such areas.

Similarly, in Kenya, alienation of millions of acres of land by Europeans in the white highlands and the post-independence sale of such land to favoured groups have laid the basis of a class structure with rich farmers or plantation owners at the top and agricultural labourers or squatters on the formerly white highlands at the bottom. In many of these countries the polarization between rich farmers and landless workers is yet incomplete. (On the general issues of conversion of tribal people into class-differentiated peasantry, see Fallers, 1971 and Saul and Woods, 1971). In some countries, such as Tanzania, the government has taken measures which seem to have arrested any such potential polarization (see the article by Ghai and Green, in Ghai, et al., 1979). But as we shall see when we review the results of land reforms in Mexico, in order to be effective, differentiation among the rural classes cannot be permanently arrested by once-for-all measures of redistribution or co-operativization, particularly when they are not accompanied by other policies to support such measures. Hence in judging the prospects for the success of the Tanzanian experiment and other similar efforts in other parts of the world, it is necessary to study the general influences acting on the evolution of rural class structures in third world countries.

6.4 SOME INFLUENCES ACTING ON THE RURAL CLASS STRUCTURES IN THE THIRD WORLD

We can approach the analysis of the evolution of the class structure by studying the process of generation of a surplus and its mode of utilization on the one hand, and the rate of increase of the numbers of poor peasants and agricultural labourers, their prospects of employment and the mode of such employment, on the other.

In the five-class scheme sketched in section 6.2, it is clear that the poor peasants or agricultural labourers do not earn any surplus above their normal subsistence needs. The middle peasants may or may not earn a surplus in normal years. If they do earn a surplus in normal years and have no means of employing it except in purchasing land, then the degree of concentration of landholdings will go up, provided, of course, the landlords and rich peasants do not lose the land systematically. Even if the middle peasants can employ their surplus to intensify cultivation on their land, or expand their non-agricultural pursuits such as marketing, moneylending or transport business, their control over local resources may go up at the cost of poor peasants. What applies to middle peasants applies *a fortiori* to rich peasants and landlords, who earn a surplus and choose to employ at least part of it in the purchase of land, intensification of farming or expansion of rural non-agricultural enterprises. We can see at once the weakness of land reform measures which aim at redistributing some land from the landlords to the other groups, but which do not follow this up with further policies to help the poor peasants and labourers and to arrest a renewed process of concentration of landholdings.

Where the middle peasants generate surpluses in some years and get into debt in bad years and where the prospects of profitable capital formation in a real form are dim, we generally get traditional landlord-dominated class structures. We then expect the concentration of land ownership to be high, and many tenants and agricultural labourers to be bound to the landlords or employers in some form of personal bondage. This was, for example, the situation in most parts of pre-communist China and pre-independence South Asia.

The employment prospects of the poor peasants and rural workers are determined by the rate at which the whole economy grows, the way the technology evolves and the way control over labour is exercised by the employers. When landlords or plantation companies began producing for external markets, they often used precapitalist methods of labour control (cf. section 2.2 above). Tribal people and indigenous peasants were denied access to good, uncultivated land, as in Spanish America or Indonesia, and were often corralled in 'native reserves', 'Indian communities', etc. Their able-bodied people were then made to work for sugar plantations, haciendas, or other such enterprises by using fiscal devices or direct methods of coercion. Even today in many parts of Latin America such as Guatemala, there are Amerindians who migrate in times of peak activity to coffee plantations or other plantations and go back to their villages after the work is over. Their wages remain low and their position insecure. Subsistence farming in the Amerindian villages and capitalist agriculture can be said to have a symbiotic relation with each other.

There were other plantations (particularly sugar plantations) in the nineteenth century which used slave labour, and which changed over to the use of workers imported mainly from India when slavery was abolished. However, these 'indentured' labourers were generally treated practically as slaves, and it involved a long hard fight before they could earn some minimal rights as free wage labourers (Adamson, 1972, Tinker, 1974). Similar systems of use of unfree labour were also instituted in the tea plantations of India (Guha, 1977) requiring long trade union and political struggles before these plantation workers were treated as free wage-earners. Although modern coffee, sugar or tea plantations generally employ a core of permanent workers in the factory and in the field, seasonal or casual workers are still important to them. These seasonal workers often come from the surrounding peasantry. Hence, in their case, the distinction between a proletariat working for capitalistic enterprises and dependent peasantry attached to estates becomes blurred. In the Brazilian North-east, plantation work was predominantly carried on by various categories of peasants – some landless workers working for wages and living on the estate, some tenants working regularly in exchange for the use of a piece of estate land, some other tenants owing casual labour service or payments in kind (vegetables or food crops), and even some formally independent peasantry providing the estate with some supplemental goods and labour service (Riegelhaupt and Forman, 1970). So the distinction of class structures on the basis of organizational forms of enterprises is not always clear cut.

In other cases, where either traditional landlordism of the type found in pre-communist China or pre-independence India prevailed, or where there were haciendas with numerous dependent peasantry having obligations of providing labour to the hacienda, the opening of new opportunities of making profits through the growing of cash crops led often to a greater degree of exploitation of the tenants or dependent peasantry. Thus, in Chile, increased opportunities of exporting grain after the 1860s apparently led the landlords to demand more labour from *inquilinos*, who were tenants with labour service obligations and also to restrict their access to the land on the hacienda (Bauer, 1975, and 'Introduction' to Duncan and Rutledge, 1977). In China and India also the poor peasants were often denied some of the customary rights of use of what had earlier been common land, and the shares of the tenants were effectively depressed.

If the economy grows fast enough and a tight labour market develops, the conditions of agricultural labourers can be expected to improve. But such improvement is not inevitable as is most vividly shown by the case of the Union of South Africa, where the ruling clique deprived black workers of many fundamental human rights and kept their wages low. In fact, it has been claimed that imposition of slavery or other institutions of unfree labour is a response on the part of landlords or capitalists to a situation of labour shortage (Domar, 1970). However, the degree of resistance of the peasantry or labourers and their organization for self-defence may determine whether the ruling classes succeed in their design to enslave or enserf free peasants or tribesmen, or to repress the struggle of unfree labour to obtain their rights and improve their material conditions (cf. Brenner, 1976).

We have already referred to the way in which organizational forms such as plantations or haciendas can influence the class structure. The influence of the market on the class structure in the era of capitalism is all-pervasive. But the particular way in which the market works depends on the specific types of state intervention for controlling labour, creating infrastructure, regulating the ownership and use of land, providing information and inputs for the use of agriculturists and arranging for special price support or subsidy schemes.

6.5 TYPICAL PATTERNS OF STATE INTERVENTION AND PREDOMINANT FEATURES OF CLASS STRUCTURES IN TODAY'S THIRD WORLD

We have already noticed some of the ways in which the state apparatus acted in shaping the class structure in colonial times and after. It legalized slavery, it restricted the movement of people, it alienated land which had traditionally been used by tribal people for pasture of shifting cultivation, it imposed taxes on particular groups with a view to influencing their behaviour. In many countries, perhaps the most important enactment was to render land a commodity for purchase and sale. From the nineteenth century onwards, the state took measures to create a more or less free labour and land market. It abolished slavery and declared (in Latin America) communal land to be partitionable and convertible into personal property. At the same time, to retain control over labour, it often brought in new laws of vagrancy which compelled poor people or particular ethnic groups to work for others. In some authoritarian states, there are laws forbidding workers' organizations and strikes.

Besides such legislative acts, the colonial state apparatus or its successors in Latin America created infrastructures to facilitate the diffusion and marketing of cash crops. Railways and port facilities in the third world were built primarily with these ends in view, although strategic objectives could also be served thereby, as in north-west India (see chapter 4 above). Besides railways, irrigation works were built in many countries such as India, Egypt and Indonesia to facilitate production of exportable crops. Such schemes were often financially profitable. Irrigation schemes, in combination with other measures, fostered plantation enterprises (as in Indonesia) or the growth of large farms (as in the Punjab in British India), and raised productivity in favoured parts of the country (for discussion of adverse side-effects of large scale irrigation works, see chapter 4).

In many colonial territories the state effectively subsidized the creation of infrastructure facilities for the benefit of dominant groups of foreign businessmen. When ex-colonial countries gain independence, naturally, the landlords and rich farmers use the state apparatus to subsidize irrigation and transport facilities. In fact, much of the productivity increase in such favoured regions as the Mexican north-west, East and West Punjab, and the Nile valley can be attributed to the spread of irrigation schemes, but peasants continued to use traditional techniques of cultivation. The later Green Revolution – that is, production of high-yielding varieties of grain with heavy doses of fertilizers – has mainly affected these irrigated areas which were already favoured.

The state apparatus has also often helped the big landowners and prosperous farmers with the provision of cheap credit. In Argentina, for example, the control of credit given by the important banks was a main source of power of the landowners before 1914. In Mexico, the National Agricultural Credit Bank helped large landowners, combining in credit unions, with loans on easy terms. At a later stage, it also helped large landowners to take over the land of poor colonists (De Alcantara, 1976, chapter IV). Similarly, in India, the state provided large landowners with cheap credit through co-operative banks, and, after 1968, through commercial banks as well. In fact, in most of the countries of Asia seeking to diffuse high-yielding varieties of paddy or wheat, the state has taken an initiative either in creating new institutions providing agricultural credit or in stepping up its flow through existing channels (Palmer, 1976).

Besides these infrastructure building activities, the state has increasingly intervened in the organization of production activities, and to redistribute rights of landownership or land use. In Algeria, the state has taken over farms which earlier belonged to foreigners (mainly Frenchmen) and run them as state farms or co-operative enterprises. In Tunisia also, Tunisians have taken over land that formerly belonged to foreigners. In both cases, since land distribution was already uneven under French rule, and few measures of drastic redistribution of land among the indigenous people were taken, the new distribution of income from, or property in, land among Algerians and Tunisians has become highly skewed. A new group of privileged owners and managers has come to occupy positions vacated by the foreign *colons* (Amin, 1970). In Kenya, similarly after independence, the state decided to *sell* the formerly European-owned ('white') highlands to Africans, instead of redistributing the land in an egalitarian fashion (the British government helped with a loan to effect the sales). Naturally only the more wealthy Africans, or those who were politically well-connected, could buy the land. (Foreigners continued to hold large estates even in 1971; see ILO, 1973, Technical Paper No. 17). The majority of the people who had been dispossessed in colonial times became poor peasants or landless workers (Leys, 1976).

In many countries, the state has tried to abolish absentee landlord-ism, redistribute land more equitably and organize co-operatives among the peasantry, with very mixed and often disappointing results. In independent India, for example, the Government abolished the system of revenue farming through the *zamindars* and other intermediary rights between the Government and the cultivators or legal owners that had grown up under British rule. Compensation was paid but at a diminishing rate in relation to net income. However, the Government often allowed the *zamindars* or other intermediaries to retain, or resume the possession of large amounts of land, under various pretexts (Thorner, 1976).

Another step taken by the Government in India was to pass legislation giving some security of tenure and better terms to tenants-at-will (who often had only verbal agreements with the landlords and were rack-rented). The government tried also to check concentration of landownership and give the poor and landless peasants some land, by putting a ceiling on landholdings (the ceiling varied from state to state). However, both these measures were ineffective, because of large-scale evasion. Tenants were evicted, or retained on condition that they did not register themselves as tenants or sharecroppers. Land above the ceiling was registered in the name of relatives, domestic servants or even farm servants (Appu, 1971, 1975). Only in a few states such as Jammu and Kashmir, Kerala and West Bengal, where peasant organizations are strong or where landlords belonged to a minority community and could be isolated, have the land reforms been even partially effective. In most other areas, taking advantage of the poor and landless peasants' illiteracy and their desperate poverty and lack of organization, and often using illegal methods of coercion, the landlords have been able to deny sharecroppers their legal rights and aggrandize land in quantities above those permitted by law.

In Egypt, at the beginning of the 1950s, the landless families constituted a majority among rural families. The major part of the cultivated land was cultivated by tenants (Abdel-Fadil, 1975 and Radwan, 1977). Major land reforms, carried out in 1952 and 1961, led, at first, to a decline in land concentration, particularly at the top, and to a fall in the proportion of landless families. However, private property in land was retained and ceiling laws were widely evaded. Between 1961 and 1972, the proportion of landless families to the total number of agricultural families increased from 45.3 per cent to 50.0 per cent (Radwan, 1977, p. 22). Moreover, small landowners leased out more than half of their land and the real wages of agricultural workers remained stagnant or fell. All this happened, in spite of the fact that peasants were organized into co-operatives on a compulsory basis and that major industries were all nationalized (Ghai et al., 1979, chapter 1). This apparent paradox will resolve itself when we discuss the fate of Mexican land reforms in the next section.

There are now studies all over the world which bear on the evolution of the rural class structure since colonial times. Although most of these studies do not use the Lenin–Mao scheme of classification, the basic features at the lower end of the class structures are clear. In the 1960s, under the auspices of the CIDA (Spanish initials for Interamerican Committee for Agricultural Development), studies of farm structure were carried out in seven Latin American countries. Farms were divided into large or medium multi-family units, employing wage labour on a regular basis, family units which might be enough to support an average family, or sub-family units which were too small to provide enough employment and income to a typical family (Barraclough and Domike, 1966, Stavenhagen, 1975, chapter 7). It was found that landless workers together with operators of subfamily farms ('poor peasants' in the Lenin–Mao scheme) constituted a majority in all the countries, ranging from 60.9 per cent of agricultural families in Argentina to 88.4 per cent in Guatemala (Peru is excluded because of non-comparability of data). Studies carried out for India, Pakistan and Bangladesh (Ahmad, 1973, Chandra, 1972, 1975, Gough, 1977, Khan, 1977, Mencher, 1974, Naseem, 1977 and Patnaik, 1976) have found a tendency for the numbers of poor peasants and landless workers to rise over time. In Pakistan and Bangladesh, in 1960/61, the percentage of landless agricultural workers was low in comparison with India. But in all three countries this percentage has risen over time, and in many areas, if not most, real wages of agricultural labour have tended to stagnate or decline. The Green Revoltution has often had a contradictory impact on rural employment and wages. By raising the productivity of land and making it possible to grow two or even three crops on a piece of land, it has made it possible for rural workers to obtain more employment for the year as a whole. In some particularly prosperous parts, it has led to the replacement of paternalistic relations between employers and workers by formal contracts (Bhalla, 1976). But, at the same time, mechanization and migration of workers from less-favoured areas have depressed the bargaining position of the original workers of the Green Revolution areas.

From our discussion so far, it is clear that the position of the middle peasant (who has often been taken as the archetypal peasant) in the class structure is a rather precarious one. He might prosper and might become a regular employer of labour; or bad harvests, low prices, or growth in numbers uncompensated by rise in productivity, or indebtedness might depress him to the position of a poor or landless peasant. For analysing the behaviour of the peasantry, therefore, it is necessary to analyse the relations between the different rural classes and their relation with the larger world of national markets, state patronage and international movements in markets, prices and technology.

While, in most countries, capitalist relations between employers and rural workers are becoming the norm, some of the precapitalist features of the rural scene, such as subsistence farming and sharecropping tenancy, have displayed a surprising degree of tenacity. One reason for this is that, as capitalists acquire control over more resources, they continue to utilize the older types of exploitation as long as they can, so that vestiges of precapitalist bondage continue to exist. Another reason is that by impoverishing whole masses of peasantry in regions on the margin of capitalist development, capitalism compels these peasants to cling to subsistence farming – with little capital on impoverished land – for survival. These marginal regions serve as labour reserves. But such regions need not always be physically separated from the regions of capitalist development. If capitalism develops in such a fashion as to create and maintain a large volume of unemployed or underemployed labour in the countryside, many landless labourers or poor peasants are compelled to establish ties of bondage with their employers in the hope of some security. Such bondage is the result of a retarded capitalism, rather than precapitalist in origin. It can take the form of sharecropping on onerous terms, and often in return for labour service on the employer's farm. We shall analyse the nature of socalled 'subsistence farming' and tenancy in more detail in section 6.7. In the next section, we use the history of land reforms in Mexico to discuss how radical land reform measures are often nullified by later developments.

6.6 THE FATE OF LAND REFORMS IN MEXICO AND IN CHINA

A clear analysis of the conditions for success of land reform measures which aim at redistributing land to the actual cultivators and speeding up the development of forces of production in agriculture was provided by Lenin. In the early twentieth century, in tsarist Russia, the left-wing Narodniks wanted to redistribute all land to the cultivating peasantry, without paying any compensation to the former owners, whereas the right-wing party of the Cadets wanted only a limited redistribution of land. When the tsar's minister, Stolypin, carried out land reforms (in 1910), peasants were allowed to buy up their allotments or sell them and withdraw from the communes. Lenin pointed out that only the left Narodniks' programme of complete expropriation of landlords and thorough redistribution among peasants could eliminate bondage and labour service (Lenin, 1912a, 1912b). For, under the Stolypin reforms, many dispossessed peasants would join the ranks of the proletariat. The landlords who obtained compensation, could use their economic power to dominate the peasantry. Moreover, if very large landholdings survived, the owners of adjacent small holdings (*minifundias*, in Latin American usage) would inevitably remain 'paupers in bondage', depending on the large landholder for employment, credit and so on (Lenin, 1912b, p. 251). In a capitalist setting, the sustainability of land reforms depends on employment in the non-agricultural sector expanding at a sufficiently high rate to prevent the emergence of a permanent reserve army of labour in the rural areas.

In Mexico, the struggle for liberation from Spanish rule started with a call to end exploitation of the Indians and the peasants. But power was eventually captured by a coalition of landlords, merchants and former public functionaries, as in other parts of Latin America. In the late nineteenth century, under Porfirio Diaz, landlords and foreign capitalists took complete control of the economy. The vestigial rights of most of the Indian communities vanished, and, in province after province, whole village populations came to be manorial serfs in all but name. Despite the brave resistance put up by Indian communities in the central region, 1 per cent of the population came to own 97 per cent of the land by the beginning of the twentieth century (Stavenhagen, 1970b, p. 227, and Wolf, 1973, pp. 17–18).

Then Diaz was overthrown and one of the fiercest peasant wars in modern history started in Mexico. By 1917, most of the great peasant leaders had been defeated by the so-called 'constitutionalists' (Pendle,

1971, Womack, 1972, Wolf, 1973, chapter 1), who still had to appease the peasantry. Article 27 of a new constitution drawn up in 1917 gave the state the right to impose restrictions on private property in the interest of 'the conservation and equitable distribution of the public wealth' (Pendle, 1971, pp. 193–4). Since neither the peasantry nor the proletariat were able to create a political party which would exercise power on their behalf and in their interest, the actual implementation of land reforms depended very much on the political will of the president of the country selected by the ruling coalition. Up to 1934, only about 3.5 per cent of the national territory had been distributed to the peasants. In 1934, Lazaro Cardenas, a Zapotec Indian and a participant in the peasant revolution, became president, and proceeded vigorously to carry out land reforms – very often in the teeth of opposition by ruling classes, including former revolutionaries who had developed vested interests in land. Under Cardenas, 31.6 million hectares of land were distributed and this came to almost a third of the total amount distributed between 1915 and 1966 (Carr, 1974, p. 168).

The Mexican land reform measures created two sectors, the private sector, in which only small-sized holdings were supposed to be allowed; and the *ejidos* or the co-operative sector, where peasants were allotted land as members of a community, and where the land was inalienable. The Cardenas government tried to ensure the viability of the *ejidos* by providing them with roads, irrigation works, schools and medical services. Credit and technical assistance was to be provided to the *ejidos* through the newly-established Banco Nacional de Credito Ejidal (BNCE). A whole network of marketing and purchasing services was also built to service producers' and consumers' co-operatives. As a result of the redistributive measures adopted by the Cardenas government, the percentage of landless labourers in Mexico dropped from 68 to 36 per cent between 1930 and 1940 (De Alcantara, 1976, pp. 4–5).

However, even while Cardenas was effecting drastic redistribution, in many areas the provisions of a law imposing a ceiling of 100 hectares on private landholdings were being evaded. After the end of the presidency of Cardenas, power passed back to an oligarchy which wanted to halt the land reform process and channel resources to the big landholders. Public investment was again directed to irrigation works primarily benefiting big estates. The ceiling on private landholdings was raised to 200 hectares of seasonally cultivated land or 100 hectares of perennially cultivated land; in fact, for selected plantation crops the ceiling was raised to 150 hectares of irrigated or 300 hectares of seasonally cultivated land. However, these ceilings are widely and openly evaded by registering the landholdings in separate names but keeping the operations under single control (Stavenhagen, 1970b, and De Alcantara, 1976, parts I and II).

Apart from such deliberate reversal and sabotage of land reform measures, three other factors have contributed to the sharpening of inequalities among the rural classes after 1940: first, structural weaknesses of a co-operative sector which is surrounded by large private landholdings and which is regarded as a sphere of bureaucratic and political patronage; second, the deliberate channelling of the benefits of public investment in agriculture to the latifundias in pre-Green Revolution days; third, the aggravation of regional inequalities as a result of pricing and other policies designed to support the quickening of the Green Revolution.

At the time of expropriation of the latifundias, the estate-owners were allowed to choose the land they would like to retain. Naturally they chose the most fertile and best-irrigated land. Hence many *ejidos* started with poorer endowments than the large-sized estates. Many problems generally occur in creating a democratically run co-operative farming sector when peasants have been used to individual farming and when many of them are illiterate. Such problems can be successfully tackled only with continuing political support for co-operative ventures. After Cardenas, the 'counter-reform' presidents and their associates deliberately set out to subvert *ejidos* and encourage individual farming by members of *ejidos*. For, they were afraid of the economic and political competition that might be posed by efficient co-operatives managed in the interest of the poor peasants (De Alcantara, 1976, pp. 192–200). When they tried to operate on their own, many *ejido* farmers found that they could not obtain adequate credit or the required inputs in competition with large farmers, and they leased out their land to others. So even though individual ownership was not conferred on the *ejido* farmers, many of them in effect became tenants of their more energetic or more affluent neighbours.

Secondly, credit, public investment and research efforts of the government and associated agencies were increasingly directed towards raising the productivity of irrigated, large farms. In 1943, after considerable discussions between the Mexican and US governments and the Rockefeller Foundation, an Office of Special Studies was created within the Ministry of Agriculture in Mexico to give effect to a programme of technical assistance by the Rockefeller Foundation to Mexican agriculture. The head of the Office was at the same time the field director of the Foundation in Mexico. The work carried out by the Office was directed towards raising the productivity of the irrigated areas as rapidly as possible, for that seemed to provide the most promising avenue for accelerating agricultural growth. Simultaneously, the government and big farmers spent large amounts on providing irrigation to hitherto unirrigated areas. However, the extension of irrigation benefited only a few select states of the North and North-west, and the major part of Mexico remained unirrigated. The majority of poor farmers remained engaged in raising maize, beans and such other crops on unirrigated land. Considering this situation and considering the difficulty of reproducing hybrid maize seeds except in special seed farms, the Institute for Agricultural Investigation (IAI), which had come into existence before the Office of Special Studies, tried to promote another approach. This approach concentrated on popularizing better yielding varieties of maize which could be reproduced through open pollination on farmers' fields. However, this approach did not get adequate government support. In any case, for the strategy of the IAI to succeed, an extensive network of extension and credit reaching into the remotest corners of the country would have been needed. Such a network did not exist in Mexico in those days.

The Office of Special Studies succeeded in producing higher yielding varieties of wheat and maize which required assured irrigation, and the large farmers obtained the major share of credit and at a relatively low cost through official banks and private credit agencies. Productivity growth was hence achieved through the increase in yields of wheat and maize under irrigated conditions. The credit supplied by the BNCE to the *ejido* sector failed to expand in the crucial years in step with output or requirements. Also the *ejido* and small farmers obtaining BNCE credit or credit through other official banks had to buy approved inputs through selected agencies. In effect, they became captive victims of private input-supplying organizations working through official banks, whereas large farmers could obtain the same or better inputs at a lower cost by working through their own purchasing agencies or operating in the open market.

The government also subsidized a programme of mechanization, mostly with imported tractors and other machinery, during the period from the 1940s to 1960s. Apart from causing an unnecessary drain of national resources, this programme primarily benefited the large farmers, and speeded up the process of conversion of many small peasants into landless labourers. Under Cardenas, central machinery stations had been set up with a view to instructing *ejido* farmers in the operation and maintenance of machinery. These later became inefficient and stagnant organizations, often selling off their machinery or allowing the machines to be scrapped for lack of adequate maintenance.

The break-through to the 'Green Revolution' in Mexico (and through diffusion, in other parts of the third world) came with the finding of dwarf varieties of wheat which could absorb fertilizers in heavy doses without the plants 'lodging' (falling over). However, the basis of regional and classwise inequality in the distribution of gains of agricultural productivity had already been laid in the earlier years through the working out of the policies and processes sketched above. In Mexico, a special problem was created by the fact that the poorer peasantry generally cultivated maize for subsistence needs and (in irrigated areas, especially) for supplementary income. While seeds of high-yielding varieties of wheat can be reproduced for several years through open pollination, hybrid maize seeds have to be reproduced every year by combining the original genetic strains. Seeds of HYV wheat came soon to be reproduced on seed farms controlled by large farmers, but hybrid maize seeds were reproduced only by a centralized official agency with inadequate extension and distribution facilities. Thus, the poorer peasants, mostly of Amerindian origin, in the central region of Mexico missed out most of the putative benefits of HYV maize (Myren, 1970).[1]

It is not necessary here to discuss in detail the question of the relative efficiency of co-operative *ejidos* and individual farming by large or small farmers. It has been found that given similar credit, marketing and transport facilities, co-operative *ejidos* can perform as well as private farms (Mueller, 1970), but in most cases conditions have not been the same. Co-operative *ejidos* have declined in number in most areas, and *ejido* farmers are now highly differentiated among themselves in respect of income and access to means of production (Ishii, 1973, and De Alcantara, 1976).

The upshot of all these processes has been a high degree of differentiation among Mexican peasantry, completely reversing the changes that were brought about by the Cardenas administration. In a study of the rural class structure in Mexico around 1960, Stavenhagen (1970b) divided the farm units into five categories. First came the large landowners possessing more than 200 hectares of land. They made up 3 per cent of all private farm units in number, but accounted for 84 per cent of all the land in the private sector and well above 40 per cent of all cultivated land. Then came the medium-sized farms, with between 25

1 A vivid contrast is provided by People's China where diffusion is ensured by organizing research and development in almost every commune (cf. Science for the People, 1974, pp. 50–1).

and 200 hectares of land-holding, which accounted for 13 per cent of all private farm units and 10 per cent of all privately held land. The owners of what Stavenhagen calls family farms (roughly corresponding to middle peasants) accounted for 7.8 per cent of all heads of farm units and 3.6 per cent of the labour force, thus forming a tiny minority of all peasants. Stavenhagen then grouped together the peasants on the *ejidos* and holders of farm units less than five hectares in size (which were too small to support a family or employ it fully). They together formed 84 per cent of all farm units and held 49 per cent of the cultivated area. Finally, there were 3.3 million landless labourers, who formed over half of the active population in agriculture. There is no indication that this process of polarization of the Mexican peasantry into a small group of large farmers and the vast majority of poor peasants and landless labourers has been arrested since.

The land reforms effected by Cardenas were reversed because while they fulfilled one of the conditions laid down by Lenin, viz. that large landowners must be expropriated without any compensation (Flores, 1970), they did not fulfil the other conditions. A very powerful sector dominated by large farmers survived, and this sector was allowed to aggrandize itself in later years. The political conditions for sustenance of land reforms were, of course, upset as soon as Cardenas quitted the presidency, for the ruling party did not want to continue his programme.

In communist countries land reforms have succeeded under very different political conditions. In China, for example, land tenure policies pursued by the Communist Party changed with changes in the political conditions in the country. In the early years of struggle against the Kuomintang in the late 1920s and early 1930s there was a tendency to attempt too radical a land reform programme, without adequate political preparation. Later, as the Communist Party acquired greater experience and as victory in the war against Japan was given priority over any other objective, the policies pursued by the Party became more flexible and also more moderate. An attempt was made to win over the majority of the peasantry and even patriotic landlords for conducting the struggle against the common enemy. Hence the main stress was on rent reduction, debt moratoria or interest reduction rather than on a drastic redistribution of land. However, in the final stages of the war against Japan and the civil war against the Kuomintang from 1946 onwards, the pace of land redistribution away from landlords and rich peasants and towards the poor and landless peasants accelerated. This was particularly true of north and north-eastern China. This policy was given legal expression in the Chinese Agrarian Law promulgated on 10 October 1947. (For a classic account of land reform in a north Chinese village, see Hinton, 1968; the text of the Agrarian Law and supplementary measures are reproduced in the appendix of the same book.)

An attempt was made to carry out land reform in China on the basis of the Lenin–Mao scheme of class analysis (see Hinton, 1968, Appendix C for Chinese Communist Party directives on how to analyse class status in the countryside). While the party provided the leadership and the policy guidelines, the actual execution was left to peasants' meetings and peasants' organizations. This is a major difference between land reforms in China (and many other socialist countries) and land reforms carried out under bureaucratic fiat (often of an occupying power, such as the US government in postwar Japan). During the civil war in China, most of the landlords and many rich peasants lost the major part of their land which was redistributed to poor and landless peasants. However, after the triumph of the Communist revolution, in the Land Reform Law of June 1950, an attempt was made to halt the process of dispossession of the rich peasants, in the interest of reconstruction and stimulation of agricultural growth. But the drive towards achieving a nearly egalitarian distribution of land among the peasantry went on. By the end of 1952, this process was practically completed. The movement for organizing mutual aid teams and elementary agricultural co-operatives (which gave some recognition still to individual ownership of land and other means of production) had already made some headway in the older liberated areas; this movement now spread all over the country, but with variations in speed and form to suit local conditions (see Shillinglaw, 1974, Moise, 1978). The final stage was the organization of communes, each of which integrated production, administration and political activity for group of villages together. To summarise, in China, as in other communist countries, the power of the landlords and rich peasants was destroyed by dispossessing them wholly or partially, and by giving poor peasants and the proletariat overwhelming political authority over the exploiting classes. Such conditions, of course, are the very antithesis of the societies based on private property in the third world countries we discussed earlier.[2]

2 It is reported that land distribution is South Korea is more even than in most other third world countries. The Americans exerted pressure for land reforms in South Korea, Taiwan, and other countries heavily dependent on them, in order to stem the tide of communism in Asia bred by peasant revolt against centuries of exploitation. An initial redistribution of land was sustained by government policies to curb land transfers, and by a remarkably high rate of absorption of the labour force achieved by South Korea in

6.7 SUBSISTENCE FARMING, SHARECROPPING TENANCY AND CAPITALIST DEVELOPMENT

In spite of considerable development of production for the market in most countries of the third world, there remain large sectors which raise crops primarily for peasant subsistence. Similarly, although employment of hired labour has become widely prevalent in these countries, such institutions as sharecropping tenancy continue to survive and even spread further in some cases. Both subsistence farming and sharecropping tenancy are integrated with 'advanced' sectors of the economy, and their persistence is characteristic of retarded capitalist development.

First, let us look at the nature of subsistence farming in the third world. An analytical distinction can be made between subsistence farming in a more or less closed tribal economy and what may be called 'last-resort subsistence farming'. In the former case, the products produced were directly used in consumption or in the mechanism of redistribution through ritual presentations to chiefs (who in turn gave them back to his tribal brethren) and gift exchange. They were not generally determined by the dictates of the market or an external tribute-raising authority. Many of the tribes might produce a surplus above their physiological needs in normal years, but it was used up within the tribe and did not enter a wider commercial nexus in any major way. (For studies of tribal economies, see Allan, 1971, Conklin, 1969, and Sahlins, 1968, 1974.)

The second type of subsistence farming occurs directly or indirectly in the wake of commercialization. This may be practised by the dependent peasantry on or around a large estate (cf. sections 6.3 and 6.4 above and Pearse, 1975, pp. 44–50). Or this may be practised by members of a tribe which has been driven out of its lands and confined to reserves. The land on the reserves (which was often marginal to start with) becomes less and less fertile since population grows and people have no surplus to invest in it. Even when there are no tribal reserves or shifting cultivation, the advance of commercial farming could induce the growth of subsistence farming by the exploited tenantry and other small peasants. Thus the Irish tenants of Anglo-Irish landlords in the nineteenth century planted a patch of ground with potato for subsistence while labouring on the landlord's land for raising com-

recent years (Lee, 1979). In these respects, South Korea and to a lesser extent, Taiwan, remain exceptions in the third world. Their size and their positions favour them and their experience is unlikely to be replicated in populous third world countries under present socio-political conditions.

mercial crops most of the time. If exploitation by money-lenders, traders or the state apparatus is excessive, even nominally independent peasants are compelled to eat up their livestock, cut down the forests and effectively mine the land. So the standard of fertility may decline, and peasants are compelled to reserve a large part of their land for mere subsistence. Such eroded lands serve as cheap labour reserves for mines and plantations. A regular pattern of migration of labour from such areas to plantations, mines or factories emerges and is kept going by the logic of exploitation (Arrighi, 1970a and Stavenhagen, 1975).

Within tribal reserves or outside them, the so-called subsistence farmers are generally compelled to raise some cash crops in order to pay taxes and dues to the landlord, tax-collector or money-lender – often to the detriment of their normal subsistence needs (Holmberg and Dobyns, 1970, Bharadwaj, 1974, Stavenhagen, 1975). The growing of poppy by Indian and Chinese peasants, or the growing of jute by small peasants in India and Bangladesh is (or was) dictated by such compulsions. Very often the capitalists in the advanced sector use the poor peasants as experimental guineapigs, or, when they can get away with it, reserve for themselves the more remunerative crops. In colonial Indonesia, cultivators on Outer Islands grew pepper, coffee and tobacco. When the latter two crops became sufficiently profitable, European firms moved in; in the case of tobacco, the latter took over the whole operation from the growing of the crop to its processing and marketing overseas (Boeke, 1946, pp. 4–6). In pre-independence Kenya, when the 'advanced' European farms could not compete on equal terms with Kenyan subsistence farmers, they used their political power to monopolize the supply of farm products to urban areas. What distinguishes today's 'subsistence farmers' is thus not their intrinsic behaviour pattern, but the high degree of exploitation they are subjected to and their low standard of living.

Not only has subsistence farming persisted alongside development of capitalist farming in the third world; a fully free labour or land market has also failed to emerge. Share-cropping tenancy has been taken as a sign of survival of precapitalist modes of exploitation in the countryside. However, it can be easily shown that so long as a large reserve army of underemployed or fitfully-employed labour persists in the countryside, under conditions of traditional agriculture, share-cropping tenancy can be a profitable mode of employment of labour by the landowner. Hence its persistence is entirely consistent with commercial agriculture.

Under conditions of traditional agriculture, with little investment of capital in the land, the productivity per acre on land holdings tends to vary inversely with the size of such holdings (Bharadwaj, 1974). A sufficient explanation of such a finding is that smallholdings are typically owned and operated by families who cannot expect to find full employment for all the working members outside the family farm, and large holdings are operated by landowners who depend mainly on hired labour. The small peasants operating family farms will try to maximize total output on the farm, so that at the margin the productivity of labour will be very nearly zero. But the landowner employing hired labour will try to maximize the surplus above wage costs, so that the marginal productivity of labour on these large holdings will be equal to the wage, but for some uncertainty about locating the point at which the surplus ceases to grow.

If the landowner now employs tenants on the understanding that the latter will surrender half of the gross output to the landowner, what happens to productivity? If the tenant can normally expect alternative employment at the going market wage, he will work on the rented land only up to the point where the marginal product of his labour is double the market wage. Thus with a declining marginal product curve, he will end up by employing less labour per unit of land than the landlord who directly hires labour to work the land. Hence employing tenants on a sharecropping basis is inefficient from the landlord's point of view. This is the traditional (Marshallian) answer.

However, if the tenant cannot expect full employment for members of his family at the going market wage and has to struggle to survive by getting as large a return from the land leased in as possible, then he will again be compelled to stretch his labour per unit of land to the point where the marginal productivity of labour is as near zero as possible. Thus the labour-intensity and productivity of land per acre on sharecropped land may be as high as that of small landholdings operated mainly with family labour (some labour may be hired in at peak seasons even by such farms).

If the marginal productivity of land declines very slowly as intensity of work increases, if the share obtained from the tenant is high (say, half or more of the crop) and if the market wage is high enough, the landlord may even get a larger surplus with sharecropping than by cultivating the land with hired labour.

The different possibilities are illustrated in figure 6.1, where labour employed per unit of land is measured on the x axis, and marginal product and wage (in terms of the crop) are measured on the y axis.

In Figure 6.1, M_1L_1 is the marginal product curve, M_2L_1 is the marginal product curve relevant to the tenant, who gets a k-th share of the product $(0 < k < 1)$, and W_1W_2 is the market wage curve. Where

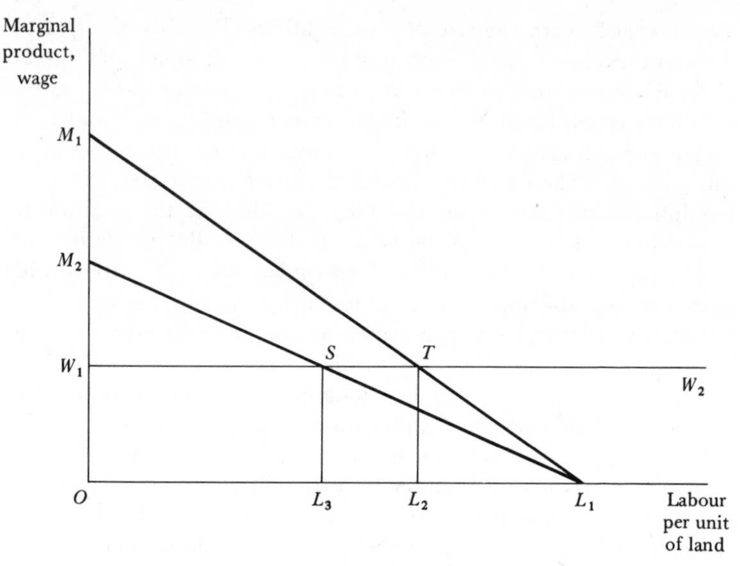

Figure 6.1

family labour is spent so as maximize total output, OL_1 is the amount of labour spent on the land. If the landlord employs wage labour to maximize the surplus, OL_2 is the amount of labour spent. If the tenant takes the wage curve as the opportunity cost of his own (and family) labour, OL_3 is the amount of labour used. Obviously, $OL_1 > OL_2 > OL_3$. However, if the tenant also has to maximize total output for survival, then he extends the labour spent from OL_3 to OL_1, whereby he gains the amount given by the area SL_3L_1. If the tenant does not try to maximize total output, but discounts his prospects of alternative employment sufficiently, then he will equate his share of the marginal product to a 'discounted wage' well below W_1W_2. It can be seen that the labour employed in that case may well lie to the right of L_2, though to the left of L_1.

The surplus obtained by the landlord relying on hired labour is given by the area M_1W_1T. In the case in which the tenant maximizes output, the landlord's surplus is given by the area $M_1M_2L_1$. Again, it can be seen that under some conditions, $M_1M_2L_1$ may be larger than M_1W_1T.

The above is a rather schematic discussion of possibilities where human labour is the main input, where the basic conditions of production are the same on both owner-operated and leased land, where the lessee generally has a smaller landholding than the typical landlord, and where the choices of modes of employment of labour and land are not interdependent and where labourers and small peasants are at least nominally free to choose between wage-employment and tenancy (for further discussion, see Bagchi, 1976b).

Suppose we introduce non-labour inputs into the picture. In traditional, non-irrigated agriculture, apart from seeds, draught animals are the main capital employed. Landowners who also own draught animals are expected to prefer own cultivation to sharecropping tenancy. However, if human labour and draught animals are strictly complementary inputs, and if landlords can recover the cost of maintenance of the animals from the tenant, then again we may find the same level of productivity on tenant-cultivated land and land operated with family labour. (In fact, if middle peasants do not own draught animals they may be at a disadvantage in relation to tenants who have access to the draught animals owned by their landlords.)

In traditional agriculture, the choices of modes of employment of labour and land are very often interdependent. Very often, the landlord gives out a piece of land to a tenant on condition that the latter labours on the landlord's land for most of his time. In this way, he may try to exploit not only the tenant but his whole family and seek to attain maximum levels of output both on self-cultivated and on tenant-cultivated land. Debt-bondage or traditional bondage gives the landlord an additional lever of control on the tenant (cf. Bhaduri, 1973). Even with the introduction of modern techniques under irrigated conditions, landlords seek to constrain the choice of the labourers and tenants in various ways when they face the possibility of labour shortage in peak seasons.

When cultivation is carried on with irrigation, water becomes a crucial non-labour input. The introduction of new implements, fertilizers and high-yielding varieties of seeds increase the importance of non-labour inputs even further. Owners of small pieces of land may then find it impossible to attain the levels of productivity reached by large farmers because they cannot afford to buy the complementary inputs on the same scale. In fact, a new type of tenancy (which may be characterized as capitalist tenancy) now arises under which a landlord or a capitalist leases in land from poor small owners and operates it with the help of the new technology.

In irrigated areas of the third world, such as the Punjab, the Nile valley or Java, intensification of non-labour inputs on peasants' land had started before the Second World War (cf. Palmer, 1976, chapter 1). This intensification has accelerated in the post-1945 period. What we observe in typical third world countries is a series of systems of agriculture – extending from unirrigated, extensive agriculture, unirrigated, intensive agriculture, to extensive and intensive agriculture with partial coverage by irrigation, and finally to fully capital-intensive agriculture in areas with assured and controlled water supply. Corresponding to these, the nature of tenancy varies from semi-feudal exploitation of poor peasants (by means of usury and rack-renting), to leasing in of land by rich peasants from others and its cultivation according to best-practice methods.

As the importance of non-labour inputs increases and as peasants struggle for liberation from traditional bondage, purely capitalist relations between employers and landless labourers spread. But since landlords dominate the rural areas, and landless labourers and poor peasants do not have adequate opportunities for employment and subsistence, the landlords continue to exploit them by using a variety of institutions, particularly forms of share-tenancy. We have seen that middle peasants, who form the archetype in much of the conventional literature on peasant bahaviour, are a small minority in most countries and occupy a precarious niche. The coming in of new inputs for which cash has to be paid tends to make their position even more precarious. If they have access to cheap credit and various types of state patronage, they aggrandize themselves and become rich peasants, depending greatly on hired labour for cultivation. If they do not have access to credit or cheap sources of new inputs, they become impoverished and are threatened with demotion to the position of poor peasants. Today's countryside in the third world rings with the struggle between the different rural classes, even if it does not always express itself in a violent form.

6.8 THE GREEN REVOLUTION, FARMERS' LOBBIES AND TECHNOLOGICAL DEPENDENCE IN THIRD WORLD AGRICULTURE

The phrase, 'Green Revolution', has been used to indicate the supposedly revolutionary increases in agricultural output in the third world made possible by the discovery and diffusion of new high-yielding varieties of seeds, particularly of wheat, rice and maize primarily under the auspices of the International Rice Research Institute in the Philippines and the Centro International de Mejoramiento de Maiz y Trigo (CIMMYT) in Mexico. We have already seen (in section 6.6) how the Rockefeller Foundation assisted the Mexican government in its effort to raise the productivity of wheat and maize. The interest of the Rockefeller Foundation and the US government in this programme probably sprang from their eagerness to pacify Mexican nationalism (the Cardenas government had nationalized the oil industry) and to keep Germany from acquiring a foothold in the western hemisphere during the Second World War (Cleaver, 1974). However it may be, after the success of the breeding programme in Mexico, the Rockefeller Foundation helped set up the CIMMYT, which became the nucleus for training agricultural scientists from other third world countries and exporting the 'Green Revolution' to those countries.

In the 1950s, the Ford Foundation moved into the field of agricultural development and so-called community development in India. In the 1960s, it sponsored the Intensive Agricultural Districts Programme for a few selected districts – usually those which were well-endowed with irrigation facilities. Along with this involvement came US style agricultural universities, training of administrators and agronomists in US-financed programmes and the thorough penetration of India's agricultural sector by the USAID, World Bank and other agencies affiliated to the western bloc (cf. Galbraith, 1969, pp. 85–6, 139–40, 160–2, 190). In 1962, the Ford and Rockefeller Foundations joined together to found the International Rice Research Institute in the Philippines. This became the centre of diffusion of the high-yielding IR varieties of paddy (higher-yielding varieties of paddy were, however, already being developed independently in other parts of south-east Asia).

Whether the 'Green Revolution' did raise the rate of agricultural growth in the affected countries has been doubted. In Mexico, for example, it has been noted that, over the period 1942–70, the highest rate of crop output growth (6.9 per cent p.a.) was recorded for the years 1945–56, well before the dwarf varieties had been diffused, and that the lowest rate of growth (1.2 per cent p.a.) was recorded for the years 1965–70, which have been hailed as the years of the Green Revolution (De Alcantara, 1976, p. 103). In India, it has been found (Reddy, 1978) that agricultural production grew at best at a constant rate on an average over the period from 1950–51 to 1973–74; at best the Green Revolution might have arrested a tendency towards decline in the agricultural growth rate observed in the late 1950s.

The Green Revolution primarily stimulated the growth of those regions which were well endowed with irrigation and those crops which could be marketed on a wide scale through channels of large-scale commerce. In these respects, irrigated areas of the third world had already made considerable advances before the high-yielding varieties came along. However, the proponents of the Green

Revolution strategy found a ready constituency among governments which wanted to increase the marketable surplus of agriculture, among agronomists who felt that not enough money was spent on agricultural education, research and extension, among large farmers who wanted more government subsidies and higher prices for their output, and among industrial firms (primarily multinationals, but also domestic input-producing enterprises) which wanted wider markets among farmers for producer and intermediate goods.

In most colonial countries of the third world, expenditure on agricultural research had been very small and had been concentrated on plantation crops which were of interest to capitalists of the ruling country (cf. Hall, 1936). In the independent countries of Latin America, the experience of the agricultural depression beginning in the late 1920s had made governments very reluctant to spend money on agricultural research. The productivity per acre of foodgrains in many third world countries had remained stagnant for decades. So when the US government and US Foundations wanted to promote agricultural research in the concerned countries, they found an enthusiastic response among the agricultural scientists and bureaucrats concerned with agricultural administration.

In the irrigated areas of the third world and in other areas concentrating on cash crops, there had grown up a class of large farmers who gradually organized themselves as farmers' lobbies. They demanded and obtained irrigation water at rates subsidized by the government, and very often fertilizers and agricultural implements were also supplied at cheap rates to them. Commercial banks and co-operative credit societies gave them loans on easy terms, and often special financial institutions were set up for their benefit. In some countries, with US and World Bank backing, they also extracted price support programmes from the government.

It has been found in many country studies that farmers as a group in the third world respond to *relative* price changes of farm products by increasing the acreage under the crops which become more profitable (Krishna, 1963, Narain, 1965, and Behrman, 1970). However, they do not switch over to the more profitable crops completely, for the changes in prices may not last, and, moreover, the farmers generally like to spread their risks. This could be particularly true of poor peasants who would strive to ensure survival by growing subsistence crops (cf. Lipton, 1968). If, nonetheless, a strong positive response to increased profitability of cash crops is found, it is to be at least partly explained by the pressure exerted on the poor peasants by the landlords, moneylenders and traders who have the whole commercial network and the tributary apparatus of the state backing them.

Under the usual conditions of a highly unequal distribution of land and incomes, in fact, an increase in prices of food grains (particularly, superior grains such as wheat and rice) can have very different implications for the landlords or rich peasants, and the poor peasants or landless labourers. While the former would gain, the latter, who have to buy a major part of their food on the market can lose badly. However, under the pressure of rich farmers' lobbies (backed by the US-affiliated agencies and input-supplying farms), many governments in the third world have instituted programmes of price support, very often at higher prices than ruled in the market, and thus transferred resources and incomes from the industrial sector and from poor and landless peasants to the landlords and rich peasants. In Mexico, for example, in the 1953/54 season, the government raised the guaranteed price of wheat from 750 to 830 pesos a ton, and the next season the price was raised further to 913 pesos a ton. This policy was in operation for the next ten years (De Alcantara, 1976, chapter IV). In India, the government began a policy of procuring wheat (and to a much lesser extent, rice) at higher-than-market prices from the mid-1960s onwards.

Farm price support policies for all major products combined with a national system of distribution of essential commodities at fixed prices can have a stabilizing effect on production and prices. However, selective support for prices of commercial crops and systematic increases in such support prices without a national system of distribution of essential commodities at stable prices can lead to, and have resulted in, the enrichment of landlords, rich peasants and traders connected with the trade in agricultural commodities at the cost of industrial workers and poor peasants. Such policies have often fed the forces of inflation, particularly since third world governments have been unwilling or unable to tax rich farmers whom they have subsidized so generously.

We have seen in the context of Mexico how government support for cash crop cultivation under irrigated conditions has aggravated intercrop (wheat vs. maize or beans), interregional (North and North-west vs. Central Mexico) and interclass inequality. Similarly, in India, the farm policies pursued by the government from the 1960s onwards have tended to increase the degree of inequality between perennially irrigated regions and regions mainly depending on rainfall for cultivation. This has been accompanied by unequal rates of growth of favoured crops, particularly wheat, and so-called inferior grain crops such as *bajra*, *jowar* or *ragi*, which are the staple diets of the poor in many regions, or pulses, which are the main source of protein for the poor. The processes serving to increase rural class differences have been quickened by the so-called Green Revolution. The number of landless labourers and their proportion to the rural population have grown in most regions. Many tenants have lost their land. Landlords have been able to defeat the purpose of legislation conferring security of tenure on tenants (including sharecroppers) by evicting the tenants before they could claim their rights under the law. In areas benefiting from the new technology, landowners have also found it profitable to manage the land on their own. The degree of inequality of rural incomes and assets has also increased over the years (Rajaraman, 1975, Saini, 1976).

While in the heartland of the Green Revolution, such as Haryana in northern India, contractual employment on a year-long basis is reported to be replacing attachment of labourers on the basis of verbal contracts and traditional loyalty (Bhalla, 1976), in most other parts of the country attached labourers are simply being thrown out and converted into casual day labourers (cf. Gough, 1977). Cropsharing tenancy is still continuing in most parts, but landlords often make the terms more stringent than before, while helping the sharecroppers to buy non-labour inputs to irrigate, fertilize and protect the crops. But in many other areas, particularly in unirrigated regions, traditional systems of cropsharing tenancy are continuing, with little change in techniques.

In an attempt to spread the Green Revolution, credit agencies have tended to spread their tentacles to the remotest villages. However, the credit has been generally monopolized by the rural rich. The Philippines illustrates the obstacles in the way of channelling credit to poor peasants. Although serving as the home of the International Rice Research Institute she has experienced the lowest rate of growth of her staple food, rice, among her neighbours. Credit was channelled through rural banks which were dominated by merchants and landlords. The rich landlords and farmers got easy credit on subsidized terms and lack of credit for poor peasants was judged to be a major bottleneck in the way of achieving a Green Revolution (Palmer, 1976, chapter II).

Credit institutions, nationwide marketing networks for procured grains and extension services have cemented the alliance between the rural and urban rich in most countries (even though generous farm price support policies have bred the seeds of dissension between the industrial bourgeoisie and landlords in some cases). Industrial capitalism has now been able to penetrate the agricultural sector of the third world to a degree formerly unknown. The importance of non-labour inputs that have to be purchased from the market for raising farm output or even maintaining it at current levels has greatly increased. It has been estimated that in Mexico, for example, the index of purchased inputs in agriculture (including chemical fertilizers, seeds, insecticides and irrigation water) went up from 18 in 1940 to 143 in 1965 (De Alcantara, 1976, p. 50). The implicit rate of growth of purchased inputs was several times higher than the rate of growth of crop output. Similar trends are observable in many other third world countries. Since, for producing purchased inputs such as fertilizers and insecticides or farm implements, technology has to be borrowed from advanced capitalist countries, this system of agriculture has brought about a situation of technological dependence in third world agriculture and strengthened the technological dependence in industry (and the military establishment). Alternatives in the form of increases in the supply of organic fertilizers, production of fertilizers or other inputs with indigenous technology, or the potential of native varieties of crops which can yield higher levels of output under irrigated conditions have been little explored in most countries. In many cases, attempts at finding such alternatives have been deliberately sabotaged at the instigation of multinationals or aid-giving agencies attached to the western bloc in the name of modernity, progress or quick results.

Multinational companies are moving on a massive front into the business of producing and processing various types of food products in the third world for the rich people everywhere, but particularly for the developed capitalist countries. They are being supported in the name of progress and efficiency by the World Bank, USAID and related organizations (Feder, 1976a, 1976b, and George, 1977). Many national governments have subsidized the use of labour-saving machinery – very often imported from abroad – by means of cheap loans, facility of importing at official exchange rates (when the black market price of foreign exchange is much higher), and outright subventions. Labour-saving machinery has often served the interest of large landowners and rich farmers (cf. Janvry, 1973) by increasing the landowners' control of workers, but it has aggravated the tendency towards increasing landlessness among poor peasants in the third world. All these developments are making inroads into the standard of living of the poor in the third world, whose employment prospects are being continually threatened, and whose staple foods are being sacrificed to make room for the luxuries of the rich. They are also helping to integrate third world agriculture in the network of international capitalism with an intensity never observed before. However, the further penetration of the market into the rural areas of the third world has sharpened the contradictions among the rural classes. It is also threatening the labour reserves and the 'subsistence sector' which have in the past acted as buffers for capitalism facing sharp opposition in other regions. Thus the completion of the historic tasks of capitalism in third world villages, while helping the capitalist classes to acquire a firmer grip over the economy, is also sowing the seeds of disintegration of the system, at least in its current form.

In the meantime, of course, the state apparatus in the third world, with the help of exploiting classes in the rural and urban areas, keeps the system running. In the next chapter, we briefly sketch some typical modes of differentiation among the classes in urban areas and the way the repressive apparatus helps to keep the different components of the system articulated together.

7

LABOUR, CAPITAL AND THE STATE

7.1 INTRODUCTION

In the preceding chapter we considered how rural classes are differentiated under the impact of colonialism and retarded capitalism in the third world. The rural class structure provides the basis of power of the ruling classes. But among the exploited classes besides the peasantry there is the industrial proletariat, and the poorer traders and artisans, mostly concentrated in urban areas. Among the ruling classes figure landlords and capitalist farmers with their economic base in rural areas (although they often have urban interests and an urban domicile), industrial capitalists and big merchants, and finally the bureaucracy running the state apparatus and public enterprises. In this chapter, we propose briefly to describe some relevant characteristics of the industrial and urban proletariat and semi-proletariat, and the industrial capitalists (see also chapter 2 above). We shall see how colonialism, and later on dominant foreign capital, affect the political configuration of the typical third world state, and how the attitudes of the native capitalists are shaped by the relative balance of forces between the indigenous exploiting classes, foreign capital and the exploited classes.

7.2 THE RECRUITMENT OF LABOUR UNDER CAPITALISM

The peasantry of the third world are the source of labour for the mines, plantations and factories of the indigenous and foreign bourgeoisie. The rise and growth of chattel slavery under mercantile capitalism may be seen as a response to problems posed by depopulation in Spanish America, and by the inability of the Spaniards or the Portuguese to convert Amerindians outside New Spain, Peru and Gran Colombia into serfs or slaves. Before industrial capitalism raised the productivity of labour and cut down transport costs, it would also have been much too expensive to induce free wage labour to migrate to the Americas.

Slavery 'worked' for the capitalists practising it, just as smuggling, establishment of offices in tax-free havens, the running of oil sheikhdoms by giant oil corporations, work for present-day capitalism. It was forcibly abolished by Great Britain and the American North, because it proved inconsistent with the political and economic requirements of advanced, industrial capitalism represented by the abolitionist powers.[1]

Outside the strict framework of slavery, Europeans often complained about their inability to recruit native labour for enterprises such as road-building, working in mines, etc. They resorted to such devices as poll taxes, hut taxes, compulsory requisitioning of labour, etc., in order to get over the shortage of labour. The rationale of regressive taxation for conquered populations was lucidly stated by Lord Grey, a British Secretary of State for the Colonies in his despatch dated 24 October 1848. Lord Grey complained about the ease with which the natives (in this case, the people of Sri Lanka) could raise their subsistence, their refusal to purchase luxuries or other benefits of civilization, such as liquor, and their unwillingness to work for hire. If they could not be taxed by levying imposts on articles of consumption, or if they could not be induced to work for 'the maintenance of civilized society', then a 'direct impost must be laid upon them' (in the form of a poll tax or hut tax or some other such measure) and thus they must uphold that 'machinery of government and those institutions which were essential to progress' (Curtin, 1971, p. 168).

To other problems of moving labour out of a tribal organization was added a strong disincentive against working in capitalist or colonial enterprises. In the case of southern Africa, Miracle and Fetter have shown that it was perfectly rational, on grounds of self-preservation and income-maximization, for Africans to be reluctant to migrate to European-controlled urban centres (Miracle and Fetter, 1970, Miracle, 1976). Death from diseases and epidemics was frequent. For example, 'in 1911, one year after the beginning of Belgian rule, the head of Katanga's medical service estimated the annual death rate among Africans in Elizabethville to be 24 per cent per year' (Miracle and Fetter, 1970, p. 247). The racist attitudes of white employers who treated Africans (or for that matter, Indians in Assamese or Caribbean plantations or on the Uganda railways) worse than animals, the inability of the workers to bring families with them, the in-

1 The debate about the 'efficiency' and profitability of slavery sparked off by the work of Conrad and Meyer in 1958, has shed a great deal of light on the lives of the plantation slaves and on the working of the southern US plantation economy (see Conrad and Meyer, 1973, Genovese, 1965, and David and Temin, 1974).

sufficiency of rations and the lack of supply of foods familiar to the Africans, exploitation by shopkeepers, relatively high prices of agricultural goods in the mines or plantations or towns – all acted as deterrents. (On the conditions of Indian plantation workers, see Das, 1931, and Guha, 1977.) In truth, the 'civilizing' mission of the European powers proved to be as murderous as the wars let loose by them in Africa and other continents (see Emil Faure's statement quoted by Hodgkin, 1972, p. 108).

As population grew and the tribal societies broke down, and as Africans took to consuming western goods, the situation changed. The working of the market, oligopolistically rigged in favour of the employers, could be expected to push the workers into plantations, mines and factories, not only in Latin America and Asia, but also in Africa. Some regimes were not content with rigging the market. The racist regime of South Africa, for example, deprived the Africans of most of their land. The process, beginning in the nineteenth century, was practically completed in 1913. The Native Land Act allotted only 13 per cent of all national land (generally less fertile than average) to the Africans who then constituted over 90 per cent of the total population (Moyana, 1975, and Wilson, 1972, chapter 1). The later 'Bantustans' were established in these overcrowded enclaves. A system of indentured labour was organized to bring labour from India and China. A migrant labour system was built to bring labour from the neighbouring territories of Mozambique, Malawi, Lesotho, etc. The advanced capitalist powers have supported a system which promises a high rate of profit on invested capital by combining the technology of space age and the repressive apparatus of the mercantile era (First, Steele and Gurney, 1973).

In countries where colonial powers overthrew established kingdoms and empires with settled agriculture as their production base, they found it easier to recruit labour for modern enterprises. (For the Indian case, see Das, 1923, 1931, Buchanan, 1964, Mukherjee, 1951, Morris, 1965, and Bagchi, 1972a, chapter 5). Policy-makers were often aware that the ease of recruitment and cheapness of labour were contingent upon the peasants' or tribesmen's habitat remaining poor, and hence were not too eager to improve it (for evidence in the case of India, see Bagchi, 1972a, p. 138n). But they also knew that a plot for subsistence of the family left at home by the wage-earner was a wonderful way of compelling the whole family to practise the maximum degree of self-exploitation. This would then make it possible for the 'breadwinner' to work at a wage which was really below the level of subsistence of a family (see chapters 2 and 6 above). With massive de-industrialization in many parts of the third world, growing landlessness among the peasantry, and slow growth of employment opportunities, in most countries, the potential labour force for capitalistic enterprises has grown enormously. In spite of the low probability of getting a job in towns and the extremely insanitary conditions of housing and living, urban areas in most third world countries act as a strong magnet for the rural labour force (see Knight and Mabro, 1972, Turner and Jackson, 1972, and Todaro, 1973).

7.3 MAINTAINING CONTROL OVER WORKERS IN CAPITALISTIC ENTERPRISES

Once the workers are brought into the plantations, mines or factories, they are subjected to the concentrated and intense exploitation process characteristic of capitalism. Where planters were reasonably sure of obtaining cheap replacements for slaves, the labour process to which slaves were subjected was extremely wasteful of their lives. They also used punitive laws and regulations which literally permitted the planters to get away with murder (see Dunn, 1973, chs. 6–9, for descriptions of the labour process under slavery). Life for indentured labour on and outside the plantations was very similar to that of slaves, at least until the First World War. The labourers were often put under the authority of the planters who exercised the right of private arrest, imprisonment and chastisement of the workers (Adamson, 1972, chapter 4, Kondapi, 1951, chapter 7, and Tinker, 1974, chapters 4–6). When laws were changed to restore personal liberty to the workers, they often remained ignorant of, or incapable of enforcing, their newly-acquired rights. It generally took decades of struggle to acquire even the rights that had been formally granted to them.

Where plantations were organized in the middle of a peasant population, as in Assam or Sri Lanka, the planters imported indentured labour and paid them a wage which was below the locally prevalent one. The indentured labourers belonged to ethnic groups different from those of the surrounding peasantry. This made it relatively easy for the planters to deprive them of a share in any improvement that might come about in the conditions of living of the local peasantry or workers in other industries. Even today, for example, the wages of Indian plantation labourers in Sri Lanka are a fraction of the wages of even unskilled workers in other sectors of the economy (ILO, 1971a, chapter 8, and ILO, 1971b, chapter 6).

With certain privileged exceptions, such as the workers in the Copper Belt of Zambia, or workers in the oil industry in most countries, the conditions of mine workers in the third world are usually no better than those of plantation workers. Their hours of work are long, the equipment they handle is primitive and safety precautions are observed more in the breach than in the observance.[2] Management has often acted brutally to break up trade union organizations and suppress workers' resistance. Now, in most countries, mine-owners are legally required to grant provident fund benefits, medical benefits, compensation for injury, etc., to the workers. But the latter are often cheated of such rights when the owners and managers hand the job over to raising contractors (i.e. contractors responsible for raising coal or other minerals from the mines) or labour contractors. (Employment of contract labour is also practised by owners of factories, for similar reasons). There are other devices used by mine-owners to control the workers: the mine-owners also own the land and houses on which workers' families live, and run liquor shops and 'tuck shops' where the workers spend their money. Because mines are often located in inaccessible places, it is easier for mine-owners and managers to evade their legal responsibility and to suppress workers' movements.

We have seen that the survival of rural connections of labour, though they can be a nuisance in increasing absenteeism among workers, are useful to factory-owners in many other ways (see chapter 2). The capitalists can pay little more than the subsistence of the worker. The workers tolerate inadequate housing facilities, when they have a village home to return to. Also, it becomes more difficult to organize workers with real rural moorings. During the course of a long strike, the workers may simply disappear into the villages.

But, of course, in most third world countries, there are now substantial sections of the working class with no rural roots. Factory workers were often recruited through intermediaries who acted as direct or indirect agents of the managers in keeping control over the workers by fining them on the slightest pretext, dismissing them for minor offences, lending them money at extortionate rates of interest, and herding them into overcrowded and insanitary slums. Workers have had to form trade unions and launch long-drawn-out strikes in order to obtain a living wage or to protect whatever earnings they had. In the early period of establishment of manufacturing industry,

2 In India, coal mines have proved a graveyard for miners, and several hundreds have died every year even as late as 1975 and 1976. Ironically enough, the guilty management in public sector mines have obtained more protection from the government than the owners of private collieries had. See in this connection, Subrahmanyam, 1977a and 1977b.

capitalists tolerated a high degree of absenteeism and 'slacking at work' which were the costs of maintaining abysmally low wages. With the growing sophistication of techniques in many industries and with the growth of technology-intensive industries, management finds it less and less profitable to have semi-starved workers working at a desultory pace. It has been suggested by Arrighi (1970b) that labour-intensive techniques are associated with a pattern of employment in which unskilled labour (not attuned to the discipline of wage employment) and skilled labour (mechanics, carpenters, etc.) predominate, whereas capital-intensive techniques are associated with a pattern of employment in which semi-skilled labour[3] and high-level man-power (with formal training besides training on the job, for example, maintenance and production engineers, designers, etc.) are predominantly employed.

However, the pattern of employment of labour with different degrees of skill or training is not dictated solely by the nature of technology. Nor is technology in retarded societies chosen mainly with an eye to the local supply of different types of labour. Techniques in modern industries were evolved in advanced capitalist countries, and were naturally adapted to their specific skill or capital endowments, and to the needs of management of those countries to bring the labour process under management control (Braverman, 1974, and Bagchi, 1978). This process of dissociation of industrial techniques from local conditions in the third world has been accelerated by the growth of transnational corporations, which choose their techniques on the basis of global considerations of profit and manageability. The presumed skill or educational requirements for industrial employment in such countries as India, Pakistan or Sri Lanka have generally been raised over time in response to the emergence of excess supply of practically all types of labour. Raising of educational qualifications without reference to specific job requirements has been a device of job rationing. The ILO study group on Kenya complained that, even in that country, the paper qualification syndrome was being fostered (ILO, 1973, p. 254).

The proportion of so-called supervisory personnel to ordinary workers in a country such as India is raised over time by several other factors. The importance of 'technology-intensive' industries has increased, thus raising the proportion of supervisors to ordinary workers. Also, padding the management with family members is a

3 Arrighi does not define this category properly. It may consist of people who have just learned one or two narrowly specialized and easily acquired skills.

device both for ensuring family or group control and of taking out some of the company earnings in the shape of inflated salaries, tax-free perquisites, etc. The recruitment pattern of employees in relatively high-wage industries and firms tends to reinforce the existing structure of inequality, since the recruitment is based formally or informally on the connections of the recruits with the existing employees and management (see, for example, Markensten, 1972, chapter 4). In India, the share of wages and salaries in value added and the share of production (as against clerical and administrative) workers in the wages and salaries have declined since the 1950s (Sethuraman, 1971, and Shetty, 1973).

The rise of some firms in some industries paying relatively good wages hardly implies the growth of an aristocracy of labour in the third world, however. The main beneficiaries of the high-wage enclaves are supervisory personnel and non-production workers. Production workers in most third world industries continue to receive a pittance by international standards. In the next section we briefly sketch the role of trade unions.

7.4 THE INFORMAL SECTOR, SMALL ENTERPRISES AND TRADE UNIONS

Effective trade unions are generally found in industries characterized by large units, or in the public sector. One of the major features of the 'informal sector' is the absence or ineffectiveness of workers' organizations. There is a large degree of overlap between small enterprises and the informal sector. Small enterprises vary greatly in origin and function. Many are essentially one-man or family affairs, with few hired workers. These are generally characterized – as in the case of poor peasant farms – by a high degree of self-exploitation. Other units often carry on because they pay the workers lower wages than those prevailing in the large-scale sector. Some of these are organized deliberately by large enterprises in order to evade labour laws and other restrictive regulations, and to take advantage of privileges extended by the governments in some countries to small-scale units (see in this connection, Basu, 1977a, 1977b). Even those enterprises which are not formally under the umbrella of a large business organization have to become subservient to large capital in order to obtain access to markets, credit, etc. Many transnational enterprises have taken advantage of the fragmented nature of the labour markets in the third world to subcontract their production to sweated-labour enterprises, or to employ labour through the intermediary of contractors (see, for example, George, 1977, parts 2 and 3, and Kreye, 1977). Naturally, in the sweatshops, women, including young girls, get the worst of the deal (see Banerjee, 1978).

Few self-employed artisans, craftsmen or small enterprises have any chance of owning or growing into large enterprises. In the third world, typical units in many branches of modern industry started out as large units with considerable local monopoly power. So long as workers' political consciousness and trade union organization are weak, the large units try to play off unorganized against organized labour, and production in sweatshops under their control against production in centralized factories, wherever possible.[4]

Trade unions in the third world grew out of workers' resistance against the employers' attempt to cut down an already meagre standard of living. For example, workers' militancy in India reached new peaks in the wake of the two World Wars which had witnessed a drastic fall in the real wages of labour. Trade unions also got caught up in political struggles against colonialism. This leads to problems in disentangling the effects of unionism from the effects of political movements on wages and working conditions of workers (see Warren, 1966, 1969, and Berg, 1969).

The relations of trade unions bosses with the rulers of the country are strongly influenced by the balance of class forces and the nature of the state apparatus which is used to control the workers. In Argentina, for example, the urban workers enjoyed an increase in real wages and even a rise in their share of national income under the early Peronist regime. That memory provided the ground-work of trade union loyalty to Peron, even after he had capitulated to the forces of capitalism (see Epstein, 1975). However, in countries such as India or Pakistan, trade unions have played a rather marginal role in bolstering up the existing regime. Very often, they have had to fight the government (as during the great railway strike of 1974 in India) in order to protect the workers' interests. In between there are many cases in which political leaders have first used workers to attain ascendancy and then tried to control them through recognized trade unions (see, Amin, 1970, pp. 206–11, for developments in the Maghreb).

Trade unions have not been able to raise real wages of workers generally in many third world countries. Nor has the intention of authoritarian regimes to control trade unions been realized in many

4 See Bienefeld, 1975, for a study of the informal sector in Tanzania. Bienefeld found that about 22 per cent of those employed in shops, bars, hotels or domestic service received considerably less than the legal minimum, and that almost half of these low-paid employees were treated as casual labour.

cases. Not only in South Asia, where a considerable volume of surplus labour is generated by the existing system, but also in Argentina where the level of per capita income is much higher and where surplus rural labour is not much in evidence, real wages of workers have hardly risen since the 1950s (see Sau, 1977, and Epstein, 1975). This stagnation is related to the slow growth or decline of employment in industry, and to the existence of the so-called informal sector which acts as a labour reservoir for the organized sector. In Kenya, where the regime of Jomo Kenyatta tried to regiment all trade unions, individual unions were forced to defend their members' rights in order to conserve their base (Sandbrook, 1975). For total control of workers' movements, we have to look to the current right-wing military regimes of Brazil, Chile and Argentina, which have used terror and violence to crush workers' struggles.

7.5 GROWTH OF OLIGOPOLY AND BUSINESS OLIGARCHY IN THE THIRD WORLD

At the top of the capitalist pyramid in trade, industry and finance in the third world is native big bourgeoisie, but in many fields foreign capital still rules the roost. In the late eighteenth or early nineteenth century, in such countries as China and India, a hierarchy of merchants and bankers could be found. The trade connections of the biggest businessmen and bankers spanned several regions, and even extended beyond the frontiers of the country. There were smaller bankers and traders who conducted their operations within particular regions. The conquering Europeans curtailed the operations of the big merchants and drove many of them out altogether. Some relatively independent bankers and merchants survived in areas where European capital could not penetrate deeply. The Europeans initially helped some collaborating native businessmen to prosper but later on severely restricted their area of operation.

From the late nineteenth century onwards, some modern industry began to grow up in the third world partly under the control of foreign capital and partly under the ownership of native trading and banking capital. By then the typical size of a factory and the capital required to start one had increased enormously. Only indigenous businessmen with command over relatively large amounts of capital could venture in the field. Many of the modern capitalistic enterprises were large in relation to the sector or area they operated in and commanded some monopoly power. The organizational forms of modern capitalistic enterprises (such as joint-stock companies) were imported from abroad. The indigenous businessmen found that it was legally convenient for them to adopt the recommended forms of organization. But they carried on with the methods of traditional and familial control behind the facade, and resembled many industrial enterprises in Britain and France in this regard (see Landes, 1965, and Payne, 1974; Hazari, 1965, and White, 1974).

In some cases, family ties were strengthened in response to the challenge of capitalism, since the family provided a network of communication and control which assisted in the competitive struggle (Shoji Ito, 1966). In India, the British and Indian businessmen together developed the managing agency system. Under this system, the control of a business firm was vested in a managing agency, which might or might not hold a controlling share in the company (Rungta, 1970, chapter 12). The reality of control of firms and industries by a small group was not, however, contingent upon particular legal forms. In post-independence India, despite the legal abolition of the managing agency system, the conglomerate business combine, generally controlled by a family or a group of families, continues to thrive (Hazari, 1965). In Pakistan also, in spite of a vacuum left by the migration of Hindu businessmen, within twenty-one years of independence, according to the Chief Economist for the Planning Commission, economic power came to be concentrated in the hands of 20 families (White, 1974, p. 43).

To some extent, the monopolization of business sought after by indigenous business groups is a defensive reaction to the domination of the field by large foreign firms. India was one of the few countries in which indigenous businessmen had managed to wrest control over a significant fraction of industry, trade and banking even before political independence. The survival of some large-scale trade and finance in western India under British rule, partly under the patronage of the so-called native states, contributed to this success. In other parts of India, indigenous businessmen, primarily from the ranks of traders, had to struggle to compete in the organized sector with Europeans who enjoyed open or implicit official backing. And they had to wait until the crisis of the British Empire triggered off by the First World War, to make any real headway (Bagchi, 1972a, chapter 6).

In Latin America too, large enterprises dominated the organized sector from the beginning of the process of industrialization, and the members of the industrial bourgeoisie were mainly recruited from the ranks of the existing upper classes (Cardoso, 1965, 1966, 1973, Johnson, 1967–1968, Derossi, 1971, and Polit, 1968). The so-called 'entrepreneurial elites' were formed in an environment in which all profitable economic opportunities were directed outward, and which brought about a cohesion among the members of the elites on the basis of subordination to the dominant foreign capitalist groups or countries of the time. The gateways into the ruling oligarchy were extremely narrow. The state apparatus was run by a coalition of the landed magnates, financiers and big traders. When it became profitable to start industrial enterprises, they were organized by the established members of the ruling coalition, or by immigrant groups which had made money in trade and which became integrated into the oligarchy. There is little evidence of any major conflict between the industrial bourgeoisie and the other members of the coalition (except perhaps in the case of the overthrow of President Balmaceda in Chile), for generally the powerful families had a finger in every pie (cf. Cardoso, 1966, p. 150, and Polit, 1968, pp. 401–2).

In political dependencies and countries newly liberated from colonial rule, native businessmen were discriminated against by the foreign ruling power and foreign firms. A formal and informal network (in the form of exclusive clubs, trade associations, religious societies, chambers of commerce, etc.) could be found among the top Europeans in officialdom, in railway companies, and in big foreign firms dominating their respective fields of operation – be it shipping, banking, insurance, inland transport, plantations, mining, or export-oriented industries. This network was used before, say, 1939, systematically to discriminate against the native in dependent India or Indonesia or even China (see Bagchi, 1972a, chapter 6, Mackenzie, 1954, pp. 68–9, and chapter 4 above).

In newly independent Nigeria, Schatz found that large foreign firms called the tune in the business world, and aspiring local businessmen were at a disadvantage (Schatz, 1965, 1968 and 1972). The government might supply them with finance, but it would take time for them to acquire the needed experience in production control, management and marketing. With restricted markets dominated by big foreign firms, demand limitation proved to be a major constraint for local business. Even if some ancillary business resulted from the operations of foreign enterprises, local entrepreneurs could not take advantage of it since they lacked experience and faced racial discrimination. Schatz's summary of their position is reminiscent of that of Indian businessmen in pre-independence India. First, 'African businessmen miss out on opportunities because of lack of social contact.' Secondly, Africans are subject to what is called *probabilistic discrimination.*

Foreign firms find it very difficult to differentiate – to distinguish among the many Africans with business aspirations who may be inefficient, incapable of turning out a product of uniform quality and making regular deliveries, less than punctual in meeting business obligations, etc., and those indigenous entrepreneurs who run their business capably and carefully. In these circumstances, African businessmen (including the capable ones) tend to be passed over in various business dealings simply on the basis of probabilities (Schatz, 1972).

Apart from other factors, lack of familiarity with the language in which official work and business dealings are conducted also acts as a barrier against the emergence of native business groups in political dependencies or the entry of members of large, repressed communities into large-scale business. Thus English in former British colonies, French in former French colonies, or Spanish in former Spanish America acted and often continues to act as a filtering agent, keeping most Asian, African or Amerindian businessmen out of the charmed circle of business magnates.

Some of the state policies for encouraging industrialization, by the logic of capitalism itself, favour the large capitalists at the expense of the small (Weeks, 1973). These include, for example, the tariffs and quotas restricting imports. The quotas favour the established traders, or where the established traders do not belong to the politically dominant community, the privileged few with the right political connections (cf. Leys, 1976, chapter 5). Extension of cheap credit by the state or state-managed institutions also favours established business groups. Even where, as in India, explicit policies aimed at curbing monopoly are pursued, the large business groups are able to use those policies to their own advantage. For example, licences for industrial investment above a certain limit were supposed to be used as an instrument of planning and of curbing monopoly power. But established business groups used to pre-empt industrial licences, because they were much better-equipped than small businessmen with project reports, credit supply guarantees, etc., and they used the industrial licences as a means of restricting entry into various fields (see GOI, 1969, for details). The attempt to encourage private entrepreneurship in the era of monopoly capital inevitably tends to encourage monopolies in the retarded capitalist societies.

7.6 CONFLICT AND COLLABORATION BETWEEN INDIGENOUS AND FOREIGN BOURGEOISIE

In chapter 2, we argued that, by the very logic of capitalism, late-developing indigenous bourgeoisie in third world countries are brought into a relation of subordination to the bourgeoisie of the advanced capitalist countries. This happens both in the case where the indigenous bourgeoisie originate as collaborating or 'comprador' bourgeoisie, and where pre-existing capitalist strata are overwhelmed by the incursion of a colonial capitalist power. Because of the competition for markets, raw materials and labour, however, conflict between the foreign and indigenous bourgeoisie remains latent, and erupts into an open struggle for control of the state apparatus in the era of world capitalist crisis and world-wide movement for national liberation.

In the post-Second-World-War period, after an initial phase in which indigenous capital entered some of the areas such as internal banking, wholesale trade, railway transport, plantations and mining, in which foreign capital had been earlier dominant, a technological dependence on foreign capital emerged. In many countries, this went hand in hand with a dependence on the dominant capitalist countries (and partly also the Soviet bloc) for loans and grants to tide over balance of payments problems (see Patnaik, 1972a, and chapters 5 and 9).

Technology in the newer fields of industry such as synthetic drugs, inorganic fertilizers, electronics, electrical equipment, etc., in capitalist countries has come to be the exclusive preserve of a few hundred transnational corporations. Small companies continue to play a part in making innovations, but they are usually absorbed by conglomerate firms who 'develop' and market the innovations (see Kennedy and Thirlwall, 1972, and Freeman, 1974, for surveys of the economics of innovation in advanced capitalist countries). One consequence of the increasing monopolization of techniques by a few transnationals is that, in the third world, even those entrepreneurs who show some capacity for initiative in the field of industrial technology and its marketing are ultimately compelled to enter into (subordinate) collaboration with foreign firms, or face the prospect of elimination.

Thus, for example, in Argentina, Torcuato Di Tella, an Italian immigrant, started out as an innovator (in association with a fellow-Italian, Guido Allegrucci), producing bread-making machines, petrol pumps, and refrigerators (mainly domestic ones). He utilized his personal friendship with the Director of the State oil monopoly, YPF., to expand his petrol-pump producing business. Initially an agent for Wayne Pump, with which he terminated his agreement in 1930 he got his own (and French) pump specifications recognized as the only ones legally permissible. This, of course, antagonized American interests selling pumps. The overthrow of the liberal government of Yrigoyen through a *coup* and the depression of the

1930s, causing, among other things, the end of the automobile boom, adversely affected Di Tella and his firm, SIAM (Di Tella was also the retailing agent of the British oil company, Shell Mex). Di Tella then changed both his product-mix, moving into the production of ice boxes and commercial refrigerators, and his strategy regarding foreign collaboration. In the words of his biographers: 'Two basic policies came increasingly to govern Di Tella's choice of new products: (1) to make machines that required skilled engineers and workers, which Avellaneda [the place at which SIAM's plant was located] possessed and many competitors did not; and (2) to work on models licensed by leading foreign companies rather than risk the costs and delays of experimentation' (Cochran and Reina, 1971, p. 91).

Paradoxically enough, it was when Di Tella's firm acquired some technical expertise in technology-intensive fields and needed a larger market to go on growing that it had to give in to transnational firms. The latter could draw not only on their own large national and global markets and organizations but also on the huge R & D effort massively supported by their national governments. No third world country could match such a research effort within the context of problems defined by capitalism.[5]

In India, there is almost an exact parallel in the story of the house of Kirloskar (Hazari, 1965, and Baldwin, 1959, pp. 284–303). The founder of the house started in business with a bicycle shop at the end of the nineteenth century. He soon added a small workshop which fabricated crude agricultural implements such as ploughs and chaff-cutters. In the interwar period, Kirloskar Brothers moved into the production of oil engines and irrigation pumps, sugarcane crushers, and other products 'within the original company's general field of competence, not so much in the design sense as in the sense of using basic metalworking process with which they had become familiar' (Baldwin, 1959, p. 286). The Second World War affected the production of pumps and engines, since certain imported items were crucial for their manufacture. Near the end of the War, Kirloskar Oil Engines was formed with the collaboration of British Oil Engines; soon after, Kirloskar Electric Company was organized in collaboration with Brush Electricals of Britain. Thereafter, the house of Kirloskar has consistently followed a policy of diversifying their products with the help of technical (and sometimes, financial) collaboration with

5 Di Tella's firm moved into a relationship of subordinate collaboration with Wayne Pump, Nash-Kelvinator, and Westinghouse. This collaboration proved crucial when SIAM expanded into Brazil and Chile.

foreign companies. (The initial stage of their collaboration with Cummins, in the field of manufacture of diesel engines, has been the subject of a detailed study by Baranson, 1967.) The house of Kirloskar, though critically dependent on foreign collaboration, had emerged by 1971 among the top twenty Indian business houses (see CMIE, 1977, table 9.10). Contrariwise, there are many firms whose refusal or inability to enter into foreign collaboration and diversify production into new products has condemned them to stagnation or even extinction in this capitalist world governed by relations of dominance and subordination. (Old drug and pharmaceutical companies in India such as Bengal Chemical and Bengal Immunity which had been founded in a spirit of economic nationalism but then became sick exemplify the destructive logic of capitalism.)

These and similar examples illustrate the limits of self-help in the field of business in third world countries. The retardation of society in the third world necessarily leads to the phenomenon of dependent capitalism. But, of course, because of the inherent contradictions of the system, individual capitalists or even the indigenous capitalist class as a whole try to break away from such dependence at times of crisis (cf. Lauterbach, 1966, chapter VII, and Derossi, 1971, pp. 76–80). In politically independent countries, the manipulation of the state apparatus does to some extent help particular indigenous entrepreneurs, but, as we shall see, transnationals in many countries have successfully used the state apparatus to subordinate the indigenous capitalists of the host country (cf. Evans, 1977).

7.7 NATION STATES, LOCAL BOURGEOISIE AND TRANSNATIONAL CORPORATIONS

Even before the Second World War, major parts of the third world had come to be dominated by transnational companies based in the USA and western Europe. The United Fruit Company controlled the economies and dictated the politics of the 'banana republics' of Central America and the Caribbean; it also had a major stake in Colombia (see Galeano, 1973, pp. 119–29). Unilever, based in Britain and the Netherlands, accounted for a major share of the agricultural exports of West Africa and owned huge plantations in the Belgian Congo. It continues to have large interests in West Africa and Zaire (see Nzimiro, 1975, and Kabala Kabinda, 1975). Oil companies had already spread across several national frontiers long before 1945. Standard Oil, Royal Dutch Shell, Caltex and other giants owned oil fields in Venezuela at one end and Indonesia at the other. They regularly interfered in the internal politics of the oil-producing states, and eliminated any threat to their own interests. In 1953, for example, the Americans openly interfered in Iran, and toppled Mohammed Mossadegh, the nationalist Prime Minister, who had nationalized the Anglo-Iranian Oil Company. By this action, the Americans also stole a march over the British, who were their main imperialist rivals in the Middle East (for a treatment of modern imperialism, see Magdoff, 1968).

By and large, the transnational companies operating in the third world before 1945 were active in mining, plantations, trading and banking. However, manufacturing companies had by then gone transnational in Europe and Canada, with production facilities in many countries. After 1945, transnational manufacturing companies also began to set up factories in the third world. Several factors were decisive in this process. Economies of scale were continually increasing in importance in communications, management, inventory control and finance (Murray, 1972). Furthermore, the attaining of independence by practically all the third world countries and the ushering in of protectionist regimes committed to 'development' meant that transnational companies had to jump tariff barriers and set up production facilities in these countries in order to retain old markets and win new ones.

Since large transnational firms numbered only a few hundred in the world as a whole, the market structure became oligopolistic on a world scale. Not only production but also technology and its development came to be controlled by these few giants. A substantial share of international trade came to consist of movements of raw materials and capital goods between transnational firms or their subsidiaries and the sales of the outputs of such firms to final consumers or other firms constituted another major share. Movements of hot money and long-term capital in response to the global strategies of transnational firms often upset the external balance of developed as well as retarded capitalist countries. The 'transfer prices' used by transnational firms for valuing goods and services flowing between their branches or subsidiaries have no relation to costs, and are not market prices at which any quantities can be bought by an outside buyer (Vaitsos, 1974, chapters 6 and 7).

Meanwhile, third world governments were engaged in various plans and public expenditure programmes, which had the aim of accelerating economic growth. Some states also invested in manufacturing enterprises on a large scale. Such policies generally helped both indigenous and foreign enterprises. In fact, in many cases such policies ultimately helped the foreign firms more (see Galeano, 1969, and Baer, Kerstenetzky and Villela, 1973).

Third world governments have tried in some cases to curb the power of foreign enterprises by regulatory measures, such as industrial licensing, monitoring of foreign collaboration agreements, etc. They have also sought help from the Soviet bloc, particularly in setting up public sector plants. But powerful international forces have operated on the other side. The IMF and the World Bank from their inception had supported private enterprise, including foreign enterprise, against national governments whenever any major conflict arose. The World Bank set up the International Finance Corporation in 1956, in order to promote the development of private enterprise and the flow of foreign private investment (cf. Konig, 1973). Many governments were specifically penalized for nationalizing foreign enterprises without 'adequate compensation'. The United States government emerged as the dominant capitalist world power and the biggest giver of aid and loans to 'friendly' governments. It championed the cause of private enterprise, channelled funds to American private capital operating abroad, and used other instruments for furthering the ends of foreign enterprise in other countries – generally with the support of the countries organized in the OECD. Through official and unofficial agencies, the advanced capitalist countries also sponsored moves towards organizing regional common markets among the weak capitalist classes of the countries involved, such moves have been seen as part of the strategy of expanding the areas of operation and control of transnational corporations, at the expense of the autonomy of the governments concerned (Girvan and Jefferson, 1973, and Teubal, 1968).

However, the ability of third world countries to fight the power of transnational companies has been impaired not only by the explicit pressure exerted by advanced capitalist countries and their agencies, but also by the inherent contradictions of the dependent capitalism that has grown up in those countries. Indigenous private firms have been unable to set up viable units in industries such as iron and steel, petroleum, etc., that require a great deal of finance. For that reason, and also for strategic reasons, the state has set up steel-making or oil-exploring and refining concerns in countries as diverse as India, Brazil, and Indonesia. These public sector units have often had to depend on foreign firms for technology, particularly because most third world countries recognize international patent rights even though they derive little benefit from patent protection. The transnational firms also find that public sector units can raise resources on a scale which is beyond the capacity of indigenous private firms. So in India, in the 'joint sector', and in Brazil, under the *tri-pé* arrangements, we find the state, private sector, and foreign firms collaborating in the same project, with the transnationals often calling the tune. (For data on the incidence of foreign collaboration in the public sector and the restrictive clauses imposed by foreign firms in India, see RBI, 1974, chapters 2 and 6; for *tri-pé* arrangements in Brazilian petrochemicals industry, see Evans, 1977).

In chapter 9, we shall see how, in Turkey, promotion of industry through the public sector as such has failed to deliver the country from the toils of retarded capitalism. In Brazil, under Getulio Vargas and Juscelino Kubitschek, enormous amounts of public investment went into the development of roads, public utilities, city-building, and into basic and capital goods sectors supplying inputs to other industries, such as iron and steel, and electricity generation. Such investment, and state protection to industry, made Brazil a more attractive field for foreign capital penetration. In the electricity industry, a scheme of division of labour sprang up: the state bore the brunt of the investments in production facilities and the foreign countries assumed charge of distribution (Tendler, 1968).

When the military regime took over in 1964, the foreign enterprises soon utilized their superior financial position and the special privileges granted by the government to foreign capital – for example, allowing foreign enterprises to have direct access to the international capital market where local capital was denied such access – to gobble up many Brazilian firms and industries. Thus a situation came about in which many of the big industries were divided between foreign and public sector enterprises, with the foreign enterprises controlling the most profitable industries (Baer, Kerstenetzky and Villela 1973). Foreign firms were also given fantastic concessions and American financiers like Daniel Ludwig, bought up whole counties in the interior of Amazonia, at the expense of the poor Brazilians, particularly the Amerindians.

7.8 AUTHORITARIANISM AND UNSTABLE REGIMES IN THE THIRD WORLD

The majority of third world countries are ruled by some variety of authoritarian regimes. These authoritarian regimes are toppled at irregular intervals by other authoritarian regimes. There have been some countries (for example, Chile) which had long histories of formally democratic regimes. But faced with a real threat to their own power, the ruling classes conspired to overthrow the formal democracy and replace it by an authoritarian regime generally ruled by the army. In other cases, a formal democracy continues along with systematic or sporadic repression of popular revolts (this would be true of Turkey, Sri Lanka and India).

The so-called instability of governments in the third world arises from several phenomena acting together or singly; (a) the weakness of the ruling classes – particularly capitalists – in relation to advanced capitalist countries, and foreign capital, (b) the lack of homogeneity among the ruling classes and consequent intra-coalition conflicts, and (c) the revolts of the ordinary people stemming from the inability of the rulers to ensure the availability of the basic amenities of the people.

That foreign capital can cause instability of the local regimes, where the native ruling classes are weak, has been long recognized (Kling, 1968, Lattimore, 1960, Schmitt, 1970). Apart from the classic case of China in the nineteenth century, there were the republics of Central America where US marines toppled regimes that big US companies or the US government disliked and installed more 'loyal' dictatorial regimes. Even when foreign capital does not intervene directly, the local contenders for power are often eager to show that they are more sympathetic towards the claims of legitimate business and thus curry favour with the foreigners. (On the influence exercised by British capital on Argentine politics without explicit intervention by the British government, see Rock, 1975).

In a world dominated by a few advanced capitalist countries, naturally, big foreign powers with aid and military hardware at their command act as the ultimate sanction of authority for many regimes. These regimes tend to be authoritarian, because they are legitimized by force rather than popular support, and because foreign powers and capitalists seek to ensure the security of their own interests through the centralization of the locus of authority in the client state.

But the ruling classes generally form a coalition, and hence, whether in a formal democracy or in an authoritarian regime, there are latent conflicts. The capitalists themselves may belong to different regional, linguistic, religious or ethnic groupings, and each section contends for supremacy in the national market. Then the capitalists with their major base in industry may want to override landowners with their major interest in high agricultural prices and rents. Such conflicts will break out into open intra-coalition struggles and one section of the coalition comes to control the apparatus of repression and gain certain advantages at the expense of other sections of the coalition.[6]

Authoritarian regimes, as such, are not necessarily unpopular.

6 See, for example, Keyder's explanation of the imposition of a military regime in Turkey between March 1971 and October 1973 (Keyder, 1979).

Many authoritarian regimes have explicitly tried to build bases among the people and have claimed to represent the popular will better than earlier regimes. In Nasser's Egypt, Peron's Argentina, or Sukarno's Indonesia, the regime explicitly sought the support of the urban poor and petty bourgeoisie including shopkeepers, professional classes, etc., and the general mass of the peasantry (Worsley, 1973, Kalecki, 1972b). Coming in the wake of excessively inefficient regimes or foreign rules these governments tried to use the state apparatus to provide for the unemployed, redistribute incomes towards the poor in rural and urban areas, promote the growth of industry and education, and minimize the influence of foreign capital.

But none of these regimes really tried to destroy the power of top bureaucrats or propertied classes and take their countries out of the network of dominance–dependence relationships inherent in world capitalism. Soon they were caught up in the contradictions of retardation, and were unable to meet the minimum needs of the poor in respect of employment, education or even subsistence. Decision-making remained concentrated among the upper bureaucrats, army officers, and businessmen who knew how to utilize the state apparatus to their own advantage. These decision-makers continued to repress trade unions or autonomous peasant organizations even when 'Arab socialism' or 'African socialism' was the official regime.

After some initial successes, such as Nasser's triumphant nationalization of the Suez Canal in 1956, or Sukarno's eviction of the Dutch capitalists of Indonesia, the populist regime inevitably runs into crisis. Moreover, through its own policies it augments the power of bureaucrats, military personnel and private businessmen. When these elements fear that the whole system might be overturned by a genuine popular revolt, they either overthrow the regime through an explicit *coup*, as in Sukarno's Indonesia, or stage a silent coup, as in the case of the reversal of Nasser's policies by his successor, President Sadat. Of course, in the overthrow of the populist regimes, foreign abetting and help has played an important role. But the ground for the coup was laid by the failures of the populist regimes.

The military–authoritarian regimes succeeding populist and democratic regimes have generally enjoyed the support of the educated middle classes as well as that of capitalists or landowners threatened with the loss of power (Nun, 1968). Technically qualified personnel working for these regimes have not been able to solve problems whose solution requires a drastic change in the social structure.[7] However,

7 Hirschman, 1968, put forward the fallacious notion that, when the capitalists of the third world failed to overcome the contradictions of import-substituting industrialization, technocrats could somehow take their place and master the difficulties.

technocrats and social scientists trained in US universities have played an important role in running the extremely repressive regimes of Indonesia under General Suharto and Chile under General Pinochet (see Ransom, 1974 and Frank, 1975).

The military–authoritarian regimes succeed in repressing popular discontent and forcibly containing intra-coalition conflicts, at least for a while. But do they succeed in much else, such as distributing incomes more equitably, pushing up the rate of growth or fostering the development of a more nationally-orientated capitalist class? In East Asia, as we have discussed in chapter 5, Hong Kong, Singapore, Taiwan and South Korea have become enclaves in which firms and capitalists from many countries escape many of the regulations of their home countries and utilize the cheap local labour. Their rates of growth have been higher than those of most third world countries. But their aggregate population in mid-1975 was only 59.1 million as against 71.3 million for Pakistan, or 135.2 million for Indonesia, not to speak of 620.4 million for India (WB, 1978, table 1.) Moreover, though there is a Chinese business community linking most of these enclaves they remain greatly dependent for technology, markets and to lesser extent, finance on Japan, the USA and the European Common Market.

Among the Latin American countries on which military–authoritarian regimes have been imposed, only Brazil recorded a fast rate of growth between 1968 and the early 1970s. Much of this growth was triggered off by foreign investment. The foreign firms, many of them transnational corporations, found in the under-populated interior provinces of Brazil a new frontier (they treated the Amerindians in Brazil almost the same way as US frontiersmen had treated the Amerindian peoples of the USA), and in the repressive apparatus of the military *junta* an assurance that workers and peasants would be kept on a tight leash. The massive investment in infrastructure under the earlier, democratic regimes of Kubitschek and Goulart had made private investment more profitable. Moreover, over the initial years of the military regime, 1964–67, there was stagnation in the economy. Later investment could also take account of this slack. The wage-control policies of the military regime, combined with their other policies for rewarding the private investor, led to income concentration among the top ten per cent and created a potentially large market for consumer durables. Besides, state enterprises proved able and willing to collaborate with foreign capital and came to replace domestic private enterprises as the major partner of transnationals (Evans, 1977). In fact, as far as private Brazilian capital was concerned, there was substantial denationalization of Brazilian industry (Galeano, 1969, Baer, 1973, and Baer, Kerstenetzky and Villela, 1973). After 1975, Brazil has piled up a huge debt to financial institutions abroad, and the rate of growth has come down to 4 per cent or so. Very recently, there are signs that a limited degree of liberalization of the regime is under way, probably under pressure from some sections of technocrats who regard the extreme degree of repression as counter-productive and fraught with dangers of revolution.

The Brazilian case cannot be used either as an illustration of the state apparatus for fostering a 'national capitalism' (see De Barros and Graham, (1978) or as a replicable model for promoting economic growth even within Latin America (O'Donnell, 1978). For, if anything, it is foreign capital which has benefited most, in association with domestic state enterprises which have played a major role in a regime avowedly wedded to the principles of private enterprise. And few other Latin American countries can offer the kind of attraction for foreign capital that Brazil has offered. Pinochet's Chile, for example, has become a byword for extreme repression and stagnation.[8]

Many of these military–authoritarian regimes continue to depend on the USA and the countries of the western bloc, and, much more rarely, on countries of the Soviet bloc, for military hardware, aid, advice and diplomatic relations. However, the current economic and political crises in the countries of the Western bloc have rendered them less willing to support these regimes. Furthermore, as the overthrow of the Shah of Iran demonstrates, even apparently invulnerable power structures can be destroyed like a cardboard box by popular anger. Such possibilities have alerted the World Bank and other watchdog agencies of advanced capitalism to the necessity of a greater degree of diffusion of the results of growth among ordinary people. But even with the Green Revolution, the rates of growth in the third world remain very low. So redistribution cannot be effected in most countries without hurting the interests of the entrenched rich. Nor can growth be speeded up in all countries without demolishing the capitalist network of dominance and dependence under which the mechanisms of growth in some countries or regions create conditions of retardation in other countries or regions.

The aid-giving agencies and their client governments are essential

8 Our concentration on openly repressive societies is not meant to suggest that in parliamentary regimes open repression of the working class or peasantry is absent. Police forces have used brutal violence and killed hundreds of persons, in such 'democratic' regimes as Sri Lanka, India and Pakistan under Bhutto (for examples of use of police and upper class violence in India, see Sen, Panda and Lahiri, 1978). But in authoritarian regimes, even the right of protest or organization in defence of the under-privileged is taken away.

links in this chain of causation which can only be broken by a drastic social change. The spread of the Green Revolution technology, and the push by transnationals into third world agriculture, will aggravate the contradictions in the third world and further proletarianize the peasantry. The new ideology of the World Bank emphasizing agriculture and small-scale industries as a means of fighting poverty in the third world will inhibit the nationalistic programmes of industrialization in the third world, without either speeding up growth or eradicating poverty. Meanwhile, third world governments dependent on the Western bloc for loans and aid are hamstrung in their bargaining with transnationals for control of technology and vital sectors of their national economies.

At one stage, aid from the Soviet bloc helped some third world countries, such as India and Algeria, to withstand the more extreme types of blackmail by the advanced capitalist countries. But the Soviet bloc has become greatly dependent on the Western capitalist countries for supply of technology in vital areas (such as petrochemicals and electronics), and the ability of the socialist countries to aid the third world countries has not kept in step with the needs of the latter. Further problems have surfaced because of the suspicion of many third world countries that the distribution of gains of direct and indirect trade of the third world with the Soviet bloc may have been skewed in favour of the Soviet bloc countries (Chandra, 1977). In any case, the mode and the efficiency of utilization of aid, received from whatever source, depend more on the internal socio-political structure of the country than on the intentions of the aid-giver. Soviet aid given to China in the 1950s was almost certainly more productive than it would have been if the same aid had been given to a retarded society ruled by a coalition of landlords, dependent capitalists, bureaucrats and military leaders. For the third world countries, the real significance of the existence of socialist countries lies in the hope that they too can change their destiny through revolution.

In the meantime, most people in the third world remain poor. Some third world countries, with generally rather small populations, have experienced a substantial rate of growth in recent years (WB, 1978). But many of them have been caught up in the general crisis of the world capitalist economy, and have piled up large external debts, and their rates of growth are tending to slow down. In many fast-growing countries, high rates of growth have been attained at the cost of the misery of large masses of people, and in fast- or slow-growing countries alike, benefits of development have been slow to trickle down to substantial sections of the people. So far, reforms within the present system have done little to overcome or ameliorate such contradictions.

8

POPULATION GROWTH AND THE QUALITY OF LIFE IN THE THIRD WORLD

8.1 INTRODUCTION

Many politicians and publicists have long voiced their concern about the harmful effects of population growth in poor countries, and many have attributed their poverty either to a large absolute population or to a high rate of population growth. This voicing of concern became a chorus among many so-called development economists in the wake of the Second World War, when a noticeable acceleration in the rate of growth of population was observed in almost all countries of the third world. These development economists have been joined by those who see the quality of life on this 'spaceship earth' threatened by the consequences of unrestrained population growth (see, for example, Ward and Dubos, 1973).

In this chapter we shall be concerned mainly with the issue of the consequences of population growth for economic development in the third world, and leave aside the issue of population growth and quality of life in relatively affluent countries.[1] We shall begin with a very brief summary of the history of population growth in the third world since the nineteenth century.

1 World population growth and attempts of the poor countries to imitate the development patterns of the affluent countries have been viewed as grave threats to scarce resources, and, particularly, to the very limited reserves of fossil fuels and other currently exploitable energy sources of the world. In order to put the problem in proper perspective and to underscore the primary responsibility of the affluent countries in causing the present strain on energy resources, it is only necessary to point out that well over half of the commercial energy consumption of the world is accounted for by the minority of the population belonging to the OECD countries (see CMIE, 1979). The oil-poor third world countries are in an extremely precarious position. Their access to oil is severely limited by their poverty, and their ability to develop alternative sources of energy is limited by their technological backwardness and by the propensity of their ruling classes to adopt the production techniques and the consumption patterns of the affluent countries.

8.2 COMPARATIVE POPULATION GROWTH RATES SINCE 1800

One very striking fact about nineteenth-century population growth is that the people of European stock then increased at a faster rate than during any other period in their history, whereas the native populations of other continents remained practically constant in number. Among the third world regions, only Latin America recorded a sizeable growth in population. However, migration from southern Europe to Argentina and Brazil accounted for much of this growth (Glass and Grebenik, 1965). It is only since 1900, and more particularly since 1930, that the rate of growth of the third world population overtook that of the population in Europe and North America (excluding Mexico) (Bairoch, 1975, chapter 1). Even so, the rate of growth of people of European stock between 1750 and 1950 was far higher than that of the rest of world population. In the words of Kuznets,

> people of European stock increased from about 150 million in 1750 to about 800 million in 1950, a rise of 433 per cent; whereas the rest of the world's population grew from about 580 million to about 1,600 million, or less than 200 per cent. An alternative calculation shows that the population of the European countries that are now fully developed (Germany, France, the United Kingdom excluding Ireland, the Scandinavian countries, Belgium, and the Netherlands), combined with North America and Oceania, rose from 59 million in 1950 to about 372 million in 1950, or over 500 per cent; whereas population in the rest of the world rose from 669 to 2,137 million, respectively, or slightly over 200 per cent (Kuznets, 1966, p. 36).

However, it is true that after 1940 the population of the third world as a whole has been growing at a faster rate than the population of either the advanced capitalist or socialist countries. And in major regions of the third world the rate of population growth seemed even to be accelerating up to 1970. Demographers had modelled a 'theory of demographic transition' on the basis of the experience of the advanced capitalist countries. According to this theory, with the onset of industrial revolution, the mortality rate falls as a result of improvements in diet, public health facilities and personal hygiene. With constant fertility rates, the rate of population growth accelerates. After a time, as a result of rapid industrialization and urbanization, the birth rate begins to decline. When the gap between the mortality and fertility rates narrows down, the population growth slows down. If the fertility rate falls further, the net population growth rate may approach zero or even become negative.

There is controversy about the exact reasons for the first phase of acceleration in population growth rates in western Europe. Furthermore, the population growth rate has not shown a uniformly declining trend in all affluent countries (see McKeown, Brown and Record, 1972, and Razzell, 1974). However that may be, this model does not fit the experience of the third world in some major respects. Population growth has not been accompanied by industrialization in most poor countries. Fall in mortality in such countries was not caused by a rise in private living standards nor even by an improvement in public health facilities and sanitation. It seems rather to have been caused by spectacular advances in the medical technology for controlling such bacterial diseases as malaria, smallpox and cholera (Meegama, 1967 and Gray, 1974). What alarmed many publicists was that in most third world countries, declines in mortality were not accompanied or even followed by, declines in fertility. Thus transition to the final phase of population growth rates seemed to be only a remote possibility. This provided one of the most potent arguments for introducing governmentally sponsored birth control programmes in all, or practically all, third world countries (see, for example, Meier, 1971, pp. 589–93).

In fact, there are clear signs of transition to a phase of declining fertility and population growth in many third world countries. In several countries of east Asia, such as Taiwan, Hong Kong, Singapore, and, most important of all, China, fertility has come down substantially since the 1960s. In Argentina and Uruguay, the fertility levels have been close to those of western Europe and the USA for some years (Schultz, 1969). In some recent studies of Latin American and Caribbean countries, it has been found that, not only Argentina and Uruguay, but also Chile, Cuba, Costa Rica, Barbados, Puerto Rico, Trinidad and Tobago recorded relatively low birth rates (less than 30 per thousand) in recent years and that, moreover, the 'demographic transition' seems to be occurring much more rapidly than in the corresponding phase of the affluent countries (Oechsli and Kirk, 1975, Stycos, 1978). Even the state of Kerala in India, whose income per head was probably below the all-India average until recently, seems to be experiencing a rapid fall in fertility levels (Panikar, Krishnan, and Krishnaji, 1977). The crude birth rate in Kerala declined from well above 40 in the 1940s to 28 in 1975. A World Bank study has found that the rate of growth of the Indian population, which had reached a peak level of 2.3 per cent in the 1960s has fallen below 2 per cent and is expected to go down to 1.6 per cent in the late 1980s (*Economic Times*, 8 June 1980).

In general, a relatively long and unbroken period of decline in mortality rates seems to have preceded a sustained fall in birth rates. For example, over the period 1900–60, death rates in Kerala were consistently lower than in the rest of India. By 1972, the Keralan death rate had come down to 9.20 per 1,000 as against the national average of 16.09. The level of literacy – particularly among women – is far higher in Kerala than in the other states of India. Kerala is characterized by a high rate of literacy, a low per capita income but apparently a low proportion of people below the poverty line.[2] The case of Costa Rica also pinpoints the importance of education and of increased social contact between couples adopting family planning measures and others in lowering fertility (Stycos, 1978). Her case provides a clue as to why a rise in average per capita incomes as such may not have a noticeable effect in reducing fertility rates in the third world, if the conditions of the poor do not improve at the same time. Without an improvement in the income prospects or life expectations of the poor, the poor will have neither the incentive nor the means for planning their family sizes.

8.3 FACTORS INFLUENCING FERTILITY

Decisions by individuals about the number of children they would like to have are not all explicable in terms of narrowly economic factors. The place of the parents in the class structure of the society concerned, and the general level of health care would normally influence such decisions (see Espenshade, 1972, for a survey of socio-economic theories of fertility). In general, the lower the chances of the offspring surviving to adulthood, the more reluctant the parents are likely to be to adopt birth control measures. Contrariwise, a big drop in mortality – particularly infant mortality – may lead to a *fall* in the net rate of population growth, because of the stimulus it may provide for family planning (see Rao, 1976). Thus poverty and associated insecurity of health and life can be a direct cause of a high birth rate.

While the majority of the people in the third world are poor and insecure, there are differences between classes regarding desired family size. Professional persons with high levels of education and expecting to incur high levels of expenditure on their children's education will be motivated to limit their families. Among the landless agricultural labourers or the floating, casually employed labour force in urban

2 The poverty line is usually defined as the income which just allows an average person to satisfy his basic nutritional needs. The conventional measures of poverty found the proportion of the Keralan population below the poverty line to be as high as 80 per cent or more in the 1960s, but a careful study of the economy of Kerala found less than 40 per cent of the people living in poverty (UN, 1975).

areas, any addition to the family may be welcome or at least costless – particularly from the father's point of view. For, among them, even a child of five may earn its keep by tending goats, cattle and other livestock, by serving as domestic help, or as sweated labour in shops and factories. Infant mortality is particularly high among these classes, so that parents will be right to rate the chance of survival of an individual child rather low. However, once the child reaches adulthood, it has little economic reason (such as stems from property ties) for keeping within the parents' family. Thus, the effective size of the family among the poor is generally smaller than among the propertied classes.

Sizes of rural families are found to vary positively with land holding sizes. If agriculture is labour-intensive, and shortage of labour develops at peak periods, a farmer will gain from being head of a large family (Mamdani, 1976). Again, where control over property and people is important (as in the case of landlords, traders and industrialists) and the family remains the basic network for gathering information and transmitting decisions, a large-sized family confers an advantage on the controlling group (Rao, 1976). In India, Pakistan and many other underdeveloped countries, the family remains the controlling thread for the concentration of economic power (cf. Bagchi, 1972a and White, 1974).

There is some evidence that, among propertied people, family partition takes place at a later stage of an individual's life-cycle than in the case of the propertyless. This also contributes to the positive relation between landholdings and family size.

Where the preferences of different groups in a class society are so different, how is a policy of strict family limitation, even if it is considered socially desirable, to be enforced?

Some advocates of family planning would want state action and at least indirect coercion. For, according to their way of looking at things, population growth is one of the biggest impediments against development in the third world and the benefits conferred by birth control are very great. It is necessary now to look more closely at the likely effects of population growth on economic development.

8.4 RELATION OF POPULATION GROWTH AND ECONOMIC DEVELOPMENT

The growth of population is part of the whole process of change in society. It is difficult to separate out its effects from those of the existing or changing relations of production, and we are not going to attempt that task. Instead, we shall critically evaluate some propositions about what are considered to be the unambiguous effects of population growth.

Much of the recent work emphasizing limits to economic growth (see, for example, Meadows et al., 1972; and for critiques see Cole, Freeman, Jahoda and Pavitt, 1972, and Nordhaus, 1973) and the harmful effects of population growth in poor countries generally take the total resources or the volume of investment to be given. Such writings derive from the work of T. R. Malthus' *Essay on the Principle of Populations as it Affects the Future Improvement of Society*, first published in 1798. This work was really based on the misleading truism that if resources are given, the more people there are, the less there is to go round for each person. Malthus' work was also based on the assumption that, wherever human beings obtain more than mere subsistence, their numbers go up, until everybody is back at the level of subsistence. From this followed a conclusion which has been very comforting to the ruling classes of unequal societies, viz. that there is no point in trying to improve the condition of ordinary people, for it will only end up in more people being poor.

This second assumption has been already falsified in the affluent countries (where wage rates have risen along with falling rates of fertility and population growth) and is on its way to being falsified in many third world countries (such as the East Asian countries, the Caribbean and several Latin American countries and even parts of India). Furthermore, man has found new resources (bronze in place of stone, iron in place of bronze, coal in place of timber, water power in place of human power) to suit his needs as numbers have gone on increasing. Taking the restricted field of agriculture alone, it has been found that increasing numbers stimulated a change from hunting to slash-and-burn cultivation, then to long-fallow cultivation and finally to short-fallow cultivation, increasing the output per unit of land, at the cost of more labour spent on producing the crops. The sequence might have varied from region to region but the picture of increasing output with increasing numbers seems to be generally valid (Boserup, 1965; see also Simon, 1977, chapters 5 and 7).

We find that in recent years also food production has kept pace with population growth in the third world as a whole. Even in densely populated Kerala, with a high rate of population growth between 1900 and 1960, there was no fall in the standard of living of the people (Panikar, Krishnan and Krishnaji, 1977). There are countries plagued by food shortages, and food imports of the third world are rising fast, but the main problem here is that of maldistribution of purchasing power within, and between, countries. It has been argued that growth in population stimulates innovations and permits economies of scale in production over time (Simon, 1977, chapters 2 and 4). Even if we discount the applicability of such general theories to the densely populated regions of the third world, there are many countries in Africa and Latin America where the sparseness of population necessitates too much investment in social overhead facilities per head and impedes development. For example, Tanzania's programme of 'villagization' aims at concentrating people in villages and stimulating their co-operative, or at least, mutually interrelated, activities.

Another favourite argument of proponents of population control as the supreme developmental instrument in the third world is that a high fertility rate leads to a high ratio of children below working age to the total population (this ratio is called the dependency ratio). This puts a pressure on current resources and results in a lower rate of saving since more current income has to be spent on maintaining and educating the children.

Such an argument might have some validity in a socialist economy where existing resources are fully utilized, wasteful consumption is minimized, and all savings are invested, and where roughly equal amounts of private and social goods are supplied to all people (except for age or sex differences). But it has little validity elsewhere. First, in actual capitalist economies, available resources are not fully utilized and there is avoidable excess capacity and unemployment. Secondly, there is an enormous amount of wasteful consumption. In third world economies, society does not provide enough schools and medical facilities for the poor, so that it is difficult to argue that population growth makes a large dent on social savings. (The evidence on the relation of savings to dependency ratios is not at all clear-cut. In India, for example, the savings rates and the dependency ratio rose together in the 1960s and 1970s. For a summary of the debate on this issue, see Mikesell and Zinser, 1973). Under the peculiarly contradictory conditions of third world societies, it is possible that an abrupt slowing down of population growth will worsen problems of shortage of effective demand for mass consumption goods (such an effect, of course, is more probable in the affluent capitalist countries).

If a more effective use is to be made of potential savings in the third world with a view to population control, more expenditure on schools and hospitals may well lead to a transition to lower fertility and a slower population growth rate. For education, particularly women's education, has been found to lead to lower fertility in most cases and decreased infant mortality may provide the parents with an incentive for family limitation.

8.5 SENSE AND NONSENSE IN THE CASE FOR FAMILY PLANNING

It is easy to agree that, given the strictly limited resources of the world as a whole, global population control is desirable, perhaps with some large-scale migrations between the relatively densely and the relatively sparsely populated regions. But when existing social arrangements lead to blatant misuse of available resources, in the absence of a global population policy it is difficult to argue that, everywhere in the third world, family planning should receive top priority to the exclusion of measures for improving the standard of living of the current generation (especially when many affluent countries pursue a policy of subsidizing large families). This does not mean that all governmental opposition to family planning programmes springs from a concern for the people. It has been argued, for example, that in Brazil a high rate of population growth is an instrument in the hands of the ruling classes for keeping wages low, and this phenomenon may well explain the lack of enthusiasm of the military *junta* for family planning programmes (Daly, 1970). However, if the poor of the third world are to control their numbers, they must be induced to do so through education and a progressive improvement in their expectation of and from life, and not through authoritarian solutions, rationalized by apparently sophisticated cost–benefit analyses.

In one variant of the cost–benefit analysis (Enke, 1966), the present value of the product expected from adding another member to the labour force is compared with the present value of the expected consumption of the new entrant over his lifetime. At the discount rates used, the latter is found to far exceed the former (the consumption in the years 1–15 gets a larger weight, the higher is the discount rate). Hence, naturally, the 'net benefit' of a birth prevented (= present value of consumption of the marginal worker – the present value of the output of that worker) is found to be far above the cost of introducing the usual birth control devices. The acceptance of such an analysis would dictate spending most of the investible funds on family planning programmes not only in the third world but also in developed capitalist countries. Even if such a programme were feasible in a perfectly controllable socialist economy, it would almost certainly lead to severe dislocation of the actual capitalist (or even socialist) economies of today's world.

The argument has been alternatively cast in the form of macroeconomic projections, but they do not generally take account of the kinds of objections against equating potential with actual saving (= investment) we have raised earlier; nor do they admit the possibility of innovations resulting from the pressure of population growth, even in the long run. Julian Simon, who was earlier a practitioner of the art of cost–benefit analysis of family planning programmes has recanted (Simon, 1977, preface). Objections have been raised against the rejection of private preferences and the neglect of class differences in motives and effects of birth control implied in these analysis (Leibenstein, 1969, and Blandy, 1974). But aid-giving agencies often give high priority to adoption of governmentally sponsored family planning programmes and sometimes even insist on them as a precondition for aid for other programmes.

Our arguments are not meant to support a blanket case against family planning programmes. Rather, family planning programmes should start from the *felt* needs of the people. And, for such a situation to come about, it is necessary that people should be well nourished and possess a reasonable chance of survival to an adult working life and beyond. The success of family planning programmes is also vitally dependent on improvement of women's position in society. For women to want to plan their families and to be able to do so it is necessary that they should be educated and that they can take major decisions about work and life without always being subject to the dictates of tradition or a patriarchal family set-up. Thus family planning programmes need to be embedded in a wider programme for education, health care and liberation of women.

When governments try to introduce family planning programmes cheaply by concentrating only on the spread of contraceptive devices, their efforts are often met by the passive resistance of the people. There have been some cases, as in India in 1975 and 1976, where the government has adopted brutal methods for propagating birth control. Not only has such a course of action meant repression of the peasantry and the workers, it has often resulted in a major setback for the family planning programme (cf. Banerji, 1977).

8.6 PLANNING FOR NUTRITION AND HEALTH CARE IN THE THIRD WORLD

Any rational plan for limiting the rate of population growth must include a plan for feeding the people adequately and taking care of their health. A very large proportion of the people of the third world are ill-nourished – in countries such as Bangladesh or India, a majority of the people may be suffering from malnutrition. Malnutrition and ill-health are the direct products of the system of inequality spawned by international capitalism – an inequality which is both inter- and intranational in character. While millions of people in the third world do not get the root crops or cereals needed to supply their basic calorie needs, millions of tons of good grain are used as fodder for the production of animal foods consumed by the rich in affluent countries (this would apply also to the livestock economy of the Soviet Union). As we have seen in earlier chapters, the 'commercialization' of agriculture geared towards export crops has diverted a major part of the resources of the third world from the satisfaction of their own needs to the meeting of the market demand emanating primarily from advanced capitalist countries. (For an overview of world food problems, see Poleman, 1977, and Barraclough, 1977).

In the area of nutrition, the basic deficiency in the third world is that of calories, since the poor peasants and workers cannot buy the minimum quantities needed of their staple foods. There are associated deficiencies in respect of vitamins, proteins, etc. Such deficiencies expose a major part of the children in these countries to debilitating and killing diseases (see Ehrlich and Ehrlich, 1972, pp. 89–92). These deficiencies may even permanently impair the intelligence of children (Rose and Gyorgy, 1970, and Selowsky and Taylor, 1973). However, the solution to such problems is not to have transnationals produce high-cost proteins at the expense of the daily food of the poor, but to find locally producible foods that can be sold cheaply, and in adequate quantities, to the poor (for the story of how soybean processing by American transnationals in Brazil and fishing by Norwegian companies in Kerala priced proteins out of the reach of the local consumers, see George, 1977).

Inducing the poorer countries to produce more proteins or implementing special programmes for giving nutritious foods to selected children or nursing mothers will be cosmetic remedies without changes in income distribution and social customs that will permit the poor to buy basic foods. As it is, in many Latin American countries (see Dumont, 1965) thousands of hectares are devoted to ranches for breeding livestock, while the poor peasants do not have enough land to raise basic foods, and the country suffers from food shortage. Stress on special types of food in this situation will merely help the big firms, particularly transnationals, to push their particular products and further damage the interests of the poor. (The promotion of babyfood by transnationals in African countries is said to have damaged the health of children and mothers since the latter stopped breastfeeding their babies while depriving themselves of basic foods in order to buy the costly babyfood sold by the transnationals.) A more sensible solution can be found by producing the basic foods (mostly cereals, rootcrops and vegetable proteins) in adequate quantities and ensuring that all the people can buy them (see Ramachandran, 1977).

What applies to the solution of food problems also applies, with only minor modifications, to problems of protection against disease. The decline in mortality in the third world countries since the Second World War is widely attributed to the control of malaria through the spraying of DDT and other pesticides, and to elimination of other killer diseases through the widespread use of antibiotics (Meegama, 1967). However, a large proportion of the population of these countries continues to suffer from various enfeebling diseases and the infant mortality rates in many Asian and African countries continue to be high (Cassen, 1976, Rado and Sinha, 1977). It is ironic that while India and Pakistan continue to suffer from shortage of western-educated doctors and nurses, they export trained doctors to the UK and other advanced capitalist countries in large numbers. (This is part of the wider problem of 'brain drain' from the third world to western Europe, the USA and Canada.) Most of the patents for the newer drugs for controlling disease are held by transnationals based in the USA, UK, Switzerland and Western Germany (Mansfield et al., 1972, chapter 8), and these transnationals exact high prices for selling the drugs to the third world (cf. Vaitsos, 1974). Efforts to monitor the pricing policies of these companies in such countries as India and Argentina have at best met with limited success so far. The lack of faith of the general run of western-trained doctors in alternative remedies or courses of treatment and the need of the rich of the third world for the remedies for obesity or stress-related diseases familiar in the affluent countries are not the least of the obstacles against the adoption of effective measures for controlling transnational corporations and for finding more widely diffusible remedies.

Meanwhile, it has been found that the bacteria causing the spread of killer diseases are becoming immune to pesticides and the malaria that was supposed to have been eradicated earlier is re-appearing in an epidemic form (FER, 1978). Whether or not one believes with Harry Cleaver (1977) that the concern of the watchdog organizations of capitalism for the crisis in healthcare systems in the third world just now may be rather lukewarm because labour is abundant in comparison with the needs of capitalism in crisis, there is little doubt that third world countries will have to find more ecologically sound and less costly remedies if the mortality and morbidity rates are to be brought down to acceptable levels. What will be needed in these countries is ever-vigilant control over the environment (including water supply, the degree of air pollution etc.) and advances in medical technology and treatment procedures adapted to local needs. However, the present social organization and the unholy alliance between powerful drug companies, governmental health departments and western-educated professional classes pose a serious obstacle to the adoption of such sensible solutions for the health and nutrition problems in the third world.

8.7 SOIL EROSION, SALINITY AND FLOODS

Both the quality of life in cities and villages and the productivity of man and land are greatly influenced by the way the forests, rivers and land are used and the way cities grow up. Under the prevalent system of production for private profit, individuals, business firms and even governments are allowed to pass on many of the ill-effects of their activities to other people (what economists call 'external diseconomies'). The result is all too frequently a ravaged landscape, a cancerous growth of big, dirty, smoke-filled cities, and polluted rivers, lakes and seas.

As far back as 1867, Marx had referred to the characteristic social irrationality of agriculture under capitalism: 'all progress in capitalistic agriculture is a progress in the art, not only of robbing the labourer, but of robbing the soil; all progress in increasing the fertility of the soil for a given time is a progress towards ruining the lasting sources of that fertility' (Marx, 1887, p. 506). Such behaviour has often resulted in devastated landscapes both in developed capitalist countries (cf. the 'dust bowls' of the Midwest in the USA) and in the retarded societies of the third world. We shall be here concerned only with the latter.

Geographers, other scientists and colonial administrators have commented upon the poverty of tropical soils, and the disastrous consequences of allegedly irrational practices on the part of tropical peasants for the fertility of the soil (see, for example, Dumont, 1966, Gourou, 1973, and Hall, 1936). Even a cursory view of the marginal lands on which tribal or semi-tribal people in Africa, Latin America, or central India eke out a living conveys an impression of a rapidly deteriorating environment.

Thus in the upper Damodar valley in India it was found around 1952 that deforestation, over-grazing by domestic livestock, and cultivation of steep inclines had combined to render large areas (which had been covered by forests in the nineteenth century) unfit for cultivation. Forests in this region have been cut down on a large scale for timber ever since it was penetrated by the British. Mica and coal mines were opened up, driving the tribal people from their habitual grounds of food-gathering, hunting and cultivation, and increasing the demand on the forest resources for timber and other products. The original inhabitants were compelled to shorten the fallow periods in their usual pattern of cultivation, and to over-graze the increasingly restricted forest undergrowth and grass lands available to them. The upshot was soil exhaustion and erosion, leaching of soluble nutrients from the subsoil, and formation of gullies. Gullies then expanded at an alarming rate, thus rendering increasing quantities of land uncultivable, and denuding the soil of any cover other than some miserable scrub (Gorrie, n.d.).

Soil erosion on hilly terrain not only damages the productivity of that particular region but also causes havoc in the valley into which streams of rivers from the hills flow. As, more and more silt is carried downstream, the river bed rises over time – sometimes above the level of the surrounding valley, and the whole valley is exposed to frequent flooding. Reservoirs and dams can be built to control the regime of the rivers downstream, but without control of soil erosion upstream, reservoirs get silted up, so that their capacity to moderate floods declines progressively.

The fundamental reason for these phenomena is not population growth or the irrational practices of the tribal people, but irresponsible exploitation of land resources by outsiders. Before Europeans or plainspeople invaded the tribal regions, the local people had generally maintained a system of low-density equilibrium. The European conquerors and other exploiters such as mine-owners, traders and moneylenders interfered with the traditional system of management of land and livestock, took away some of the most valuable land and water resources from the local people, and left them with little or no surplus so that they were unable to make the investment necessary to change over to a new, intensive system of cultivation without damaging their own environment (cf. chapter 6 above).

As we have noted in chapter 6 already, most of the colonial rulers put in little investment or research in agriculture anyway, and what little there was went to serve the interests of European settlers and businessmen and of export crops. In the 1930s, Hall, a British scientist investigating agricultural conditions in Kenya and other British colonies in east Africa found that there were only a few scientific officers in the colonies, that they mostly either did pure research on problems they had been trained to recognize back at home or applied research on crops or methods that were likely to prove valuable for plantations or growers of crops. Hall remarked: 'Research has enabled wheat to be grown in Kenya but I am not conscious of any systematic work on the native millets' (Hall, 1936, pp. 89–90). Similar comments could be made regarding agricultural research in Nigeria or India before independence (cf. Bagchi, 1972a, chapter 4).

After political independence, the focus of agricultural investment or research shifted towards the interest of large farmers or landlords. The people most affected by the invasion of the market, viz. the poor peasants, and tribal people brought into the network of capitalist relations, gained little from such investment or research. The government generally regarded the forests as commercial resources to be exploited jointly by private contractors and the government. In these circumstances, the rural and sylvan environment has often continued to deteriorate through the dual action of the exploiting capitalists and landlords and the desperate struggle of the poor peasants and the landless workers to make their ends meet.[3]

Large-scale public works have often added to the damage caused by individual action. Colonial railways often ran on wood fuel for which vast forests were cut down. Their alignment took little notice of natural drainage channels. This led to the blocking of drainage channels, silting up of rivers and formation of swampy terrain. Frequent flooding, breeding of mosquitoes and the spread of malaria – the biggest killer disease in many parts of the world at one time – were some of the consequences. Similarly, the construction of large-scale irrigation works without adequate provision for drainage in nineteenth-century Egypt led to widespread incidence of the snail-borne disease, *bilharzia* or schistosomiasis, because snails bred in the stagnant channels and their banks. Again, lack of adequate drainage led to problems of waterlogging, salinity and alkalinity in vast tracts irrigated by large-scale irrigation works in India (see Whitcombe, 1972, and Michel, 1973).

Similar experiences have been repeated in many countries in more recent times. In Afghanistan, for example, peasants in the Helmand valley had been using seasonal inundation canals for centuries. In 1946, it was decided to extend irrigation facilities in the valley and the project was handed over to an American firm which would use 'advanced technology' in the form of 'heavy earth-moving equipment, rock-fill dams and reinforced concrete barrages and canal structures' (Michel, 1973, p. 263). The Boghra Canal was opened in 1949, and the irrigation was extended to the hilly terraces. Within four years, the water table rose by 16 feet, mainly because of the impenetrable

3 For the story of the change of the Brazilian North-east from a fertile region with a diversified agriculture to one with monoculture of sugarcane, exhausted soils and a perennially hungry population, see Castro, 1969, and Galloway, 1974.

substratum of the irrigated area. This caused serious problems of salinity, and expensive reclamation projects had to be undertaken for restoring the cultivability of the soil (for other stories of a similar nature, see Dasmann, Milton and Freeman, 1973, chapter 7; Dumont, 1966, chapter 3).

With the coming of the Green Revolution and the introduction of new high-yielding varieties and their accompanying doses of fertilizers and pesticides, many third world regions now suffer seriously from water pollution, depletion of fish-breeding grounds, and lowering of plant resistance to the disease owing to the introduction of plant varieties which are not adapted to the local climate and pests (Cleaver, 1974, Dasmann, Milton and Freeman, 1973, chapter 6). Exotic varieties often prove too delicate and native varieties are neglected; this makes agriculture much riskier, particularly for the poor peasants. Monoculture of the most profitable crops accentuates the evil.

Scientists and technologists are often puzzled by the endless repetition of avoidable errors affecting such vital decisions (Michel, 1973, p. 265). The repetitions are not too difficult to explain if we remember that in the case of the Helmand project, for example, neither the American firm involved nor the Afghan bureaucrats and technologists had to account for their actions to the peasants who were most immediately affected by their decisions.

8.8 URBANIZATION, SLUMS AND POLLUTION

The third world is still largely rural. The percentage of people living in urban areas (defined as agglomerations of 20,000 inhabitants or more) of less-developed countries as late as 1960 was 16.7 per cent whereas the corresponding percentage for Europe was 47.1 (Bairoch, 1975, chapter 8). The proportion of urban dwellers in some Latin American countries such as Argentina and Chile was of the same order of magnitude as in western Europe, so that in fact, in the majority of the third world countries, the proportion of urban to total population could be taken as less than 16 per cent.

Urbanization in the third world is a different type of phenomenon from urbanization in the developed capitalist countries. First of all, starting from a very low proportion of town-dwellers to the population as a whole, urbanization in recent decades in many third world countries has proceeded much faster than urbanization in the industrialized countries when those countries were themselves urbanizing. In contrast to the industrialised countries again, urbanization in the third world (that is, the rate of growth of the proportion of urban to total population) has generally moved faster than industrialization (as measured by the growth in the proportion of workers in secondary industry to the total workforce). Indeed, many countries which have not experienced any significant degree of industrialization at all have still seen a rapid rise in the urban population. This has meant, among other things, the formation of large pools of underemployed or unemployed labour in urban areas, and the swelling of the so-called informal sector. Finally, it is also generally found that the gap between urban and rural earnings or wages is generally considerably higher than the rural–urban earnings or wage gap in North American or Western Europe at the time those regions were in the initial phase of industrialization (Datta, 1952, and Bagchi, 1972b).

The most extreme cases of urbanization are found in Latin America. The percentages of urban population in large urban centres and the rates of transfer of rural people to towns are very high in such countries as Argentina, Chile, Brazil and Colombia (Blakemore and Smith, 1974, table 1.1, and Barraclough, 1970, p. 936). These phenomena have been explained in terms of the colonial heritage and ensuing developments in the nineteenth century. The towns of Spanish America were primarily centres of rule over the surrounding countryside, and wealth and power came to be centred on the towns (Morse, 1964). The Amerindian tribes were broken up and their communities became atomized units isolated from one another. The settlements on or around the haciendas or plantations had little of the solidarity of villages proper.

In the nineteenth century, policies were pursued to break up the surviving Amerindian communities, and the rural settlements became orientated more towards ports and external commerce. The proletarian character of the rural poor was exposed through the dissolution of semi-servile ties of dependence and the spread of capitalist relations. While the growth of large towns exerted a pull on this proletariat, the extremely uneven distribution of land and other means of production acted as a factor pushing the rural poor to the towns.

Many of these migrants have swollen the ranks of poorly remunerated workers in the service sector. The growth of towns and the growth of the tertiary sector have gone hand in hand in many third world countries. However, 'tertiarization' is not *caused* by the growth of towns as such (More, 1971). Even in rural Egypt, a large proportion of the population is found to be working in the service sector; and in India and Indonesia, while the rate of urbanization has been slow, the tertiary sector has grown relatively to the other two sectors.

In the towns, two streams have contributed to the growth of the services sector. The first is the growth of organized banking, trade, etc., and administration and defence services, which help the centralized gathering of the surplus from the economy, and the second is the inflation of the category of residual workers who eke out a living on the margins of society.

The poorly-paid, often self-employed, workers who work in small factories under sweatshop conditions or carry on as street vendors, rag-pickers, porters, casual construction workers, etc., naturally increase the overcrowding of third world cities. Theirs are the shantytowns and the slums that sprawl alongside palatial buildings. In Brasilia, the new, architecturally innovative capital of Brazil, for example, large numbers of people move continually from one squatment to another, because they occupy unauthorized plots, and lack the money or the qualifications to occupy houses in authorized settlements (Epstein, 1973). The residents of the so-called Social Security Invasion either work as sweated labour in factories and shops, or take in work at home as seamstresses, carpenters and so on. The maladorous, overcrowded, insanitary slums (Sen, 1960) are as much part of the exploitation system in the third world as the palaces and suburbs of the rich and the comfortable. Slum clearance projects might beautify the cities and remove the worst eyesores from the ken of the casual tourist, but a radical change in the living conditions of the urban and rural poor will require a radical redistribution of income and assets from the rich to the poor.

The ruling classes of the third world who have so long sustained such an unequal system and who are conscious of having to compete in both international and internal markets with the ruling classes of the affluent countries with their much vaster resources are unlikely to pay much attention to a demand for less industrial pollution, since measures for curbing industrial pollution are often expensive. Even a relatively affluent country such as Japan allowed the Minimata Bay disease to develop unchecked for a number of years, because the alternative would have been costly for the firm responsible for the disaster.[4] Third world governments or public authorities have either

4 Near the tiny fishing village of Minimata, a chemical factory discharged its untreated effluent into the sea. The result was a steep rise in the level of methyl mercury in the sea-fish. People eating the fish were afflicted by a painful disease attacking the nervous system and a quick, or slow, death. The managers of the factory apparently knew of the danger but decided to ignore it because the cost of effluent treatment would have been high (Haggett, 1975, chapter 7).

not insisted on environmental (or even plant-level) safety measures or have enforced them very loosely when these are in existence. In eastern India, for example, the water of the river Damodar, which flows through an industrial and mining belt was found in 1974 to be so polluted as to be unfit for almost any kind of human use (see *Statesman* (Calcutta), 20 December 1974 and 27 September 1975).

The destruction or degradation of the environment in cities or in villages is attributed by economists to external diseconomies of economic activity. It is often argued that such side effects of industrial or agricultural growth can be controlled by regulatory or fiscal and monetary measures, or even by passing laws that allow the people adversely affected to sue the wrong-doers. Such a view has proved to be too optimistic even in affluent countries which can afford large expenditures for reclaiming the environment. In most third world countries, little has actually been attempted in the way of controlling environmental degradation. Environmental damage seems to be the systematic result of the working of the capitalist system, and it can hardly be regarded as an easily remediable side-effect of the working of the market (cf. Hymer and Roosevelt, 1972, p. 652).

Even in normal times, transnationals have paid scant attention to problems of environmental damage. In times of war, the concern of governments of capitalist countries for the protection of enemy territory has been on a par with their concern for the lives of the enemy population – military or civilian. In Vietnam, for instance, the US military authorities systematically set about to destroy the environment by spraying forests and crops with defoliants, using herbicides to kill growing crops and destroying mangrove forests, which play a vital role in sustaining fisheries, and dropping millions of tons of 500 to 700 pound bombs to create a moon landscape, by obliterating villages, forests, fields, dykes, dams, water supply and transport systems (Ehrlich and Ehrlich, 1972; Kehl, 1977). The credibility of any concern about the environment expressed by spokesmen from advanced capitalist countries naturally appears to be rather low to the average citizen of the third world. The alternative is to build environmental protection into a more egalitarian system as the Chinese have sought to do in their planning.

9

PLANNING FOR CAPITALISM IN THE THIRD WORLD

9.1 INTRODUCTION

State intervention as a way of countering western European domination and, if possible, of catching up with the West, has formed part of the middle and upper class ideology of the third world since the days of Mohammed Ali in Egypt. After the collapse of Mohammed Ali's bid for independence under the onslaught of British imperialism, the examples, first of Prussia and then of Japan, acted as beacons to many nationalist leaders of the colonial countries. In 1928, the Soviet Union launched its first five-year plan and, from then on, the desire for state intervention to stimulate economic development became clothed in the demand for planning of economic activities. The desired content of 'planning' has varied from planner to planner; for some, it has simply meant state action in support of private enterprise; for others, it has meant the entry of the state into fields which private enterprise finds it unprofitable to explore and develop; for yet a third segment, it has meant the gradual replacement of private enterprise by collective action and co-ordination of all economic activities according to criteria of social welfare (for expositions of the ideology of state intervention and planning, see Chandra, 1966, and Myrdal, 1970, chapter 15).

The objectives of state intervention have rarely been explicity stated in terms of class interests. It has been generally assumed that the growth of private or public enterprises will benefit not only the businessmen, top executives and others near the centre of power, but also the workers and peasantry through some kind of percolation process. Correspondingly, the apparatus of planning has escaped any analysis in class terms. Planners have often been seen as wise men who can somehow remain above class and political strife. Sometimes, supporters of private enterprise, after watching the disappointing performance of state-aided private enterprise systems, have seized on supposedly supra-class technocrats to execute policies which will advance the general welfare of the people rather than sectional interests (cf. Hirschman, 1968). The working of state intervention and 'planning' in third world economies has also belied these expectations.

In this chapter, we shall take three case studies and discuss the problems which have bedevilled the planning efforts in these cases. Some particular problems will be highlighted in the case of each country. For example, in the case of Turkey, the focus will be on the problem of stimulating private investment through state support in a retarded economy. In the case of India, the problems of raising the rates of saving and investment and, in that connection, the problem of poverty on the one hand and of technological dependence on the other will be brought into focus. In the case of Pakistan, the problems of regional inequality and rapid growth of concentration in industry will be the focus of our attention. This does not mean at all that the other problems do not crop up in the cases mentioned; it is only that the literature on certain particular problems is more abundant in the cases of some countries than those of others – although the majority of the countries are plagued by very similar problems.

9.2 ETATISM IN TURKEY AND ITS GYRATIONS

At the end of the First World War, the empire of Ottoman Turkey broke up. Turkey was saved from complete western domination through the heroism of the Turkish people (who threw out the Greek invaders and the Caliphate). But the new Republic inherited a desperately poor country. Anatolia, that is, Asiatic Turkey, was a sparsely populated land of peasants and shepherds, and Istanbul was the outpost of an empire that had vanished. For the first few years, Kemal Ataturk's government was engaged simply in reconstructing the region ravaged by the Greek invaders. Many of the foreign concessionaires tried to enforce the 'rights' they had obtained by putting pressure on the previous regime. By a special commercial treaty signed in 1924, Turkey had to agree that she would not change customs tariffs or restrictions on imports or exports for five years. Only from 1929 was she free to pursue an independent commercial policy. However, she had to assume the burden of the Ottoman Debt, repayment of which ate up as much as 13–18% of the budget in the 1930s – a proportion that gradually declined to 5%. The nationalization of foreign enterprises in railways, mining, banking, tobacco, etc., involved further financial outlay (for a summary of economic development in Republican Turkey up to 1939, see Hershlag, 1964, part seven).

In the 1920s, very little industrial or agricultural growth took place, although Ataturk established the Is Bank, a private bank under governmental patronage, specifically for the purpose of financing and stimulating industrial growth. This bank established several new industrial enterprises. In spite of the pronounced anti-communist stance of the government, no major foreign investment took place in Turkey either in the 1920s or in the 1930s (with the sole exception of a loan of 10 million gold dollars raised from the Swedish–American concern of Ivar Kreuger). A law was passed in 1927 for the encouragement of industry. It stipulated, among other things, that industrial enterprises above a certain size would enjoy a number of tax concessions and concessions in public utility rates, a government subsidy of up to 10% of annual output, and a guarantee of purchase of their products by government departments and enterprises so long as their price did not exceed that of foreign-made goods by more than 10%.

Despite all the encouragement given to private enterprise, there was very little growth under private auspices, since the Turkish capitalist class was tiny and weak. This class, moreover, had long been habituated to control by the feudal–bureaucratic Caliphate. Turkey was hit hard, in common with other primary producing countries, by the depression of the thirties. On the other side of the Black Sea, the Soviet Union was able to escape the effects of the general capitalist crisis through her socialist planning. These factors induced the ruling People's Republican Party to go in for *etatism*. The first Five Year Plan was announced in 1933, and Turkey received aid from the Soviet Union, the only foreign country to offer her aid. This took the form of a 20-year loan of 8 million gold dollars without interest, training of Turkish students in the Soviet Union, and the despatch of Soviet experts to help establish industrial enterprises (Hershlag, 1964, p. 179). In particular, the Russians helped in the construction of a large textile mill at Kayseri (Hanson, 1959, p. 120). However, neither the class character of the ruling party nor its objectives were changed by its decision to embrace planning. Prime Minister (later President) Inönü, emphasized in 1933 that nationalization of key industries would 'give considerable stimulus to private initiative and capital' (Hanson, 1959, p. 116). The major instruments for state intervention in industry were two government-controlled banks, the Sumerbank and the Etibank (Hanson, 1955, and 1959). Characteristically enough – and as a precursor of things to come – although Turkish planning was inspired by the Soviet example, the plan was drawn up by an American commission (Hershlag, 1964, p. 185). It gave priority to the development of consumer goods industry. The Sumerbank had a wide range of planning and executive functions, and it came to own iron and steel works at Karabuk, cement plants, textile mills, footwear factories, and so on. It also controlled a buying and selling organization for the inputs and products of its enterprises; and through share-holding it controlled, among other enterprises, sugar factories, a fertilizer factory, and a flour mill. The Etibank was primarily concerned with mines. Most of the new industrial investment during the first two five year plans was either directly undertaken by the public sector or promoted by it.

The number and output of factories grew significantly. Factory output doubled between 1929 and 1938. The number of factory employees rose from about 27,000 in 1927 to about 90,000 in 1939. The income per capita went up from 75 Turkish pounds in 1927 to 95 Turkish pounds in 1939 (both measured at constant, 1938 prices). The share of industry and construction in national income rose from 13 per cent in 1929 to 16 per cent in 1938 (Hanson, 1959, p. 124). It was the public sector again which was mainly responsible for an increase of 80 per cent in factory output up to about 1948–49.

However, the failure of the Turkish state to effect any fundamental change in production relations in agriculture, which sustained 80 per cent of the people, the bureaucratic management of the state factories, essentially in the interest of the ruling coterie, and the way the plans were financed—all these ensured that planning would have little impact in changing the economic or social structure of the nation. In the period 1923–34, poor peasants obtained about 700,000 hectares of land comprising farms and homes abandoned by the Greeks, *waqf* lands (i.e. lands belonging to religious foundations), and surplus lands. A further 200,000 hectares were distributed to them between 1934 and 1939. But there was little effort at destroying the landlordism characterizing the Turkish countryside (Hershlag, 1964, p. 182). Even the lands distributed were generally in units that were too small to allow the poor peasants to become independent of their traditional overlords. No attempt was made to introduce co-operation among the peasants.

The major instrument for improving agricultural production was extension of credit by the Agricultural Bank. Its operations were on a modest scale, until the 1940s (Hanson, 1959, pp. 122–3), and, in any case, the benefits of its loan operations naturally accrued to the landlords and rich farmers. Finally, the poor people, among whom the poor peasants were naturally in a majority, bore the brunt of financing industrial growth in Turkey. The income and property taxes began to be of any importance in the state budget (from which much of the funds for industrial development came) only from the middle of the 1930s onwards. Even then, they together amounted to no more than 15% of the state budget. The state ran several monopolies, which provided 20–25 per cent of its total revenues. The remaining 60 per cent of the revenue came from turnover and consumption taxes and customs duties, all of which fell mainly on the common people. Even then, the state budget had large deficits which were met by raising loans (Hershlag, 1964).

A highly bureaucratic structure of management of state enterprises, continued toleration and mild expansion of private enterprises, and a class structure dominated by property-owners, naturally led to a demand from the latter that private enterprise should be given its head. It is with this demand spearheading its programme that the Democratic Party came to power in 1950. It also thrived on American encouragement in the Cold War period. The irony was that, in spite of an apparently more benign attitude to private enterprise, the major part of the growth in industry in the 1950s took place again in the public sector (Land, 1971, Rockwell, 1971, and Fry, 1971). The government tried to encourage private investment by using existing laws which accorded special favour to private industry. But until the mid-1950s at least, most industrial investment took place in joint ventures in which state enterprises played the role of the entrepreneur and major investor (Hanson, 1955).

During this period, the government vastly expanded the credit institutions servicing agriculture. It also provided a 'one-way bet' to landlords and rich farmers (cf. the experience in India from the 1960s onwards) by buying up grain from them at guaranteed prices while leaving them free to sell it at market prices. At the same time, it refused to institute any land reforms, or tax the rich in urban or rural areas. It was then forced to resort to deficit financing on a vast scale. And the public sector mainly invested in slow-yielding infrastructure projects. One result was a fast rate of inflation and balance of payments crises. The Americans and western aid-giving agencies who were major backers of the pro-private enterprise government of Adnan Menderes put pressure on him to change his policies (although the government also unreservedly welcomed foreign investment). A 'free enterprise' ideology as such could do little to stimulate private industrial investment.

The slow rate of growth (with per capita income registering an increase of about 1–2 per cent over the decade), the high rate of inflation and social unrest led to a military coup in 1960. When the military government restored civilian rule in 1962, the civilians promptly restored many of the features of 'private enterprise first'. For the growth of the bureaucratically controlled public sector had also fostered the growth of entrenched private interests and the upper-class civilians represented these interests. From 1963 onwards, a new First Five Year Development plan was undertaken. The plan perhaps made for a little more co-ordination in the development effort than under the preceding regime. It seemed to be eminently successful. Whereas the plan target was an annual rate of growth of GNP of 6.8% per year over the period 1963–67, the actual rate was about 6.5% (Fry, 1971, p. 314). This was primarily import-substituting industrialization, and the public sector was responsible for approximately half the amount of investment between 1963 and 1971, concentrating mainly on intermediate goods (Keyder, 1979, p. 27).

However, much of the growth was due to developments outside the plan as such. While public investment fell short of the target, private investment exceeded it. Agricultural output (growing at the rate of only 2.2%) also fell short of target, whereas services grew at a much faster rate than was planned for (Paine, 1972). Hence 'structural change' in Turkey followed the parasitic pattern characteristic of other third world economies except for the fact that the population dependent on agriculture declined absolutely in the 1960s and 1970s (Keyder, 1980). Furthermore, the Turkish government failed to implement land reforms. It continued to rely for its major sources of revenue on indirect taxes and foreign aid (it received an unlooked-for relief by way of remittances from Turkish workers abroad). The government also continued to put money in the pockets of landlords by raising prices of grain. The unemployment situation worsened in spite of migration of a large number of Turkish workers, and surplus labour continued to remain a serious problem in the countryside (Hamurdan, 1971).

By the beginning of the 1970s, the industrial and agricultural growth rates had fallen to 2.5 and 1.1 respectively owing to the multiple problems left unsolved by the 1963–67 plan (Paine, 1972). Income distribution, which was already highly skewed in 1962 shifted further against low income groups by 1966 (Griffin and Enos, 1970, pp. 204–9). In order to resolve the balance of payments crisis, Turkey had to devalue her official exchange rate by two thirds. Once the possibilities of import-substitution were exhausted (at least temporarily), the advocates of an export-led growth strategy became more vocal. However, the prospects of a fast expansion of exports were dimmed by the trade restrictions imposed by Turkey's main trading partners among the OECD countries (Keyder, 1979). Meanwhile, the IMF dictated their usual package of deflationary policies, cities continued to grow faster than villages, mechanization of agriculture went forward at the expense of the poor peasants and workers, and Turkish society was plagued by endemic violence originating from neo-fascist groups.

The Turkish revolution seems to have gone back on its tracks. It started with Kemal Ataturk's determination to westernize the nation. He outlawed traditional dress, abolished the Caliphate, introduced the principle of secularism, the Roman script in place of Arabic, and made an attempt to educate the masses (some of these efforts are reminiscent of Sarmiento's reform activities in Argentina in the 1860s). But as the property structure and class relations changed but slowly, this 'modernization' failed to trigger off autonomous growth. Her experience demonstrates that expansion of the public sector by itself is not a means of achieving or even advancing towards socialism of any kind. Increased public expenditure and creating infrastructural facilities at public expense while continuing to recognize the right of private property led to private aggrandizement. Private interests then resisted the expansion of the public sector into fields that were privately profitable. At the same time, with a landlord-dominated agriculture (in 1963, 3.7% of land-owning families owned 28% of the land), and with the property-owners extremely reluctant to pay taxes for development, the technological and the market base for industrial growth remained insecure. However, agricultural productivity and output seem to have grown more rapidly in recent years. This change has been partly stimulated by a migration of workers to the towns and to western Europe, which has in its turn speeded up (capital-intensive) technical change (Keyder, 1980).

The experience of Turkey illustrates how in a retarded society the public sector becomes a bastion of privilege. The pattern and timing of its expansion is dictated by the needs of the narrow ruling class and is financed either by raising the prices of consumer goods turned out by the public sector, or through other inflationary policies. There is often an alternation between the demand for expansion of the public sector and the demand for unbridled expansion of the private sector. When this alternation does not reflect the state of the Cold War and the position of the particular country between the two super-powers (viz. the Soviet Union and the USA), it reflects the shifting requirements of the ruling clique and changes in its composition, rather than the shifting fortunes of a battle for attaining socialism.

9.3 PROBLEMS OF ENSURING CONSISTENCY IN INDIAN PLANNING

Since the 1930s, Indian nationalists of various shades as well as Indian capitalists had advocated planning in order to foster economic growth and eradicate poverty. Even socialism had been talked about as a goal to aim at. Rulers of independent India drew up economic plans soon after coming to power. The Indian first five year plan (dating officially from April 1951) was simply the aggregate of programmes drawn up by different departments well before the Planning Commission had begun working. But economists attached to the Planning Commission and other advisers to the government (among whom P. C. Mahalanobis was the most important in the period 1953–62) tried to provide a formal basis for the planning effort.

9.3.1 *The plan models*

Criticism of plan models as such or attempts to verify the plan targets against actual developments often resemble the interpretation of real life phenomena in terms of the quality of dreams dreamed the night before. It is better to treat the announced plans only as a guide to the rough direction of government policy or to the type of ideology the government wanted the people to swallow.

The formalization provided for the Indian first five year plan was rather rudimentary. Given certain conventional estimates of the ratio of capital to output, the rates of saving required to support different projected rates of growth were calculated (for a critique of the conventional measurements of capital, see Robinson, 1956). If the ratio of realized net saving to national income, the rate of growth of national income, and the capital–output ratio are denoted by s, g, and k, respectively, then

$$g \equiv \frac{s}{k}$$

If planned rates of growth are derived from such considerations as the necessity of doubling national income over a period of time, or attaining a minimum average income in real terms within a specified period, and k is taken to be constant, then the planned rate of saving and investment is derived as $s = gk$. Variations on this simplistic formula for exponential growth can be made by allowing k to change on the basis of available information about likely changes in technique or in the intersectoral composition of output, or by planning for increases in s in a graduated sequence. (We are assuming that initially s

is too low to attain the desired rate of growth—why plan in this way otherwise?)

The next sophistication introduced into the Indian plan models (for surveys of the models, see Chakravarty, 1959, Tendulkar, 1974, and Blitzer, Clark and Taylor, 1975) was to distinguish between the consumer goods and capital goods sectors and to consider the allocation of investment between them. This model for the Indian second five year plan was proposed by Mahalanobis and was formally similar to that constructed by G. A. Feldman on the eve of the Soviet first five year plan. Since the capital goods sector produces the goods needed for investment, raising the rate of investment in that sector has the effect of raising the long-run rate of growth of the economy. However, while the rate of investment in the capital goods sector is being raised, the investment devoted for the time being to the consumer goods sector suffers, and in the short run, the rate of growth of output of consumer goods remains low. This can raise problems of excess demand for consumer goods (including necessities). Mahalanobis proposed to deal with such problems (to the extent that they were anticipated in 1955) by raising the output of the handicraft sector and the sector producing services with only a small dose of additional investment, since both these sectors were supposed to have low capital–output ratios. This strategy ran soon into difficulties, whose nature will be analysed presently.

The third five year plan (starting in April 1961) was drawn up primarily on the basis of a rough balancing of inputs and outputs in the economy, after taking the exports, imports, and inflows of foreign aid or loans into account. (A formal demonstration of the feasibility of the plan was provided by Reddaway, 1962.) Later models can be taken to be elaborations of the input–output framework. The basic input–output balance equation for an economy with n sectors can be written as follows:

$$X_i = \sum_{j=1}^{n} a_{ij} X_j + C_i + I_i + E_i - M_i, \quad i = 1, \ldots, n$$

where X_i = output of the ith sector
C_i = consumption of the ith sector output
I_i = investment
E_i = exports
M_i = imports
a_{ij} = amount of X_i needed to produce a unit of X_j (these coefficients are assumed to be constant)

Various further disaggregations may be effected in C_i, I_i, etc., distinguishing between public and private consumption, between investment in fixed capital and inventory investment, imports that compete with domestic output and non-competitive imports, etc. These elements of final demand and imports are also estimated on various assumptions. (The magnitudes are all flows over certain specified periods.)

Manne and Rudra in 1965 published a consistency model of the fourth five year plan—which was supposed to start in April 1966 (Manne and Rudra, 1965). Two notable features of the model were (a) that it demonstrated that the flows of current inputs and outputs within a broadly defined sector based on mining, metals and fabrication of machinery were virtually independent of another broadly defined sector utilizing mainly outputs of the agricultural sector, and (b) that it derived an endogenous estimate of the gross fixed investment on the basis of the planned growth of output over the five year period, instead of leaving it to be determined exogenously by factors not captured in the model. As it turned out, because of serious economic and political difficulties, the fourth five year plan did not begin in 1966; instead there was a 'plan holiday' of three years, and the actual fourth five year plan officially began in April 1969. But the Manne–Rudra model brought out into the open the issue of demand generated by planned investment which model-makers have at best dealt with in an imperfect fashion so far. If the virtual independence of the two aggregative sectors of metals, mining and machinery on the one hand and the agriculture-based industries on the other is taken at its face value, then it would appear that the rates of growth of the two sectors can be planned for separately. (In order to support the growth of either sector, activities such as transport, power supply, etc., would have to be expanded *pari passu*, but that is a different issue.) However, if the demand generated by expansion of the metal and mineral-based industries is to be satisfied, then the supply of consumer goods (which directly or indirectly need agricultural inputs) has to be expanded. The usual input–output models could not take account of such demands, except in an *ad hoc* manner.

An input–output model was proposed for India's fifth five year plan (starting in 1974). The model was supplemented by an explicit estimation of the demand for consumer goods after allowing for some redistribution of incomes. It was assumed that logarithms of consumption expenditures of different expenditure classes conformed to a normal distribution so that if the average consumption expenditure and its variance were known, the absolute levels of consumption expenditure of a particular expenditure class could be predicted. For the exercise with redistribution of consumption an arbitrary increase in the level of expenditure of the bottom 30 per cent of the population (arranged according to levels of expenditure in both urban and rural areas) was assumed. However, such redistribution was not organically linked to the investment programmes proposed for the plan, nor were any specific policy instruments proposed for effecting such redistribution (Tendulkar, 1974). The *Draft Plan 1978–83* and later revisions did not fare better in formulating a strategy for generating more employment for the poor and redistributing incomes towards them. While they provided for some concrete rural works programmes, the consistency of a vast increase in labour-intensive activities catering to the poor with a stress on exports and on industrial efficiency to be achieved through more foreign collaboration and foreign investment was never demonstrated in a convincing manner.

9.3.2 *Macroeconomic imbalances, administrative controls and aid*

Now that we have provided a very rapid overview of the general nature of the Indian plan models, what can we say about the actual plan performance? There is first the question of macroeconomic balance, and the degree of success of the planners in correcting imbalances. Secondly, there is the question of the use of policy instruments as they are usually understood by economists – such as monetary and fiscal policies, administrative controls, and foreign trade policies adopted during the plan period. Thirdly, there is the question of the social basis of planning in India, and, connected with that, the degree of decentralization and devolution of the planning effort. We shall concentrate mainly on the third aspect.

The basic failure in the macroeconomic field consisted in the inability to match supplies with demands over short or long periods, for consumer, as well as capital, goods. Excess demand for some goods co-existed with excess supplies of others. There was a persistent deficit in the Indian balance of payments up to about 1974–75. This does not mean that excess demand predominated in most sectors, as it must have done in the aggregate. Demand for mass consumer goods very often fell short of supply. Even in the case of consumer durables, the narrow internal market tended to be quickly saturated. The balance of payments crises were largely caused by the failure of the government to limit the import of intermediate goods entering into the production of agricultural and industrial commodities, by its eagerness to receive food and other kinds of aid as a means of budgetary support and by the continual expansion of the civil and military establishment.

In the input–output planning model for a single, short period, the aim is to achieve consistency of supplies of intermediate goods with demands for such goods thrown up by the production process. Final demand (consisting of investment, public and private consumption, exports) is also to be satisfied with the available supplies of goods – either domestic or foreign. The input–output model as such does not include the determination of final demands. In the more ambitious input–output models, an attempt is made, plan targets being given, to estimate the aggregate value and sectoral composition of needed investment. The objective here is to match the supplies of capital goods and the demands for those goods on the part of the user sectors (cf. Tendulkar, 1974).

In the partially planned economies of the third world, the different agents belonging to the private sector make their decisions in the light of profit opportunities as perceived by them. Governmental directives or inducement mechanisms can have but a confused and uncertain impact on such decisions (Bagchi, 1970). We have seen in chapter 5 that in a retarded economy (such as that of India), the typical path of evolution of consumption patterns creates problems of excess capacity for both mass consumer goods and for newer types of consumer goods which are invented in affluent capitalist economies. In South Asia, planners failed to take account of the uncertainty of output, incomes and employment of poor farmers and agricultural labourers, and eliminate the problems of survival for the poorest strata of population (cf. chapter 6 above). The supply of wage goods depends too much on the vagaries of weather. The demand for wage goods fluctuates with fluctuations in national economic activity. It is typical of these private enterprise economies that in a year of good harvest an excess supply of wage goods and people barely managing to stave off starvation exist side by side. In a socialist economy, by contrast, the supply of, and demand for, basic necessities are planned for simultaneously. In such an economy an adequate supply of basic necessities in the aggregate and the access of all the people to those necessities are sought to be ensured simultaneously. In a market-dominated, retarded economy such a dual guarantee is virtually ruled out.

The prediction or control of the course of private investment proves even more intractable for the planners. In India, in a bid to guide private investment, the bureaucrats in charge of planning used controls on the setting up of industrial enterprises and their expansion, on issues of fresh capital or of bonus shares by new or existing firms, on the import of raw materials and capital goods from abroad, and on the issue of foreign exchange for settling external obligations. From the middle 1960s onwards, when industrial growth in India entered into a long phase of recession, these controls were blamed for all the ills that beset the economy. (The Report of the Bell Mission sent by the World Bank to evaluate the performance of the Indian economy set the tone of such criticisms, although similar complaints had been voiced by Indian economists also earlier on; see Bell, 1965). The major argument against the administrative controls was that they were arbitrary in operation and had little relation to the plan objectives. But the troubles that beset planning in India are traceable to more fundamental causes than administrative controls.

Looking at the post-independence history of private investment in India, we find that industrial production and investment picked up after the post-Korean War recession under the stimulus of massive doses of public expenditure. The protection afforded by the combination of import tariffs and import quotas, regulation of investment in specified fields and various subsidies in the form of low-interest loans and tax exemptions for investment, also lured investors in search of easy, monopolistic profits. Private industrial investment boomed over the decade 1955–64 or so. Provisions for industrial licensing, control of capital issues, etc., can be regarded as a way of rationing the scarce resources when the private sector on its own was unable to generate enough finance, or usable capital goods and import-saving technology to sustain its own expansion (cf. Bagchi, 1971b). Private investment and the partial planning process were soon caught up in their own contradictions – contradictions that were brought sharply into focus by the harvest failures of 1965–66 and 1966–67.

The fragility of planning in India had been revealed in the continuous balance of payments deficits from 1957–58 onwards. The Indian government sought and accepted massive doses of foreign 'aid' (mostly loans) as a means of overcoming the balance of payments crisis, thus avoiding unpleasant decisions that would have been otherwise needed to balance its own budget and to feed the politically sensitive metropolitan areas. Most of the aid in these years came in the shape of food imports from the United States. (This helped keep up the world market price of US wheat exports, and sustained American shipping, since the food had to be transported in US ships even though American freight charges were higher than market rates.) The Indian government used the counterpart funds of the food imports under PL 480 to balance its budget. With these 'easy' supplies of foodgrains, it could provide metropolitan areas with cheap food, without having to mobilize the marketable surplus of agriculture through a procurement drive. (For the cost and impact of aid to India, see Chaudhuri, 1978, chapter 4.)

9.3.3 *Demand limitations, industrial stagnation and planning in India*

It was not only the government that became enmeshed in the toils of imperialism in the process. Foreign business – primarily British-controlled – had already been occupying a major position in manufacturing, plantations, wholesale trade and finance – especially finance involving foreign exchange transactions. With an upsurge in private investment, and the inability of the Indian private sector to acquire independently (through outright purchase or innovation) technology for such industries as oil refining, drugs and pharmaceuticals, synthetic fibres, and consumer durables of various kinds, foreign private capital often came to dominate these technology-intensive fields. Many firms which had been importing industrial goods from abroad entered into collaboration agreements with their foreign majors, or the foreign firms themselves set up subsidiaries. Meanwhile, many of the foreigners in the more traditional industries sold their holdings to Indians. Thus there was a change in the nature of foreign control on Indian industry from the mid-1950s onwards. Foreign private capital was supported by the obligatory use of a part of the PL 480 loan funds for promoting American enterprise, and by the setting up of a new term-lending institution, the Industrial Credit and Investment Corporation of India, with funds from foreign agencies, and with the specific objective of extending credit to firms with foreign collaboration.

Contradictions between the interests of foreign capital and those of Indian capital rarely induced the Indian bourgeoisie to make common cause with ordinary people in fighting imperialist penetration (see Bagchi, 1973a; and Patnaik, 1972a). The official reluctance of the Western bloc countries and the World Bank to aid public sector projects and the willingness of the Soviet Union in the atmosphere of Cold War diplomacy to provide the assistance needed initially limited penetration of the public sector by foreign capital. But, even in that early stage, two steel plants were constructed for the public sector by German and British steel-making firms. Public sector plants in technology-intensive fields came more and more to depend on foreign private capital (and in some fields, on Soviet bloc technical and financial assistance) and accepted the restrictions imposed by their foreign collaborators. (These restrictions included a limitation on the area to which the outputs could be exported, a ban on licensing of the technology to any third party, a reversion of all blueprints, designs, etc., to the technology-supplying firm at the expiry of the agreement, and a virtual ban on R & D by the Indian firm without explicit permission from the collaborators).

From 1964 onwards, private companies producing consumer goods suffered from a recession. At the same time, the capital goods industries in the public and private sectors experienced a massive decline in sales, because the demand emanating from agriculture or small-scale industries was not nearly enough to compensate for the shortfall of demand from large-scale industry and government. (By contrast, in China, the growth of demand for capital goods by agriculture and light industry has been so fast that industrialization of the villages has been necessary in order to cope with it.)

In chapter 6, we have already touched upon some of the problems of rural social transformation in third world countries, including India. When the Rockefeller Foundation was trying to render Mexico safe for the 'free world' by helping to breed high-yielding varieties of wheat, the Ford Foundation was extending its influence in the Indian countryside with the help of the so-called Community Development programmes. (The latter were, in fact, programmes for further commercialization of agriculture and for channelling funds to the rural upper classes.) The Indian government's eagerness to obtain food aid gave the American government and its agencies a wonderful opportunity to penetrate Indian agriculture and agricultural education in a massive way. It sent experts to agricultural colleges, to agronomy departments of universities and helped set up new agricultural universities (see, for a vivid description of the activities of American agencies in these directions in India, Galbraith, 1969; see also George, 1977, chapters 3–5).[1]

The major thrust of American-inspired Indian policy in the field of agriculture was 'technology first'. Land reforms, which had been already stalled by the resistance of landlords and big farmers, were practically shelved in the 1960s. The spread of the 'Green Revolution' in wheat, and to a lesser extent in paddy, helped to raise outputs above the disastrous levels of 1965–66 and 1966–67, but it is doubtful whether it raised the *trend rate* of growth of output. In any case, in most parts of India, the Green Revolution failed to raise the incomes of the rural poor. In many parts real earnings of agricultural labourers and

1 Galbraith's book also provides ample testimony to the extent to which American diplomats and agency personnel, Indian civil servants, Indian businessmen, and Indian technocrats were hand-in-glove to increase foreign influence in various fields.

poor peasants may have been lower at the beginning of the 1970s than in 1960–61 (see the studies of Punjab, Uttar Pradesh, Bihar and Tamil Nadu by I. Rajaraman, R. Nayyar and C. T. Kurien, in ILO, 1977). Thus the Green Revolution failed to resolve the market problem of private industry (see also chapter 6 above).

The contradictions in the planning process revealed by the developments in the mid-1960s, the growth of private enterprise under the stimulus of protected markets and massive public expenditure and subsidy programmes, the further growth of monopoly houses dominating the industrial sector and the dependence on foreign capital and technology led, for a time, to a demand by the Indian ruling classes that planning should be given a low priority. The officially declared 'plan holiday' for the three years of 1966–67 to 1968–69 was partly a response to this demand.

The plan holiday plus the devaluation of the Indian rupee in 1966, however, failed to resolve the crisis of the Indian economy. Reasonably satisfactory harvests from 1967–68 onwards did not answer either. Capital and basic goods industries such as engineering and iron and steel – often owned by the state – had to seek markets abroad. Recession in the economy helped in the growth of exports of some types of manufactured goods. When the demand for capital goods produced by public sector enterprises declined, they also had to try to export their products (often at prices that were below world levels). Some of them went into partnership with firms from advanced capitalist or socialist countries for executing projects in other third world countries. Recession accentuated the process of concentration of economic power in private industry. The rate of private investment remained low, even through huge subsidies in the form of low-interest loans from banks, and various export incentives were made available to all types of industrial enterprises. Foreign private capital in new industries came out a clear winner during the pocess of recession, and transnational corporations and their Indian collaborator made huge profits.

The crisis of the economy was deepened by an inflationary spiral which reached its peak in 1974–75. After the adventure of Bangladesh was over in 1971, there were no more spectacles to make the Indian people forget their daily struggle for existence. A sense of insecurity generated by repeated countrywide strikes of workers and rural class struggles led Prime Minister Indira Gandhi to declare an emergency in June 1975, and people's freedoms were severely curtailed. Although her government continued to pour out populist slogans, foreign capital was made more welcome than it had been in the early 1960s. In a reversal of fortune through a major miscalculation by Mrs Gandhi, a regime which was more openly committed to private enterprise and the Western bloc (although it also preached nonalignment) came to power in 1977. But that regime also faced the problem of sluggish growth in industrial production and investment. It broke up through contradictions among the ruling partners and Indira Gandhi came back to power.

These political changes have not altered the basic factors keeping the rate of growth – particularly industrial growth – low and the mass of the people abjectly poor. Private investment remains sluggish, because of the narrowness of the home market, and because of the inability of Indian industrialists to compete with transnationals and their subsidiaries in the world market. The Indian government is now deliberately encouraging a greater degree of involvement of Indian capital with external markets and is making welcoming gestures to foreign capital and technology. This is being done while retaining slogans about removal of poverty. The more predatory sections of capitalists who have done well in some new products or in speculative activities are being given their head, and it is intended to diffuse capitalist (and capital-intensive) agriculture, which was earlier confined to a few regions, throughout the country. Public sector organizations are urged to make more profits, and this often means making them more dependent on foreign technology. Artificial expansion of the home market is sought through expansion of public expenditure, and massive subsidies are provided to encourage exports. Anti-monopoly measures have been practically shelved, and there are few effective programmes for redistributing incomes. What is intended through such measures is a boost for industrial growth on the basis of more exports (including exports of foodgrains, if possible), without removing the patronage enjoyed by Indian large-scale industry. This kind of dynamism will almost certainly require more repressive measures for keeping labour in line, and for checking any popular unrest that might result from squeezing the living standards of the ordinary people. In today's world, such a two-pronged strategy combining populism and authoritarianism and more state intervention and a greater degree of involvement in the world capitalist network may be blessed by both the Soviet and the OECD blocs – the former, for the sake of greater power for the Indian state (as a balancing force against China) and the latter because of their solicitude for private and, especially, transnational, enterprise.

Some problems in the fields of technology and product choices faced by third world countries (including India) are dealt with in a later section (see also Bagchi, 1978).

9.4 PLANNING AND REGIONAL INEQUALITY IN PAKISTAN

Capitalism has a tendency to produce uneven development between regions within a country as well as between countries. Once growth along capitalist lines begins to take place in particular regions and particular locations, they tend to attract resources away from other regions. Capital gravitates there and a local capital market springs up; growth of certain industries creates demand for the outputs of ancillary industries and also generates demand for consumer goods through the familiar multiplier effects. Public funds—and, more rarely, private—are devoted to the creation of various types of infrastructure facilities such as roads, ports, railway lines, hospitals, power stations and educational institutions. A skilled labour force springs up at the nodes of growth. The growing regions tend to attract the capital, and the young, skilled and enterprising persons from other regions. These tend naturally to have adverse effects on the latter regions (Gunnar Myrdal has termed these 'backwash effects'; see Myrdal, 1957).

It has been claimed that, in advanced capitalist countries, after industrial growth has proceeded far enough, the 'spread effects' of industrialization begin to overcome the backwash effects even in the lagging regions. In the initially advanced regions, the cities and the suburbs become overcrowded, the wages of skilled and unskilled labour rise steeply, and the costs of urban renewal become astronomical. As a result, the more backward regions eventually appear to be new frontiers. The flows of capital and skilled labour begin to lap the neglected shores again, and backwardness tends to get eradicated over time (see Williamson, 1965). Doubts have been expressed as to whether this is an adequate characterization of regional equalization in advanced capitalist countries even today: Northern Ireland is only a notorious, but not the lone, example of regional backwardness in an advanced capitalist economy.

Be that as it may, as far as the third world is concerned, the story of eventual equalization as between the 'advanced' and 'backward' regions still remains a fairy tale. The advance of the advanced regions in such countries remains rather limited in most cases. The ports remain advanced in relation to the vast hinterland but, compared with the affluent capitalist countries, they develop slowly at best. For, much of the investible resources of the littoral areas are drained away as profits of foreign capital, and the non-investing rich squander a major part of the residual in conspicuous consumption. In the advanced agricultural regions of the third world also, capitalist farming grows only fitfully (cf. chapter 6 above). Nonetheless, a tendency to create man-made deserts out of temporarily prosperous hinterlands is noticeable in most large third world countries (witness the tragic case of the Brazilian North-east).

In the Indian subcontinent before independence, the whole of Pakistan could be regarded as industrially backward. In the West wing of the new country, Punjab and Sind were agriculturally advanced because of the large-scale irrigation works and because of the relatively large-sized farms which produced wheat and cotton – mainly for export or consumption in other parts of India. This region had relatively widespread small-scale industries and handicrafts, but few large-scale factories. When, in 1947, Pakistan was carved out of British India, less than half of the population of the newly created political entity lived in West Pakistan. However, the upper stratum of the less populous West wing dominated the whole country and effectively constituted its ruling class. Several factors combined to increase the disparities between the two wings (see Lewis, 1970; Griffin and Khan, 1972). First, it was at Karachi (in West Pakistan) that the decisions about import control and investment allocation were taken, and these decisions tended naturally to be biased in favour of the West wing. Secondly, with the migration of the Hindu merchants and industrialists from Pakistan, and the influx of Muslim trading communities primarily into West Pakistan, the West Pakistani traders emerged as the dominant elements in Pakistan's trade and, later, in her industry. Thirdly, with an earlier base of large-scale irrigation works and with lavish government subsidies for private investment, agricultural output increased fast in the West while it stagnated in the East. Fourthly, West Pakistan also received a disproportionately large share of public investment, including investment in defence installations. Pakistan had a large balance of payments deficit in the sixties, which was financed by an inflow of foreign assistance. This in turn formed a large proportion of public investment. Hence West Pakistan also appeared to receive the lion's share of foreign aid.[2]

2 Taking the balances of trade of the two wings separately, we find that East Pakistan had a positive balance with the external world (excluding West Pakistan) throughout the period from 1950/51 to 1964/65. Because the import-substituting consumer goods industries (mainly textiles, footwear, etc.) grew up in West Pakistan under the umbrella of protection, East Pakistan had a deficit in balance of trade with the west wing. She had a net balance of trade surplus up to 1959/60, and even during the Second Plan period (1960/61–1964/65) she had an overall deficit of only Rs. 383.4 million. As against that, West Pakistan had net deficits in balance of trade in each of the three periods, 1950/51 – 1954/55, 1955/56 – 1959/60 and 1960/61 – 1964/65 amounting to Rs. 200.3

Pakistan's economic policy throughout had an explicit bias towards private enterprise. This had the effect of rapidly enriching the trading and landlord classes. The system of tariff protection, licences for import of goods and for the use of foreign exchange, even the schedule of approved investments (which was not rigorously adhered to) and the links between the bureaucracy, army and the top businessmen all favoured a siphoning of resources into the coffers of the established business groups and of businessmen with connections. (The rise and growth of Gandhara Industries, controlled by ex-President Ayub's family, is the most notorious – but by no means isolated – example of the tie-up of business fortunes and careers in the army and the bureaucracy.) The government floated the Pakistan Industrial Development Corporation, whose task was to promote industrial enterprises and then transfer them to the private sector, wherever possible. Since Pakistan had started out with a weak capitalist class (Bagchi, 1972a, chapter 14), that class had to seek a coalition with landlords, bureaucrats and military top brass, in order to aggrandize itself. Objectively speaking, the other ruling classes could not preserve themselves without pursuing a basically capitalist goal either. (The position of the Pakistani capitalist class is perceptively discussed in MacEwan, 1971.)

Once the authoritarian coalition of the ruling classes was achieved, the Pakistani capitalists, mainly based in West Pakistan, did not look back. Since members of the upper classes of West Pakistan headed the army and the bureaucracy, this concentration of effective power ensured that there should be no business houses of any significance based in East Pakistan. (On the concentration of economic power in Pakistan's trade and industry, see White, 1974, and Amjad, 1977.) For very similar reasons, and because of a pre-existing infrastructure of widespread canal irrigation, resources for development of agriculture were also channelled primarily to the landlords of Punjab and Sind. Because Hindus had been the main landlord class in East Pakistan, their exodus had helped to alleviate the problems of landlordism there. In West Pakistan, however, the landlords were mainly Muslims and were virtually unaffected by the derisory land reforms decreed by the government (see Naseem, 1977). Hence the expenditures incurred by the government on irrigation, supply of fertilizers and other farm-inputs at subsidized rates mainly benefited the large landlords and farmers in the West wing.

---

million, Rs. 908.7 million and Rs. 1,915.5 million respectively (see Lewis, 1970, table 6.4). So, objectively speaking, East Pakistan received little foreign aid until 1964/65.

The outcome of all this is reflected in the balance between saving and investment in the two wings (Griffin and Khan, 1972). In order to estimate the saving rates, and take care of the overvaluation of the currency, the exports and inflows of capital have to be valued at a premium. We have already indicated (see p. 238 n. 2) that, in the period up to 1964/65, most of the aid was being used in West Pakistan, and the more rural and poorer East Pakistan was in effect being forced to subsidize the industrialization of the West wing. In the four-year period 1964/65 to 1967/68, the picture did not change much. Again West Pakistan ran up a large import surplus with the rest of the world but a large export surplus with East Pakistan; whereas East Pakistan had only a small import surplus with the rest of the world. Officially, investment in East Pakistan was estimated at only 35 per cent of national investment.

The nominal savings rate (as a percentage of regional product) and the nominal ratio of capital inflow to regional investment in the two wings over the period from 1964/65 to 1967/68 are indicated below (Griffin and Khan, 1972, pp. 194–5):

	East Pakistan	West Pakistan
Nominal savings rate	10.2	9.4
Ratio of nominal capital inflow from abroad to nominal investment	17.1	48.8

After making several adjustments for currency depreciation, Griffin and Khan arrived at the following figures:

	East Pakistan	West Pakistan
True savings rate	11.4	5.1
Ratio of true capital inflow to true investment	15.7	74.5

These figures bring out the degree of dependence of West Pakistan on the inflow of foreign (mostly official) capital, and the massive proportions of the transfer of resources from East to West Pakistan. Under the military – bureaucratic regime of Pakistan, this transfer led to growing disparity between the two regions, whose per capita incomes were already different at the time of independence. And just when, with the record of rapid industrialization through import substitution in consumer goods, expanding exports of agricultural goods and simple manufactured consumer goods and rapidly expanding agricultural output in West Pakistan, Pakistan was becoming the favourite success story of the World Bank, USAID and the Harvard Development Advisory Service, the country was involved in a popular struggle which first led to the overthrow of President Ayub and then to the secession of East Pakistan which emerged as the new country of Bangladesh.

The overthrow of Ayub and the independence of Bangladesh did not solve the basic social problems either of West Pakistan (now Pakistan) or Bangladesh. In the West, the Green Revolution led to a worsening of income distribution in the countryside, and growing landlessness. In spite of ex-President Bhutto's symbolic gesture in 1972 of nationalizing ten industries (where government ownership and control was already significant) and arresting two top industrialists, the degree of concentration of economic power in Pakistan remains very great indeed. (Although comparisons are difficult, it is probably greater than in India; see White, 1974, chapter 4.) Real wages in Pakistan's industry have hardly risen; the experience is very similar to India's where the rate of industrial growth was much lower in the decade 1965–74. Within the new territorial limits of Pakistan, the regional disparities between the conurbation of Karachi and the province of Punjab on the one hand, and the rest of the country, on the other, remain very great, and are believed to be even more extreme than the disparity between East and West Pakistan before 1972 (Naseem, 1977). These regional tensions, and the class struggles in the countryside and in the industrial areas have led repeatedly to the suspension of civil liberties, culminating yet again in the imposition of military rule in 1977.

In Bangladesh, things have developed in an even more cataclysmic fashion, if that is possible. Under West Pakistani hegemony, local bourgeoisie and managerial expertise had remained weak. Without any socialist perspective and without any changes in the class structure nationalization of enterprises belonging to West Pakistanis led to a fall in the output and investment of those enterprises. In the villages, the income distribution was already worsening in the late 1960s, and this process probably continued thereafter. According to the calculations of A. R. Khan (1977a), by 1975, 61.8 per cent of the rural population in Bangladesh could be classed as absolutely poor, and 41.0 per cent as extremely poor.[3] Real wages in the countryside displayed a steady downward trend. All these unfavourable developments in the economy and the heightened consciousness of the people who had recently won independence led to repeated political struggles and the ruling classes resorted to extreme measures of repression to contain these struggles. (For a moving testament of one of the leaders of the struggle, see Lifschultz, 1977.) The identification of the first post-independence regime of Mujibur Rahman as being pro-Russian and pro-Indian made it easy for the later military regime of Ziaur Rahman to drag Bangladesh closer to the Western bloc. There has also been an attempt to denationalize many of the industrial enterprises and hand them over to the private sector. The experience of Bangladesh again suggests that, in the absence of a social revolution, creating a public sector from the top and adopting anti-capitalist postures is no way of moving towards socialism and a planned economy. In fact, the interest of retarded capitalism and neocolonialism is well served by the debasement of socialist slogans in the mouths of populist leaders.

9.5 A PAMPERED CAPITALIST CLASS, AN INADEQUATE RATE OF INVESTMENT AND AN INAPPROPRIATE TECHNOLOGY BASE

After two decades of planning in major third world countries, the rate of growth of output remains low and that of employment is even lower. In country after country, industrial employment has grown more slowly than output, and sometimes more slowly than population. At the same time, the Green Revolution has often aggravated the problem of providing employment for the rural masses, since it has converted disguised into open unemployment (see chapter 6 above).

One of the major obstacles to development has been the character of the techniques of production that have been embodied in new investment in agriculture and industry (see Sen, 1968, and Bagchi, 1978). These techniques have mostly been borrowed from advanced capitalist countries and have demanded a very large amount of capital per man employed. Moreover, the structure of employment generated by the new investment has been characterized by a higher-than-

3 Khan considered the FAO norm of 2,150 calories per day per person as unrealistically high. He took 90 per cent of this (i.e. 1,935 calories) as indicating a level of intake below which people were 'absolutely poor', and 80 per cent of the recommended intake (i.e. 1,720 calories) as indicating a level below which people were 'extremely poor'.

average share of supervisory personnel to other manpower and by a higher-than-average proportion of purely administrative and clerical labour to productive labour. In India, for example, not only did the share of wages in industrial value added tend to fall over time (Shetty, 1973) but the share of the wages of production workers to the salaries of non-production workers also fell (Sethuraman, 1971). These effects were produced by a rise in the weight of industries with lower-than-average shares of wages and salaries to net value added and of wages of production workers to salaries of non-production workers, and by an increase in the proportion of managerial salaries and capitalists' profit in almost all industries. There was also a steep rise in the capital–labour ratios in industry.

In agriculture, the use of farm machinery (such as tractors, mechanical harrows, harvesters, etc.) and of increased doses of intermediate inputs, such as fertilizers and pesticides, has meant a rise in the capital–labour ratios in the pockets undergoing Green Revolution. Hence the employment generated by a given value of investment (measured at constant prices) has steadily decreased over time, so that greater and greater effort is needed to make a dent on the unemployment situation.

The causes of these developments have been identified as: (a) the low rate of interest at which large or medium industrial firms and business houses have been able to borrow from banks and from term-leading institutions specially set up by the government; (b) the specially favourable terms on which capital goods have been imported from abroad in many countries; (c) the special treatment meted out to investment in fixed capital for tax purposes (see Khan, 1970). For example, in Pakistan, while the average profit rate was roughly 30 per cent in the large-scale industrial sector (Haq, 1963, p. 41), the weighted average of interest rates on bank advances during the years 1960–67 was between 5.28 and 7.34 per cent (Khan, 1970, p. 200). Effective profit rates in large-scale industry and the rates of interest at which loans could be raised by industry and large-scale commerce differed greatly in India as well as in Pakistan. Capital goods were imported into Pakistan at a specially low tariff rate (amounting to about 15 per cent of value), and, since the currency was overvalued by anything between 50 and 100 per cent, the import of capital goods at official exchange rates was especially profitable. Finally, the system of taxation in India and Pakistan was weighted in favour of investment in fixed capital because of a whole paraphernalia of tax exemptions on new investment, investment allowances and so on.

In Turkey also, an overvalued exchange rate, tariff concessions on imported capital goods or spcial facilities for payment of import duties on capital goods, income tax exemption for investment in fixed assets, accelerated depreciation for industrial investments and concessional terms for loan specified projects – all favoured the use of capital-intensive techniques in industry. Ongut (1971) examined two projects for the manufacture of matches. One would employ 600 workers and labour-intensive methods for producing a given number of matches (Project I). The other would employ automatic machinery, and only 106 workers for producing about the same output, but the cost of capital would be 50 per cent more (Project II). With the existing incentives, and at the official exchange rate, Project II had a higher present value than Project I. But if the incentives were withdrawn, Project I would have considerably higher present value than Project II (Ongut, 1971, p. 680).

While the factors mentioned definitely create a bias in favour of the use of capital-intensive production methods, to regard them as 'distortions' in the factor market or in the foreign exchange market, whose correction will lead to the adoption of more employment-generating techniques or products, is misleading. For a start, some of those distortions are the very essence of planning for building up capitalism in retarded economies with relatively weak capitalist classes. Elimination of some of these distortions does not guarantee the adoption of techniques or products generating enough employment. For example, Argentina has not allowed the import of capital goods on favoured terms. Yet, in that country, industrial employment actually *fell* steadily over the period 1955–64 (Epstein, 1975).

In a capitalist economy, controllers of large volumes of capital *will* have access to credit on particularly easy terms. Again, capitalists *will* divert capital somehow or other to uses which are highly profitable, even if they are considered undesirable from a social point of view. In India, under the assumption that easy terms of lending would lead to a high rate of investment, a system of institutional credit was operated practically throughout the 1950s which tended greatly to favour large borrowers. Then it was found that a large fraction of the loans was being used to support speculation and inventory build-up and feed the forces of inflation. At first, the situation was sought to be controlled primarily by curbing lending for avowedly commercial purposes. However, this merely led to increased borrowing in the name of financing industrial production and investment and to the build-up of stocks in support of price-escalation. In the late 1960s, when industrial production was stagnant or on the decline, bank loans to industry were rising by large percentages (Dehejia Committee, 1969).

Greater controls over bank lending and a steep rise in their lending rates have not led to a reversal of the trend, and bank loans to industry continue to rise faster than industrial output (Ghosh, 1979, chapter 13).

But apart from the feasibility of correcting the so-called distortions of the market, it is erroneous to identify such distortions as the primary causes of the capital-intensive nature of production techniques. The primary causes have to do with the antinomies of capitalist development, of which the above-mentioned distortions are only symptoms or offshoots (see chapter 2 above and Bagchi, 1978). When capitalist colonialism invaded the third world, it caused de-industrialization and destroyed traditional skills. No new skills developed on any scale to replace the old ones. Other bases for the development of an indigenous technology, or a technology that is imported from abroad but is rapidly adapted to local conditions, were also lacking. Formal education was woefully inadequate, capital goods industries, which have often served as centres for diffusion of new equipment and skills hardly developed, and links between different sectors of the economy were weakened rather than strengthened. These sectors became adjuncts of the world capitalist network. When attempts at industrialization began, techniques were imported from abroad. And the rich demanded the new luxuries which were developed in the advanced capitalist countries. Naturally the new techniques were highly capital-intensive, and the products absorbed on unduly large proportion of the nation's capital, skill and foreign exchange.

Attempts were made to provide the missing links in the process of learning required skills, adaptation of imported techniques to local needs and innovation of new skills. But the logic of dominance inherent in capitalism and the inherited patterns of retardation continually snapped these links.

For example, in the Punjab (Pakistan), an industry grew up on the basis of repair of farm equipment and manufacture of the simpler kinds of tool. However, the subsidized import of tractors and other farm equipment threatened this industry (see Child and Kaneda, 1975). Were the government to discontinue such a policy, even then, Pakistani industrialists would probably have to seek the help of foreign firms, when they wanted to manufacture more sophisticated types of equipment. For the patents and knowhow in most cases are monopolized by transnational firms based in advanced capitalist countries. So long as Pakistan adheres to private property rights nationally and internationally, the scope for choice must remain very limited.

Would the development of a base for capital goods industries help overcome these problems of interrupted or truncated learning processes, and blockages in the diffusion of industrial skills and equipment? So long as the logic of capitalism operates, large firms would generally enjoy an advantage over small firms struggling to develop their skills and capital. In Brazil, the capital goods industry is dominated by foreign enterprises. In India, in the manufacture of iron and steel, and electrical equipment, public and private sector firms have sought the collaboration of either transnationals or of countries of the Soviet bloc. India's need for such help and her failure to provide the conditions for a rapid growth of the basic and capital goods industries (see section 9.3 above) have sapped her bargaining strength, and many obstacles have impeded the processes of learning and diffusion (for surveys of foreign collaboration agreements in the public and private sectors in India, see RBI, 1968, 1974).

In advanced capitalist countries, the capital-intensive techniques have had as their basic rationale not only the substitution of (increasingly expensive) labour by capital but also the *control* of labour by management and capital. Capital goods, industrial processes, and managerial methods have been designed to increasingly eliminate the participation of the workers in production as autonomous beings. Craftsmanship or creative adaptation has been taken away from the workers, and the functions of research and product development have been concentrated in laboratories manned by specialized personnel (Braverman, 1974). When the manufacturing process is transplanted from advanced capitalist countries to a third world country with foreigners retaining control, the control of the workers by the management is transformed into the dependence of the host country on the transnationals (or in some cases, on Soviet bloc countries). Even if foreigners are not in formal control, they can retain the design or construction of the plant in their own hands, and they can arrange for supply of intermediate inputs from their other installations and associate enterprises abroad. Explicit restrictions on research and development and independent product diversification by the third world collaborators are also often imposed.

Of course, R & D efforts, with the existing product-mix and the existing pattern of dominance of foreign enterprises, will often have but a marginal significance. For the types of techniques and products they have developed, the advanced capitalist countries, led by the USA, enjoy a head start and stupendous economies of scale. Trying to beat them along the same lines might be a Sisyphean task. Even if genuine research is undertaken in order to build a base of national information and adaptation generally, it gets caught up in the existing relations of dominance and their results are largely nullified. Thus, in Turkey, a national research organization was set up to promote scientific research. But it was found to be really subsidizing university research that was simply an adjunct to research in similar fields in advanced capitalist countries, or technological development that subserved the transnationals dominating the technology-intensive fields (Cooper, 1974).

All this is not to say that even within the present structures of third world countries there is no advantage to be reaped from well-directed research or that no adaptation of techniques to local conditions ever takes place. Where there is scope for economizing on costs by easy substitution of cheap labour for capital, private entrepreneurs do adopt labour-intensive methods. This is particularly true of ancillary operations such as lifting, and transport of things from one part of the factory to another. In some countries, such as Argentina or India, some research is directed even towards the adaptation of techniques to local conditions. It has been claimed in the case of Argentina that 'local expenditure on research and development has a significant effect at the margin upon the observed rate of technological change' (Katz, 1973, p. 212). However, 'most of what is presently going on in terms of local "technological effort" takes the form of "adaptive" R & D expenditure, whose major purpose is that of supporting a "product differentiation" game typical of oligopolistic confrontations. The larger part of these efforts are carried out, and their benefits appropriated, by local subsidiaries of large multinational corporations' (Katz, 1973, p. 221).

In spite of all these caveats, some independent research either by government financed laboratories or by public sector organizations with a large enough base will be beneficial for finding out adaptations that are less costly than foreign imports. Some R & D is necessary in order even to know what to buy from foreign sources in the way of technology and machinery, and in order to bargain effectively. The research carried out by Constantine Vaitsos (1974) and his associates into the real magnitude of the profits realized by foreign companies in the form of transfer prices for imported materials has apparently been used by Andean Pact countries to impose certain norms on payments to foreign subsidiaries operating in such countries.

While a deliberate policy of encouraging research into relevant technology may minimize foreign control of technology, the history and structure of third world economies inhibit the widespread use and development of appropriate technologies, that is, technologies that generate employment and incomes for the poor people and can supply them with the bare necessities of food, clothing, medical treatment, housing and education. Different sectors of a typical third world economy are currently linked more with the world capitalist system than with one another. When, sometimes, a link is established between two sectors (such as agriculture and a local equipment-manufacturing industry), it is again snapped by the entry of large firms buying many of their inputs directly and indirectly from abroad. Imperialist organizations and transnational corporations are constantly on the look-out for products and techniques that can be introduced into the third world and used as profit-making and control instruments (see George, 1977, chapter 5–7, and chapter 6 above).

In the same way, world capitalist development renders many skills obsolete and they are not automatically replaced by the development of new skills. Advanced capitalist countries play a dominating role in designing jobs and the workforce, and workers are rendered more and more impotent in the face of techniques that dominate them. (In this connection, the controversy as to whether foreign or local enterprises are better at adapting techniques to local conditions seems to be of only marginal significance, for both groups follow highly alienating techniques, and adaptation takes place only in peripheral occupations.) The educational system is also generally geared towards the production of a small group of rulers for the class-riven society, and of scientists and technicians whose expertise can usually be utilized only in operations and enterprises characterized by techniques developed in advanced capitalist countries. Any new type of skill or innovation developed by a minority cannot support a movement towards an autonomous technological development, because the market-dominated society cannot protect these innovations or skills against take-over or subversion by large indigenous or foreign-controlled capitalist organisations.

What applies to sectors, techniques, skills and innovations in the way of risk of domination or subversion by the international capitalist network, also applies to products. It has been said that the major problem is not so much that the usual techniques are inappropriate to the third world as that products themselves are inappropriate (Stewart and Streeten, 1973). In particular, the products sold are over-sophisticated and cater essentially to rich men's needs. While this is true, recommending a change in the product-mix as such does not take us very far. So long as there are rich men in the third world keen to imitate the life-styles of their peers in affluent lands, there will be a financial incentive for selling these products to them. These products will then be produced, if necessary, behind tariff and quota barriers. While foreign or indigenous firms can make a profit by producing white bread and are permitted to subvert the tastes of the poor (as well as the rich) through costly sales campaigns, it will be difficult to prevent the gradual elimination of brown bread, un-leavened home-made bread, or bread made with so-called 'inferior cereals' (which are often more nutritious than high-yielding varieties of wheat). The only way to change the product-mix ultimately is thus to change the social structure and eliminate private profit-making at the cost of society as a whole. This is, of course, something that planning for capitalism has no use for.

9.6 EPILOGUE: PLANNING FOR CAPITALISM CAN ONLY RE-PRODUCE THE CONTRADICTIONS OF CAPITALISM

That 'planning' as such has nothing to do with socialism or an egalitarian order of society became clear when Turkey followed the Soviet Union in formulating five year plans. One of the first proponents of planning in India, M. Visvesvaraya, wanted planning in order to encourage private enterprise. When the most influential Pakistani economist in the authoritarian regime of President Ayub wrote a book explaining the rationale of planning, he made it brutally clear that reducing inequality was not the major objective (Haq, 1963, chapter 1). Maximizing the surplus and the rate of growth was the main goal for him.

Maximizing the surplus in the hands of the rich in the third world is not, however, necessarily a way of maximizing the rate of growth. For, much of the surplus is consumed by the rich, some of it is invested in enterprises which are too small by the standards of world capitalism, some of it is wasted through cyclical movements, some of it is sent abroad openly or clandestinely both by rich natives and by foreigners and some gets hoarded or diverted to unproductive uses because the capitalists do not have access to the technology that is profitable. Besides those quoted already, other sophisticated models for planning in third world countries have been constructed. For Pakistan, for example, MacEwan (1970) explicitly tackled the problem of in-terregional allocation of investment over the period from 1964/65 to 1974/75. He postulated the objective of leading the economy to the highest possible consumption path by 1974/75. The recognized constraints were shortages of investment funds and foreign exchange earnings, and limited agricultural growth possibilities. The optimal solution was found to involve a reduction in disparity of per capita consumption and a transfer of capital from West to East Pakistan. Exactly the opposite happened, for the political and economic forces operating in Pakistan ordained it that way. Thus MacEwan's study remained a purely academic exercise, and for a more realistic assessment of what was likely to happen we have to turn to his exercise in political economy (MacEwan, 1971).

In yet other cases, planning studies have been aimed at rationalizing aid programmes and policies pursued by various agencies of the advanced capitalist countries. Thus a series of 'planning' studies on the Chilean economy were sponsored by the ODEPLAN of the Christian Democratic Government of Frei and the Centre for International Studies of MIT, and were published after Allende's government had been toppled by the military coup of General Pinochet (Eckaus and Rosenstein-Rodan, 1973). Some of the studies take the aim of closely integrating the third world economies with the major forces of world trade and investment as an explicit goal. The method of cost – benefit analysis propagated by Little and Mirrlees under the auspices of the OECD and World Bank is best regarded in this light (see, Layard, 1972). The Little–Mirrlees method takes 'border prices' or world prices as the norm for computing the costs and benefits. However, the prices of products sold and bought by third world countries are greatly influenced by such 'non-competitive' factors as virtual monopsony in the sales outlets controlled by advanced capitalist countries, oligopoly in most of the technology-intensive manufacturing industries, various arrangements for tying of aid, and sheer lack of access of third world buyers and sellers to relevant information. Moreover, a very large amount of guesswork is needed to find the relevant prices for non-tradable goods and services, which account for about 50 per cent of total costs. Thus the Little–Mirrlees method even loses the virtue of definiteness (see for example, ICICI, 1975). The application of this method and other similar methods to derive shadow wages which turn out to be generally lower than market wages also serves the purpose of rationalizing the extremely low wages paid to labour by highly profitable enterprises including transnational corporations (for examples see George, 1977, chapter 7).

The use of planning in third world countries to promote dependent capitalism may also be seen in the scramble for aid on the part of most countries apparently attempting to reach self-reliance, even though 'aid' generally inhibits efforts at gaining autonomy. Indeed, planning exercises are often carried out to make out a case for more aid from the World Bank and its soft-interest affiliate, IDA, the US government and other members of the OECD. Planning aimed at reinforcing capitalism in third world countries can only reinforce the tendency towards retardation as analysed in the earlier chapters.

A GUIDE TO FURTHER READING

Many of the basic books and articles used in writing this book have been listed in the relevant chapters and are collected in the list of references at the end of the book. Students will benefit by consulting those references directly. The following notes are meant to indicate to the students the kind of sources he has to consult if he wants to go more deeply into particular questions that are dealt with in a summary fashion in this book. The references cited here are supplementary to, and not substitutes for, the references already listed. These supplementary references cannot act as a full bibliography, and are no more than a guide.

The appropriate framework for the study of societies in general and the correct way of looking way at the history of human society and the history of economic ideas, particularly in recent times, are generally debated together. For Marxist, or, more generally, radical or unconventional, perspectives on such problems, the following books will prove stimulating and informative to students:

Althusser, L. 1969. *For Marx*, London, New Left Books.

Amin, S. 1979. *Unequal Development*, New Delhi, Oxford University Press.

Anderson, P. 1974. *Passages from Antiquity to Feudalism*, London, New Left Books.

Berger, P. L. and Luckmann, T. 1971. *The Social Construction of Reality*, Harmondsworth, Middlesex, Penguin Books.

Blackburn, R. (ed.) 1972. *Ideology in the Social Sciences*, Glasgow, Fontana/Collins.

Deane, P. 1979. *The Evolution of Economic Ideas*, London, Cambridge University Press.

Dobb, M. 1967. *Papers on Capitalism, Development and Planning*, New Delhi, Allied Publishers.

Hilton, R. 1976. *The Transition from Feudalism to Capitalism*, London, New Left Books.

Meek, R. L. 1967. *Economics and Ideology and Other Essays*, London, Chapman and Hall.

Myrdal, G. 1953. *The Political Element in the Development of Economic Theory*, London, Routledge & Kegan Paul.

Robinson, J. 1964. *Economic Philosophy*, Harmondsworth, Middlesex, Penguin Books.

Wallerstein, I. 1974. *The Modern World-System*, New York, Academic Press.

Students are encouraged to compare the perspectives on economic thought in

Marx (1963), Dobb (1973) and the books of Deane, Meek, Myrdal and Robinson listed above with the view propounded in Schumpeter, J. A. 1954. *History of Economic Analysis*, London, Allen and Unwin.

For differing, but related views on the evolution of societies and their organization, see

Dalton, G. 1968. *Primitive, Archaic and Modern Economies: Essays of Karl Polanyi*, New York, Anchor Books.

Gerschenkron, A. 1965. *Economic Backwardness in Historical Perspective*, New York, Praeger.

Hicks, J. 1969. *A Theory of Economic History*, London, Oxford University Press.

Work on the histories of third world countries, some of it of very fine quality, is proceeding apace. On the state of knowledge up to the middle 1960s, the relevant portions of the volumes of the *New Cambridge Modern History* are still very useful. For detailed studies of Latin America, the volumes of the Latin American Studies series published by the Cambridge University Press, many of them written by Latin American scholars, are generally of a high quality. The volumes in the South Asian Studies series of the same publishers (covering India, Pakistan, Bangladesh and Sri Lanka) are perhaps less uniform in standard, but most of them embody a considerable amount of new research. Much of the new work on Indian economic and social history is appearing in journals or proceedings published in India, such as the *Proceedings of the Indian History Congress, Indian Economic and Social Historical Review, Indian Historical Review, Bengal Past and Present, Economic and Political Weekly* and *Social Scientist.* For coverage of work on various aspects of Latin American history and society, the *Latin American Research Review* is an essential guide. New journals in the field are coming out all the time. Two journals worth noticing are *Journal of Latin American Studies* and *Latin American Perspectives.* In the field of African studies also, several journals have made their mark: *Journal of African History, Journal of South African Studies, African Economic History* and *African Social Research.*

Some notable attempts have been made to write comprehensive histories of Asian countries from a radical perspective. Three recent books in this *genre* are noted below:

Caldwell, M. and Utrecht, E. 1979. *Indonesia: An Alternative History*, Sydney, Alternative Publishing Company.

Chesnaux, J., Le Barbier, F. and Bergere, M. C. 1976. *China from the Opium Wars to the 1911 Revolution*, Hassocks, Sussex, Harvester Press.

Chesneaux, J., Le Barbier, F. and Bergere, M. C. 1978. *China from the 1911 Revolution to Liberation*, Hassocks, Sussex, Harvester Press.

Sarkar Sumit. *History of Modern India*, Macmillan (forthcoming).

Two of the books on earlier epochs which have profoundly influenced the writings on modern Indian history are:

Habib, I. 1963. *The Agrarian System of Mughal India*, Bombay, Asia Publishing House.

Kosambi, D. D. 1956. *An Introduction to the Study of Indian History*, Bombay, Popular Prakashan.

For radical perspectives on political economy in general (with application to particular situations and countries) the following journals are worth consulting: *Cambridge Journal of Economics, Capital and Class, Economy and Society,*

Monthly Review, New Left Review, Race and Class, Review of Radical Political Economics and *Science and Society*.

For following current economic developments in the third world countries, there is no alternative to the study of current periodicals concerned with them. But the following journals may perhaps be singled out as especially valuable: *Comercio Exterior* (published in Mexico), *CEPAL Review* (formerly *Economic Bulletin of Latin America*, United Nations), *Economic and Political Weekly* (India) and *Far Eastern Economic Review*. In this book, we have concentrated on developments in poor capitalist economies. For a good analysis of the organization of economic life in socialist countries and references to the literature, see

Ellman, M. 1979. *Socialist Planning*, London, Cambridge University Press.

The material on the People's Republic of China, which is a poor socialist country, and whose development path has often been considered to be a model for other poor countries, is immense. The following English-language journals are exclusively devoted to Chinese developments: *China Quarterly, Modern China*, and *Bulletin of the Society for Anglo-Chinese Understanding*. The documentation section of *China Quarterly* and *Far Eastern Economic Review* together provide an easily accessible base for keeping abreast of policy decisions and current affairs. The papers compiled by the Joint Economic Committee of the U.S. Congress and published by it from time to time generally contain a mass of useful material and analyses on China. Besides, important articles on China appear in the *Bulletin of Concerned Asian Scholars. Journal of Contemporary Asia, Economic and Political Weekly*, and *U.S.–China Business Review*.

Attempts have been made from time to time to compare and contrast the developments in India and China, the two biggest third world countries with contrasting social systems. A useful book-length study of this *genre* is

Byres, T. J. and Nolan, P. 1976. *Inequalities between Nations*, Milton Keynes, The Open University.

REFERENCES

Notes:

(a) In cases where an old book or paper has been reprinted, the date, within brackets, after the author's name, refers to the original date of publication.

(b) Where the place of publication is London, it is not explicitly mentioned; for all Penguin Books the place of publication is Harmondsworth, Middlesex, UK.

(c) *List of abbreviations used*

CUP	Cambridge University Press
HUP	Harvard University Press
MRP	Monthly Review Press
OUP	Oxford University Press
PUP	Princeton University Press
YUP	Yale University Press
EDCC	Economic Development and Cultural Change
EHR	Economic History Review
EJ	Economic Journal
EPW	Economic and Political Weekly
IAEA	Inter-American Economic Affairs
JDS	Journal of Development Studies
JEH	Journal of Economic History
JPE	Journal of Political Economy
LARR	Latin American Research Review
OEP	Oxford Economic Papers
PS	Population Studies
QJE	Quarterly Journal of Economics
RRPE	Review of Radical Political Economics
WD	World Development

Abdel-Fadil, M. 1975. *Development, Income Distribution and Social Change in Rural Egypt, 1952–1970* Cambridge, CUP.

Adams, R. (ed.), 1969. *Contemporary China*, Peter Owen.

Adamson, A. H. 1972. *Sugar without Slaves: the Political Economy of British Guiana 1838–1904*, YUP.

Adler, J. H. (ed.), 1967. *Capital Movements and Economic Development*, Macmillan.

Agra Bank 1875. The Agra Bank Limited, *Bankers' Magazine*, vol. 35.

Ahmad, S. 1973. Peasant classes in Pakistan, in Gough and Sharma, 1973.
Aitken, H. G. J. (ed.), 1965. *Explorations in Enterprise*, Cambridge, Mass HUP.
Allan, W. 1971. The normal supply of subsistence agriculture, in Dalton, 1971.
Allen, G. C. and Donnithorne, A. G. 1962. *Western Enterprise in Far Eastern Economic Development: China and Japan*, Allen & Unwin.
Amin, S. 1970. *The Maghreb in the Modern World*, Penguin.
Amjad, R. 1977. Profitability and industrial concentration in Pakistan, JDS, April.
Anstey, R. T. 1975. *The Atlantic Slave Trade and the British Abolition, 1760–1810*, Macmillan.
1977. The slave trade of the Continental powers, 1760–1810, EHR, Second Series, May.
Anstey, V. 1952. *The Economic Development of India*, Longmans, Green & Co.
Appu, P. S. 1971. Ceiling on Agricultural Holdings (mimeographed), New Delhi, Ministry of Agriculture, Government of India.
1975. Tenancy reform in India, EPW, Special Number, August.
Arrighi, G. 1970a. Labour supplies in historical perspective: A study of the proletarianisation of the African peasantry in Rhodesia, JDS, April.
1970b. International corporations, labour aristocracies and economic development in tropical Africa, in Rhodes, 1970.
Arrow, K. J. 1959. Towards a theory of price adjustment in M. Abramovitz and others, *The Allocation of Economic Resources*, Stanford, California, Stanford University Press.
Bacha, E. L. and Taylor, L. 1978. Brazilian income distribution in the 1960s, JDS, April.
Baer, W. 1973. The Brazilian boom 1968–72: An explanation and an evaluation, WD, August.
Kerstenetzky, I. and Villela, A. V. 1973. The changing role of state in the Brazilian economy, WD, November.
Bagchi, A. K. 1970. Long-term constraints on India's industrial growth 1951–68, in Robinson and Kidron, 1970.
1971. The theory of efficient neo-colonialism, EPW, Special Number, July.
1972a. *Private Investment in India 1900–1939*, CUP.
1972b. Some international foundations of capitalist growth and underdevelopment, EPW, Special Number, August.
1973a. Foreign capital and economic development in India: A schematic view, in Gough and Sharma, 1973.
1973b. Some implications of unemployment in rural areas, EPW, Special Number, August.
1973c. An estimate of the gross domestic material product of Bengal and Bihar in 1794 from Colebrooke's data, *Nineteenth Century Studies* (Calcutta), No. 3, July.
1975. Some characteristics of industrial growth in India, EPW, Annual Number, February.
1976a. De-industrialization in India in the nineteenth century, JDS, January.
1976b. Crop-sharing tenancy and neo-classical economics, EPW, January 17.

1976c. Reflections on patterns of regional growth in India during the period of British rule, *Bengal Past and Present*, January–June.

1977. Export-led growth and import-substituting industrialization, EPW, Annual Number, February.

1978. The political economy of technological choice and development, *Cambridge Journal of Economics*, June.

Bairoch, P. 1975. *The Economic Development of the Third World since 1900*, Methuen.

Balazs, E. 1972. *Chinese Civilization and Bureaucracy*, YUP.

Baldwin, G. B. 1959. *Industrial Growth in South India*, Glencoe, Illinois, Free Press.

Baldwin, R. E. 1956. Patterns of development of newly settled areas, *Manchester School*, May.

Banerjee, N. 1978. Women workers and development, *Social Scientist* (Trivandrum, India), No. 68.

Banerji, D. 1977. Community response to the intensified family planning programme, EPW, Annual Number, February.

Baran, P. A. 1962. *The Political Economy of Growth*, Indian edition, New Delhi, People's Publishing House.

Baran, P. A. and Sweezy, P. M. 1968. *Monopoly Capital: An Essay on the American Economic and Social Order*, Penguin.

Baranson, J. 1967. *Manufacturing Problems in India: The Cummins Diesel Experience*, Syracuse, New York, Syracuse University Press.

Barraclough, S. 1970. Agricultural policy and land reform, JPE, Supplement to July/August.

1977. Agricultural production prospects in Latin America, WD, May–July.

Barraclough, S. and Domike, A. L. 1966. Agrarian structure in seven Latin American countries, *Land Economics*, November.

Basu, T. 1977a. Calcutta's sandal makers, EPW, August 6.

1977b. Hosiery workers of Calcutta, EPW, December 17.

Bauer, A. J. 1975. *Chilean Rural Society from the Spanish Conquest to 1930*, London, CUP.

Baxter, P. and Sansom, B. (eds.), 1972. *Race and Social Difference*, Penguin.

Beattie, J. H. M. 1967. Bunyoro: An African feudality?, in Dalton, 1967.

Behrman, J. R. 1970. Supply response and the modernization of peasant agriculture: A study of four major annual crops in Thailand, in Wharton, 1970.

Belden, J. 1973. *China Shakes the World*, Penguin.

Bell, D. R. 1965. *Report to the President of the International Bank for Reconstruction and Development and the International Development Association on India's Development*, vol. VIII, *Administrative Controls*, Washington, DC, IBRD.

Berg, E. J. 1969. Urban real wages and the Nigerian trade union movement, 1939–60: A comment, EDCC, July.

Bergsman, J. 1970. *Brazil: Industrialization and Trade Policies*, OUP.

Bernstein, H. (ed.) 1973. *Underdevelopment and Development*, Penguin.

Bettison, D. G. 1961. Factors in the determination of the wage rate in Central Africa, *Rhodes Livingstone Journal*, vol. 28.

Bhaduri, A. 1973. Agricultural backwardness under semi-feudalism, EJ.
Bhalla, S. 1976. New relations of production in Haryana agriculture, EPW, 27 March.
Bharadwaj, K. 1974. *Production Conditions in Indian Agriculture*, CUP.
Bienefeld, M. 1975. The informal sector and peripheral capitalism, *IDS Bulletin*, February.
Blakemore, H. 1974. Chile, in Blakemore and Smith, 1974.
Blakemore H. and Smith, C. T. (eds.) 1974. *Latin America: Geographical Perspectives*, Methuen.
Blandy, R. 1974. The welfare analysis of fertility reduction, EJ, vol. 34, March.
Blitzer, C. R., Clark, P. B. and Taylor, L. 1975. *Economy-wide Models and Development Planning*, OUP.
Bloch, M., 1962. *Feudal Society*, Routledge & Kegan Paul.
Boeke, J. H. 1946. *The Evolution of the Netherlands Indies Economy*, New York, Institute of Pacific Relations.
Borah, W. W. 1951. New Spain's century of depression, *Ibero-Americana*, No. 35.
Boserup, E. 1965. *The Conditions of Agricultural Growth*, Allen & Unwin.
Boxer, C. R. 1973a. *The Portuguese Seaborne Empire 1415–1825*, Penguin.
1973b. *The Dutch Seaborne Empire, 1600–1800*, Penguin.
Braudel, F. and Spooner, F. 1967. Prices in Europe from 1450 to 1750 in Rich and Wilson, 1967.
Braverman, H. 1974. *Labour and Monopoly Capital: The Degradation of Labour in Twentieth Century*, MRP.
Breman, J. 1974. *Patronage and Exploitation: Changing Agrarian Relations in South Gujarat, India*, Berkeley, California, University of California Press.
Brenner, R. 1976. Agrarian class structure and economic development in pre-industrial Europe, *Past and Present*, No. 70.
1978. Dobb on the transition from feudalism to capitalism, *Cambridge Journal of Economics*, June.
Britannica, 1881. *Encyclopaedia Britannica*, Ninth edition, vol. 12, Edinburgh, Adam and Charles Black.
1884. *Encyclopaedia Britannica*, Ninth edition, vol. 17, Edinburgh, Adam and Charles Black.
BRPF, 1972. *Subversion in Chile: A case study in US Corporate Intrigue in the Third World*, Nottingham, Bertrand Russell Peace Foundation.
Buchanan, D. H. 1964. *Development of Capitalistic Enterprise in India*, Frank Cass.
Bukharin, N. 1972. *Imperialism and World Economy*, Merlin.
Burn, D., and Epstein, B. 1972. *Realities of Free Trade: Two Industry Studies*, Allen & Unwin.
Cameron, R. E. 1961. *France and the Economic Development of Europe 1800–1914*, Princeton, NJ, PUP.
Cardoso, F. H. 1965. The structure and evolution of industry in Sao Paulo, 1930–1960, *Studies in Comparative International Development*, vol. 1.
1966. The entrepreneurial elites of Latin America, *Studies in Comparative International Development*, vol. 2.

1973. The industrial elite in Latin America, in Bernstein, 1973.
Carr, R. 1974. Mexican agrarian reform 1910–1960, in E. L. Jones and S. J. Woolf (eds.), *Agrarian Change and Economic Development: The Historical Problems*, Methuen.
Cassen, R. 1976. Development and population, EPW, Special Number, August.
Castro, J. de. 1969. *Death in the Northeast*, New York, Vintage Books.
Census, 1901. Census of India, 1901, vol. VI, *Bengal*, Part I, *Report* by E. A. Gait, Calcutta, Bengal Secretariat Press.
Chakravarty, S. 1959. *The Logic of Investment Planning*, Amsterdam, North-Holland.
Chandra, B. 1966. *The Rise and Growth of Economic Nationalism in India*, New Delhi, People's Publishing House.
Chandra, N. K. 1972. Agrarian classes in East Pakistan, *Frontier*, 8 January, 15 January and 22 January.
1977. USSR and the third world: Unequal distribution of gains, EPW, Annual Number, February.
Chandra, N. K. and associates, 1975. Survey of Peasant Organisations, Part II, Studies in Burdwan (mimeographed), Calcutta, Indian Institute of Management.
Chang, Kia-Ngau. 1958. *The Inflationary Spiral: The Experience in China, 1939–1950*, New York, John Wiley.
Chang, J. K. 1966. Industrial development of mainland China, 1912–1947, JEH, vol. 26.
Chaudhuri, P. 1978. *The Indian Economy: Poverty and Development*, Delhi, Vikas.
Chen Han-Seng (1936). *Landlord and Peasant in China: A Study of the Agrarian Crisis of Southern China*, New York, International Publishers, reprinted by Hyperion Press, Westport, Connecticut, 1973.
Chen, Jerome, 1969. Historical background, in J. Gray (ed.): *Modern China's Search for a Political Form*, OUP.
Chesnaux, J. 1973. *Peasant Revolts in China 1840–1949*, Thames and Hudson.
Child, F. C. and Kaneda, H. 1975. Links to the Green Revolution: A Study of small scale, agriculturally related industry in the Pakistan Punjab, EDCC, January.
Chuan, H. S. and Kraus, R. A. 1975. *Mid-Ching Rice Markets and Trade, An Essay in Price History*, Cambridge, Mass., East Asian Research Centre, Harvard University.
Cipolla, C. M. 1973. *The Fontana Economic History of Europe: The Emergence of Industrial Societies*, Part One, Collins/Fontana.
Clairmonte, F. 1976. World banana economy: Problems and prospects, EPW, Annual Number, February.
Cleaver, H. 1974. Will the Green Revolution turn red? in Weissman, 1974.
1977. Malaria, the politics of public health and the international crisis, RRPE, Spring.
CMIE, 1977. *Basic Statistics relating to the Indian Economy*, vol. 1, *All India*, Bombay, Centre for Monitoring Indian Economy.
1979. *World Economy and India's Place in It*, Bombay, Centre for Monitoring Indian Economy.

Cochran, T. C. and Reina, R. E. 1971. *Capitalism in Argentine Culture: A Study of Torcuato Di Tella and SIAM*, Philadelphia, University of Pennsylvania Press.

Cole, H. S. D., Freeman, C., Jahoda, M. and Pavitt, K. L. R. (eds.). 1973. *Thinking about the Future: A Critique of the Limits to Growth*, Chatto & Windus.

Colebrooke, H. T. and Lambert, A. 1795. *Remarks on the Present State of Husbandry and Commerce in Bengal*, Calcutta.

Collis, M. 1965. *Wayfoong; the Hongkong and Shanghai Banking Corporation*, Faber & Faber.

Conklin, H. C. 1969. An ethnoecological approach to shifting agriculture, in A. P. Vayda (ed.), *Environment and Cultural Behaviour*, Garden City, New York, Natural History Press.

Conrad, A. H. and Meyer, J. R. 1973. The economics of slavery in the Antebellum South, in Temin, 1973.

Cooke, C. N. 1863. *The Rise, Progress, and Present Condition of Banking in India*, Calcutta.

Cooper, C. 1974. Science policy and technological change in developing countries, WD, March.

Cooper, R. N. 1973. An analysis of currency devaluation in developing countries, in M. B. Connolly and A. K. Swoboda (eds.), *International Trade and Money*, Allen & Unwin.

CR. 1975. How imperialism brought monetary disaster in China, *China Reconstructs*, April.

Curtin, P. D. 1969. *The Atlantic Slave Trade: A Census*, University of Wisconsin Press.

Curtin, P. D. (ed.) 1971. *Imperialism*, Macmillan.

Dalton, G. (ed.) 1967. *Tribal and Peasant Economies*, Garden City, New York, Natural History Press.

1971. *Economic Development and Social Change*, Garden City, New York, Natural History Press.

Daly, H. E. 1970. The population question in Northeast Brazil: Its economic and ideological dimensions, EDCC, July.

Das, R. K. 1923. *Factory Labour in India*, Berlin, Walter de Gruyter.

1931. *Plantation Labour in India*.

Dasmann, R. F., Milton, J. P. and Freeman, P. H. 1973. *Ecological Principles for Economic Development*, John Wiley.

Datta, B. 1952. *The Economics of Industrialization*, Calcutta, World Press.

David, P. and Temin, P. 1974. Slavery, the progressive institution? JEH, September.

De Alcantara, C. H. 1976. *Modernizing Mexican Agriculture: Socioeconomic Implications of Technological Change 1940–1970*, Geneva, United Nations Research Institute for Social Development.

Deane, P. and Cole, W. A. 1967. *British Economic Growth 1688–1959*, 2nd ed., CUP.

De Barros, J. R. M. and Graham, D. H. 1978. The Brazilian economic miracle revisited: Private and public sector initiative in a market economy, LARR, 13 (2).

De Cecco, M. 1974. *Money and Empire: The International Gold Standard 1890–1914*, Oxford, Basil Blackwell.
Dehejia Committee, 1969. Report of the Study Group on the extent to which credit needs of industry and trade are likely to be inflated and how such trends could be changed, *Reserve Bank of India Bulletin*, November.
Derossi, F. 1971. *The Mexican Enterpreneur*, Paris, OECD Development Centre.
Diaz Alejandro, C. F. 1965. *Exchange Rate Devaluation in a Semi-Industrialized Economy*, Cambridge, Mass, MIT Press.
1970. *Essays on the Economic History of the Argentine Republic*, YUP.
Dobb, M. 1940. *Political Economy and Capitalism*, George Routledge & Sons.
1963. *Studies in the Development of Capitalism*, Routledge & Kegan Paul.
1973. *Theories of Value and Distribution*, CUP.
Domar, E. 1970. The causes of slavery or freedom, JEH, March.
Dumont, R. 1965. *Lands Alive*, Merlin Press.
1966. *False Start in Africa*, Andre Deutsch.
Duncan, K. and Rutledge, I. (ed.) 1977. *Land and Labour in Latin America*, London, CUP.
Dunn, R. S. 1973. *Sugar and Slaves: The Rise of the Planter Class in the English West Indies 1624–1713*, Jonathan Cape.
Dutt, R. C. 1963. *The Economic History of India under Early British Rule*, Delhi, Manager of Publications, Government of India.
Eckaus, R. S. and Rosenstein-Rodan, P. N. (ed.) 1973. *Analysis of Development Problems: Studies of the Chilean Economy*, Amsterdam, North-Holland.
Ehrlich, P. R. and Ehrlich, A. H. 1972. *Population, Resources and Environment*, San Francisco, W. H. Freeman & Co.
Elliot, J. H. 1963. *Imperial Spain 1469–1716*, Edward Arnold.
Enke, S. 1966. The economic aspects of slowing population growth, EJ, March.
Epstein, D. G. 1973. *Brasilia: Plan and Reality*, Berkeley, California, University of California Press.
Epstein, E. C. 1975. Politicization and income redistribution in Argentina: The case of the Peronist worker, EDCC, July.
Epstein, S. 1971. Customary systems of rewards in rural South India, in Dalton, 1971.
Espenshade, T. J. 1972. The price of children and socio-economic theories of fertility, PS, July.
Evans, P. 1977. Multinationals, state-owned corporations, and the transformation of imperialism: a Brazilian case study, EDCC, October.
Fairbank, J. K., Reischauer, E. O. and Craig, A. M. 1969. *East Asia: The Modern Transformation*, Allen & Unwin.
Falkus, M. E. (ed.) 1968. *Readings in the History of Economic Growth*, Nairobi, OUP.
Fallers, L. A., 1971. Are African cultivators to be called 'Peasants'?, in Dalton, 1971.
Feder, E. 1976a. McNamara's little Green Revolution: World Bank Scheme for self-liquidation of Third World peasantry, EPW, 3 April.
1976b. Agribusiness in underdeveloped agriculture: Harvard Business School myths and reality, EPW, 17 July.

Felix, D. 1968. The dilemma of import substitution – Argentina, in Papanek, 1968.

FER. 1978. The great malaria disaster, *Far Eastern Economic Review*, 18 August.

Ferns, H. S. 1960. *Britain and Argentina in the Nineteenth Century*, Oxford, Clarendon Press.

Feuerwerker, A. 1958. *China's Early Industrialization: Sheng Hsuan-Huai (1844–1916) and Mandarin Enterprise*, Cambridge, Mass, HUP.

1968. The Chinese Economy 1912–1949, *Michigan Papers in Chinese Studies*, No. 1.

1970. Handicraft and manufactured cotton textiles in China 1871–1910, JEH, vol. 30.

First, R., Steele, J. and Gurney, C. 1973. *The South African Connection: Western Investment in Apartheid*, Penguin.

Fisher, H. E. S. 1969. *The Portugal Trade: A Study of Anglo-Portuguese Commerce 1700–1770*, Methuen.

Flores, E. 1970. The economics of land reform, in Stavenhagen, 1970a.

Ford, A. G. 1962. *The Gold Standard 1880–1914: Britain and Argentina*, Oxford, Clarendon Press.

Frank, A. G. 1971. *Capitalism and Underdevelopment in Latin America*, Penguin.

1975. An open letter about Chile to Arnold Harberger and Milton Friedman, RRPE, Autumn.

Freeman, C. 1974. *The Economics of Industrial Innovation*, Penguin.

Fry, M. J. 1971. Turkey's First Five Year Development Plan: an assessment, EJ, vol. 81.

Fukazawa, H. 1972. Rural servants in the 18th century Maharashtrian village – demiurgic or *jajmani* system? *Hitotsubashi Journal of Economics*, February.

1974. Structure and change of the 'sharehold village' (*Bhagdari* or *Narwadari* village) in the nineteenth century British Gujarat, *Hitotsubashi Journal of Economics*, February.

Furber, H. 1951, *John Company at Work*, Cambridge, Mass., HUP.

Furnivall, J. S. 1967. *Netherlands India*, CUP.

Furtado, C. 1971. *Economic Growth of Brazil, A Survey from Colonial to Modern Times*, University of California Press.

1972. *Economic Development of Latin America*, CUP.

1973. The Brazilian model, *Social and Economic Studies*, March.

Galbraith, J. K. 1967. *The New Industrial State*, Hamish Hamilton.

1969. *Ambassador's Journal*, New York, New American Library.

Galeano, E. 1969. The de-nationalization of Brazilian industry, *Monthly Review*, December.

1973. *Open Veins of Latin America*, MRP.

Galloway, J. H. 1974. Brazil, in Blakemore and Smith, 1974.

Gedicks, A. 1973. The nationalization of copper in Chile: Antecedents and consequences, RRPE, Fall.

Geertz, C. 1963. *Agricultural Involution: The Process of Ecological Change in Indonesia*, Berkeley, California, University of California Press.

Genovese, E. D. 1965. *The Political Economy of Slavery: Studies in the Economy and Society of the Slave South*, MacGibbon & Kee.

George, S. 1977. *How the Other Half Dies: The Real Reasons for World Hunger*, Penguin.

Germani, G. 1966. Mass immigration and modernization in Argentina, *Studies in Comparative International Development*, vol. 2.

Ghai, D. et al. 1979. *Agrarian Systems and Rural Development*, Macmillan.

Ghosh, D. N. 1979. *Banking Policy in India: An Evaluation*, Bombay, Allied Publishers.

Gibson, C. 1969. Spanish exploitation of Indians in Central Mexico, in Hanke, 1969a.

Girvan, N. 1972. *Copper in Chile*, Kingston, Jamaica, University of the West Indies.

Girvan, N. and Jefferson, O. 1973. Corporate vs. Caribbean integration, in Bernstein, 1973.

Glamann, K. 1974. European trade 1500–1750, in C. M. Cipolla (ed.), *The Fontana Economic History of Europe*, vol. 2, Collins/Fontana.

Glass, D. V. and Grebenik, E. 1965. World population 1800–1950, in Habakkuk and Postan, 1965.

GOI, 1969. *Report of the Industrial Licensing Policy Inquiry Committee*, New Delhi, Ministry of Industrial Development, Government of India.

Goodwin, A. (ed.) 1965. *The New Cambridge Modern History*, vol. VIII, *The American and French Revolutions 1763–93*, CUP.

Goody, J. 1971. Feudalism in Africa?, in Dalton, 1971.

Gorrie, R. M. n.d. *Forestry Development and Soil Conservation in the Upper Damodar Valley – A 15-year Scheme*, Alipore, India, Damodar Valley Corporation.

Gough, K. 1977. Agrarian change in Thanjavur, in K. S. Krishnaswamy et al. (eds.) *Society and Change: Essays in Honour of Sachin Chaudhuri*, Bombay, OUP.

Gough, K. and Sharma, H. 1973. *Imperialism and Revolution in South Asia*, MRP.

Gourou, P. 1973. *The Tropical World*, Longman.

Graham, R. 1968. *Britain and the Onset of Modernization in Brazil 1850–1914*, CUP.

1969. Sepoys and imperialists: Techniques of British power in nineteenth century Brazil, IAEA, Autumn.

Gray, R. H. 1974. The decline of mortality in Ceylon and the demographic effects of malaria control, PS, July.

Greenberg, M. 1969. *British Trade and the Opening of China 1800–42*, CUP.

Griffin, K. 1969. *Underdevelopment in Spanish America*, Allen & Unwin.

1973. The effect of aid and other resource transfers on savings and growth in less developed countries: A comment, EJ, vol. 83.

Griffin, K. and Enos, J. L. 1970. *Planning Development*, London, Addison – Wesley Publishing Co.

Griffin, K. and Khan, A. R. (eds.) 1972. *Growth and Inequality in Pakistan*, Macmillan.

Grunig, J. E. 1969. Economic decision making and entrepreneurship among Columbian latifundistas, IAEA, Summer.

Guha, A. 1977. *Planter Raj to Swaraj*, New Delhi, People's Publishing House.

Guha, R. 1963. *A Rule of Property for Bengal*, Paris, Mouton.

Habakkuk, H. J. and Postan, M. M. (eds.). 1965. *The Cambridge Economic*

History of Europe, vol. VI, *The Industrial Revolution of Europe and After*, Parts I and II, CUP.

Haberler, G. 1949. The market for foreign exchange and the stability of the balance of payments, a theoretical analysis, *Kyklos*, vol. 3.

Haggett, P. 1975. *Geography: A Modern Synthesis*, New York, Harper & Row.

Hall, A. D. 1936. *The Improvement of Native Agriculture in relation to Population and Public Health*, OUP.

Halperin-Donghi, T. 1975. *Politics, Economics and Society in Argentina in the Revolutionary Period*, CUP.

Hamilton, A. (1791) *Report on Manufactures, to the House of Representatives*, December 5, 1791, excerpted in J. Grunwald, Some reflections on Latin American industrialization policy, JPE, supplement to July–August 1970.

Hamurdan, Y. 1971. Surplus labour in Turkish agriculture, in Ridker and Lubell, 1971, vol. I.

Hanke, L. (ed.). 1969a. *History of Latin American Civilization: Sources and Interpretations*, vol. I, Methuen.

1969b. *History of Latin American Civilization: Sources and Interpretations*, vol. II, Methuen.

Hanson, A. H. 1955. The system of State banks and their role in the development of public enterprise in Turkey, in Hanson (ed.) *Public Enterprise*, Brussels, International Institute of Administrative Sciences.

1959. *Public Enterprise and Economic Development*, London, Routledge & Kegan Paul.

Haq, M. 1963. *The Strategy of Economic Planning: A Case Study of Pakistan*, Karachi, OUP.

Harris, P. 1975. Industrial workers in Rhodesia, 1946–1972: Working class elites or lumpen proletariat? *Journal of Southern African Studies*, April.

Hayter, T. 1971. *Aid as Imperialism*, Penguin.

Hazari, B. R. 1967. Import intensity of consumption in India, *Indian Economic Review*, New Series, vol. 2, October.

Hazari, R. K. 1965. *The Structure of the Corporate Private Sector*, Bombay, Asia.

Helleiner, G. K. 1972. *International Trade and Economic Development*, Penguin.

Hershlag, Z. Y. 1964. *Introduction to the Modern Economic History of the Middle East*, Leiden, E. J. Brill.

Hicks, J. R. 1950. *A Contribution to the Theory of the Trade Cycle*, Oxford, Clarendon Press.

Higgins, B. 1971. A critique of Boeke's 'dualistic theory', in Meier, 1971.

Hilton, R. H. (ed.) 1976. *The Transition from Feudalism to Capitalism*, New Left Books.

Hindess, B. and Hirst, P. Q. 1975. *Pre-capitalist Modes of Production*, Routledge & Kegan Paul.

Hinton, W. 1968. *Fanshen: A Documentary of Revolution in a Chinese Village*, New York, Vintage Books.

Hirschman, A. O. 1968. The political economy of import substituting industrialization in Latin America, QJE, February.

Hobsbawm, E. 1968. *Industry and Empire*, Weidenfeld & Nicolson.

1975. *The Age of Capital 1848–1875*, Weidenfeld & Nicolson.

Hobsbawm, E. (ed.) 1964. *Karl Marx: Pre-capitalist Economic Formations*, Lawrence & Wishart.

Hodgkin, T. 1972. Some African and third world theories of imperialism, in Owen and Sutcliffe, 1972.

Holmberg, A. R. and Dobyns, H. F. 1970. The Cornell programme in Vicos, Peru, in Wharton, 1970.

Holub, A. 1970. A brief review of structural development in the developing ECAFE countries, *UN Bulletin of the Economic Commission for Asia and the Far East*, June/Sept.

Hopkins, A. G. 1973. *An Economic History of West Africa*, Longman.

Hsiao Liang-lin. 1974. *China's Foreign Trade Statistics, 1864–1949*, Cambridge, Mass., HUP.

Huberman, L. 1976. *Man's Worldly Goods*, New Delhi, People's Publishing House.

Humphreys, R. A. 1965. The emancipation of Latin America, in C. W. Crawley (ed.) *The New Cambridge Modern History*, Vol. IX, *War and Peace in an Age of Upheaval 1793–1830*, CUP.

Hymer, S. and Resnick, S. 1969. A model of the agrarian economy with nonagricultural activities, *American Economic Review*, September.

Hymer, S. and Roosevelt, F. 1972. Economics of the New Left: Comment, QJE, November.

ICICI. 1975. *Economic Rate of Return: ICICI Projects*, Bombay, Industrial Credit and Investment Corporation of India Ltd.

ILO. 1971a. *Matching Employment Opportunities and Expectations: A Programme of Action for Ceylon*, Geneva, International Labour Office.

1971b. *Matching Employment Opportunities and Expectations, A Programme of Action for Ceylon, Technical Papers*, Geneva, International Labour Office.

1973. *Employment, Incomes and Equality: A Strategy for Increasing Productive Employment in Kenya*, Geneva, International Labour Office.

1977. *Poverty and Landlessness in Rural Asia*, Geneva, International Labour Office.

Indonesian Economics, 1961. *Indonesian Economics: The concept of Dualism in Theory and Policy*, The Hague, W. Van Hoeve.

IPR. 1939. *Agrarian China: Selected source Materials from Chinese Authors* compiled and selected by Research Staff of Secretariat, Institute of Pacific Relations, with an introduction by R. H. Tawney, Allen & Unwin.

Iqbal, Z. 1975. The Generalised System of Preferences examined, *Finance & Development*, September.

Ishii, A. 1973. Ejidos in Mexico: Actual situation and problems, *Developing Economies*, September.

Israel, J. I. 1974. Mexico and the 'General Crisis' of the seventeenth century, *Past and Present*, No. 63, May.

Janvry, A. de. 1973. A socio-economic model of induced innovations for agricultural development, QJE, August.

Jefferson, M. 1926. *Peopling the Argentine Pampa*, New York, American Geographical society.

Jenks, L. H. 1963. *The Migration of British Capital to 1875*, Thomas Nelson.

Johnson, D. L. 1967–68. Industrialization, social mobility and class formation in Chile, *Studies in Comparative International Development*, vol. 3.

Johnson, D. L. (ed.) 1973. *The Chilean Road to Socialism*, Garden City, New York, Anchor Books.

Jolly, R. et al. 1973. *Third World Employment: Problems and Strategy*, Penguin.

Kabala Kabinda, M. K. K. 1975. Multinational Corporations and the installation of externally oriented economic structure in contemporary Africa, the example of the Unilever-Zaire group, in Widstrand, 1975.

Kahn, A. E. 1946. *Great Britain in the World Economy*, New York, Columbia University Press.

Kalecki, M. 1972a. *Selected Essays on the Economic Growth of the Socialist and the Mixed Economy*, CUP.

1972b. Social and economic aspects of 'intermediate regimes', in Kalecki, 1972a.

Kang Chao, 1975. The growth of a modern cotton textile industry and the competition with handicrafts, in Perkins, 1975.

Katz, J. M. 1973. Industrial growth, royalty payments and local expenditure on research and development, in Urquidi and Thorp, 1973.

Kehl, F. 1977. Approach to environmental problems, *Social Scientist* (Trivandrum, India), May–June.

Kennedy, C. and Thirlwall, A. P. 1972. Technical progress: A survey, EJ, March.

Keyder, C. 1979. Turkey: Dictatorship and democracy, *New Left Review*, May–June.

1980. Paths of rural transformation in Turkey (mimeo.).

Keynes, J. M. 1913. *Indian Currency and Finance*, Macmillan.

1973. *The Collected Writings of John Maynard Keynes*, vol. XIII, *The General Theory and After*, Part I, *Preparation* (ed. by D. Moggridge), Macmillan.

Khan, A. R. 1970. Some problems of choice of techniques in a mixed economy: The case of Pakistan, in Robinson and Kidron, 1970.

1977. Poverty and inequality in rural Bangladesh, in ILO, 1977.

Kindleberger, C. 1965. *Economic Development*, 2nd edition, New York, McGraw-Hill.

Kling, M. 1968. Toward a theory of power and political instability in Latin America, in Petras and Zeitlin, 1968.

Knight, J. B. and Mabro, R. 1972. The determination of the general wage level: A comment, EJ, June.

Kondapi, C. 1951. *Indians Overseas 1838–1949*, New Delhi, Indian Council of World Affairs & OUP.

Konig, W. 1973. International financial institutions and Latin American development, in Urquidi and Thorp, 1973.

Kosminsky, E. A. 1956. *Studies in the Agrarian History of England in the Thirteenth Century*, Oxford, Basil Blackwell.

Kreye, O. 1977. World Market – Oriented Industrialization of Developing Countries: Free Production Zones and World Market Factories, (mimeo) Max-Planck-Institute, Starnberg, W. Germany.

Krishna, R. 1963. Farm supply response in India-Pakistan: A case study of the Punjab region, EJ, September.

Krishnan, T. N. 1964. *The Role of Agriculture in Economic Development*, PhD thesis, Massachusetts Institute of Technology, Cambridge, Mass.

Kumar, R. 1968. *Western India in the Nineteenth Century*, Routledge & Kegan Paul.

Kuznets, S. 1966. *Modern Economic Growth: Rate, Structure and Spread*, YUP.

Kuznets, S., Moore, W, J., and Spengler, J. J. (eds.) 1955. *Economic Growth: Brazil, India, Japan*, Durham, NC, Duke University Press.

Land, J. W. 1971. The role of public enterprise in Turkish economic development, in Ranis, 1971.

Landes, D. S. 1965. French business and the businessman: A social and cultural analysis, in Aitken, 1965.

1968. Some thoughts on the nature of economic imperialism, in Falkus, 1968.

Lattimore, O. 1960. The industrial impact on China 1880–1950, *First International Conference of economic History, Stockholm, 1960*, The Hague, Mouton & Co.

Lauterbach, A. 1966. *Enterprise in Latin America: Business Attitudes in a Developing Economy*, New York, Cornell University Press.

La Valette, J. de. 1938a. Holland today, *Journal of the Royal Society of Arts*, vol. 87.

1938b. The Netherlands East Indies today, *Journal of the Royal Society of Arts*, vol. 87.

Layard, R. (ed.) 1972. *Cost–Benefit Analysis*, Penguin.

Lee, E. 1979. Egalitarian peasant farming and rural development: The case of South Korea, in Ghai et al., 1979.

Lehmann, D. (ed.) 1974. *Agrarian Reform and Agrarian Reformism*, Faber & Faber.

Leibenstein, H. 1969. Pitfalls in benefit–cost analysis of birth prevention, PS, July.

Lenin, V. I. (1899). *The Development of Capitalism in Russia*, in Lenin, 1963–70, vol. 3.

(1900a). Capitalism in agriculture (Kautsky's book and Mr. Bulgakov's article), in Lenin, 1963–70, vol. 4.

(1900b). The Agrarian question and the 'Critics of Marx', in Lenin, 1963–70, vol. 5.

(1903). To the rural poor: An explanation for the peasants of what the Social-Democrats want, in Lenin, 1963–70, vol. 6.

(1908a). The agrarian programme of Social Democracy in the First Russian Social Revolution, 1905–1907, in Lenin, 1963–70, vol. 13.

(1908b). The agrarian question in Russia towards the close of the nineteenth century, in Lenin, 1963–70, vol. 15.

(1912a). A comparison of the Stolypin and the Narodnik agrarian programme, in Lenin, 1963–70, vol. 18.

(1912b). The last valve, in Lenin, 1963–70, vol. 18.

(1917). *Imperialism: The Highest Stage of Capitalism*, in Lenin, 1963–70, vol. 22.

(1920). Preliminary draft theses on the agrarian question for the Second Congress of the Communist International, in Lenin, 1963–70, vol. 31.

1963–70. *Collected Works*, vols. 1–45, Moscow, Progress Publishers.

Lewis, S. R. 1970. *Pakistan: Industrialization and Trade Policies*, OUP.

Lewis, W. A. 1954. Economic development with unlimited supplies of labour, *Manchester School*, May.
1956. *The Theory of Economic Growth*, Allen & Unwin.
Lewis, W. A. (ed.) 1970. *Tropical Development 1880–1913*, Allen & Unwin.
Leys, C. 1976. *Underdevelopment in Kenya*, Heinemann.
Lifschultz, L. 1977. Abu Taher's last testament – Bangladesh: The unfinished revolution, EPW, Special Number, August.
Lipton, M. 1968. The theory of the optimising peasant, JDS, April.
List, F. 1857. *The National System of Political Economy*, Philadelphia.
Little, I., Scitovsky, T. and Scott, M. 1970. *Industry and Trade in Some Developing Countries: A Comparative Study*, OUP for the Development Centre of the OECD.
Luxemburg, R. 1963. *The Accumulation of Capital*, Routledge & Kegan Paul.
McBride, G. M. 1936. *Chile: Land and Society*, New York, American Geographical Society.
MacEwan, A. 1970. Problems of interregional and intersectoral allocation. The case of Pakistan, *Pakistan Development Review*, Spring.
1971. Contradiction in capitalist development: The Case of Pakistan, RRPE, Spring.
Mackenzie, C. 1954. *Realms of Silver*, Routledge & Kegan Paul.
McKeown, T., Brown, R. G. and Record R. G. 1972. An interpretation of the modern rise of population in Europe, PS, November.
Magdoff, H. 1968. The age of Imperialism, Parts 1–3, *Monthly Review*, June, October and November.
Mamalakis, M. 1971. The role of government in the resource transfer and resource allocation process: The Chilean nitrate sector 1880–1930, in Ranis, 1971.
Mamdani, M. 1976. The ideology of population control, EPW, Special Number, August.
Manne, A. S. and Rudra, A. 1965. A consistent model of India's fourth plan, *Sankhya*, Series B, vol. 27.
Mansfield, E. et al. 1972. *Research and Innovation in the Modern Corporation*, London, Macmillan.
Mao Tse-tung (1926). Analysis of the classes in Chinese society, in Mao Tse-tung, 1967, vol. 1.
(1933). How to differentiate the classes in rural areas, in Mao Tse-tung, 1967, vol. 1.
(1967). *Selected Works of Mao Tse-tung*, vols. 1–4, Peking, Foreign Language Press.
Markensten, K. 1972. *Foreign Investment and Development: Swedish Companies in India*, Lund, Student Litteratur.
Martinez, A. B. and Lewandowski, M. 1911. *The Argentine in the Twentieth Century*, T. Fisher Unwin.
Marx, K. (1853). The British rule in India, *New York Daily Tribune*, 25 June 1853, reprinted in K. Marx and F. Engels, *On Colonialism*, Moscow, Foreign Language Publishing House, n.d.
(1859). *A Contribution to the Critique of Political Economy*, translated from the German by S. W. Ryazanskaya and edited by M. Dobb, Moscow, Progress Publishers, 1970.

(1887). *Capital: A Critical Analysis of Capitalist Production*, vol. I, translated from German by S. Moore and E. Aveling and edited by F. Engels, reprinted, n.d., Moscow, Foreign Languages Publishing House.
1963. *Theories of Surplus Value*, Parts I, II, III, Moscow, Progress Publishers.
1976. *The German Ideology*, Moscow, Progress Publishers.
Mason, P. 1970. *Patterns of Dominance*, OUP.
Massel, M. S. 1973. Non-tariff barriers as an obstacle to world trade, in H. B. Thorelli (ed.). *International Marketing Strategy*, Penguin.
Matsuo, H. 1970. *The Development of Javanese Cotton Industry*, Tokyo, The Institute of Developing Economies.
Matthews, R. C. O. 1959. *Trade Cycle*, CUP.
Meadows, D. H., Meadows, D. L. et al., 1972. *The Limits to Growth*, New York, Universe Books.
Meegama, S. A. 1967. Malaria eradication and its effects on mortality levels, PS, November.
Meier, G. M. (ed.) 1971. *Leading Issues in Economic Development*, OUP.
Mencher, J. P. 1974. Problems in analysing rural class structure, EPW, 31 August.
Michel, A. A. 1973. The impact of modern technology in the Indus and Helmand basins of Southwest Asia, in M. T. Favar and J. P. Milton (eds.), *The Careless Technology: Ecology and International Development*, Tom Stacey.
Mikesell, R. F. and Zinser, J. E. 1973. The nature of the savings function in developing countries: A survey of the theoretical and empirical literature, *Journal of Economic Literature*, March.
Minchinton, W. E. (ed.) 1969. *The Growth of English Overseas Trade in the 17th and 18th Centuries*, Methuen.
Miracle, M. P. 1976. Interpretation of backward-sloping supply curves in Africa, EDCC, January.
Miracle, M. P. and Fetter, B. 1970. Backward-sloping labour supply function and African economic behaviour, EDCC, January.
Mitchell, B. R. and Deane, P. 1976. *Abstract of British Historical Statistics*, CUP.
Mitchell, K. L. (1942). *Industrialization of the Western Pacific*, reprinted New York, Russell, 1971.
Moise, E. 1978. Comment: Radical, moderate and optimal patterns of land reforms, *Modern China*, January.
Moore, Jr, B. 1967. *Social Origins of Dictatorship and Democracy*, Allen Lane.
Morris, M. D. 1965. *The Emergence of an Industrial Labour Force in India*, Berkeley, California, University of California Press.
Morse, H. B. 1909. *The Guilds of China with an Account of Guild Merchant or Co-hong of Canton*, Longmans, Green & Co.
Morse, R. M. 1964. Latin American cities: Aspects of function and structure, in J. Friedman and W. Alonso (eds.). *Regional Development and Planning: A Reader*, Cambridge, Mass., MIT Press.
1971. Trends and issues in Latin American urban research, 1965–1970, *Latin American Research Review*, Summer.
Moyana, J. K. 1975. The political economy of the migrant labour system:

Imperialism, agricultural growth and rural development in Southern Africa, (mimeo.), paper presented at the UNIDEP Conference, Tananarive, 4–14 July.
Mueller, M. W. 1970. Changing patterns of agricultural output and productivity in the private and land reform sectors in Mexico, 1940–1960, EDCC, January.
Mukherjee, R. 1951. *The Indian Working Class*, Bombay, Hind Kitabs.
Mulhall, M. G. 1896. *Industries and Wealth of Nations*, Longmans, Green & Co.
Murray, R. 1972. Underdevelopment, international firms and the international division of labour, in *Towards a New World Economy*, Rotterdam, Rotterdam University Press.
Myers, R. H. 1965. Cotton textile handicrafts and the development of cotton textile industry in China, EHR, Second Series, vol. 18.
1970. *The Chinese Peasant Economy: Agricultural Development in Hopei and Shantung 1890–1949*, Cambridge, Mass, HUP.
Myint, H. 1958. The 'classical' theory of international trade and the underdeveloped countries, EJ, vol. 68.
1965. *The Economics of the Developing Countries*, London, Hutchinson.
Myrdal, G. 1957. *Economic Theory and Underdeveloped Regions*, London, Duckworth.
1970. *An Approach to the Asian Drama: Methodological and Theoretical*, New York, Vintage Books.
Myren, D. T. 1970. The Rockefeller Foundation programme in corn and wheat in Mexico, in Wharton, 1970.
Nanavati, M. B. and Anjaria, J. J. 1951. *The Indian Rural Problem*, Bombay, Vora & Co.
Narain, D. 1965. *The Impact of Price Movements on Areas under Selected Crops in India 1900–1939*, CUP.
Naseem, S. M. 1977. Rural poverty and landlessness in Pakistan, in ILO, 1977.
Needham, J. 1969. *Within the Four Seas: The Dialogue of East and West*, Allen & Unwin.
Newlyn, W. T. 1973. The effects of aid and other resource transfers on savings and growth in less developed countries: A comment, EJ, vol. 83.
Niedergang, M. 1971. *The Twenty Latin Americas*, vols. 1 and 2, Penguin.
Nisbet, C. T. (ed.). 1969. *Latin America: Problems in Economic Development*, Collier-Macmillan.
Njonjo, A. 1975. Agrarian capitalism: The basis of capitalist industrialization with some observations on Africa (mimeo.), paper presented to the UNIDEP Conference held at Tananarive, 4–14 July.
Nordhaus, W. D. 1973. World dynamics: Measurement without data, EJ, vol. 83.
Nun, J. 1968. A Latin American phenomenon: The middle class military coup, in Petras and Zeitlin, 1968.
Nzimiro, I. 1975. The political and social implications of multinational corporations in Nigeria, in Widstrand, 1975.
O'Conor, J. E. 1887. *Review of the Trade of India 1886–87*, Simla (India) Government Central Branch Press.

O'Donnell, G. 1978. Reflections on patterns of change in the bureaucratic authoritarian state, *Latin American Research Review*, vol. 13.

Oechsli, F. M. and Kirk, P. 1975. Modernization and demographic transition in Latin America and the Caribbean, EDCC, April.

Oliver, R. and Fage, J. D. 1969. *A Short History of Africa*, Penguin.

Ongut, I. 1971. Economic policies, investment decisions and employment in Turkish industry, in Ridker and Lubell, 1971, vol. II.

Opium War, 1976. *The Opium War*, by the Compilation Group for the History of Modern China series, Peking, Foreign Languages Press.

Outline History. 1958. *An Outline History of China*, Peking, Foreign Language Press.

Owen, R. and Sutcliffe, B. (eds.) 1972. *Studies in the Theory of Imperialism*, London, Longman.

Paine, S. 1972. Turkey's First Five Year Development Plan (FFYDP) 1963–67: A different assessment, EJ, vol. 82.

Palmer, I. 1976. *The New Rice in Asia: Conclusions from Four Country Studies*, Geneva, United Nations Research Institute for Social Development.

Panikar, P. G. K., Krishnan, T. N. and Krishnaji, N. 1977. Population Growth and Agricultural Development: A Case Study of Kerala (mimeo.), Centre for Development Studies, Trivandrum, India.

Panikkar, K. M. 1970. *Asia and Western Dominance*, Allen & Unwin.

Papanek, G. F. (ed.) 1968. *Development Policy – Theory and Practice*, Cambridge, Mass., HUP.

1973. The effect of aid and other resource transfers on saving and growth in less-developed countries, A reply, EJ, vol. 83.

Parry, J. H. 1948. *The Audiencia of New Galicia in the Sixteenth Century: A Study in Spanish Colonial Government*, CUP.

1963. *The Age of Reconnaissance*, Weidenfeld and Nicolson.

1973. *The Spanish Seaborne Empire*, Penguin.

1974. *Trade and Dominion*, Sphere Books.

Patnaik, P. 1972a. Imperialism and the growth of Indian capitalism, in Owen and Sutcliffe, 1972.

1972b. Disproportionality crisis and economic growth, EPW, Annual Number, February.

Patnaik, U. 1976. Class differentiation within the peasantry: An approach to analysis of Indian agriculture, EPW, Review of Agriculture, September 25.

Payer, C. 1974. *The Debt Trap*, Penguin.

1975. Was the Chinese peasant exploited?, *Journal of Peasant Studies*, January.

Payne, P. L. 1974. *British Enterpreneurship in the Nineteenth Century*, Macmillan.

Paz, O. 1961. *The Labyrinth of Solitude: Life and Thought in Mexico*, New York, Grove Press.

Pearse, A. 1975. *The Latin American Peasant*, Frank Cass.

Pearson, H. W. 1957. The economy has no surplus: Critique of a theory of development, in K. Polanyi, C. M. Arensberg and H. W. Pearson (eds.), *Trade and Market in Early Empires*, Glencoe, Illinois, The Free Press.

Pendle, G. 1971. *A History of Latin America*, Penguin.

Perkins, D. (ed.) 1975. *China's Modern Economy in Historical Perspective*, Cambridge, Mass., HUP.

Petras, J. and Zeitlin, M. (eds.) 1968. *Latin America: Reform or Revolution?* Greenwich, Conn., Fawcett Publications.

Pike, F. B. 1968. Aspects of class relations in Chile, 1850–1960, in Petras and Zeitlin, 1968.

Poleman, T. T. 1977. World food: Myth and reality, WD, May–July.

Polit, G. 1968. The Argentinian industrialists, in Petras and Zeitlin, 1968.

Pratten, C. F. 1971. *Economies of Scale in Manufacturing Industry*, CUP.

Price, B. J. 1971. Prehispanic irrigation agriculture in Nuclear America, *Latin American Research Review*, Fall.

Prinsep, G. A. (1823). *Remarks on the External Commerce and Exchanges of Bengal*, in K. N. Chaudhuri (ed.): *The Economic Development of India under the East India Company 1814–1858*, CUP, 1971.

Rado, E. and Sinha, R. 1977. Africa: A continent in transition, WD, May–July.

Radwan, S. 1977. The Impact of Agrarian Reform on Rural Egypt (1952–75) (mimeo.) Geneva, International Labour Office.

Rajaraman, I. 1975. Poverty, inequality and economic growth: Rural Punjab, 1960–61 – 1970–71, JDS, July.

Ramachandran, L. 1977. *India's Food Problem: A New Approach*, Calcutta, Allied Publishers.

Ramsunder, A. V. 1965. Relative rates of growth: Agriculture and industry, *Economic Weekly* (Bombay).

Ranis, G. (ed.). 1971. *Government and Economic Development*, YUP.

Ransom, D. 1974. Ford Country: Building an elite for Indonesia, in S. Weissman, 1974.

Rao, S. K. 1976. Population growth and economic development: A counter-argument, EPW, Special Number, August.

Razzell, P. E. 1974. An interpretation of the modern rise of population in Europe – A critique, PS, March.

RBI. 1968. *Foreign Collaboration in Indian Industry: Survey Report*, Bombay, Reserve Bank of India.

1974. *Foreign Collaboration in Indian Industry: Second Survey Report*, Bombay, Reserve Bank of India.

Reddaway, W. B. 1962. *The Development of the Indian Economy*, Allen & Unwin.

1963. The Argentine economy: A visiting economist's questions, *The Review of the River Plate*, September.

Reddy, V. N. 1978. Growth rates, EPW, 13 May.

Remer, C. F. 1933. *Foreign Investment in China*, New York, Macmillan.

Rennie, Y. F. 1945. *The Argentine Republic*, New York, Macmillan.

Rhodes, R. I, (ed.) 1970. *Imperialism and Underdevelopment*, MRP.

Rich, E. E. 1967. Colonial settlement and its labour problems, in Rich and Wilson, 1967.

Rich, E. E. and Wilson, C. H. (eds.), 1967. *The Cambridge Economic History of Europe*, vol. IV, *The Economy of Expanding Europe in the Fifteenth and Sixteenth Centuries*, CUP.

Ridker, R. G. and Lubell, H. (eds.), 1971. *Employment and Unemployment*

Problems of the Near East and South Asia, vols. I and II, Delhi, Vikas.
Riegelhaupt, J. F. and Forman, S. 1970. Bodo was never Brazilian: Economic integration and rural development among a contemporary peasantry, JEH, March.
Rippy, J. F. and Pfeiffer, J. 1948. Notes on the dawn of manufacturing in Latin America, *Hispanic American Historical Review*, vol. 28.
Riskin, C. 1975. Surplus and stagnation in modern China, in Perkins, 1975b.
Robinson, E. A. G. and Kidron, M. 1970. *Economic Development in South Asia*, Macmillan.
Robinson, J. 1937. *Essays in the Theory of Employment*, Oxford, Basil Blackwell.
1956. *The Accumulation of Capital*, Macmillan.
1971a. *Exercises in Economic Analysis*, Macmillan.
1971b. *Essays in the Theory of Economic Growth*, Macmillan.
1972. *Freedom and Necessity*, Bombay, Allen & Unwin.
Robinson, J. and Eatwell, J. 1974. *An Introduction to Modern Economics*, New Delhi, Tata McGraw-Hill.
Rock, D. 1975. *Politics in Argentina 1890–1930*, CUP.
Rockwell, C. R. 1971. 'Comments' (on Land, 1971) in Ranis, 1971.
Rodney, W. 1973. *How Europe Underdeveloped Africa*, Bogle-L'ouverture Publishers.
Rose, C. S. and Gyorgy, P. 1970. Malnutrition in children in Indonesia, in H. W. Beers (ed.) *Indonesia: Resources and their Technological Development*, Lexington, USA, The University Press of Kentucky.
Royal Commission on Opium. 1894. Royal Commission on Opium, Vol. II, *Further Evidence*, UK Parl. Papers, 1894, Vol. LXI.
Rudra, A. and Paul, P. 1964. Demand elasticity for foodgrains, *Economic Weekly* (Bombay), 28 November.
Rungta, R. S. 1970. *Rise of Business Corporations in India, 1851–1900*, CUP.
Sahlins, M. 1968. *Tribesmen*, Englewood-Cliffs, NJ, Prentice-Hall.
1974. *Stone Age Economics*, Tavistock.
Saini, G. R. 1976. Green Revolution and the distribution of farm incomes, EPW, 27 March.
Sandbrook, R. 1975. *Proletarians and African Capitalism, The Kenyan Case, 1960–1972*, CUP.
Sau, R. K. 1977. Share of wages, EPW, 25 June.
Saul, J. S. and Woods, R. 1971. African peasantries, in T. Shanin (ed.), *Peasants and Peasant Societies*, Penguin.
Saul, S. B. 1960. *Studies in British Overseas Trade 1870–1914*, Liverpool, Liverpool University Press.
Saville, J. 1969. Primitive accumulation and early industrialization in Britain, in R. Miliband and J. Saville (eds.), *The Socialist Register 1969*, Merlin Press.
Sayers, R. S. 1956. *Financial Policy 1939–45*, London, Her Majesty's Stationery Office.
Schatz, S. P. 1965. The capital shortage illusion: Government lending in Nigeria, OEP, New Series, July.
1968. The high cost of aiding business in developing economies: Nigeria's loans programmes, OEP, New Series, November.

1972. Development in an adverse economic environment, in Schatz (ed.), *South of the Sahara: Development in African Economies*, Macmillan.
Schmitt, H. O. 1970. Foreign capital and social conflict in Indonesia, in Rhodes, 1970.
Schultz, T. P. 1969. Demographic conditions of economic development in Latin America, in Nisbet, 1969.
Schurman, F. and Schell, O. (eds.) 1967. *China Readings*, I, *Imperial China*, Penguin.
1968. *China Readings*, 3, *Communist China*, Penguin.
Science for the People. 1974. *China: Science Walks On Two Legs*, New York, Avon Books.
Scobie, J. R. 1960. The implications of Argentine wheat economy 1870–1915, IAEA, Autumn.
1964. *Argentina: A City and a Nation*, New York, OUP.
1968. Buenos Aires of 1910: the Paris of South America that did not take off, IAEA, Autumn.
Selden, M. 1972. *The Yenan Way in Revolutionary China*, Cambridge, Mass., HUP.
Selowsky, M. and Taylor, L. 1973. The economics of malnourished children: an example of disinvestment in human capital, EDCC, October.
Sen, A. K. 1968. *Choice of Techniques*, third edition, Oxford, Basil Blackwell.
Sen, S. N. 1960. *The City of Calcutta: A Socioeconomic Survey, 1954 to 1957–58*, Calcutta, Bookland.
Sen, S., Panda, D., and Lahiri, A. (eds.) 1978. *Naxalbari and After: a Frontier Anthology*, Calcutta, Kathasilpa.
Sethuraman, S. V. 1971. Prospects for increasing employment in the Indian manufacturing sector, in Ridker and Lubell, 1971, vol. II.
Sharpston, M. 1975. International subcontracting, OEP, NS, March.
Sheridan, R. B. 1965. The wealth of Jamaica in the nineteenth century, EHR, Second Series, vol. 18.
1976. 'Sweet Malefactor': the social costs of slavery and sugar in Jamaica and Cuba, EHR, Second Series, May.
Shetty, S. L. 1973. Trends in wages, salaries and profits of the private corporate sector, EPW, October 13.
Shillinglaw, G. 1974. Land reform and peasant mobilization in southern China 1947–50, in Lehmann, 1974.
Shoji Ito. 1966. A note on the 'Business Combine' in India – with special reference to the Nattukottai Chettiars, *The Developing Economies*, vol. 4.
Simon, J. L. 1977. *The Economies of Population Growth*, Princeton, NJ, PUP.
Simon, M. 1967. The pattern of new British portfolio foreign investment 1865–1914, in Adler, 1967.
Singh, S. B. 1966. *European Agency Houses in Bengal (1783–1833)*, Calcutta, Firma K. L. Mukhopadhyay.
Sinha, J. C. 1927. *Economic Annals of Bengal*, London, Macmillan.
Sinha, N. K. 1970. *The Economic History of Bengal*, vol. III, 1793–1848, Calcutta, Firma K. L. Mukhopadhyay.
Sivasubramonian, S. 1965. National Income of India 1900–01 to 1946–47, (mimeo.) Delhi, Delhi School of Economics.

Smedley, A. 1972. *The Great Road: Life and Times of Chu Teh*, MRP.
Smith, A. (1776). *The Wealth of Nations*, reprinted in Everyman edition in 2 vols., Dent, 1911.
Snow, E. 1958. *Journey to the Beginning*, New York, Random House.
Stavenhagen, R. 1975. *Social Classes in Agrarian Societies*, Garden City, New York, Anchor Books.
(ed.) 1970a. *Agrarian Problems and Peasant Movements in Latin America*, Garden City, New York, Anchor Books.
1970b. Social aspects of agrarian structure in Mexico, in Stavenhagen, 1970a.
Stein, S. J. 1955. The Brazilian cotton textile industry, in Kuznets, Moore and Spengler, 1955.
Stewart, F. and Streeten, P. 1973. Conflicts between output and employment objectives, in Jolly et al., 1973.
Stilwell, J. W. 1948. *The Stilwell Papers*, ed. by T. H. White, New York, William Sloan.
Stokes, E. 1969. *The English Utilitarians and India*, OUP.
Stycos, J. M. 1978. Recent declines in Latin American fertility, PS, November.
Subrahmanyam, K. V. 1977a. Indian coal mines: Graveyards of miners, EPW, 6 August.
1977b. Shielding the guilty of Chasnala, EPW, December 17.
Sun, E-tu Zen, 1955. The pattern of railway development in China, *Far Eastern Quarterly*, February.
Sweezy, P. M. 1964. *The Theory of Capitalist Development*, New York, MRP.
Sweezy, P. M. (ed.) 1975. *Karl Marx and the Close of His System by E. von Böhm-Bawerk and Böhm-Bawerk's Criticism of Marx by R. Hilferding*, London, Merlin.
Tan Chung. 1973. The triangular trade between China and India (1771–1840) – a case of commercial imperialism, *Proceedings of the Indian History Congress*, Chandigarh.
Tawney, R. H. 1964. *Land and Labour in China*, Allen & Unwin.
Taylor, C. C. 1948. *Rural Life in Argentina*, Baton Rouge, Louisiana, Louisiana University Press.
Temin, P. (ed.) *New Economic History*, Penguin.
Tendler, J. 1968. *Electric Power in Brazil*, Cambridge, Mass., HUP.
Tendulkar, S. 1974. Planning for growth, redistribution and selfreliance in the Fifth Five Year Plan, EPW, 12 and 19 January.
Teubal, M. 1968. The failure of Latin America's economic integration, in Petras and Zeitlin, 1968.
Thomas, B. 1967. The historical record of capital movements to 1913, in Adler, 1967.
Thorner, D. 1956. Feudalism in India, in R. Coulborn (ed.), *Feudalism in History*, Princeton, NJ, PUP.
1976. *The Agrarian Prospect in India*, second edition, Bombay, Allied Publishers.
Tinker, H. 1974. *A New System of Slavery: The Export of Indian Labour Overseas 1830–1920*, OUP.

Titow, J. Z. 1969. *English Rural Society 1200–1350*, Allen and Unwin.
Todaro, M. P. 1973. Income expectations, rural–urban migration and employment in Africa, in Jolly et al., 1973.
Trevelyan, C. E. 1835. *Report upon Inland Customs and Duties of the Bengal Presidency*, Calcutta.
Triffin, R. 1969. The myth and realities of the so-called Gold Standard, in R. N. Cooper (ed.), *International Finance*, Penguin.
Turner, H. A. and Jackson, D. A. S. 1972. The determination of the general wage level; a reply, EJ, June.
UN. 1975. *Poverty, Unemployment and Development Policy: A Case Study of Selected Issues with Reference to Kerala*, New York, United Nations.
Urquidi, V. L. and Thorp, R. (eds.) 1973. *Latin America in the International Economy*, Macmillan.
Vaitsos, C. V. 1974. *Intercountry Income Distribution and Transnational Enterprise*, Oxford, Clarendon Press.
Vanek, J. 1967. *Estimating Foreign Resource Needs for Economic Development: Theory, Method and a Case Study of Colombia*, New York, McGraw-Hill.
Vernon, R. 1970. Organization as a scale factor in the growth of firms, in Markham, J. W. and Papanek, G. F. (eds.), *Industrial Organization and Economic Development*, Boston, Houghton Mifflin.
Ward, B. and Dubos, R. 1973. *Only One Earth*, Penguin.
Warren, W. M. 1966. Urban real wages and the Nigerian trade union movement, 1939–60, EDCC, October.
1969. Urban real wages and the Nigerian trade union movement, 1939–60: A rejoinder, EDCC, July.
Watanabe, S. 1976. *International Subcontracting and Transfer of Technology and Skills* (mimeo.), Geneva, International Labour Office.
WB. 1978. *World Development Report 1978*, Washington, DC, World Bank.
Weeks, J. 1973. Uneven sectoral development and the role of the state, *IDS Bulletin*, October.
Weisskoff, R. 1971. Demand elasticities for a developing economy: An international comparison of consumption patterns, in H. B. Chenery and others (eds.), *Studies in Development Planning*, Cambridge, Mass., HUP.
Weissman, S. et al. 1974. *The Trojan Horse*, San Francisco, USA, Ramparts Press.
Wells, J. 1974. Distribution of earnings, growth and structure of demand in the 1960s, WD, vol. 2.
1977. The diffusion of durables in Brazil and its implications for recent controversies concerning Brazilian development, *Cambridge Journal of Economics*, September.
Wertheim, W. F. 1959. *Indonesian Society in Transition*, The Hague, W. Van Hoeve.
Wharton, Jr., C. R. (ed.) 1970. *Subsistence Agriculture and Economic Development*, Chicago, Aldine.
Whitaker, A. P. 1941. *The Huancavelica Mercury Mines*, Cambridge, Mass., HUP.
Whitcombe, E. 1972. *Agrarian Conditions in Northern India*, vol. 1, *1860–1900*, Berkeley, California, University of California Press.

White, L. J. 1974. *Industrial Concentration and Economic Power in Pakistan*, Princeton, NJ, PUP.

Widstrand, C. (ed.) 1975. *Multinational Firms in Africa*, Dakar, African Institute for Economic Development and Planning.

Wiens, T. B. 1975. Review of Myers, 1970, in *Modern Asian Studies*, April.

Williams, E. 1944. *Capitalism and Slavery*, New York, Russell & Russell.

Williams, J. H. 1920. *Argentine International Trade under Inconvertible Paper Money 1880–1900*, Cambridge, Mass., HUP.

Williamson, J. G. 1965. Regional inequality and the process of national development: a description of the patterns, EDCC, vol. 13.

Willoughby, W. W. 1920. *Foreign Rights and Interests in China*, Baltimore, The Johns Hopkins Press.

Wilson, F. 1972. *Labour in the South African Gold Mines 1911–1969*, CUP.

Wolf, E. 1973. *Peasant Wars of the Twentieth Century*, Faber.

Womack, J. Jr 1972. *Zapata and the Mexican Revolution*, Penguin.

Woodruff, W. 1966. *Impact of Western Man*, Macmillan.

Worsley, P. 1973. *The Third World*, Weidenfeld and Nicolson.

Zuvekas, Jr, C. 1966. Economic growth and income distribution in postwar Argentina, IAEA, Winter.

1968. Argentina economic policy, 1958–1962: The Frondizi government's development plan, IAEA, Summer.

INDEX

Afghanistan, 215–16
Africa, 31, 47–8, 180–1, 211, 213
agriculture, 9–10, 54–6, 72–3, 76–7, 86–7, 107–8, 112–19, 168–9, 171, 173, 175, 223–5, 234–5; commercialization of, 18, 85–7, 107–9, 134–6, 176–7, 225, 234, 239; fluctuations in, 131–6, 231.
Algeria, 156, 201
Ali, Mohammed, 220
Allegrucci, G., 191
Allende, S., 62, 66–7, 250
Alley, R., 109n.
Amerindians, 41–2, 44, 48–52, 56, 59–60, 196, 199, 217
Amherst, Lord, 96
Anaconda, 61, 66
Anstey, R., 44n
Argentina, 30, 33, 54–9, 65–6, 131, 186, 191–2, 204, 216–17
Arrighi, G., 184
Ataturk, K., 221–2, 226
Australia, 30, 33, 88
authoritarianism, 196–201, 236, 239
Ayub, President, 241, 249

backwash effects, 237
balance of payments crises, 65, 130, 136–43, 224, 232
Baldwin, R., 114n.
Balmaceda, President, 61, 189
Bangladesh, 69, 158, 241–2
Baran, P., 20
Belgian Congo, 193
Bell, D. R., 232
Bienefeld, M., 186n.
Bloch, M., 4–6
Boeke, J., 77
Borah, W. W., 42
bourgeoisie, comprador and national, 27–8, 99–100, 111; foreign and indigenous, 190–3; (see also 'capitalist classes')
Braverman, H., 115n.
Bray, J. F., 3
Brazil, 25, 27, 44, 52–3, 63–6, 128–9, 131, 145, 196, 199–200, 217; North-east, 53, 154, 211
Brenner, R., 6–7
Britain (and the British), 26, 30, 78–94, 97–9, 102, 141, 142, 190
British-American Tobacco Company, 108
British and Chinese Corporation, 104
Bukharin, N., 29
Bunyoro, 8
bureaucratic feudalism, 95

Caltex, 193
Canada, 30, 33, 88
capital stock adjustment, 122
capitalism, bureaucratic, 109–10; contradictions of, 38–40; dependent, 195; defined, 12; industrial, 14–15; retarded, 159.
capitalist classes, 26–31, 77, 87–8, 121, 146, 190–6, 201, 248; (see also 'bourgeoisie')
Cardenas, L., 161–5, 173
Caribbean, 25, 44, 193, 204
Centro International de Mejoramiento de Maiz y Trigo (CIMMYT), 172–3
Chen brothers, 109–10
Chen Han-seng, 107–8
Chiang Kai-shek, 104–5, 109
Ch'ien-lung, Emperor, 95–6
Chile, 59–63, 66–7, 154, 189, 196, 204, 216–17
China, 27, 31, 69, 94–111, 154, 165–6, 187, 189, 204
Chu Teh, 101, 108n
class analysis, 110–11; Lenin–Mao scheme for, 147–9, 158, 166; and planning, 220–1
classes, ruling (or upper), 55–6, 67–8, 196–201, 217–18; rural, 11, 147–9, 151–9, 164–5
transitional, 149–52
Cleaver, H., 212
Clive, R., 78
Coen, J. P., 70
Colebrooke, H. T., 79–80
Colombia, 193, 217
colonialism, 54–8, 63–4, 69–78, 78–94; and semi-colonialism, 98–111; capitalist, 28–31, 117, 121; 'voluntary', 48, 53

colonies of exploitation, 45; of settlement, 26, 45
Communists in China, 69, 104–5, 110–11, 165–6
comparative costs, theory of, 16
Conrad, A. H., 180n
Cook, S. F., 42
Cornwallis, Lord, 81, 96
Costa Rica, 204–5
cost–benefit analysis, 209, 250
culture system, 71–2
Curtin, P., 44

Darwin, C., 43n
debt bondage, 22, 37, 49, 56, 86–7
de-industrialization, 24, 31–5, 51–4, 82, 101–2
Dent & Co., 97
devaluation, 58, 137–41, 225, 235
Di Tella, T., 191–2
Diaz, P., 160
dual society, 77

East India Company, British, 78–82, 96–7
East India Company, Dutch (VOC), 70–1, 75, 77–8
Eatwell, J., 16
Egypt, 31, 34, 102, 155, 157–8, 215
Elphinstone, M., 81
Engels, F., 3
Enke, S., 209
Europe, 88, 141, 203–4
exploitation, defined, 15–16; methods of, 21–5
export-led exploitation, 115–20; growth, 112, 143–6
export surplus, 33, 46–7, 58, 73–5, 81, 88–90
exports, 34, 55–6, 58, 60–7, 70–1, 96–8, 100–1, 144–6

Fel'dman, G. A., 228
Fetter, B., 180
feudalism, 4–8, 13, 30, 95, 111
fiscal policy, 92–3, 115–19, 123–4, 235, 243
floods, 214–15
Ford Foundation, 135, 173–4, 234
foreign aid, 105, 143n., 200–1, 222, 224, 232–3, 240–1, 250
foreign capital, 25–31, 188–98, 233; (see also 'transnational corporations')
foreign investment, 30, 33, 58, 88, 106–7
France (and the French), 26, 98–9, 102, 190
free trade, 17–18, 32, 60, 82, 88–90
Frei, E., 67, 250

Galbraith, J. K., 234n
Gandhi, I., 235–6
Geertz, C., 72, 76
General Motors, 93
Ghana, 151
Girvan, N., 62
Gobineau, Count de, 43n
Goulart, President, 129, 199
Green Revolution, 156, 158, 164, 172–8, 200, 216, 234, 241
Greenberg, M., 97
Grey, Lord, 180
Griffin, K., 240
Guatemala, 150, 153

Hall, A. D., 214–15
Hamilton, A., 17
Hicks, J. R., 134
Hidalgo, M., 51
Hirschman, A. O., 198n
Hobson, J. A., 35n
Hodgskin, T., 3
Hong Kong, 28, 98, 199, 204
Hong Kong and Shanghai Banking Corporation, 102, 104
Humboldt, A. von, 51n
Hymer, S., 114n

Imperial Chemical Industries, 93
import-substituting industrialization, 58–9, 65–6, 90–4, 126–43, 248–9
indentured labour, 48, 153–4, 182
India (and the Indians), 10–11, 24, 26–7, 31–2, 34, 69, 78–94, 96–7, 123–4, 141, 149–50, 155–6, 173, 184, 187–8, 192–3, 227–36
Indonesia, 27, 32–3, 69–78, 153, 193
industrial capitalism, 21–2, 39, 102, 176, 179; and the British in India, 84–91 and the Dutch in Indonesia, 71–2
Industrial Revolution, 14, 21, 96
industry (and industrial growth), 58–9, 62, 77–8, 90–4, 106–7, 120–30, 223–5, 232–3
infrastructure, 32–4, 55–7, 60, 64, 85–7, 156, 162–3, 199, 226
Inönü, President, 222
input–output models, 229–31
International Monetary Fund (IMF), The 112, 137, 140, 195, 226
International Rice Research Institute, 172
international subcontracting, 146
irrigation works, 34, 86–7, 155, 163–4, 171–2, 215–16
Ivory Coast, 151

Jajmani system, 11
Jamaica, 33, 44, 46–7, 72
Japan, 28, 99, 102–5, 109, 111, 141, 145, 199, 218, 220
Jardine Matheson & Co., 97, 102, 104
Jefferson, M., 56n

Kalecki, M., 3, 25n., 133
Kennecott, 61, 66
Kenya, 24, 151–2, 156–7, 168, 187, 214
Kenyatta, J., 187
Keynes, J. M., 3
Khan, A. R., 240, 241–2
Kirloskar, The house of, 192–3
Kreuger, I., 222
Krishnan, T. N., 133
Kubitschek, J., 126, 196, 199
Kung, H. H., 109
Kuomintang, 104–6, 109–10, 165
Kuznets, S., 203

labour, control over, 21–5, 76, 182–4, 246
  wages of, 8, 22–3, 61, 107, 182–3, 185–7, 241, 243
labour power, defined, 15
Lambert, A., 79–80
Land reforms, 157–8, 160–7, 201–2, 234
Landes, D. S., 23n
landless labourers, 147–8, 157–8, 176, 243–5
landlords, 37, 48–51, 59, 61, 84–5, 87, 95, 101, 104, 106, 109, 111, 147–9, 153–4, 201, 223, 234, 239
Las Casas, B., 43
Lattimore, O., 99
Lenin, V. I., 3, 8, 29, 35–6, 147, 149, 158, 160, 166
Li Hung-chang, 103
linkages, 36–7
Lin Tse-hsu, 98
List, F., 17–18
Little, I.M.D., 250
Long, E., 33, 46
Luxemburg, R., 3, 23

Macartney, Lord, 95
MacEwan, A., 249–50
Mahalanobis, P.C., 228
Malthus, T. R., 3, 207
Manne, A., 229
Mao Tse-tung, 3, 8, 105, 110–11, 147, 149, 158, 166
Marx, K., 2–3, 10, 12, 15–16, 21–2, 85, 213
Maua, Baron, 64
Menderes, A., 224
mercantilism (and mercantile capitalism), 12–15, 31, 38, 70–1, 78–82, 179, 187
Mexico, 41, 48–9, 131, 145, 150, 160–5, 234
Meyer, J. R., 180n
Minimata Bay, 218
Miracle, M. P., 180
Mirrlees, J. A., 250
monetary policy, 57–8, 110, 119–20, 123–4, 233, 243–5
monopoly, 26, 71–2, 80, 103, 109, 188–90, 232–6
monopoly capital and imperialism, 35–6
Morelos, J. M., 51
Mossadegh, M., 194
Munro, T., 81
Myers, R., 109n
Myint, H., 113n
Myrdal, G., 237

Nadel, S. F., 7
Nasser, G. A., 198
Needham, J., 95
neoclassical economics, 18
neocolonialisms, defined, 78
Netherlands, the (and the Dutch), 26, 69–78,
Nigeria, 189–90
North, J. T., 61
nutrition and health care, 210–13

Ongut, I., 244
opium, production and trade, 96–101
Opium War, 98, 102

Pakistan, 69, 158, 184, 199, 237–41
Panikkar, K. M., 99n
Patnaik, P., 133–4
peasant revolts, 98–9, 160
peasants, as suppliers of labour, 153, 179, 181–2; differentiation among, 76–7, 147–9, 164–5; middle, 148, 172; poor, 147–8, 157, 172, 174, 223, 234–5; rich, 147–8, 156, 174, 224; (see also 'landlords')
Peron, J., 65–6, 186, 198
Peru, 41, 44
Philippines, The, 145, 172–3
Pinochet, General, 199, 250
Pirenne, H., 6
plan models, 227–31
plantations, 22, 43–6, 72, 87, 115, 153–4, 182
population, and its growth, 42, 203–6; and economic development, 206–8; and family planning, 209–10
Portugal (and the Portuguese), 26–7, 30, 52–3
poverty, measurement of, 205n; in Kerala, 204–5; in Bangladesh, 241–2
private investment, 34–5, 90–3, 122–3, 221, 224–5, 231–6, 238–9
property, communal, 9–11, 149, 155; private, 81, 155, 231–2
public enterprises (and sector), 193–6, 222–4, 226, 233–6, 242, 246–7

Quesnay, F., 94

racialism and discrimination, 28, 43–4, 77, 88–9, 150, 189–90

Rahman, M., 242
Rahman, Z., 242
railways, 29, 33, 56–7, 60, 64, 85–6, 103–6, 215
regional inequality, 237–41
Resnick, S., 114n.
retardation and underdevelopment, defined, 20
Rhodesia, 24
Ricardo, D., 2–3, 16–17
Robinson, J., 16, 142n
Roca–Runciman Pact, 59
Rockefeller Foundation, 135, 172–4, 234
Rosas, J. M., 54
Royal Dutch Shell, 193
Rudra, A., 229
Russia (and the Soviet Union), 149, 220, 222

Sadat, A., 198
salinity, 215–16
Sarmiento, D. F., 54, 226
Schatz, S. P., 189–90
semi-feudalism, defined, 8
Sharpston, M., 145
Sheridan, R. B., 47
Simon, J. L., 210
Singapore, 28, 149, 199, 204
slave trade, 42–5, 63
slavery, 22, 25, 42–7, 52–3, 63, 85, 114, 154–5, 179–80, 186
Smith, A., 2, 16–17, 23n., 54n., 71
Snow, E., 109n
soil erosion, 213–16
Soong, T. V., 109
Spain (and the Spanish), 26–7, 30, 41–5, 48–53, 179, 190
Sri Lanka, 138, 182, 197
Standard Oil, 193
Stavenhagen, R., 164–5
stratification systems, 149–52
subsistence farming, 113, 159, 167–8, 180
Suharto, General, 199
Sukarno, President, 198
Sun Yat-sen, 104
surplus value, defined, 12

Taiwan, 28, 145, 166n., 199, 204
taxes, 23–4, 71–2, 76, 78–80, 83–4, 101–2, 107, 180–1
Taylor, C., 56
technology, 39–40, 127–8, 141, 146, 184–5, 191–5, 201, 233–5, 242–9
tenants and sharecroppers, 56, 59, 101, 107–8, 167–72, 148–9, 176
third world, defined, 4
Tod, J., 7
trade unions, 183–4, 185–7
transnational (or multinational) corporations, 37, 127, 130, 145–6, 177–8, 185–6, 193–6, 211–12, 235, 246, 248
tribesmen and tribal organizations, 8–10, 23, 153, 167–8, 180–1
Tseng Kuo-fan, 103
Tunisia, 156
Turkey, 33, 140, 196–7, 221–6

unemployment, 24–5, 35, 76, 85, 169–71
Unilever, 193
Union of South Africa, The, 23, 30, 88, 154
United States of America (USA), The, 23, 25, 30, 33, 88, 135–6, 138, 142–3, 145, 173–4, 195, 199, 212, 219
urbanization and slums, 216–19

Vaitsos, C., 247
Van den Bosch, Governor, 247
Vargas, G., 65, 129, 196
Venezuela, 193
Vietnam, 219
Visvesvaraya, M., 249

Wales, Nym, 109n
West Indies, The, 23, 45–6, 47
Wheelwright, W., 60
Williams, E., 47n
World Bank (IBRD), The, 112, 137, 143n., 173–4, 177, 195, 200–1, 204, 232, 241, 250

Yrigoyen, President, 191–2
Yuan Shih-kai, 104
Yugoslavia, 145